ALSO BY SCOTT RUSSELL SANDERS

NONFICTION

*A Conservationist Manifesto*
*A Private History of Awe*
*The Force of Spirit*
*The Country of Language*
*Hunting for Hope*
*Writing from the Center*
*Staying Put*
*Secrets of the Universe*
*The Paradise of Bombs*
*In Limestone Country*

FICTION

*The Invisible Company*
*The Engineer of Beasts*
*Bad Man Ballad*
*Terrarium*
*Wonders Hidden*
*Fetching the Dead*
*Hear the Wind Blow*
*Wilderness Plots*

# earth works

# earth works

## SELECTED ESSAYS

*Scott Russell Sanders*

Indiana University Press

BLOOMINGTON & INDIANAPOLIS

*This book is a publication of*

INDIANA UNIVERSITY PRESS
601 North Morton Street
Bloomington, Indiana 47404-3797 USA

iupress.indiana.edu

*Telephone orders*   800-842-6796
*Fax orders*   812-855-7931

♾ The paper used in this publication meets
the minimum requirements of the American
National Standard for Information Sciences—
Permanence of Paper for Printed Library
Materials, ANSI Z39.48-1992.

Manufactured in the
United States of America

Library of Congress
Cataloging-in-Publication Data

Sanders, Scott R. (Scott Russell), 1945-
  Earth works : selected essays / Scott Russell
Sanders.
     p. cm.
  ISBN 978-0-253-00094-1 (cloth : alk. paper)
  — ISBN 978-0-253-00095-8 (pbk. : alk. paper)
  I. Title.
  PS3569.A5137E26 2012
  814'.54—DC23
                                    2011030599

1 2 3 4 5   17 16 15 14 13 12

*For the community of writers, readers,*
*editors, artists, scientists, activists, and Earth lovers*
*gathered by Orion magazine.*

Sometimes I think that is all we are really here for:
to look at the world, and to see
as much as we can.

JOHN HAINES

# CONTENTS

# CONTENTS

# PREFACE

All of us ponder our lives, more or less often, more or less deeply, and all of us likewise reflect on the larger webs in which our lives are enmeshed, from families and communities to nations and nature, and on out to the farthest reaches of imagination. Essayists choose to do such reflecting, remembering, and imagining in public, on the page. They differ from scholars in claiming no expertise, from journalists in disclosing their opinions, and from novelists in refusing to make things up.

I have gathered here thirty essays that best represent what I have tried to do in this versatile, inquisitive, and sometimes revelatory art form over the past three decades. Twenty-one of the essays have appeared in my previous books, nine are collected here for the first time. In revisiting them, I have made small deletions, for the sake of economy, and slight changes in wording, for the sake of clarity. But I have refrained from making significant revisions, allowing the essays to remain, for better or worse, essentially as they first appeared in print. They are arranged in roughly chronological order, by date of composition. Where I have varied that order, I have done so in order to juxtapose certain essays that cast what seems to me an interesting light on one another. The "Notes and Acknowledgments" section at the back of this volume records, for each essay, when it was composed and where it was first published, along with a few of the circumstances and concerns that influenced the writing. I also list there the chief sources of quotations, and the names of editors who have been especially supportive of my work.

The writing of an essay usually begins for me in a state of strong emotion and equally strong puzzlement. Some event, recollection, journey, or notion bewilders me, distresses me, fascinates me, or otherwise provokes me, and sets me asking questions that drive the writing forward. Such answers as I come up with are always partial and tentative, subject to rethinking in light of new knowledge or further reflection—just like the findings of science, my first intellectual love.

Although the answers vary from essay to essay, certain questions have persisted over the years. Some of them pertain to my own life—my midwestern background, my father's drinking, my resistance to war, my literary debts, my feeling for wildness. But most of the questions that drive my essays are impersonal, for they must occur to every inquisitive soul: What is a good life, and how might one come closer to leading such a life? What is a good society, and how might we shift our society in that direction? How do family and culture shape a person's character? Why are humans so violent, toward one another and toward Earth? What is our place in nature? What role, if any, do humans play in the universe? What is this inwardness we call mind, which fills our awareness, and what is it good for? Are we connected, through the core of our being, to anything eternal? These are perennial human questions, and my response to them is only one among a host of responses. That they can never be definitively answered does not mean one can avoid asking them.

We humans are exceedingly clever animals, but we are animals nonetheless. Along with our millions of fellow species, we carry an evolutionary inheritance that stretches back billions of years, and we are wholly dependent for our well-being on the health of this planet. Because my essays embody this awareness, I am sometimes asked if I am a "nature" writer, as if paying attention to our membership in the web of life were a specialized interest, like following sports or fashion or cuisine. What I am is an *Earth* writer: I'm interested in life on this planet—all life. Since I know most about my own species, I think mostly about human affairs, but I do so while seeking to understand how our kind arises from and affects the living world. Hence the title of this book. *Works* serves here as both noun and verb. Like all works of art, my essays are products of Earth, as are you, as am I, and we are able to make books and babies, to wonder and sing, to spend our brief time under the sun, only because Earth works miraculously well, providing us a benign habitation in the void of space.

Scott Russell Sanders
BLOOMINGTON, INDIANA
JANUARY 2012

# earth works

# The Singular First Person

The first soapbox orator I ever saw was haranguing a crowd beside the Greyhound station in Providence, Rhode Island, about the evils of fluoridated water. What the man stood on was actually an upturned milk crate, all the genuine soapboxes presumably having been snapped up by antique dealers. He wore an orange plaid sport coat and matching bow tie and held aloft a bottle filled with mossy green liquid. I don't remember the details of his spiel, except his warning that fluoride was an invention of the Communists designed to weaken our bones and thereby make us pushovers for a Red invasion. What amazed me, as a tongue tied kid of seventeen newly arrived in the city from the boondocks, was not his message but his courage in delivering it to a mob of strangers. I figured it would have been easier for me to jump straight over the Greyhound station than to stand there on that milk crate and utter my thoughts.

To this day, when I read or when I compose one of those curious monologues we call the personal essay, I often think of that soapbox orator. Nobody had asked him for his two cents' worth, but there he was declaring it with all the eloquence he could muster. The essay, although enacted in private, is no less arrogant a performance. Unlike novelists and playwrights, who lurk behind the scenes while distracting our attention with the puppet show of imaginary characters; unlike scholars and journalists, who quote the opinions of others and shelter behind the hedges of neutrality, the essayist has nowhere to hide. While the poet can lean back on a several-thousand-year-old legacy of ecstatic speech, the essayist inherits a much briefer and skimpier tradition. The poet is allowed to quit after a few lines, but the essayist must hold our attention for pages and pages. It is a brash and foolhardy form, this one-man or one-woman circus, which relies on the tricks of anecdote, conjecture, memory, and wit to enthrall us.

Addressing a monologue to the world seems all the more brazen or preposterous an act when you consider what a tiny fraction of the human chorus any single voice is. At Boston's Museum of Science an electronic meter records with flashing lights the population of the United States. Figuring in the rate of births and deaths, emigrants leaving the country and immigrants arriving, the meter calculates that we add one fellow citizen every twenty-one seconds. When I looked at it one day in 1987, the count stood at 249,958,483. As I wrote that figure in my notebook, the final number jumped from 3 to 4. Another mouth, another set of ears and eyes, another brain. A counter for Earth's population, somewhere past five billion at that moment, would be rising in a blur of digits. Amid this avalanche of selves, it is a wonder that anyone finds the gumption to sit down and write one of those naked, lonely, quixotic letters to the world.

A surprising number do find the gumption. In fact, I have the impression there are more essayists at work in America today, and more gifted ones, than at any time in recent decades. Whom do I have in mind? Here is a sampler: Edward Abbey, James Baldwin, Wendell Berry, Carol Bly, Joan Didion, Annie Dillard, Stephen Jay Gould, Elizabeth Hardwick, Edward Hoagland, Barry Lopez, Peter Matthiessen, John McPhee, Cynthia Ozick, Paul Theroux, Lewis Thomas, Tom Wolfe. No doubt you could make up a list of your own—with a greater ethnic range, perhaps, or fewer nature enthusiasts—a list that would provide equally convincing support for the view that we are blessed right now with an abundance of essayists. We do not have anyone to rival Emerson or Thoreau, but in sheer quantity of first-rate work our time stands comparison with any period since the heyday of the form in the mid–nineteenth century.

Why are so many writers taking up this risky form and why are so many readers—to judge by the statistics of book and magazine publication—seeking it out? In this era of pre-packaged thought, the essay is the closest thing we have, on paper, to a record of the individual mind at work and play. It is an amateur's raid in a world of specialists. Feeling overwhelmed by data, random information, the flotsam and jetsam of mass culture, we relish the spectacle of a single consciousness making sense of a portion of the chaos. We are grateful to Lewis Thomas for shining his light into the dark corners of biology, to John McPhee for laying bare the geology beneath our landscape, to Annie Dillard for showing us the universal fire blazing in the branches of a cedar, to Peter Matthiessen for chasing after snow leopards and mystical insights in the Himalayas. No matter if they are sketchy, these maps of meaning are still welcome. As Joan Didion observes in the title essay of her collection, *The White Album,* "We live entirely, especially if we are writers, by the imposition of a narrative line upon disparate images, by the 'ideas' with which we have learned to freeze the shifting phantasmagoria which is our actual experience." Dizzy from a dance that seems to accelerate hour by hour, we cling to the narrative line, even though it may be as pure an invention as the shapes drawn by Greeks to identify the constellations.

The essay is a haven for the private, idiosyncratic voice in an era of anonymous babble. Like the blandburgers served in their millions along our highways, most language served up in public these days is textureless, tasteless mush. On television, over the phone, in the newspaper, wherever humans bandy words about, we encounter more and more abstractions, more empty formulas. Think of the pabulum ladled out by politicians. Think of the fluffy white bread of advertising. Think, Lord help us, of committee reports. By contrast, the essay remains stubbornly concrete and particular: it confronts you with an oil-smeared toilet at the Sunoco station, a red vinyl purse shaped like a valentine heart, a bow-legged dentist hunting deer with an elephant gun. As Orwell forcefully argued, and as dictators seem to agree, such a bypassing of abstractions, such an insistence on the concrete, is a politically subversive act. Clinging to this door, that child, this grief, following the zigzag motions of an inquisitive mind, the essay renews language and clears trash from the springs of thought. In his first book, a slender volume entitled *Nature*, Emerson called on a new generation of writers to cast off the hand-me-down rhetoric of the day, to "pierce this rotten diction and fasten words again to visible things." The essayist aspires to do just that.

As if all these virtues were not enough to account for a renaissance of this protean genre, the essay has also taken over some of the territory abdicated by contemporary fiction. Whittled down to the bare bones of plot, camouflaged with irony, muttering in brief sentences and grade school vocabulary, peopled with characters who stumble like sleepwalkers through numb lives, today's fashionable fiction avoids disclosing where the author stands on anything. In the essay, you had better speak from a region pretty close to the heart or the reader will detect the wind of phoniness whistling through your hollow phrases. In the essay you may be caught with your pants down, your ignorance and sentimentality showing, while you trot recklessly about on one of your hobbyhorses. You cannot stand back from the action, as Joyce instructed us to do, and pare your fingernails. You cannot palm off your cockamamie notions on some hapless character.

To our list of the essay's contemporary attractions we should add the perennial ones of verbal play, mental adventure, and sheer anarchic high spirits. To see how the capricious mind can be led astray, consider the foregoing paragraph, which drags in metaphors from the realms of toys, clothing, weather, and biology, among others. That is bad enough; but it could have been worse. For example, I began to draft a sentence in that paragraph with the following words: "More than once, in sitting down to beaver away at a narrative, felling trees of memory and hauling brush to build a dam that might slow down the waters of time . . ." I had set out to make some innocent remark, and here I was gnawing down trees and building dams, all because I had let that *beaver* slip in. On this occasion I had the good sense to throw out the unruly word. I don't always, as no doubt you will have noticed. Whatever its more visible subject, an essay is also about the way a mind moves, the links and leaps and jigs of thought. I might as well drag in another metaphor—and another unoffending animal—by saying that each doggy sentence, as it noses forward into the underbrush of thought, scatters a bunch of rabbits that go bounding off in all directions. The essayist can afford to chase more of those rabbits than the fiction writer can, but fewer than the poet. If you refuse to chase any of them, and keep plodding along in a straight line, you and your reader will have a dull outing. If you chase too many, you will soon wind up lost in a thicket of confusion with your tongue hanging out.

The pursuit of mental rabbits was strictly forbidden by the teachers who instructed me in English composition. For that matter, nearly all the qualities of the personal essay, as I have been sketching them, violate the rules that many of us were taught in school. You recall we were supposed to begin with an outline and stick by it faithfully, like a train riding its rails, avoiding sidetracks. Each paragraph was to have a topic sentence pasted near the front, and these orderly paragraphs were to be coupled end to end like so many boxcars. Every item in those boxcars was to bear the stamp of some external authority, preferably a footnote referring to a thick book, although appeals to magazines and newspapers would do in a pinch. Our diction was to be formal, dignified, shunning the vernacular. Polysyllabic words derived from Latin were preferable to the blunt lingo of the streets. Metaphors were to be used only in emergencies, and no two species of metaphor were to be mixed. And even in emergencies we could not speak in the first person singular.

Already as a schoolboy, I chafed against those rules. Now I break them shamelessly, in particular the taboo against using the lonely capital *I*. Just look at what I'm doing right now. My speculations about the state of the essay arise, needless to say, from my own practice as reader and writer, and they reflect my own tastes, no matter how I may pretend to gaze dispassionately down on the question from on high. As Thoreau declares in his cocky manner on the opening page of *Walden:* "In most books the *I*, or first person, is omitted; in this it will be retained; that, in respect to egotism, is the main difference. We commonly do not remember that it is, after all, always the first person that is speaking. I should not talk so much about myself if there were anybody else whom I knew as well." True for the personal essay, it is doubly true for an essay *about* the essay: one speaks always and inescapably in the first person singular.

We could sort out essays along a spectrum according to the degree to which the writer's ego is on display—with John McPhee, perhaps, at the extreme of self-effacement, and Norman Mailer at the opposite extreme of self-dramatization. Brassy or shy, stage center or hanging back in the wings, the author's persona commands our attention. For the length of an essay, or a book of essays, we respond to that persona as we would to a friend caught up in a rapturous monologue. When the monologue is finished, we may not be able to say precisely what it was about, any more than we can draw conclusions from a piece of music. "Essays don't usually boil down to a summary, as articles do," notes Edward Hoagland, one of the least summarizable of companions, in *The Tugman's Passage*, "and the style of the writer has a 'nap' to it, a combination of personality and originality and energetic loose ends that stand up like the nap of a piece of wool and can't be brushed flat." We make assumptions about that speaking voice, assumptions we cannot validly make about the narrators in fiction. Only a sophomore is permitted to ask how many children had Huckleberry Finn; but even literary sophisticates wonder in print about Thoreau's love life, Montaigne's domestic arrangements, De Quincey's opium habit, or Virginia Woolf's depression.

Montaigne, who not only invented the form but nearly perfected it as well, announced from the start that his true subject was himself. In his note "To the Reader," he slyly proclaimed:

I want to be seen here in my simple, natural, ordinary fashion, without straining or artifice; for it is myself that I portray. My defects will here be read to the life, and also my natural form, as far as respect for the public has allowed. Had I been placed among those nations which are said to live still in the sweet freedom of nature's first laws, I assure you I should very gladly have portrayed myself here entire and wholly naked.

A few pages after this disarming introduction, we are told of the emperor Maximilian, who was so prudish about exposing his private parts that he would not let a servant dress him or see him in the bath. The emperor went so far as to give orders that he be buried in his underdrawers. Having let us in on this intimacy about Maximilian, Montaigne then confessed that he himself, although "bold-mouthed," was equally prudish, and that "except under great stress of necessity or voluptuousness," he never allowed anyone to see him naked. Such modesty, he feared, was unbecoming in a soldier. But such honesty is quite becoming in an essayist. The very confession of his prudery is a far more revealing gesture than any doffing of clothes.

Every English major knows that the word *essay,* as adapted by Montaigne, means a trial or attempt. The Latin root carries the more vivid sense of a weighing out. In the days when that root was alive and green, merchants discovered the value of goods and alchemists discovered the composition of unknown metals by the use of scales. Just so the essay, as Montaigne was the first to show, is a weighing out, an inquiry into the value, meaning, and true nature of experience; it is a private experiment carried out in public. In each of three successive editions, Montaigne inserted new material into his essays without revising the old material. Often the new statements contradicted the original ones, but Montaigne let them stand, since he believed that the only consistent fact about human beings is their inconsistency. In "Why Montaigne Is Not a Bore," Lewis Thomas has remarked of him that "he is fond of his mind, and affectionately entertained by everything in his head." Whatever Montaigne wrote about—and he wrote about everything under the sun: fears, smells, growing old, the pleasures of scratching—he weighed on the scales of his own character.

It is the *singularity* of the first person—its warts and crotchets and turns of voice—that lures many of us into reading essays, and that lingers with us after we finish. Consider the lonely, melancholy persona of Loren Eiseley, forever wandering, forever brooding on our dim and bestial past, his lips frosty with the chill of the Ice Age. Consider the volatile, Dionysian persona of D. H. Lawrence, with his incandescent gaze, his habit of turning peasants into gods and trees into flames, his quick hatred and quicker love. Consider that philosophical farmer Wendell Berry, who speaks with a countryman's knowledge and a deacon's severity. Consider E. B. White, with his cheery affection for brown eggs and dachshunds, his unflappable way of herding geese while the radio warns of an approaching hurricane.

Of course for anyone who writes in the first person singular, there is always a danger of narcissism, as White himself acknowledges in his foreword to *Essays of E. B. White:*

> I think some people find the essay the last resort of the egoist, a much
> too self-conscious and self-serving form for their taste; they feel that it
> is presumptuous of a writer to assume that his little excursions or his
> small observations will interest the reader. There is some justice in their
> complaint. I have always been aware that I am by nature self absorbed and
> egoistical; to write of myself to the extent I have done indicates a too great
> attention to my own life, not enough to the lives of others.

Yet the self-absorbed Mr. White was in fact a delighted observer of the world, and shared that delight with us. Thus, after describing memorably how a circus girl practiced her bareback riding in the leisure moments between shows ("The Ring of Time"), he confessed: "As a writing man, or secretary, I have always felt charged with the safekeeping of all unexpected items of worldly or unworldly enchantment, as though I might be held personally responsible if even a small one were to be lost." That may still be presumptuous, but it is a presumption turned outward on the creation.

This looking outward helps distinguish the essay from pure autobiography, which dwells more complacently on the self. Mass murderers, movie stars, sports heroes, Wall Street crooks, and defrocked politicians may blather on about whatever high jinks or low jinks made them temporarily famous, may chronicle their exploits, their diets, their hobbies, in perfect confidence that the public is eager to gobble up every least gossipy scrap. And the public, according to sales figures, generally is. On the other hand, I assume the public does not give a hoot about my private life. If I write of hiking up a mountain with my one-year-old boy riding like a papoose on my back, and of what he babbled to me while we gazed down from the summit onto the scudding clouds, it is not because I am deluded into believing that my baby, like the offspring of Prince Charles, matters to the great world. It is because I know the great world produces babies of its own and watches them change cloud-fast before its doting eyes. To make that climb up the mountain vividly present for readers is harder work than the climb itself. I choose to write about my experience not because it is mine, but because it seems to me a door through which others might pass.

On that cocky first page of *Walden,* Thoreau justified his own seeming self-absorption by saying that he wrote the book for the sake of his fellow citizens, who kept asking him to account for his peculiar experiment by the pond. There is at least a sliver of truth to this, since Thoreau, a town character, had been invited more than once to speak his mind at the public lectern. Most of us, however, cannot honestly say the townspeople have been clamoring for our words. I suspect that all writers of the essay, even Norman Mailer and Gore Vidal, must occasionally wonder if they are egomaniacs. For the essayist, in other words, the problem of authority is inescapable. By what right does one speak? Why should anyone listen? The traditional sources of authority no longer serve. You cannot justify your words by appealing to the Bible or some other holy text, you cannot merely stitch together a patchwork of quotations from classical authors, you cannot lean on a podium at the Athenaeum and deliver your wisdom to a rapt audience.

In searching for your own soapbox, a sturdy platform from which to deliver your opinionated monologues, it helps if you have already distinguished yourself at some other, less fishy form. When Yeats describes his longing for Maud Gonne or muses on Ireland's misty lore, everything he says is charged with the prior strength of his poetry. When Virginia Woolf, in *A Room of One's Own,* reflects on the status of women and the conditions necessary for making art, she speaks as the author of *Mrs. Dalloway* and *To the Lighthouse.* The essayist may also lay claim to our attention by having lived through events or traveled through terrains that already bear a richness of meaning. When James Baldwin writes his *Notes of a Native Son,* he does not have to convince us that racism is a troubling reality. When Barry Lopez takes us on a meditative tour of the far north in *Arctic Dreams,* he can rely on our curiosity about that fabled and forbidding place. When Paul Theroux climbs aboard a train and invites us on a journey to some exotic destination, he can count on the romance of railroads and the allure of remote cities to bear us along.

Most essayists, however, cannot draw on any source of authority from beyond the page to lend force to the page itself. They can only use language to put themselves on display and to gesture at the world. When Annie Dillard tells us in the opening lines of *Pilgrim at Tinker Creek* about the tomcat with bloody paws that jumps through the window onto her chest, why should we listen? Well, because of the voice that goes on to say "And some mornings I'd wake in daylight to find my body covered with paw prints in blood; I looked as though I'd been painted with roses." Listen to her explaining a few pages later what she is up to in this book, this broody, zestful record of her stay in the Roanoke Valley: "I propose to keep here what Thoreau called 'a meteorological journal of the mind,' telling some tales and describing some of the sights of this rather tamed valley, and exploring, in fear and trembling, some of the unmapped dim reaches and unholy fastnesses to which those tales and sights so dizzyingly lead." The sentence not only describes the method of her literary search, but also exhibits the breathless, often giddy, always eloquent and spiritually hungry soul who will do the searching. If you enjoy her company, you will relish Annie Dillard's essays; if you don't, you won't

Listen to another voice which readers tend to find either captivating or insufferable:

> That summer I began to see, however dimly, that one of my ambitions, perhaps my governing ambition, was to belong fully to this place, to belong as the thrushes and the herons and the muskrats belonged, to be altogether at home here. That is still my ambition. I have made myself willing to be entirely governed by it. But now I have come to see that it proposes an enormous labor. It is a spiritual ambition, like goodness. The wild creatures belong to the place by nature, but as a man I can belong to it only by understanding and by virtue. It is an ambition I cannot hope to succeed in wholly, but I have come to believe that it is the most worthy of all.

That is Wendell Berry writing about his patch of Kentucky in *The Long-Legged House*. Once you have heard that stately, moralizing, cherishing voice, laced through with references to the land, you will not mistake it for anyone else's. Berry's themes are profound and arresting ones. But it is his voice, more than anything he speaks about, that either seizes us or drives us away.

Even so distinct a persona as Wendell Berry's or Annie Dillard's is still only a literary fabrication, of course. The first person singular is too narrow a gate for the whole writer to squeeze through. What we meet on the page is not the flesh-and-blood author, but a simulacrum, a character who wears the label *I*. Introducing the lectures that became *A Room of One's Own,* Virginia Woolf reminds her listeners that "'I' is only a convenient term for somebody who has no real being. Lies will flow from my lips, but there may perhaps be some truth mixed up with them; it is for you to seek out this truth and to decide whether any part of it is worth keeping." Here is a part I consider worth keeping: "Women have served all these centuries as looking-glasses possessing the magic and delicious power of reflecting the figure of man at twice its natural size." It is from such elegant, revelatory sentences that we build up our notion of the "I" who speaks to us under the name of Virginia Woolf.

What the essay tells us may not be true in any sense that would satisfy a court of law. As an example, think of Orwell's brief narrative "A Hanging," which describes an execution in Burma. Anyone who has read it remembers how the condemned man as he walked to the gallows stepped aside to avoid a puddle. That is the sort of haunting detail only an eyewitness should be able to report. Alas, biographers, those zealous debunkers, have recently claimed that Orwell never saw such a hanging, that he reconstructed it from hearsay. What then do we make of his essay? Or has it become the sort of barefaced lie we prefer to call a story?

Frankly, I don't much care what label we put on "A Hanging," fiction or non-fiction—it is a powerful statement either way; but Orwell might have cared a great deal. I say this because not long ago I was bemused and then vexed to find one of my own essays treated in a scholarly article as a work of fiction. Here was my earnest report about growing up on a military base, my heartfelt rendering of indelible memories, being confused with the airy figments of novelists! To be sure, in writing the piece I had used dialogue, scenes, settings, character descriptions, the whole fictional bag of tricks; sure, I picked and chose among a thousand beckoning details; sure, I downplayed some facts and highlighted others; but I was writing about the actual, not the invented. I shaped the matter, but I did not make it up.

To explain my vexation, I must break another taboo by speaking of the author's intent. My teachers warned me strenuously to avoid the intentional fallacy. They told me to regard poems and plays and stories as objects washed up on the page from some unknown and unknowable shores. Now that I am on the other side of the page, so to speak, I think quite recklessly of intention all the time. I believe that if we allow the question of intent in the case of murder, we should allow it in literature. The essay is distinguished from the short story, not by the presence or absence of literary devices, not by tone or theme or subject, but by the writer's stance toward the material. In composing an essay about what it was like to grow up on that military base, I *meant* something quite different from what I mean when concocting a story. I meant to preserve and record and help give voice to a reality that existed independently of me. I meant to pay my respects to a minor passage of history in an out-of-the-way place. I felt responsible to the truth as known by other people. I wanted to speak directly out of my own life into the lives of others.

You can see I am teetering on the brink of metaphysics. One step farther and I will plunge into the void, wondering as I fall how to prove there is any external truth for the essayist to pay homage to. I draw back from the brink and simply declare that I believe one writes, in essays, with a regard for the actual world, with a respect for the shared substance of history, the autonomy of other lives, the being of nature, the mystery and majesty of a creation we have not made.

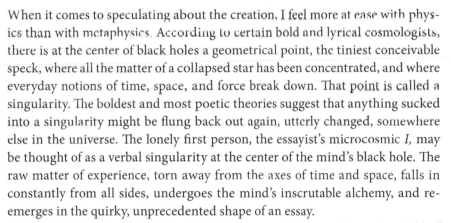

When it comes to speculating about the creation, I feel more at ease with physics than with metaphysics. According to certain bold and lyrical cosmologists, there is at the center of black holes a geometrical point, the tiniest conceivable speck, where all the matter of a collapsed star has been concentrated, and where everyday notions of time, space, and force break down. That point is called a singularity. The boldest and most poetic theories suggest that anything sucked into a singularity might be flung back out again, utterly changed, somewhere else in the universe. The lonely first person, the essayist's microcosmic *I*, may be thought of as a verbal singularity at the center of the mind's black hole. The raw matter of experience, torn away from the axes of time and space, falls in constantly from all sides, undergoes the mind's inscrutable alchemy, and re-emerges in the quirky, unprecedented shape of an essay.

Now it is time for me to step down, before another metaphor seizes hold of me, before you notice that I am standing, not on a soapbox, but on the purest air.

# At Play in the
# Paradise of Bombs

wice a man's height and topped by strands of barbed wire, a chain-link fence stretched for miles along the highway leading up to the main gate of the Arsenal. Beside the gate were tanks, hulking dinosaurs of steel, one on each side, their long muzzles slanting down to catch trespassers in a cross-fire. A soldier emerged from the gatehouse, gun on hip, silvered sunglasses blanking his eyes.

My father stopped our car. He leaned out the window and handed the guard some papers which my mother had been nervously clutching.

"With that license plate, I had you pegged for visitors," said the guard. "But I see you've come to stay."

His flat voice ricocheted against the rolled-up windows of the back seat where I huddled beside my sister. I hid my face in the upholstery, to erase the barbed wire and tanks and mirror-eyed soldier, and tried to wind myself into a ball as tight as the fist of fear in my stomach. By and by, our car eased forward into the Arsenal, the paradise of bombs.

This was in April of 1951, in Ohio. We had driven north from Tennessee, where spring had already burst the buds of trees and cracked the flowers open. Up here on the hem of Lake Erie, the Earth was bleak with snow. I had been told about northern winters, but in the red clay country south of Memphis I had seen only occasional flurries, harmless as confetti, never this smothering quilt of white. My mother had been crying since Kentucky. Sight of the Arsenal's fences and guard shacks looming out of the snow brought her misery to the boil. "It's like a concentration camp," she whispered to my father. I had no idea what she meant. I was not quite six, born two months after the destruction of Hiroshima and Nagasaki. My birth sign was the mushroom cloud. "It looks exactly like those pictures of the German camps," she lamented. Back in Tennessee, the strangers who had bought our farm were clipping bouquets from her garden. Those strangers had inherited everything—the barn and jittery cow, the billy goat fond of corn silk, the crops of beans and potatoes already planted, the creek bottom cleared of locust trees, the drawling voices of neighbors, the smell of cotton dust.

My father had worked through World War II at a munitions plant near his hometown in Mississippi. Now the company he worked for, hired by the Pentagon to run this Ohio arsenal, was moving him north to supervise the production lines where artillery shells and land mines and bombs were loaded with explosives. Later I would hear scary stories, passed down from older children, about those load lines. The concrete floors were so saturated with TNT that any chance spark would set off a quake. The workers used tools of brass to guard against sparks, but every now and again a careless chump would drop a pocket knife or shell casing, and lose a leg. Once a forklift dumped a pallet of barrels and blew out an entire factory wall, along with three munitions loaders.

In 1951 I was too young to realize that what had brought on all this bustle in our lives was the war in Korea. Asia was absorbing bullets and bombs as quickly as the Arsenal could ship them. At news conferences, President Truman meditated aloud on whether or not to spill *the* Bomb—the sip of planetary hemlock—over China. Senator McCarthy was denouncing Reds from every available podium, pinning a single handy label on all the bugbears of the nation. Congress had recently passed bills designed to hamstring unions and slam the doors of America in the faces of immigrants. The Soviet Union had detonated its own atomic weapons, and the search was on for the culprits who had sold our secret. How else but through treachery could such a benighted nation ever have built such a clever bomb? In the very month of our move to the Arsenal, Julius and Ethel Rosenberg were sentenced to death. Too late, J. Robert Oppenheimer was voicing second thoughts about the weapon he had helped build. In an effort to preserve our lead in the race toward oblivion, our scientists were perfecting the hydrogen bomb.

We rolled to our new home in the Arsenal over the impossible snow, between parking lots filled with armored troop carriers, jeeps, strafing helicopters, wheeled howitzers, bulldozers, Sherman tanks, all the brawny machines of war. On the front porch of our Memphis home I had read GI Joe comic books, and so I knew the names and shapes of these death-dealing engines. In the gaudy cartoons the soldiers had seemed like two-legged chunks of pure glory, muttering speeches between bursts on their machine guns, clenching the pins of grenades between their dazzling teeth. Their weapons had seemed like tackle worthy of gods. But as we drove between those parking lots crowded with real tanks, past guard houses manned by actual soldiers, a needle of dread pierced my brain.

Thirty years later the needle is still there, and is festering. I realize now that in moving from a scrape-dirt farm in Tennessee to a munitions factory in Ohio I had leaped overnight from the nineteenth century into the heart of the twentieth. I had landed in a place that concentrates the truth about our condition more potently than any metropolis or suburb. If, one hundred years from now, there are still human beings capable of thinking about the past, and if they turn their sights on our own time, what they will see through the cross hairs of memory will be a place very like the Arsenal, a fenced wilderness devoted to the building and harboring of the instruments of death.

Our house was one of twenty white frame boxes arrayed in a circle about a swatch of lawn. Originally built for the high-ranking military brass, some of these government quarters now also held civilians—the doctors assigned to the base hospital, the engineers who carried slide rules dangling from their belts, the accountants and supervisors, the managerial honchos. In our children's argot, this hoop of houses became the Circle, the beginning and ending point of all our journeys. Like campers drawn up around a fire, like wagons wound into a fearful ring, the houses faced inward on the Circle, as if to reassure the occupants, for immediately outside that tamed hoop the forest began, a tangled, beast-haunted woods.

Through our front door I looked out on mowed grass, flower boxes, parked cars, the curves of concrete, the wink of windows. From the back door I saw only trees, bare dark bones thrust up from the snow in that first April, snarled green shadows in all the following summers. Not many nights after we had settled in, I glimpsed a white-tailed deer lurking along the edge of the woods out back, the first of thousands I would see over the years. The Arsenal was a sanctuary for deer, I soon learned, and also for beaver, fox, turkey, geese, and every manner of beast smaller than wolves and bears. Protected by that chain-link fence, which kept out hunters and woodcutters as well as spies, the animals had multiplied to very nearly their ancient numbers, and the trees grew thick and old until they died with their roots on. So throughout my childhood I had a choice of where to play—inside the charmed Circle or outside in the wild thickets.

Viewed on a map against Ohio's bulldozed land, the Arsenal was only a tiny patch of green, about thirty square miles; some of it had been pasture as recently as ten years earlier, when the government bought the land. It was broken up by airstrips and bunkers and munitions depots; guards cruised its perimeter and bored through its heart twenty-four hours a day. But to my young eyes it seemed like an unbounded wilderness. One parcel of land for the Arsenal had belonged to a U.S. senator, and the rest was purchased from farmers, some of them descendants of the hard-bitten New England folks who had settled that corner of Ohio, most of them reluctant to move. According to the children's lore, one of the old-timers refused to budge from his house until the wrecking crew arrived, and then he slung himself from a noose tied to a rafter in his barn. By the time I came along to investigate, all that remained of his place was the crumbling silo; but I found it easy to imagine him strung up there, roped to his roof beam, riding his ship as it went down. Every other year or so, the older children would string a scarecrow from a rafter in one of the few surviving barns, and then lead the younger children in for a grisly look. I only fell for the trick once, but the image of that dangling husk is burned into my mind.

Rambling through the Arsenal's twenty-one thousand acres, at first in the safe back seats of our parents' cars, then on bicycles over the gravel roads, and later on foot through the backcountry, we children searched out the ruins of those abandoned farms. Usually the buildings had been torn down and carted away, and all that remained were the cellar holes half-filled with rubble, the skewed stone foundations, the stubborn flowers. What used to be lawns were grown up in sumac, maple, and blackberry. The rare concrete walks and driveways were shattered, sown to ferns. Moss grew in the chiseled names of the dead on headstones in backyard cemeteries. We could spy a house site in the spring by the blaze of jonquils, the blue fountain of lilacs, the forsythia and starry columbine; in the summer by roses; in the fall by the flow of mums and zinnias. Asparagus and rhubarb kept pushing up through the meadows. The blasted orchards kept squeezing out plums and knotty apples and bee-thick pears. From the cellar holes wild grapevines twisted up to ensnarl the shade trees. In the ruins we discovered marbles, bottles, the bone handles of knives, the rusty heads of hammers, and the tips of plows. And we dug up keys by the fistful, keys of brass and blackened iron, skeleton keys to ghostly doors. We gathered the fruits of other people's planting, staggering home with armfuls of flowers, sprays of pussy willow and bittersweet, baskets of berries, our faces sticky with juice.

Even where the army's poisons had been dumped, nature did not give up. In a remote corner of the Arsenal, on land that had been used as a Boy Scout camp before the war, the ground was so filthy with the discarded makings of bombs that not even guards would go there. But we children went, lured on by the scarlet warning signs: DANGER. RESTRICTED AREA. The skull-and-crossbones aroused in us dreams of pirates. We found the log huts overgrown with vines, the swimming lake a bog of algae and cattails, the stone walls scattered by the heave of frost. The only scrap of metal we discovered was a bell, its clapper rusted solid to the rim. In my bone marrow I carry traces of the poison from that graveyard of bombs, as we all carry a smidgen of radioactivity from every atomic blast. Perhaps at this very moment one of those alien molecules, like a grain of sand in an oyster, is irritating some cell in my body, or in your body, to fashion a pearl of cancer.

Poking about in the ruins of camp and farms, I felt a wrestle of emotions, half sick with loss, half exultant over the return of forest. It was terrifying and at the same time comforting to see how quickly the green wave lapped over the human remains, scouring away the bold marks of occupation. The displaced farmers, gone only a decade, had left scarcely more trace than the ancient Indians who had heaped up burial mounds in this territory. We hunted for Indian treasure, too, digging in every suspicious hillock until our arms ached. We turned up shards of pottery, iridescent shells, fiery bits of flint, but never any bones. The best arrow points and ax heads were invariably discovered not by looking but by chance, when jumping over a creek or scratching in the dirt with a bare incurious toe. This was my first lesson in the Zen of seeing, seeing by not-looking.

With or without looking, we constantly stumbled across the more common variety of mound in the Arsenal, the hump-backed bunkers where munitions were stored. Implausibly enough, they were called igloos. There were rows and rows of them, strung out along rail beds like lethal beads. Over the concrete vaults grass had been planted, so that from the air, glimpsed by enemy bombers, they would look like undulating hills. Sheep kept them grazed. The signs surrounding the igloos were larger and more strident than those warning us to keep away from the waste dumps. These we respected, for we feared that even a heavy footfall on the grassy roof of a bunker might set it off. According to tales that circulated among the children, three or four igloos had blown up over the years, from clumsy handling or the quirk of chemicals. Once a jet trainer crashed into a field of them and skidded far enough to trigger a pair. These numbers multiplied in our minds, until we imagined the igloos popping like corn. No, no, they were set far enough apart to avoid a chain reaction if one should explode, my father assured me. But in my reckoning the munitions bunkers were vaults of annihilation. I stubbornly believed that one day they all would blow, touched off by lightning, maybe, or by an enemy agent. Whenever I stole past those fields of bunkers or whenever they drifted like a flotilla of green humpbacked whales through my dreams, I imagined fire leaping from one to another, the spark flying outward to consume the whole creation. This poison I also carry in my bones, this conviction that we build our lives in minefields. Long before I learned what new sort of bombs had devoured Hiroshima and Nagasaki, I knew from creeping among those igloos full of old-fashioned explosives that, on any given day, someone else's reckless step might consume us all.

Of course we played constantly at war. How could we avoid it? At the five and-dime we bought plastic soldiers, their fists molded permanently around machine guns and grenades, their faces frozen into expressions of bravery or bloodlust. They were all men, all except the weaponless nurse who stood with uplifted lantern to inspect the wounded; and those of us who toyed at this mayhem were all boys. In the unused garden plot out back of the Circle, we excavated trenches and foxholes, embedded cannons inside rings of pebbles, heaped dirt into mounds to simulate ammo bunkers. Our miniature tanks left tread marks in the dust like those cut into the blacktop roads by real tanks. As we ran miniature trucks, our throats caught the exact groan of the diesel convoys that hauled army reservists past our door every summer weekend. When we grew tired of our Lilliputian battles, we took up weapons in our own hands. Any stick would do for a gun, any rock for a bomb. At the drugstore we bought war comics, and on wet afternoons we studied war movies on television to instruct us in the plots for our games. No one ever chose to play the roles of Japs or Nazis or Commies, and so the hateful labels were hung on the smallest or shabbiest kids. For the better part of my first three years in the Arsenal I was a villain, consigned to the Yellow Peril or the Red Plague. Like many of the runts, even while wearing the guise of a bad guy I refused to go down, protesting every lethal shot from the good guys. If all the kids eligible to serve as enemies quit the game, the Americans just blasted away at invisible foes, GIs against the universe.

Whenever we cared to we could glance up from our play in the garden battlefield and see the dish of a radar antenna spinning silently beyond the next ridge. We knew it scoured the sky for enemy bombers and, later, missiles. The air was filled with electronic threats. Every mile or so along the roads there were spiky transmitters, like six-foot-tall models of the Empire State Building, to magnify and boom along radio messages between security headquarters and the cruising guards. Imagining dire secrets whispered in code, I keened my ears to catch these broadcasts, as if by one particular resonance of brain cells I might snare the voices inside my skull. What I eventually heard, over a shortwave radio owned by one of the older boys, were guards jawing about lunch, muttering about the weather, complaining about wives or bills, or cursing deer.

Our favorite family outing on the long summer evenings, after supper, after the washing of dishes, was to drive the gravel roads of the Arsenal and count deer. We would surprise them in clearings, a pair or a dozen, grass drooping from their narrow muzzles, jaws working. They would lift their delicate heads and gaze at us with slick dark eyes, some of the bucks hefting intricate antlers, the fresh does thick-uddered, the fawns still dappled. If the herd was large enough to make counting tricky, my father would stop the car. And if we kept very still, the deer, after studying us awhile, would go back to their grazing. But any slight twitch, a throat cleared or the squeak of a window crank, would startle them. First one white tail would jerk up, then another and another, the tawny bodies wheeling, legs flashing, and the deer would vanish like smoke. Some nights we counted over three hundred.

There were so many deer that in bad winters the managers of the Arsenal ordered the dumping of hay on the snow to keep the herds from starving. When my father had charge of this chore, I rode atop the truckload of bales, watching the tire slices trail away behind us in the frozen crust. Still the weak went hungry. Sledding, we would find their withered carcasses beside the gnawed stems of elderberry bushes. A few generations earlier, wolves and mountain lions would have helped out the snow, culling the slow of foot. But since the only predators left were two-legged ones, men took on the task of thinning the herds, and naturally they culled out the strongest, the heavy-antlered bucks, the meaty does. Early each winter the game officials would calculate how many deer ought to be killed, and would sell that many hunting tags. Most of the licenses went to men who worked in the Arsenal, the carpenters and munitions loaders and firemen. But a quantity would always be reserved for visiting military brass.

They rolled into the Arsenal in chauffeured sedans or swooped down in star-spangled planes, these generals and colonels. Their hunting clothes smelled of mothballs. Their shotguns glistened with oil. Jeeps driven by orderlies delivered them to the brushwood blinds, where they slouched on canvas chairs and slugged whiskey to keep warm, waiting for the deer to run by. The deer would always run by, because local boys would have been out since dawn beating the bushes, scaring up a herd and driving it down the ravine past the hidden generals.

Each deer season of my childhood I heard about this hunt. It swelled in my imagination to the scale of myth and outstripped in glory the remote battles of the last war. It seemed even grander than the bloody feuds between frontiersmen and Indians. I itched to go along, if not as a hunter then as one of the beaters. Finally, when I turned thirteen, my father let me help round up deer for a party of shooters from the Pentagon.

A freezing rain the night before had turned the world to glass. As we fanned out over the brittle snow, our steps sounded like the shattering of windows. We soon found our deer, lurking where they had to be, in the frozen field where hay had been dumped. Casting about them our net of bodies, we left open only the path that led to the ravine where the officers waited. With a clap of hands we set them scurrying, the white tails like an avalanche, black hoofs punching the snow, taut hams kicking skyward. Not long after, we heard the crackle of shotguns. When the shooting was safely over, I hurried up to inspect the kills. The deer lay with legs crumpled beneath their bellies or jutting stiffly out, heads askew, tongues dangling like handles of leather. The wounded ones had stumbled away, trailing behind them ropes of blood; my father and the other seasoned hunters had run after to finish them off. The generals were tramping about in the red snow, noisily claiming their trophies, pinning tags on the ear of each downed beast. The local men gutted the deer. They heaped the steaming entrails on the snow and tied ropes through the tendons of each hind leg and dragged them to the waiting jeeps. I watched it all to the end that once, rubbed my face in it, and never again asked to work as a beater, or to watch the grown men shoot, or to hunt.

With the money I was paid for herding deer, I bought the fixings for rocket fuel. That was the next stage in our playing at war, the launching of miniature missiles. We started by wrapping tinfoil around the heads of kitchen matches, graduated to aluminum pipes crammed with gunpowder, and then to machined tubes that burned magnesium or zinc. On the walls of our bedrooms we tacked photos of real rockets, the v-2 and Viking; the homely Snark, Hound Dog, Bullpup, Honest John, Little John, Mighty Mouse, Davy Crockett; and the beauties with godly names—Atlas, Titan, Jupiter, Juno, Nike-Hercules—the pantheon of power. By then I knew what rode in the nose cones, I knew what sort of bombs had exploded in Japan two months before my birth; I even knew, from reading physics books, how we had snared those fierce bits of sun. But I grasped these awesome facts in the same numb way I grasped the definition of infinity. I carried the knowledge in me like an ungerminated seed.

There was a rumor among the children that atomic bombs were stored in the Arsenal. The adults denied it, as they denied our belief that ghosts of Indians haunted the burial mounds or that shades of strung-up farmers paced in the haylofts of barns, as they dismissed all our bogies. We went searching anyway. Wasting no time among the igloos, which were too obvious, too vulnerable, we searched instead in the boondocks for secret vaults that we felt certain would be surrounded by deadly electronics and would be perfect in their camouflage. Traipsing along railway spurs, following every set of wheel tracks, we eventually came to a fenced compound that satisfied all our suspicions. Through the wire mesh of fencing and above the earthen ramparts we could see the gray concrete skulls of bunkers. We felt certain that the eggs of annihilation had been laid in those vaults, but none of us dared climb the fence to investigate. It was as if, having sought out the lair of a god, we could not bring ourselves to approach the throne.

In our searches for the Bomb we happened across a good many other spots we were not supposed to see—dumps and manmade deserts, ponds once used for hatching fish and now smothered in oil, machine guns rusting in weeds, clicking signal boxes. But the most alluring discovery of all was the graveyard of bombers. This was a field crammed with the hulks of World War II Flying Fortresses, their crumpled olive-drab skins painted with enigmatic numbers and symbols, their wings twisted, propellers shattered, cockpits open to the rain. In one of them we found a pair of mannequins rigged up in flight gear, complete with helmets, wires running from every joint in their artificial bodies. What tests they had been used for in these crashed planes we had no way of guessing; we borrowed their gear and propped them in back to serve as navigators and bombardiers. Most of the instruments had been salvaged, but enough remained for us to climb into the cockpits and to fly imaginary bombing runs. Sitting where actual pilots had sat, clutching the butterfly wings of a steering wheel, gazing out through a cracked windshield, we rained fire and fury on the cities of the world. Not even the sight of the deer's guts steaming on the red snow had yet given me an inkling of how real streets would look beneath our storm of bombs. I was drunk on the fancied splendor of riding those metal leviathans, making them dance by a touch of my fingers. At the age when Samuel Clemens sat on the bank of the Mississippi River smitten by the power of steamboats, I watched rockets sputter on their firing stand, I sat in the cockpits of old bombers, hungry to pilot sky ships.

The sky over the Arsenal was sliced by plenty of routine ships, the screaming fighters, droning trainers, groaning transports, percussive helicopters; but what caught the attention of the children were the rare, rumored visitations of flying saucers. To judge by reports in the newspaper and on television, UFOS were sniffing about here and there all over the Earth. We studied the night sky hopefully, fearfully, but every promising light we spied turned into a commonplace aircraft. I was beginning to think the aliens had declared the Arsenal off-limits. But then a neighbor woman, who sometimes looked after my sister and me in the afternoons, told us she had ridden more than once in a flying saucer that used to come fetch her in the wee hours from the parking lot behind the Bachelor Officers' Quarters. Mrs. K. was about fifty when we knew her, a rotund woman who gave the impression of being too large for her body, as if at birth she had been wrapped in invisible cords which were beginning to give way. She had a pinched face and watery eyes, a mousy bookkeeper for a husband, and no children. She was fastidious about her house, where the oak floors gleamed with wax, bathrooms glittered like jeweled chambers, and fragile knickknacks balanced on shelves of glass. When my mother dropped us by her place for an afternoon's stay, we crept about in terror of sullying or breaking something. In all her house there was nothing for children to play with except, stashed away in the bottom drawer of her desk, a dog-eared pack of cards, a pair of dice, and a miniature roulette wheel. Soon tiring of these toys, my sister and I sat on the waxed floor and wheedled Mrs. K. into talking. At first she would maunder on about the life she had led on military bases around the world, about bridge parties and sewing circles; but eventually her eyes would begin to water and her teeth to chatter and she would launch into the history of her abduction by aliens.

"They're not at all like devils," she insisted, "but more like angels, with translucent skin that glows almost as if there were lights inside their bodies." And their ship bore no resemblance to saucers, she claimed. It was more like a diamond as large as a house, all the colors of the rainbow streaming through the facets. The angelic creatures stopped her in the parking lot during one of her stargazing walks, spoke gentle English inside her head, took her on board their craft, and put her to sleep. When she awoke she was lying naked, surrounded by a ring of princely aliens, and the landscape visible through the diamond walls of the ship was the vague purple of wisteria blossoms. "They weren't the least bit crude or nasty," she said, the words coming so fast they were jamming in her throat, "no, no they examined me like the most polite of doctors, because all they wanted was to save us from destroying ourselves, you see, and in order to do that, first they had to understand our anatomy, and that's why they had chosen me, don't you see, they had singled me out to teach them about our species," she insisted, touching her throat, "and to give me the secret of our salvation, me of all people, you see, *me.*"

My sister had the good sense to keep mum about our babysitter's stories, but I was so frazzled by hopes of meeting with these aliens and learning their world-saving secrets that I blabbed about the possibility to my mother, who quickly wormed the entire chronicle from me. We never visited Mrs. K. again, but occasionally we would see her vacuuming the lawn in front of her house. "Utterly crazy," my mother declared.

Mrs. K. was not alone in her lunacy. Every year or so one of the career soldiers, having stared too long into the muzzle of his own gun, would go berserk or break down weeping. More than a few of the army wives had turned to drink and drugs. Now and again an ambulance would purr into the Circle and cart one of them away for therapy. When at home, they usually kept hidden, stewing in bedrooms, their children grown and gone or off to school or buried in toys. Outside, with faces cracked like the leather of old purses, loaded up with consoling chemicals, the crazed women teetered carefully down the sidewalk, as if down a tightrope over an abyss.

The Arsenal fed on war and rumors of war. When the Pentagon's budget was fat, the Arsenal's economy prospered. We could tell how good or bad the times were by reading our fathers' faces, or by counting the pickup trucks in the parking lots. The folks who lived just outside the chain-link fence in trailers and farmhouses did poorly in the slow spells, but did just fine whenever an outbreak of Red Scare swept through Congress. In the lulls between wars, the men used to scan the headlines looking for omens of strife in the way farmers would scan the horizon for promises of rain.

In 1957, when the Arsenal was in the doldrums and parents were bickering across the dinner table, one October afternoon between innings of a softball game somebody read aloud the news about the launching of Sputnik. The mothers clucked their tongues and the fathers groaned; but soon the wise heads among them gloated, for they knew this Russian feat would set the load lines humming, and it did.

Our model rocketry took on a new cast. It occurred to us that any launcher capable of parking a satellite in orbit could plant an H-bomb in the Circle. If one of those bitter pills ever landed, we realized from our reading, there would be no Circle, no dallying deer, no forests, no Arsenal. Suddenly there were explosives above our heads as well as beneath our feet. The cracks in the faces of the crazed ladies deepened. Guards no longer joked with us as we passed through the gates to school. We children forgot how to sleep. For hours after dark we squirmed on our beds, staring skyward. "Why don't you eat?" our mothers scolded. Aged thirteen or fourteen, I stood one day gripping the edge of the marble-topped table in our living room, staring through a glass bell at the spinning golden balls of an anniversary clock, and cried, "I don't ever want to be a soldier, not ever, ever!"

On weekends in summer the soldiers still played war. They liked to scare up herds of deer with their tanks and pin them against a corner of the fence. Snooping along afterward, we discovered tufts of hair and clots of flesh caught in the barbed wire from the bucks that had leapt over. Once, after a weekend soldier's cigarette had set off a brushfire, we found the charred bodies of a dozen deer. We filled ourselves with that sight, and knew what it meant. There we lay, every child in the Arsenal, every adult, every soul within reach of the bombs—twisted black lumps trapped against a fence, with no place to run. I have dreamed of those charred deer ever since. During the war in Vietnam, every time I read or heard about napalm, my head filled with visions of those blackened lumps.

To a child it seemed the only salvation was in running away. Parents and the family roof were no protection from this terror. My notebooks filled with designs for orbiting worlds we could build from scratch and for rocket ships that would carry us to fresh, unpoisoned planets. But I soon realized that no more than a handful of us could escape to the stars; and there was too much on Earth—the blue fountains of lilacs, the red streak of a fox across snow, the faces of friends—that I could never abandon. I took longer and longer walks through the backwoods of the Arsenal, soaking in the green juices; but as I grew older, the forest seemed to shrink, the fences drew in, the munitions bunkers and the desolate chemical dumps seemed to spread like a rash, until I could not walk far in any direction without stumbling into a reminder of our preparations for doom.

Because the foundations of old farms were vanishing beneath the tangle of briars and saplings, for most of my childhood I had allowed myself to believe that nature would undo whatever mess we made. But the scars from these new chemicals resisted the return of life. The discolored dirt remained bare for years and years. Tank trucks spraying herbicides to save the cost of mowing stripped the roads and meadows of wildflowers. Fish floated belly-up in the scum of ponds. The shells of bird eggs, laced with molecules of our invention, were too flimsy to hold new chicks. The threads of the world were beginning to unravel.

In a single winter a hired trapper cleared out the beavers, which had been snarling the waterways, and the foxes, which had troubled the family dogs. Our own collie, brought as a puppy from Memphis, began to chase deer with a pack of dogs. At night he would slink back home with bloody snout and the smell of venison on his laboring breath. The guards warned us to keep him in, but he broke every rope. Once I saw the pack of them, wolves again, running deer across a field. Our collie was in the lead, gaining on a doe, and as I watched he bounded up and seized her by the ear and dragged her down, and the other dogs clamped on at the belly and throat. I preferred this wild killing to the shooting-gallery slaughter of the hunting season. If our own dogs could revert to wildness, perhaps there was still hope for the Earth. But one day the guards shot the whole wolfish pack. Nature, in the largest sense of natural laws, would outlast us; but no particular scrap of it, no dog or pond or two-legged beast, was guaranteed to survive.

There was comfort in the tales forever circulating among the children of marvelous deer glimpsed at dusk or dawn, bucks with white legs, a doe with pale fur in the shape of a saddle on her back, and, one year, a pair of snowy albinos. Several of the children had seen the all-white deer. In 1962 I spent many sunsets looking for them, needing to find them, hungering for these tokens of nature's prodigal energies. By September I still had seen neither hide nor hair of them. The showdown over the placement of Soviet missiles in Cuba took place that October; Kennedy and Khrushchev squared off at the opposite ends of a nuclear street, hands hovering near the butts of their guns. For two weeks, while these desperadoes brooded over whether to start the final shooting, I passed all the daylight hours after school outdoors, looking for those albino deer. Once, on the edge of a thicket, on the edge of darkness, I thought I glimpsed them, milky spirits, wisps of fog. But I could not be sure. Eventually the leaders of the superpowers lifted their hands a few inches away from their guns; the missiles did not fly. I returned to my studies, but gazed stupidly at every page through a meshwork of fear. In December the existence of the albino deer was proven beyond a doubt, for one afternoon in hunting season, an officer and his wife drove into the Circle with the pair of ghostly bodies tied onto the hood of their car.

The following year—the year when John Kennedy was murdered and I registered for the draft and the tide of U.S. soldiers began to lap against the shores of Asia—my family moved from the Arsenal. "You'll sleep better now," my mother assured me. "You'll fatten up in no time." During the years I spent inside the chain-link fences, almost every night at suppertime outdated bombs would be detonated at the ammo dump. The concussion rattled the milk glass and willowware in the corner cupboard, rattled the forks against our plates and the cups against our teeth. It was like the muttering of local gods, a reminder of who ruled our neighborhood. From the moment I understood what those explosions meant, what small sparks they were of the engulfing fire, I lost my appetite. But even outside the Arsenal, a mile or an ocean away, every night at suppertime my fork still stuttered against the plate, my teeth still chattered from the remembered explosions. They still do. Everywhere now there are bunkers beneath the humped green hills; electronic challenges and threats needle through the air we breathe; the last wild beasts fling themselves against our steel boundaries. The fences of the Arsenal have stretched outward until they encircle the entire planet. I feel, now, I can never move outside.

# The Men We Carry in
# Our Minds

his must be a hard time for women," I say to my friend Anneke.
"They have so many paths to choose from, and so many voices calling them."

"I think it's a lot harder for men," she replies.

"How do you figure that?"

"The women I know feel excited, innocent, like crusaders in a just cause. The
men I know are eaten up with guilt."

We are sitting at the kitchen table drinking sassafras tea, our hands wrapped
around the mugs because this April morning is cool and drizzly. "Like a Dutch
morning," Anneke told me earlier. She is Dutch herself, a writer and midwife
and peacemaker, with the round face and sad eyes of a woman in a Vermeer
painting who might be waiting for the rain to stop, for a door to open. She leans
over to sniff a sprig of lilac, pale lavender, that rises from a vase of cobalt blue.

"Women feel such pressure to be everything, do everything," I say. "Career,
kids, art, politics. Have their babies and get back to the office a week later. It's
as if they're trying to overcome a million years' worth of evolution in one lifetime."

"But we help one another. We don't try to lumber on alone, like so many
wounded grizzly bears, the way men do." Anneke sips her tea. I gave her the
mug with owls on it, for wisdom. "And we have this deep down sense that we're
in the *right*—we've been held back, passed over, used—while men feel they're
in the wrong. Men are the ones who've been discredited, who have to search
their souls."

I search my soul. I discover guilty feelings aplenty—toward the poor, the Vietnamese, Native Americans, the whales, an endless list of debts—a guilt in each case that is as bright and unambiguous as a neon sign. But toward women I feel something more confused, a snarl of shame, envy, wary tenderness, and amazement. This muddle troubles me. To hide my unease I say, "You're right, it's tough being a man these days."

"Don't laugh." Anneke frowns at me, mournful-eyed, through the sassafras steam. "I wouldn't be a man for anything. It's much easier being the victim. All the victim has to do is break free. The persecutor has to live with his past."

How deep is that past? I find myself wondering after Anneke has left. How much of an inheritance do I have to throw off? Is it just the beliefs I breathed in as a child? Do I have to scour memory back through father and grandfather? Through St. Paul? Beyond Stonehenge and into the twilit caves? I'm convinced the past we must contend with is deeper even than speech. When I think back on my childhood, on how I learned to see men and women, I have a sense of ancient, dizzying depths. The back roads of Tennessee and Ohio where I grew up were probably closer, in their sexual patterns, to the campsites of Stone Age hunters than to the genderless cities of the future into which we are rushing.

The first men, besides my father, I remember seeing were black convicts and white guards, in the cotton field across the road from our farm on the outskirts of Memphis. I must have been three or four. The prisoners wore dingy gray-and-black zebra suits, heavy as canvas, sodden with sweat. Hatless, stooped, they chopped weeds in the fierce heat, row after row, breathing the acrid dust of boll weevil poison. The overseers wore dazzling white shirts and broad shadowy hats. The oiled barrels of their shotguns flashed in the sunlight. Their faces in memory are utterly blank. Of course those men, white and black, have become for me an emblem of racial hatred. But they have also come to stand for the twin poles of my early vision of manhood—the brute toiling animal and the boss.

When I was a boy, the men I knew labored with their bodies. They were marginal farmers, just scraping by, or welders, steelworkers, carpenters; they swept floors, dug ditches, mined coal, or drove trucks, their forearms ropy with muscle; they trained horses, stoked furnaces, built tires, stood on assembly lines wrestling parts onto cars and refrigerators. They got up before light, worked all day long whatever the weather, and when they came home at night they looked as though somebody had been whipping them. In the evenings and on weekends they worked on their own places, tilling gardens that were lumpy with clay, fixing broken-down cars, hammering on houses that were always too drafty, too leaky, too small.

The bodies of the men I knew were twisted and maimed in ways visible and invisible. The nails of their hands were black and split, the hands tattooed with scars. Some had lost fingers. Heavy lifting had given many of them finicky backs and guts weak from hernias. Racing against conveyor belts had given them ulcers. Their ankles and knees ached from years of standing on concrete. Anyone who had worked for long around machines was hard of hearing. They squinted, and the skin of their faces was creased like the leather of old work gloves. There were times, studying them, when I dreaded growing up. Most of them coughed, from dust or cigarettes, and most of them drank cheap wine or whiskey, so their eyes looked bloodshot and bruised. The fathers of my friends always seemed older than the mothers. Men wore out sooner. Only women lived into old age.

As a boy I also knew another sort of men, who did not sweat and break down like mules. They were soldiers, and so far as I could tell they scarcely worked at all. During my early school years we lived on a military base, an arsenal in Ohio, and every day I saw GIs in the guard shacks, on the stoops of barracks, at the wheels of olive-drab Chevrolets. The chief fact of their lives appeared to be boredom. Long after I left the Arsenal I came to recognize the sour smell the soldiers gave off as that of souls in limbo. They were all waiting—for wars, for transfers, for leaves, for promotions, for the end of their hitch—like so many braves waiting for the hunt to begin. Unlike the warriors of older tribes, however, they would have no say about when the battle would start or how it would be waged. Their waiting was broken only when they practiced for war. They fired guns at targets, drove tanks across the churned-up fields of the military reservation, set off bombs in the wrecks of old fighter planes. I knew this was all play. But I also felt certain that when the hour for killing arrived, they would kill. When the real shooting started, many of them would die. This was what soldiers were *for,* just as a hammer was for driving nails.

Warriors and toilers: those seemed, in my boyhood vision, to be the chief destinies for men. They weren't the only destinies, as I learned from having a few male teachers, from reading books, and from watching television. But the men on television—the politicians, the astronauts, the generals, the savvy lawyers, the philosophical doctors, the bosses who gave orders to both soldiers and laborers—seemed as remote and unreal to me as the figures in tapestries. I could no more imagine growing up to become one of these cool, potent creatures than I could imagine becoming a prince.

A nearer and more hopeful example was that of my father, who had escaped from a red-dirt farm to a tire factory, and from the assembly line to the front office. Eventually he dressed in a white shirt and tie. He carried himself as if he had been born to work with his mind. But his body, remembering the earlier years of slogging work, began to give out on him in his fifties, and it quit on him entirely before he turned sixty-five. Even such a partial escape from man's fate as he had accomplished did not seem possible for most of the boys I knew. They joined the army, stood in line for jobs in the smoky plants, helped build highways. They were bound to work as their fathers had worked, killing themselves or preparing to kill others.

In college—a scholarship enabled me not only to go, a rare enough feat in my circle, but to study in a university meant for the children of the rich—I met for the first time young men who had assumed from birth that they would lead lives of comfort and power. And for the first time I met women who told me that men were guilty of having kept all the joys and privileges of the Earth for themselves. I was baffled. What privileges? What joys? I thought about the maimed, dismal lives of most of the men back home. What had they stolen from their wives and daughters? The right to go five days a week, twelve months a year, for thirty or forty years to a steel mill or a coal mine? The right to drop bombs and die in war? The right to feel every leak in the roof, every gap in the fence, every cough in the engine, as a wound they must mend? The right to feel, when the layoff comes or the plant shuts down, not only afraid but ashamed?

I was slow to understand the deep grievances of women. This was because, as a boy, I had envied them. Before college, the only people I had ever known who were interested in art or music or literature, the only ones who read books, the only ones who ever seemed to enjoy a sense of ease and grace were the mothers and daughters. Like the menfolk, they fretted about money, they scrimped and made do. But when the pay stopped coming in, they were not the ones who had failed. Nor did they have to go to war, and that seemed to me a blessed fact. By comparison with the narrow, ironclad days of fathers, there was an expansiveness, I thought, in the days of mothers. They went to see neighbors, to shop in town, on errands to school, to the library, to church. No doubt, had I looked harder at their lives, I would have envied them less. It was not my fate to become a woman, so it was easier for me to see the graces. Few of them held jobs outside the home, and those who did filled thankless roles, as clerks and waitresses. I didn't see, then, what a prison a house could be, since houses seemed to me brighter, handsomer places than any factory. I did not realize—because such things were never spoken of—how often women suffered from men's bullying. I did learn about the wretchedness of wives abandoned, single mothers, widows; but I also learned about the wretchedness of lone men. Even then I could see how exhausting it was for a mother to cater all day to the needs of young children. But if I had been asked, as a boy, to choose between tending a baby and tending a machine, I think I would have chosen the baby. (Having now tended both, I know I would choose the baby.)

So I was baffled when the women at college accused me and my sex of having cornered the world's pleasures. I think something like my bafflement has been felt by other boys—and by girls as well—who grew up in dirt-poor farm country, in mining country, in black ghettos, in Hispanic barrios, in the shadows of factories, in Third World nations—any place where the fate of men is as grim, as bleak, as the fate of women. Toilers and warriors. I realize now how ancient these identities are, how deep the tug they exert on men, the undertow of a thousand generations. The miseries I saw, as a boy, in the lives of nearly all men I continue to see in the lives of many—the body-breaking toil, the tedium, the call to be tough, the humiliating powerlessness, the battle for a living and for territory.

When the women I met at college thought about the joys and privileges of men, they did not carry in their minds the sort of men I had known in my childhood. They thought of their fathers, who were bankers, physicians, architects, stockbrokers, the big wheels of the big cities. These fathers rode the train to work, or drove cars that cost more than any of my childhood houses. They were attended from morning to night by female helpers, wives and nurses and secretaries. They were never laid off, never short of cash at month's end, never lined up for welfare. These fathers made decisions that mattered. They ran the world.

The daughters of such men wanted to share in this power, this glory. So did I. They yearned for a say over their future, for jobs worthy of their abilities, for the right to live at peace, unmolested, whole. Yes, I thought, yes yes. The difference between me and these daughters was that they saw me, because of my sex, as destined from birth to become like their fathers, and therefore as an enemy to their desires. But I knew better. I wasn't an enemy, in fact or in feeling. I was an ally. If I had known, then, how to tell them so, would they have believed me? Would they now?

# Doing Time in the
# Thirteenth Chair

*T*he courtroom is filled with the ticking of a clock and the smell of mold. Listening to the minutes click away, I imagine bombs or mechanical hearts sealed behind the limestone walls. Forty of us have been yanked out of our usual orbits and called to appear for jury duty in this ominous room, beneath the stained-glass dome of the county courthouse. We sit in rows like strangers in a theater, coats rumpled in our laps, crossing and uncrossing our legs, waiting for the show to start.

I feel sulky and rebellious, the way I used to feel when a grade-school teacher made me stay inside during recess. This was supposed to have been the first day of my Christmas vacation, and the plain, uncitizenly fact is that I don't want to be here. I want to be home hammering together some bookshelves for my wife. I want to be out tromping the shores of Lake Monroe with my eye cocked skyward for bald eagles and sharp-shinned hawks.

But the computer-printed letter said to report today for jury, and so here I sit. The judge beams down at us from his bench. Tortoise-shell glasses, twenty-dollar haircut, square boyish face: although probably in his early forties, he could pass for a student-body president. He reminds me of an owlish television know-it-all named Mr. Wizard who used to conduct scientific experiments (Magnetism! Litmus tests! Sulfur dioxide!) on a kids' show in the 1950s. Like Mr. Wizard, he lectures us in slow, pedantic speech: trial by one's peers, tradition stretching back centuries to England, defendant innocent until proven guilty beyond a reasonable doubt, and so abundantly on. I spy around for the clock. It must be overhead, I figure, up in the cupola above the dome, raining its ticktocks down on us.

When the lecture is finished, the judge orders us to rise, lift our hands, and swear to uphold the truth. There is a cracking of winter-stiff knees as we stand and again as we sit down. Then he introduces the principal actors: the sleek young prosecutor, who peacocks around like a politician on the hustings; the married pair of brooding, elegantly dressed defense lawyers; and the defendant. I don't want to look at this man who is charged with crimes against the "peace and dignity" of the State of Indiana. I don't want anything to do with his troubles. But I grab an image anyway, of a squat, slit-eyed man about my age, mid-thirties, stringy black hair parted in the middle and dangling like curtains across his face, sparse black beard. The chin whiskers and squinted-up eyes make him look faintly Chinese, and faintly grimacing.

Next the judge reads a list of twelve names, none of them mine, and twelve sworn citizens shuffle into the jury box. The lawyers have at them, darting questions. How do you feel about drugs? Would you say the defendant there looks guilty because he has a beard? Are you related to any police officers? Are you pregnant? When these twelve have finished answering, the attorneys scribble names on sheets of paper which they hand to the judge, and eight of the first bunch are sent packing. The judge reads eight more names, the jury box fills up with fresh bodies, the questioning resumes. Six of these get the heave-ho. And so the lawyers cull through the potential jurors, testing and checking them like two men picking over apples in the supermarket. At length they agree on a dozen, and still my name has not been called. Hooray, I think. I can build those bookshelves after all, can watch those hawks.

Before setting the rest of us free, however, the judge consults his list. "I am calling alternate juror number one," he says, and then he pronounces my name.

Groans echo down my inmost corridors. For the first time I notice a thirteenth chair beside the jury box, and that is where the judge orders me to go.

"Yours is the most frustrating job," the judge advises me soothingly. "Unless someone else falls ill or gets called away, you will have to listen to all the proceedings without taking part in the jury's final deliberations or decisions."

I feel as though I have been invited to watch the first four acts of a five-act play. Never mind, I console myself; the lawyers will throw me out. I'm the only one in the courtroom besides the defendant who sports a beard or long hair. A backpack decorated with NO NUKES and PEACE NOW and SAVE THE WHALES buttons leans against my boots. How can they expect me, a fiction writer, to confine myself to facts? I am unreliable, a confessed fabulist, a marginal Quaker and Wobbly socialist, a man so out of phase with my community that I am thrown into fits of rage by the local newspaper. The lawyers will take a good look at me and race one another to the bench for the privilege of having the judge boot me out.

But neither Mr. Defense nor Mr. Prosecution quite brings himself to focus on my shady features. Each asks me a perfunctory question, the way vacationers will press a casual thumb against the spare tire before hopping into the car for a trip. If there's air in the tire, you don't bother about blemishes. And that is all I am, a spare juror stashed away in the trunk of the court, in case one of the twelve originals gives out during the trial.

Ticktock. The judge assures us that we should be finished in five days, just in time for Christmas. The real jurors exchange forlorn glances. Here I sit, number thirteen, and nobody looks my way. Knowing I am stuck here for the duration, I perk up, blink my eyes. Like the bear going over the mountain, I might as well see what I can see.

What I see is a parade of mangled souls. Some of them sit on the witness stand and reveal their wounds; some of them remain offstage, summoned up only by the words of those who testify. The case has to do with the alleged sale, earlier this year, of hashish and cocaine to a confidential informer. First, the prosecutor stands at a podium in front of the jury and tells us how it all happened, detail by criminal detail, and promises to prove every fact to our utter satisfaction. Next, one of the defense attorneys has a fling at us. It is the husband of the Mr. and-Mrs. team, a melancholy-looking man with bald pate and muttonchop sideburns, deep creases in the chocolate skin of his forehead. Leaning on the podium, he vows that he will raise a flock of doubts in our minds— grave doubts, reasonable doubts—particularly regarding the seedy character of the confidential informer. They both speak well, without hemming and hawing, without stumbling over syntactic cliffs, better than senators at a press conference. Thus, like rival suitors, they begin to woo the jury.

At midmorning, before hearing from the first witness, we take a recess. (It sounds more and more like school.) Thirteen of us with peel-away JUROR tags stuck to our shirts and sweaters retreat to the jury room. We drink coffee and make polite chat. Since the only thing we have in common is this trial, and since the judge has just forbidden us to talk about that, we grind our gears trying to get a conversation started. I find out what everybody does in the way of work: a bar waitress, a TV repairman (losing customers while he sits here), a department store security guard, a dentist's assistant, an accountant, a nursing home nurse, a cleaning woman, a caterer, a mason, a boisterous old lady retired from rearing children (and married, she tells us, to a school crossing guard), a meek college student with the demeanor of a groundhog, a teacher. Three of them right now are unemployed. Six men, six women, with ages ranging from twenty-one to somewhere above seventy. Chaucer could gather this bunch together for a literary pilgrimage, and he would not have a bad sampling of small-town America.

Presently the bailiff looks in to see what we're up to. She is a jowly woman, fiftyish, with short hair the color and texture of buffed aluminum. She wears silvery half-glasses of the sort favored by librarians; in the courtroom she peers at us above the frames with a librarian's skeptical glance, as if to make sure we are awake. To each of us she now gives a small yellow pad and a ballpoint pen. We are to write our names on the backs, take notes on them during the trial, and surrender them to her whenever we leave the courtroom. (School again.) Without saying so directly, she lets us know that we are her flock and she is our shepherd. Anything we need, any yen we get for traveling, we should let her know.

I ask her whether I can go downstairs for a breath of fresh air, and the bailiff answers "Sure." On the stairway I pass a teenage boy who is listlessly polishing with a rag the wrought-iron filigree that supports the banister. Old men sheltering from December slouch on benches just inside the ground-floor entrance of the courthouse. Their faces have been caved in by disappointment and the loss of teeth. Two-dollar cotton work gloves, the cheapest winter hand-covers, stick out of their back pockets. They are veterans of this place; so when they see me coming with the blue JUROR label pasted on my chest, they look away. Don't tamper with jurors, especially under the very nose of the law. I want to tell them I'm not a real juror, only a spare, number thirteen. I want to pry old stories out of them, gossip about hunting and dogs, about their favorite pickup trucks, their worst jobs. I want to ask them when and how it all started to go wrong for them. Did they hear a snap when the seams of their life began to come apart? But they will not be fooled into looking at me, not these wily old men with the crumpled faces. They believe the label on my chest and stare down at their unlaced shoes.

I stick my head out the door and swallow some air. The lighted thermometer on the bank reads twenty-eight degrees. Schmaltzy Christmas organ music rebounds from the brick-and-limestone shop fronts of the town square. The Salvation Army bell rings and rings. Delivery trucks hustling through yellow lights blare their horns at jaywalkers.

The bailiff must finally come fetch me, and I feel like a wayward sheep. On my way back upstairs, I notice the boy dusting the same square foot of filigree, and realize that he is doing this as a penance. Some judge ordered him to clean this metalwork. I'd like to ask the kid what mischief he's done, but the bailiff, looking very dour, is at my heels.

In the hallway she lines us up in our proper order, me last. Everybody stands up when we enter the courtroom, and then, as if we have rehearsed these routines, we all sit down at once. Now come the facts.

The facts are a mess. They are full of gaps, chuckholes, switchbacks, and dead ends—just like life.

At the outset we are shown three small plastic bags. Inside the first is a wad of aluminum foil about the size of an earlobe; the second contains two white pills; the third holds a pair of stamp-sized square packets of folded brown paper. A chemist from the state police lab testifies that he examined these items and found cocaine inside the brown packets, hashish inside the wad of aluminum foil. As for the white pills, they are counterfeits of a popular barbiturate, one favored by politicians and movie stars. They're depressants—downers—but they contain no "controlled substances."

There follows half a day's worth of testimony about how the bags were sealed, who locked them in the narcotics safe at the Bloomington police station, which officer drove them up to the lab in Indianapolis and which drove them back again, who carried them in his coat pocket and who carried them in his briefcase. Even the judge grows bored during this tedious business. He yawns, tips back in his chair, sips coffee from a mug, folds and unfolds with deft thumbs a square of paper about the size of the cocaine packets. The wheels of justice grind slowly. We hear from police officers in uniform, their handcuffs clanking, and from mustachioed officers in civvies, revolvers bulging under their suit coats. From across the courtroom, the bailiff glares at us above her librarian's glasses, alert to catch us napping. She must be an expert at judging the degrees of tedium.

"Do you have to go back and be in the jail again tomorrow?" my little boy asks me at supper.

"Not jail," I correct him. "Jury. I'm in the jury."

"With real police?"

"Yes."

"And guns?"

"Yes, real guns."

On the second day there is much shifting of limbs in the jury box when the confidential informer, whom the police call 190, takes the stand. Curly-haired, thirty-three years old, bear-built and muscular like a middle-range wrestler, slow of eye, calm under the cross-fire of questions, 190 works—when he works—as a drywall finisher. (In other words, he gets plasterboard ready for painting. It's a dusty, blinding job; you go home powdered white as a ghost, and you taste the joint-filler all night.) Like roughly one-quarter of the construction workers in the county, right now he's unemployed.

The story he tells is essentially this: Just under a year ago two cops showed up at his house. They'd been tipped off that he had a mess of stolen goods in his basement, stuff he'd swiped from over in a neighboring county. "Now look here," the cops said to him, "you help us out with some cases we've got going, and we'll see what we can do to help you when this here burglary business comes to court." "Like how?" he said. "Like tell us what you know about hot property, and maybe finger a drug dealer or so." He said yes to that, with the two cops sitting at his kitchen table, and—zap!—he was transformed into 190. (Hearing of this miraculous conversion, I am reminded of Saul on the road to Damascus, the devil's agent suddenly seeing the light and joining the angels.) In this new guise he gave information that led to several arrests and some prison terms, including one for his cousin and two or three for other buddies.

In this particular case, his story goes on, he asked a good friend of his where a guy could buy some, you know, drugs. The friend's brother led him to Bennie's trailer, where Bennie offered to sell 190 about any kind of drug a man's heart could desire. "All I want's some hash," 190 told him, "but I got to go get some money off my old lady first." "Then go get it," said Bennie.

Where 190 went was to the police station. There they fixed him up to make a "controlled buy": searched him, searched his car; strapped a radio transmitter around his waist, took his money and gave him twenty police dollars to make the deal. Back 190 drove to Bennie's place, and on his tail in an unmarked police car drove Officer B., listening over the radio to every burp and glitch sent out by 190's secret transmitter. On the way, 190 picked up a six-pack of Budweiser. ("If you walk into a suspect's house drinking a can of beer," Officer B. later tells us, "usually nobody'll guess you're working for the police.") Inside the trailer, the woman Bennie lives with was now fixing supper, and her three young daughters were playing cards on the linoleum floor. 190 bought a gram of blond Lebanese hashish from Bennie for six dollars. Then 190 said that his old lady was on him bad to get her some downers, and Bennie obliged by selling him a couple of 714s (the white pills favored by movie stars and politicians) at seven dollars for the pair. They shot the bull awhile, Bennie bragging about how big a dealer he used to be (ten pounds of hash and five hundred hits of acid a week), 190 jawing along like an old customer. After about twenty minutes in the trailer, 190 drove to a secluded spot near the L & N railroad depot, and there he handed over the hash and pills to Officer B., who milked the details out of him.

Four days later, 190 went through the same routine, this time buying two packets of cocaine—two "dimes'" worth—from Bennie for twenty dollars. Inside the trailer were half a dozen or so of Bennie's friends, drinking whiskey and smoking pot and watching TV and playing backgammon and generally getting the most out of a Friday night. Again Officer B. tailed 190, listened to the secret radio transmission, and took it all down in a debriefing afterwards behind the Colonial Bakery.

The lawyers burn up a full day leading 190 through this story, dropping questions like breadcrumbs to lure him on, Mr. Prosecutor trying to guide him out of the labyrinth of memory and Mr. Defense trying to get him lost. 190 refuses to get lost. He tells and retells his story without stumbling, intent as a wrestler on a dangerous hold.

On the radio news I hear that U.S. ships have intercepted freighters bound from Beirut carrying tons and tons of Lebanese hashish, the very same prize strain of hash that 190 claims he bought from Bennie. Not wanting to irk the Lebanese government, the radio says, our ships let the freighters through. Tons and tons sailing across the Mediterranean—into how many one-gram slugs could that cargo be divided?

Out of jail the defense lawyers subpoena one of 190's brothers, who is awaiting his own trial on felony charges. He has a rabbity look about him, face pinched with fear, ready to bolt for the nearest exit. His canary yellow T-shirt is emblazoned with a scarlet silhouette of the Golden Gate Bridge. The shirt and the fear make looking at him painful. He is one of seven brothers and four sisters. Hearing that total of eleven children—the same number as in my father's family—I wonder if the parents were ever booked for burglary or other gestures of despair.

This skittish gent tells us that he always buys his drugs from his brother, good old 190. And good old 190, he tells us further, has a special fondness for snorting cocaine. Glowing there on the witness stand in his yellow shirt, dear brother gives the lie to one after another of 190's claims. But just when I'm about ready, hearing all of this fraternal gossip, to consign 190 to the level of hell reserved by Dante for liars, the prosecutor takes over the questioning. He soon draws out a confession that there has been a bitter feud recently between the two brothers. "And haven't you been found on three occasions to be mentally incompetent to stand trial?" the prosecutor demands.

"Yessir," mutters the brother.

"And haven't you spent most of the past year in and out of mental institutions?"

"Yessir."

This second admission is so faint, like a wheeze, that I must lean forward to hear it, even though I am less than two yards away. While the prosecutor lets this damning confession sink into the jury, the rabbity brother just sits there, as if exposed on a rock while the hawks dive, his eyes pinched closed.

By day three of the trial, we jurors are no longer strangers to one another. Awaiting our entry into court, we exhibit wallet photos of our children, of nieces and nephews. We moan in chorus about our Christmas shopping lists. The caterer tells about serving three thousand people at a basketball banquet. The boisterous old lady, to whom we have all taken a liking, explains how the long hairs on her white cats used to get on her husband's black suit pants until she put the cats out in the garage with heating pads in their boxes.

"Where do you leave your car?" the accountant asks.

"On the street," explains the lady. "I don't want to crowd those cats. They're particular as all get-out."

People compare their bowling scores, their insurance rates, their diets. The mason, who now weighs about 300 pounds, recounts how he once lost 129 pounds in nine months. His blood pressure got so bad he had to give up dieting, and inside of a year he'd gained back all his weight and then some. The nurse, who wrestles the bloated or shriveled bodies of elderly paupers at the city's old folks' home, complains about her leg joints, and we all sympathize. The security guard entertains us with sagas about shoplifters. We compare notes on car wrecks, on where to get a transmission overhauled, on the outgoing college football coach and the incoming Bloomington mayor. We talk, in fact, about everything under the sun except the trial.

In the hall, where we line up for our reentry into the courtroom, a sullen boy sits at a table scrawling on a legal pad. Line after line he copies the same sentence: "I never will steal anything ever again." More penance. He's balancing on the first rung of a ladder that leads up—or down—to the electric chair. Somewhere in the middle of the ladder is a good long prison sentence, and that, I calculate, is what is at stake in our little drug-dealing case.

On the third day of testimony, we learn that 190 has been hidden away overnight by police. After he stepped down from the witness stand yesterday, Bennie's mate, Rebecca, greeted the informant outside in the lobby and threatened to pull a bread knife out of her purse and carve him into mincemeat. I look with new interest at the stolid, bulky, black-haired woman who has been sitting since the beginning of the trial right behind the defendant. From time to time she has leaned forward, touched Bennie on the shoulder, and bent close to whisper something in his good ear. She reminds me of the Amish farmwives of my Ohio childhood—stern, unpainted, built stoutly for heavy chores, her face a fortress against outsiders.

When Rebecca takes the stand, just half a dozen feet from where I sit in chair thirteen, I sense a tigerish fierceness beneath her numb surface. She plods along behind the prosecutor's questions until he asks her, rhetorically, whether she would like to see Bennie X put in jail; then she lashes out. God no, she doesn't want him locked away. Didn't he take her in when she had two kids already and a third in the oven, and her first husband run off, and the cupboards empty? And haven't they been living together just as good as married for eight years, except while he was in jail, and don't her three little girls call him Daddy? And hasn't he been working on the city garbage trucks, getting up at four in the morning, coming home smelling like other people's trash, and hasn't she been bagging groceries at the supermarket, her hands slashed with paper cuts, and her mother looking after the girls, all so they can keep off welfare? Damn right she doesn't want him going to any prison.

What's more, Rebecca declares, Bennie don't deserve prison because he's clean. Ever since he got out of the slammer a year ago, he's quit dealing. He's done his time and he's mended his ways and he's gone straight. What about that sale of cocaine? the prosecutor wants to know. It never happened, Rebecca vows. She was there in the trailer the whole blessed night, and she never saw Bennie sell nobody nothing, least of all cocaine, which he never used because it's too expensive—it'll run you seventy-five dollars a day—and which he never sold even when he was dealing. The prosecutor needles her: How can she remember that particular night so confidently? She can remember, she flares at him, because early that evening she got a call saying her sister's ten-year-old crippled boy was fixing to die, and all the family was going to the children's hospital in Indianapolis to watch him pass away. That was a night she'll never forget as long as she lives.

When I was a boy, my friends and I believed that if you killed a snake, the mate would hunt you out in your very bed and strangle or gnaw or smother you. We held a similar belief regarding bears, wolves, and mountain lions, although we were much less likely to run into any of those particular beasts. I have gone years without remembering that bit of child's lore, until today, when Rebecca's turn on the witness stand revives it. I can well imagine her stashing a bread knife in her purse. And if she loses her man for years and stony years, and has to rear those three girls alone, the cupboards empty again, she might well jerk that knife out of her purse one night and use it on something other than bread.

During recess we thirteen sit in the jury room and pointedly avoid talking about the bread knife. The mason tells how a neighbor kid's Ford Pinto skidded across his lawn and onto his front porch, blocking the door and nosing against the picture window. "I took the wheels off and chained the bumper to my maple tree until his daddy paid for fixing my porch."

Everyone, it seems, has been assaulted by a car or truck. Our vehicular yarns wind closer and closer about the courthouse. Finally, two of the women jurors—the cigarillo-smoking caterer and the elderly cat lady—laugh nervously. The two of them were standing just inside the plate-glass door of the court-house last night, the caterer says, when along came a pickup truck, out poked an arm from the window, up flew a smoking beer can, and then BAM! the can exploded. "We jumped a yard in the air!" cries the old woman. "We thought it was some of Bennie's mean-looking friends," the caterer admits. Everybody laughs at the tableau of speeding truck, smoking can, exploding cherry bomb, leaping ladies. Then we choke into sudden silence, as if someone has grabbed each of us by the throat.

Four of Bennie's friends—looking not so much mean as broken, like shell-shocked refugees—testify on his behalf during the afternoon of day three. Two of them are out-of-work men in their twenties, with greasy hair to their shoulders, fatigue jackets, and clodhopper boots: their outfits and world-weary expressions are borrowed from record jackets. They are younger versions of the old men with caved-in faces who crouch on benches downstairs, sheltering from December. The other two witnesses are young women with reputations to keep up, neater than the scruffy men; gold crosses dangle over their sweaters and gum cracks between crooked teeth. All four speak in muttered monosyl-lables and orphaned phrases, as if they are breaking a long vow of silence and must fetch bits and pieces of language from the archives of memory. They were all at Bennie's place on the night of the alleged cocaine sale, and they swear in unison that no such sale took place.

Officer B., the puppet master who pulled the strings on 190, swears just as adamantly that both sales, of cocaine and of hash, did take place, for he listened to the proceedings over the radio in his unmarked blue Buick. He is a sleepy-eyed man in his mid-thirties, about the age of the informant and the defendant, a law-upholding alter ego for those skewed souls.

Double-chinned, padded with the considerable paunch that seems to be is-sued along with the police badge, Officer B. answers Mr. Prosecutor and Mr. Defense in a flat, walkie-talkie drawl, consulting a sheaf of notes in his lap, never contradicting himself. Yes, he neglected to tape the opening few minutes of the first buy, the minutes when the exchange of hashish and money actually took place. Why? "I had a suspicion my batteries were weak, and I wanted to hold off." And, yes, he did erase the tape of the debriefing that followed buy number one. Why? "It's policy to reuse the old cassettes. Saves the taxpayers' money." And, yes, the tape of the second buy is raw, indecipherable noise, because a blaring TV in the background drowns out all human voices. (Listening to the tape, we can understand nothing in the squawking except an ad for the American Express Card.) The tapes, in other words, don't prove a thing. What it all boils down to is the word of the law and of the unsavory informer versus the word of the many-times-convicted defendant, his mate, and his friends.

Toward the end of Officer B.'s testimony, there is a resounding clunk, like a muffled explosion, at the base of the witness stand. We all jump—witness, judge, jury, onlookers—and only relax when the prosecutor squats down and discovers that a pair of handcuffs has fallen out of Officer B.'s belt. Just a little reminder of the law's muscle. All of us were envisioning bombs. When Officer B. steps down, the tail of his sport coat is hitched up over the butt of his gun.

The arrest: A squad car pulls up to the front of the trailer, and out the trailer's back door jumps Bennie, barefooted, wearing T-shirt and cutoff jeans. He dashes away between tarpaper shacks, through dog yards, over a stubbled field (his bare feet bleeding), through a patch of woods to a railroad cut. Behind him puffs a skinny cop (who recounts this scene in court), shouting, "Halt! Police!" But Bennie never slows down until he reaches that railroad cut, where he stumbles, falls, and rolls down to the tracks like the sorriest hobo. The officer draws his gun. Bennie lifts his hands for the familiar steel cuffs. The two of them trudge back to the squad car, where Officer B. reads the arrest warrant and Bennie blisters everybody with curses.

The judge later instructs us that flight from arrest may be regarded as evidence, not of guilt but of *consciousness* of guilt. Oh ho! A fine distinction! Guilt for what? Selling drugs? Playing hooky? Original sin? Losing his job at Coca-Cola? I think of those bleeding feet, the sad chase. I remember the story of a distant relative who stumbled drunk down a railroad cut, fell asleep between the tracks, and died of fear when a train passed over.

On day four of the trial, Bennie himself takes the stand. He is shorter than I thought, and fatter—too many months of starchy jail food and no exercise. With exceedingly long thumbnails he scratches his jaw. When asked a question, he rolls his eyes, stares at the ceiling, then answers in a gravelly country voice, the voice of a late-night disk jockey. At first he is gruffly polite, brief in his replies, but soon he gets cranked up and rants in a grating monologue about his painful history.

He graduated from high school in 1968, worked eight months at RCA and Coca-Cola, had a good start, had a sweetheart, then the army got him, made him a cook, shipped him to Vietnam. After a few weeks in the kitchen, he was transferred to the infantry because the fodder-machine was short of foot soldiers. "Hey, listen, man, I ain't nothing but a cook," he told them. "I ain't been trained for combat." And they said, "Don't you worry; you'll get on-the-job training. Learn or die." The artillery ruined his hearing. (Throughout the trial he has held a hand cupped behind one ear, and has followed the proceedings like a grandfather.) Some of his buddies got shot up. He learned to kill people. "We didn't even know what we was there for." To relieve his constant terror, he started doing drugs. marijuana, opium, just about anything that would ease a man's mind. Came home from Vietnam in 1971 a wreck, got treated like dirt, like a baby-killer, like a murdering scumbag, and found no jobs. His sweetheart married an insurance salesman.

Within a year after his return he was convicted of shoplifting and burglary. He was framed on the second charge by a friend, but couldn't use his only alibi because he had spent the day of the robbery in bed with a sixteen-year-old girl, whose father would have put him away for statutory rape. As it was, he paid out two years in the pen, where he sank deeper into drugs than ever before. "If you got anything to buy or trade with, you can score more stuff in the state prisons than on the streets of Indianapolis." After prison, he still couldn't find work, couldn't get any help for his drug thing from the VA hospital, moved in with Rebecca and her three girls, eventually started selling marijuana and LSD. "Every time I went to somebody for drugs, I got ripped off. That's how I got into dealing. If you're a user, you're always looking for a better deal."

In 1979 he was busted for selling hash, in 1980 for possessing acid, betrayed in both cases by the man from whom he had bought his stock. "He's a snitch, just a filthy snitch. You can't trust nobody." Back to prison for a year, back out again in December 1981. No jobs, no jobs, no damn jobs: then part-time on the city garbage truck, up at four in the morning, minus five degrees and the wind blowing and the streets so cold his gloves stuck to the trash cans. Then March came, and this 190 guy showed up, wanted to buy some drugs, and "I told him I wasn't dealing any more. I done my time and gone straight. I told him he didn't have enough money to pay me for no thirty years in the can." (The prosecutor bristles, the judge leans meaningfully forward: we jurors are not supposed to have any notion of the sentence that might follow a conviction on this drug charge.)

In his disk-jockey voice, Bennie denies ever selling anything to this 190 snitch. (He keeps using the word "snitch": I think of tattletales, not this adult betrayal.) It was 190, he swears, who tried to sell *him* the hash. Now the pills, why, those he had lying around for a friend who never picked them up, and so he just gave them to 190. "They was give to me, and so I couldn't charge him nothing. They wasn't for me anyway. Downers I do not use. To me, life is a downer. Just to cope with every day, that is way down low enough for me." And as for the cocaine, he never laid eyes on it until the man produced that little plastic bag in court. "I don't use coke. It's too expensive. That's for the bigwigs and the upstanding citizens, as got the money."

Sure, he admits, he ran when the police showed up at his trailer. "I'm flat scared of cops. I don't like talking to them about anything. Since I got back from Vietnam, every time they cross my path they put bracelets on me." (He holds up his wrists. They are bare now, but earlier this morning, when I saw a deputy escorting him into the courthouse, they were handcuffed.) He refuses to concede that he is a drug addict, but agrees he has a terrible habit, "a gift from my country in exchange for me going overseas and killing a bunch of strangers."

After the arrest, forced to go cold turkey on his dope, he begged the jail doctor—"He's no kind of doctor, just one of them that fixes babies"—to zonk him out on something. And so, until the trial, he has spent eight months drowsing under Valium and Thorazine. "You can look down your nose at me for that if you want, but last month another vet hung himself two cells down from me." (The other guy was a scoutmaster, awaiting trial for sexually molesting one of his boys. He had a record of severe depression dating from the war, and used his belt for the suicide.)

"The problem with my life," says Bennie, "is Vietnam." For a while after coming home, he slept with a knife under his pillow. Once, wakened suddenly, thinking he was still in Vietnam, he nearly killed his best friend. During the week of our trial, another Vietnam vet up in Indianapolis shot his wife in the head, imagining she was a gook. Neighbors got to him before he could pull out her teeth, as he used to pull out the teeth of the enemies he bagged over in Vietnam.

When I look at Bennie, I see a double image. He was drafted during the same month in which I, studying in England, gave Uncle Sam the slip. I hated that war, and feared it, for exactly the reasons he describes—because it was foul slaughter, shameful, sinful, pointless butchery. While he was over there killing and dodging, sinking into the quicksand of drugs, losing his hearing, storing up a lifetime's worth of nightmares, I was snug in England, filling my head with words. We both came home to America in the same year, I to a job and family, he to nothing. Ten years after that homecoming, we stare across the courtroom at one another as into a funhouse mirror.

As the twelve jurors file past me into the room where they will decide on Bennie's guilt or innocence, three of them pat my arm in a comradely way. They withdraw beyond a brass-barred gate; I sit down to wait on a deacon's bench in the hallway outside the courtroom. I feel stymied, as if I have rocketed to the moon only to be left riding the ship round and round in idle orbit while my fellow astronauts descend to the moon's surface. At the same time I feel profoundly relieved, because, after the four days of testimony, I still cannot decide whether Bennie truly sold those drugs, or whether 190, to cut down on his own prison time, set up this ill-starred Bennie for yet another fall. Time, time—it always comes down to time: in jail, job, and jury box we are spending and hoarding our only wealth, the currency of days.

Even through the closed door of the courtroom, I still hear the ticking of the clock. The sound reminds me of listening to my daughter's pulse through a stethoscope when she was still riding, curled up like a stowaway, in my wife's womb. Ask not for whom this heart ticks, whispered my unborn daughter through the stethoscope: it ticks for thee. So does the courtroom clock. It grabs me by the ear and makes me fret about time—about how little there is of it, about how we are forever bumming it from one another as if it were cups of sugar or pints of blood. ("You got a minute?" "Sorry, have to run, not a second to spare.") Seize the day, we shout, to cheer ourselves; but the day has seized us and flings us forward pell-mell toward the end of all days.

Now and again there is a burst of laughter from the jury room, but it is always squelched in a hurry. They are tense, and laugh to relieve the tension, and then feel ashamed of their giddiness. Lawyers traipse past me—the men smoking, striking poses, their faces like lollipops atop their ties; the women teetering on high heels. The bailiff walks into our judge's office carrying a bread knife. To slice her lunch? As evidence against Rebecca? A moment later she emerges bearing a piece of cake and licking her fingers. Christmas parties are breaking out all over the courthouse.

Rebecca herself paces back and forth at the far end of my hallway, her steps as regular as the clock's tick, killing time. Her bearded and cross-wearing friends sidle up to comfort her, but she shrugs them away. Once she paces down my way, glances at the barred door of the jury room, hears muffled shouts. This she must take for good news, because she throws me a rueful smile before turning back.

Evidently the other twelve are as muddled by the blurred and contradictory "facts" of the case as I am, for they spend from noon until five reaching their decision. They ask for lunch. They ask for a dictionary. They listen again to the tapes. Sullen teenagers, following in the footsteps of Bennie and 190, slouch into the misdemeanor office across the hall from me; by and by they slouch back out again, looking unrepentant. At length the three-hundred-pound mason lumbers up to the gate of the jury room and calls the bailiff. "We're ready as we're going to be." He looks bone-weary, unhappy, and dignified. Raising his eyebrows at me, he shrugs. Comrades in uncertainty.

The cast reassembles in the courtroom, the judge asks the jury for its decision, and the mason stands up to pronounce Bennie guilty. I stare at my boots. Finally I glance up, not at Bennie or Rebecca or the lawyers, but at my fellow jurors. They look distraught, wrung-out and despairing, as if they have just crawled out of a mine after an explosion and have left some of their buddies behind. Before quitting the jury room, they composed and signed a letter to the judge pleading with him to get some help—drug help, mind help, any help—for Bennie.

The ticking of the clock sounds louder in my ears than the judge's closing recital. But I do, with astonishment, hear him say that we must all come back tomorrow for one last piece of business. He is sorry, he knows we are worn out, but the law has prevented him from warning us ahead of time that we might have to decide on one more question of guilt.

\\\||///

The legal question posed for us on the morning of day five is simple. Has Bennie been convicted, prior to this case, of two or more unrelated felonies? If so, then he is defined by Indiana state law as a "habitual offender," and we must declare him to be such. We are shown affidavits for those earlier convictions—

burglary, sale of marijuana, possession of LSD—and so the answer to the legal question is clear.

But the moral and psychological questions are tangled, and they occupy the jury for nearly five more hours on this last day of the trial. Is it fair to sentence a person again after he has already served time for his earlier offenses? How does the prosecutor decide when to apply the habitual offender statute, and does its use in this case have anything to do with the political ambitions of the sleek young attorney? Did Bennie really steal that $150 stereo, for which he was convicted a decade ago, or did he really spend the day in bed with his sixteen-year-old girlfriend? Did Vietnam poison his mind and blight his life?

Two sheriff's deputies guard the jury today; another guards me in my own little cell. The bailiff would not let me stay out on the deacon's bench in the hall, and so, while a plainclothes detective occupies my old seat, I sit in a room lined with file cabinets and stare out like a prisoner through the glass door. "I have concluded," wrote Pascal in his *Thoughts*, "that the whole misfortune of men comes from a single thing, and that is their inability to remain at rest in a room." I agree with him: nothing but that cruising deputy would keep me here.

This time, when the verdict is announced, Rebecca has her daughters with her, three little girls frightened into unchildlike stillness by the courtroom. Their lank hair and washed-out eyes remind me of my childhood playmates, the children of used-up West Virginia coalminers who'd moved to Ohio in a vain search for work. The mother and daughters are surrounded by half a dozen rough customers, guys my age with hair down over their shoulders and rings in their ears, with flannel shirts, unfocused eyes. Doubtless they are the reason so many holstered deputies and upholstered detectives are patrolling the courthouse, and the reason I was locked safely away in a cell while the jury deliberated.

When the mason stands to pronounce another verdict of guilty, I glimpse what I do not want to glimpse: Bennie flinging his head back, Rebecca snapping hers forward into her palms, the girls wailing.

The judge accompanies all thirteen of us into the jury room, where he keeps us for an hour while the deputies clear the rough customers from the courthouse. We should not be alarmed, he reassures us; he is simply being cautious, since so much was at stake for the defendant. "How much?" the mason asks. "Up to twenty-four years for the drug convictions, plus a mandatory thirty years for the habitual offender charges," the judge replies. The cleaning woman, the nurse, and the TV repairman begin crying. I swallow carefully. For whatever it's worth, the judge declares comfortingly, he agrees with our decisions. If we knew as much about Bennie as he knows, we would not be troubled. And that is just the splinter in the brain, the fact that we know so little—about Bennie, about Vietnam, about drugs, about ourselves—and yet we must grope along in our ignorance, pronouncing people guilty or innocent, squeezing out of one another that precious fluid, time.

And so I do my five days in the thirteenth chair. Bennie may do as many as fifty-four years in prison, buying his drugs from meaner dealers, dreaming of land mines and of his adopted girls, checking the date on his watch, wondering at what precise moment the hinges of his future slammed shut.

# The Inheritance of Tools

At just about the hour when my father died, soon after dawn one February morning when ice coated the windows like cataracts, I banged my thumb with a hammer. Naturally I swore at the hammer, the reckless thing, and in the moment of swearing I thought of what my father would say: "If you'd try hitting the nail it would go in a whole lot faster. Don't you know your thumb's not as hard as that hammer?" We both were doing carpentry that day, but far apart. He was building cupboards at my brother's place in Oklahoma; I was at home in Indiana putting up a wall in the basement to make a bedroom for my daughter. By the time my mother called with news of his death—the long-distance wires whittling her voice until it seemed too thin to bear the weight of what she had to say—my thumb was swollen. A week or so later a white scar in the shape of a crescent moon began to show above the cuticle, and month by month it rose across the pink sky of my thumbnail. It took the better part of a year for the scar to disappear, and every time I noticed it I thought of my father.

The hammer had belonged to him, and to his father before him. The three of us have used it to build houses and barns and chicken coops, to upholster chairs and crack walnuts, to make doll furniture and bookshelves and jewelry boxes. The head is scratched and pockmarked, like an old plowshare that has been working rocky fields, and it gives off the sort of dull sheen you see on fast creek water in the shade. It is a finishing hammer, about the weight of a bread loaf, too light really for framing walls, too heavy for cabinetwork, with a curved claw for pulling nails, a rounded head for pounding, a fluted neck for looks, and a hickory handle for strength.

The present handle is my third one, bought from a lumberyard in Tennessee down the road from where my brother and I were helping my father build his retirement house. I broke the previous one by trying to pull sixteen-penny nails out of floor joists—a foolish thing to do with a finishing hammer, as my father pointed out. "You ever hear of a crowbar?" he said. No telling how many handles he and my grandfather had gone through before me. My grandfather used to cut down hickory trees on his farm, saw them into slabs, cure the planks in his hayloft, and carve handles with a drawknife. The grain in hickory is crooked and knotty, and therefore tough, hard to split, like the grain in the two men who owned this hammer before me.

After proposing marriage to a neighbor girl, my grandfather used this hammer to build a house for his bride on a stretch of river bottom in northern Mississippi. The lumber for the place, like the hickory for the handle, was cut on his own land. By the day of the wedding he had not quite finished the house, and so right after the ceremony he took his wife home and put her to work. My grandmother had worn her Sunday dress for the wedding, with a fringe of lace tacked on around the hem in honor of the occasion. She removed this lace and folded it away before going out to help my grandfather nail siding on the house. "There she was in her good dress," he told me some fifty-odd years after that wedding day, "holding up them long pieces of clapboard while I hammered, and together we got the place covered up before dark." As the family grew to four, six, eight, and eventually thirteen, my grandfather used this hammer to enlarge his house room by room, like a chambered nautilus expanding his shell.

By and by the hammer was passed along to my father. One day he was up on the roof of our pony barn nailing shingles with it, when I stepped out the kitchen door to call him for supper. Before I could yell, something about the sight of him straddling the spine of that roof and swinging the hammer caught my eye and made me hold my tongue. I was five or six years old, and the world's commonplaces were still news to me. He would pull a nail from the pouch at his waist, bring the hammer down, and a moment later the *thunk* of the blow would reach my ears. And that is what had stopped me in my tracks and stilled my tongue, that momentary gap between seeing and hearing the blow. Instead of yelling from the kitchen door, I ran to the barn and climbed two rungs up the ladder—as far as I was allowed to go—and spoke quietly to my father. On our walk to the house he explained that sound takes time to make its way through air. Suddenly the world seemed larger, the air more dense, if sound could be held back like any ordinary traveler.

By the time I started using this hammer, at about the age when I discovered the speed of sound, it already contained houses and mysteries for me. The smooth handle was one my grandfather had made. In those days I needed both hands to swing it. My father would start a nail in a scrap of wood, and I would pound away until I bent it over.

"Looks like you got ahold of some of those rubber nails," he would tell me. "Here, let me see if I can find you some stiff ones." And he would rummage in a drawer until he came up with a fistful of more cooperative nails. "Look at the head," he would tell me. "Don't look at your hands, don't look at the hammer. Just look at the head of that nail and pretty soon you'll learn to hit it square."

Pretty soon I did learn. While he worked in the garage cutting dovetail joints for a drawer or skinning a deer or tuning an engine, I would hammer nails. I made innocent blocks of wood look like porcupines. He did not talk much in the midst of his tools, but he kept up a nearly ceaseless humming, slipping in and out of a dozen tunes in an afternoon, often running back over the same stretch of melody again and again, as if searching for a way out. When the humming did cease, I knew he was faced with a task requiring great delicacy or concentration, and I took care not to distract him.

He kept scraps of wood in a cardboard box—the ends of two-by-fours, slabs of shelving and plywood, odd pieces of molding—and everything in it was fair game. I nailed scraps together to fashion what I called boats or houses, but the results usually bore only faint resemblance to the visions I carried in my head. I would hold up these constructions to show my father, and he would turn them over in his hands admiringly, speculating about what they might be. My cobbled-together guitars might have been alien spaceships, my barns might have been models of Aztec temples, each wooden contraption might have been anything but what I had set out to make.

Now and again I would feel the need to have a chunk of wood shaped or shortened before I riddled it with nails, and I would clamp it in a vise and scrape at it with a handsaw. My father would let me lacerate the board until my arm gave out, and then he would wrap his hand around mine and help me finish the cut, showing me how to use my thumb to guide the blade, how to pull back on the saw to keep it from binding, how to let my shoulder do the work.

"Don't force it," he would say, "just drag it easy and give the teeth a chance to bite."

As the saw teeth bit down, the wood released its smell, each kind with its own fragrance, oak or walnut or cherry or pine, usually pine because it was the softest, easiest for a child to work. No matter how weathered and gray the board, no matter how warped and cracked, inside there was this smell waiting, as of something freshly baked. I gathered every smidgen of sawdust and stored it away in coffee cans, which I kept in a drawer of the workbench. When I did not feel like hammering nails I would dump my sawdust on the concrete floor of the garage and landscape it into highways and farms and towns, running miniature cars and trucks along miniature roads. Looming as huge as a colossus, my father worked over and around me, now and again bending down to inspect my work, careful not to trample my creations. It was a landscape that smelled dizzyingly of wood. Even after a bath my skin would carry the smell, and so would my father's hair, when he lifted me for a bedtime hug.

I tell these things not only from memory but also from recent observation, because my own son now turns blocks of wood into nailed porcupines, dumps cans full of sawdust at my feet and sculpts highways on the floor. He learns how to swing a hammer from the elbow instead of the wrist, how to lay his thumb beside the blade to guide a saw, how to tap a chisel with a wooden mallet, how to mark a hole with an awl before starting a drill bit. My daughter did the same before him, and even now, on the brink of teenage aloofness, she will occasionally drag out my box of wood scraps and carpenter something. So I have seen my apprenticeship to wood and tools reenacted in each of my children, as my father saw his own apprenticeship renewed in me.

The saw I use belonged to him, as did my level and both of my squares, and all four tools had belonged to his father. The blade of the saw is the bluish color of gun barrels, and the maple handle, dark from the sweat of hands, is inscribed with curving leaf designs. The level is a shaft of walnut two feet long, edged with brass and pierced by three round windows in which air bubbles float in oil-filled tubes of glass. The middle window serves for testing if a surface is horizontal, the others for testing if a surface is plumb or vertical. My grandfather used to carry this level on the gun rack behind the seat in his pickup, and when I rode with him I would turn around to watch the bubbles dance. The larger of the two squares is called a framing square, a flat steel elbow, so beat up and tarnished you can barely make out the rows of numbers that show how to figure the cuts on rafters. The smaller one is called a try square, for marking right angles, with a blued steel blade for the shank and a brass-faced block of cherry for the head.

I was taught early on that a saw is not to be used apart from a square: "If you're going to cut a piece of wood," my father insisted, "you owe it to the tree to cut it straight."

Long before studying geometry, I learned there is a mystical virtue in right angles. There is an unspoken morality in seeking the level and the plumb. A house will stand, a table will bear weight, the sides of a box will hold together only if the joints are square and the members upright. When the bubble is lined up between two marks etched in the glass tube of a level, you have aligned yourself with the forces that hold the universe together. When you miter the corners of a picture frame, each angle must be exactly forty-five degrees, as they are in the perfect triangles of Pythagoras, not a degree more or less. Otherwise the frame will hang crookedly, as if ashamed of itself and of its maker. No matter if the joints you are cutting do not show. Even if you are butting two pieces of wood together inside a cabinet, where no one except a wrecking crew will ever see them, you must take pains to ensure that the ends are square and the studs are plumb.

I took pains over the wall I was building on the day my father died. Not long after that wall was finished—paneled with tongue-and-groove boards of yellow pine, the nail holes filled with putty and the wood all stained and sealed—I came close to wrecking it one afternoon when my daughter ran howling up the stairs to announce that her gerbils had escaped from their cage and were hiding in my brand-new wall. She could hear them scratching and squeaking behind her bed. Impossible! I said. How on earth could they get inside my drum-tight wall? Through the heating vent, she answered. I went downstairs, pressed my ear to the honey-colored wood, and heard the scritch scritch of tiny feet.

"What can we do?" my daughter wailed. "They'll starve to death, they'll die of thirst, they'll suffocate."

"Hold on," I soothed. "I'll think of something."

While I thought and she fretted, the radio on her bedside table delivered us the headlines. Several thousand people had died in a city in India from a poisonous cloud that had leaked overnight from a chemical plant. A nuclear-powered submarine had been launched. Rioting continued in South Africa. An airplane had been hijacked in the Mediterranean. Authorities calculated that several thousand homeless people slept on the streets within sight of the Washington Monument. I felt my usual helplessness in face of all these calamities. But here was my daughter weeping because her gerbils were holed up in a wall. This calamity I could handle.

"Don't worry," I told her. "We'll set food and water by the heating vent and lure them out. And if that doesn't do the trick, I'll tear the wall apart until we find them."

She stopped crying and gazed at me. "You'd really tear it apart? Just for my gerbils? The *wall*?" Astonishment slowed her down only for a second, however, before she ran to the workbench and began tugging at drawers, saying, "Let's see, what'll we need? Crowbar. Hammer. Chisels. I hope we don't have to use them—but just in case."

We didn't need the wrecking tools. I never had to assault my handsome wall, because the gerbils eventually came out to nibble at a dish of popcorn. But for several hours I studied the tongue-and-groove skin I had nailed up on the day of my father's death, considering where to begin prying. There were no gaps in that wall, no crooked joints.

I had botched a great many pieces of wood before I mastered the right angle with a saw, botched even more before I learned to miter a joint. The knowledge of these things resides in my hands and eyes and the web of muscles, not in the tools. There are machines for sale—powered miter boxes and radial arm saws, for instance—that will enable any casual soul to cut proper angles in boards. The skill is invested in the gadget instead of the person who uses it, and this is what distinguishes a machine from a tool. If I had to earn my keep by making furniture or building houses, I suppose I would buy powered saws and pneumatic nailers; the need for speed would drive me to it. But since I carpenter only for my own pleasure or to help neighbors or to remake the house around the ears of my family, I stick with hand tools. Most of the ones I own were given to me by my father, who also taught me how to wield them. The tools in my workbench are a double inheritance, for each hammer and level and saw is wrapped in a cloud of knowing.

All of these tools are a pleasure to look at and to hold. Merchants would never paste NEW NEW NEW! signs on them in stores. Their designs are old because they work, because they serve their purpose well. Like folksongs and aphorisms and the grainy bits of language, these tools have been pared down to essentials. I look at my claw hammer, the distillation of a hundred generations of carpenters, and consider that it holds up well beside those other classics—Greek vases, Gregorian chants, *Don Quixote,* barbed fish hooks, candles, spoons. Knowledge of hammering stretches back to the earliest humans who squatted beside fires chipping flints. Anthropologists have a lovely name for those unworked rocks that served as the earliest hammers. Dawn stones, they are called. Their only qualification for the work, aside from hardness, is that they fit the hand. Our ancestors used them for grinding corn, tapping awls, smashing bones. From dawn stones to this claw hammer is a great leap in time, but no great distance in design or imagination.

On that iced-over February morning when I smashed my thumb with the hammer, I was down in the basement framing the wall that my daughter's gerbils would later hide in. I was thinking of my father, as I always did whenever I built anything, thinking how he would have gone about the work, hearing in memory what he would have said about the wisdom of hitting the nail instead of my thumb. I had the studs and plates nailed together all square and trim, and was lifting the wall into place when the phone rang upstairs. My wife answered, and in a moment she came to the basement door and called down softly to me. The stillness in her voice made me drop the framed wall and hurry upstairs. She told me my father was dead. Then I heard the details over the phone from my mother. Building a set of cupboards for my brother in Oklahoma, he had knocked off work early the previous afternoon because of cramps in his stomach. Early this morning, on his way into the kitchen of my brother's trailer, maybe going for a glass of water, so early that no one else was awake, he slumped down on the linoleum and his heart quit.

For several hours I paced around inside my house, upstairs and down, in and out of every room, looking for the right door to open and knowing there was no such door. My wife and children followed me and wrapped me in arms and backed away again, circling and staring as if I were on fire. Where was the door, the door, the door? I kept wondering. My smashed thumb turned purple and throbbed, making me furious. I wanted to cut it off and rush outside and scrape away the snow and hack a hole in the frozen earth and bury the shameful thing.

I went down into the basement, opened a drawer in my workbench, and stared at the ranks of chisels and knives. Oiled and sharp, as my father would have kept them, they gleamed at me like teeth. I took up a clasp knife, pried out the longest blade, and tested the edge on the hair of my forearm. A tuft came away cleanly, and I saw my father testing the sharpness of tools on his own skin, the blades of axes and knives and gouges and hoes, saw the red hair shaved off in patches from his arms and the backs of his hands. "That will cut bear," he would say. He never cut a bear with his blades, now my blades, but he cut deer, dirt, and wood. I closed the knife and put it away. Then I took up the hammer and went back to work on my daughter's wall, snugging the bottom plate against a chalk line on the floor, shimming the top plate against the joists overhead, plumbing the studs with my level, making sure before I drove the first nail that every line was square and true.

# Under the Influence

My father drank. He drank as a gut-punched boxer gasps for breath, as a starving dog gobbles food—compulsively, secretly, in pain and trembling. I use the past tense not because he ever quit drinking but because he quit living. That is how the story ends for my father, age sixty-four, heart bursting, body cooling and forsaken on the linoleum of my brother's trailer. The story continues for my brother, my sister, my mother, and me, and will continue so long as memory holds.

In the perennial present of memory, I slip into the garage or barn to see my father tipping back the flat green bottles of wine, the brown cylinders of whiskey, the cans of beer disguised in paper bags. His Adam's apple bobs, the liquid gurgles, he wipes the sandy-haired back of a hand over his lips, and then, his bloodshot gaze bumping into me, he stashes the bottle or can inside his jacket, under the workbench, between two bales of hay, and we both pretend the moment has not occurred.

"What's up, buddy?" he says, thick-tongued and edgy.

"Sky's up," I answer, playing along.

"And don't forget prices," he grumbles. "Prices are always up. And taxes."

In memory, his white 1951 Pontiac with the stripes down the hood and the Indian head on the snout jounces to a stop in the driveway; or it is the 1956 Ford station wagon, or the 1963 Rambler shaped like a toad, or the sleek 1969 Bonneville that will do 120 miles per hour on straightaways; or it is the robin's-egg blue pickup, new in 1980, battered in 1981, the year of his death. He climbs out, grinning dangerously, unsteady on his legs, and we children interrupt our game of catch, our building of snow forts, our picking of plums, to watch in silence as he weaves past into the house, where he slumps into his overstuffed chair and falls asleep. Shaking her head, our mother stubs out the cigarette he has left smoldering in the ashtray. All evening, until our bedtimes, we tiptoe past him, as past a snoring dragon. Then we curl in our fearful sheets, listening. Eventually he wakes with a grunt, Mother slings accusations at him, he snarls back, she yells, he growls, their voices clashing. Before long, she retreats to their bedroom, sobbing—not from the blows of fists, for he never strikes her, but from the force of words.

Left alone, our father prowls the house, thumping into furniture, rummaging in the kitchen, slamming doors, turning the pages of the newspaper with a savage crackle, muttering back at the late-night drivel from television. The roof might fly off, the walls might buckle from the pressure of his rage. Whatever my brother and sister and mother may be thinking on their own rumpled pillows, I lie there hating him, loving him, fearing him, knowing I have failed him. I tell myself he drinks to ease an ache that gnaws at his belly, an ache I must have caused by disappointing him somehow, a murderous ache I should be able to relieve by doing all my chores, earning A's in school, winning baseball games, fixing the broken washer and the burst pipes, bringing in money to fill his empty wallet. He would not hide the green bottles in his tool box, would not sneak off to the barn with a lump under his coat, would not fall asleep in the daylight, would not roar and fume, would not drink himself to death, if only I were perfect.

I am forty-two as I write these words, and I know full well now that my father was an alcoholic, a man consumed by disease rather than by disappointment. What had seemed to me a private grief is in fact a public scourge. In the United States alone some ten or fifteen million people share his ailment, and behind the doors they slam in fury or disgrace, countless other children tremble. I comfort myself with such knowledge, holding it against the throb of memory like an ice pack against a bruise. There are keener sources of grief: poverty, racism, rape, war. I do not wish to compete for a trophy in suffering. I am only trying to understand the corrosive mixture of helplessness, responsibility, and shame that I learned to feel as the son of an alcoholic. I realize now that I did not cause my father's illness, nor could I have cured it. Yet for all this grown-up knowledge, I am still ten years old, my own son's age, and as that boy I struggle in guilt and confusion to save my father from pain.

Consider a few of our synonyms for *drunk:* tipsy, tight, pickled, soused, and plowed; stoned and stewed, lubricated and inebriated, juiced and sluiced; three sheets to the wind, in your cups, out of your mind, under the table; lit up, tanked up, wiped out; besotted, blotto, bombed, and buzzed; plastered, polluted, putrefied; loaded or looped, boozy, woozy, fuddled, or smashed; crocked and shit-faced, corked and pissed, snockered and sloshed.

It is a mostly humorous lexicon, as the lore that deals with drunks—in jokes and cartoons, in plays, films, and television skits—is largely comic. Aunt Matilda nips elderberry wine from the sideboard and burps politely during supper. Uncle Fred slouches to the table glassy-eyed, wearing a lamp shade for a hat and murmuring, "Candy is dandy but liquor is quicker." Inspired by cocktails, Mrs. Somebody recounts the events of her day in a fuzzy dialect, while Mr. Somebody nibbles her ear and croons a bawdy song. On the sofa with Boyfriend, Daughter giggles, licking gin from her lips, and loosens the bows in her hair. Junior knocks back some brews with his chums at the Leopard Lounge and stumbles home to the wrong house, wonders foggily why he cannot locate his pajamas, and crawls naked into bed with the ugliest girl in school. The family dog slurps from a neglected martini and wobbles to the nursery, where he vomits in Baby's shoe.

It is all great fun. But if in the audience you notice a few laughing faces turn grim when the drunk lurches onstage, don't be surprised, for these are the children of alcoholics. Over the grinning mask of Dionysus, the leering mask of Bacchus, these children cannot help seeing the bloated features of their own parents. Instead of laughing, they wince, they mourn. Instead of celebrating the drunk as one freed from constraints, they pity him as one enslaved. They refuse to believe *in vino veritas,* having seen their befuddled parents skid away from truth toward folly and oblivion. And so these children bite their lips until the lush staggers into the wings.

My father, when drunk, was neither funny nor honest; he was pathetic, frightening, deceitful. There seemed to be a leak in him somewhere, and he poured in booze to keep from draining dry. Like a torture victim who refuses to squeal, he would never admit that he had touched a drop, not even in his last year, when he seemed to be dissolving in alcohol before our very eyes. I never knew him to lie about anything, ever, except about this one ruinous fact. Drowsy, clumsy, unable to fix a bicycle tire, throw a baseball, balance a grocery sack, or walk across the room, he was stripped of his true self by drink. In a matter of minutes, the contents of a bottle could transform a brave man into a coward, a buddy into a bully, a gifted athlete and skilled carpenter and shrewd businessman into a bumbler. No dictionary of synonyms for *drunk* would soften the anguish of watching our prince turn into a frog.

⁂

Father's drinking became the family secret. While growing up, we children never breathed a word of it beyond the four walls of our house. To this day, my brother and sister rarely mention it, and then only when I press them. I did not confess the ugly, bewildering fact to my wife until his wavering walk and slurred speech forced me to. Recently, on the seventh anniversary of my father's death, I asked my mother if she ever spoke of his drinking to friends. "No, no, never," she replied hastily. "I couldn't bear for anyone to know."

The secret bores under the skin, gets in the blood, into the bone, and stays there. Long after you have supposedly been cured of malaria, the fever can flare up, the tremors can shake you. So it is with the fevers of shame. You swallow the bitter quinine of knowledge, and you learn to feel pity and compassion toward the drinker. Yet the shame lingers in your marrow, and, because of the shame, anger.

⁂

For a long stretch of my childhood we lived on a military reservation in Ohio, an arsenal where bombs were stored underground in bunkers, vintage airplanes burst into flames, and unstable artillery shells boomed nightly at the dump. We had the feeling, as children, that we played in a mine field, where a heedless footfall could trigger an explosion. When Father was drinking, the house, too, became a mine field. The least bump could set off either parent.

The more he drank, the more obsessed Mother became with stopping him. She hunted for bottles, counted the cash in his wallet, sniffed at his breath. Without meaning to snoop, we children blundered left and right into damning evidence. On afternoons when he came home from work sober, we flung ourselves at him for hugs, and felt against our ribs the telltale lump in his coat. In the barn we tumbled on the hay and heard beneath our sneakers the crunch of buried glass. We tugged open a drawer in his workbench, looking for screwdrivers or crescent wrenches, and spied a gleaming six-pack among the tools. Playing tag, we darted around the house just in time to see him sway on the rear stoop and heave a finished bottle into the woods. In his good-night kiss we smelled the cloying sweetness of Clorets, the mints he chewed to camouflage his dragon's breath.

I can summon up that kiss right now by recalling Theodore Roethke's lines about his own father in "My Papa's Waltz":

> The whiskey on your breath
> Could make a small boy dizzy;
> But I hung on like death:
> Such waltzing was not easy.

Such waltzing was hard, terribly hard, for with a boy's scrawny arms I was trying to hold my tipsy father upright.

For years, the chief source of those incriminating bottles and cans was a grimy store a mile from us, a cinder-block place called Sly's, with two gas pumps outside and a moth-eaten dog asleep in the window. A strip of flypaper, speckled the year round with black bodies, coiled in the doorway. Inside, on rusty metal shelves or in wheezing coolers, you could find pop and Popsicles, cigarettes, potato chips, canned soup, raunchy postcards, fishing gear, Twinkies, wine, and beer. When Father drove anywhere on errands, Mother would send us kids along as guards, warning us not to let him out of our sight. And so with one or more of us on board, Father would cruise up to Sly's, pump a dollar's worth of gas or plump the tires with air, and then, telling us to wait in the car, he would head for that fly-spangled doorway.

Dutiful and panicky, we cried, "Let us go in with you!"

"No," he answered. "I'll be back in two shakes."

"Please!"

"No!" he roared. "Don't you budge, or I'll jerk a knot in your tails!"

So we stayed put, kicking the seats, while he ducked inside. Often, when he had parked the car at a careless angle, we gazed in through the window and saw Mr. Sly fetching down from a shelf behind the cash register two green pints of Gallo wine. Father swigged one of them right there at the counter, stuffed the other in his pocket, and then out he came, a bulge in his coat, a flustered look on his red face.

Because the Mom and Pop who ran the dump were neighbors of ours, living just down the tar-blistered road, I hated them all the more for poisoning my father. I wanted to sneak in their store and smash the bottles and set fire to the place. I also hated the Gallo brothers, Ernest and Julio, whose jovial faces shone from the labels of their wine, labels I would find, torn and curled, when I burned the trash. I noted the Gallo brothers' address, in California, and I studied the road atlas to see how far that was from Ohio, because I meant to go out there and tell Ernest and Julio what they were doing to my father, and then, if they showed no mercy, I would kill them.

While growing up on the back roads and in the country schools and cramped Methodist churches of Ohio and Tennessee, I never heard the word *alcoholism*, never happened across it in books or magazines. In the nearby towns, there were no addiction treatment programs, no community mental health centers, no Alcoholics Anonymous meetings, no therapists. Left alone with our grievous secret, we had no way of understanding Father's drinking except as an act of will, a deliberate folly or cruelty, a moral weakness, a sin. He drank because he chose to, pure and simple. Why our father, so playful and competent and kind when sober, would choose to ruin himself and punish his family, we could not fathom.

Our neighborhood was high on the Bible, and the Bible was hard on drunkards. "Woe to those who are heroes at drinking wine, and valiant men in mixing strong drink," wrote Isaiah. "The priest and the prophet reel with strong drink, they are confused with wine, they err in vision, they stumble in giving judgment. For all tables are full of vomit, no place is without filthiness." We children had seen those fouled tables at the local truck stop where the notorious boozers hung out, our father occasionally among them. "Wine and new wine take away the understanding," declared the prophet Hosea. We had also seen evidence of that in our father, who could multiply seven-digit numbers in his head when sober, but when drunk could not help us with fourth-grade math. Proverbs warned: "Do not look at wine when it is red, when it sparkles in the cup and goes down smoothly. At the last it bites like a serpent, and stings like an adder. Your eyes will see strange things, and your mind utter perverse things." Woe, woe.

Dismayingly often, these biblical drunkards stirred up trouble for their own kids. Noah made fresh wine after the flood, drank too much of it, fell asleep without any clothes on, and was glimpsed in the buff by his son Ham, whom Noah promptly cursed. In one passage—it was so shocking we had to read it under our blankets with flashlights—the patriarch Lot fell down drunk and slept with his daughters. The sins of the fathers set their children's teeth on edge.

Our ministers were fond of quoting St. Paul's pronouncement that drunkards would not inherit the kingdom of God. These grave preachers assured us that the wine referred to during the Last Supper was in fact grape juice. Bible and sermons and hymns combined to give us the impression that Moses should have brought down from the mountain another stone tablet, bearing the Eleventh Commandment: Thou shalt not drink.

The scariest and most illuminating Bible story apropos of drunkards was the one about the lunatic and the swine. Matthew, Mark, and Luke each told a version of the tale. We knew it by heart: When Jesus climbed out of his boat one day, this lunatic came charging up from the graveyard, stark naked and filthy, frothing at the mouth, so violent that he broke the strongest chains. Nobody would go near him. Night and day for years this madman had been wailing among the tombs and bruising himself with stones. Jesus took one look at him and said, "Come out of the man, you unclean spirits!" for he could see that the lunatic was possessed by demons. Meanwhile, some hogs were conveniently rooting nearby. "If we have to come out," begged the demons, "at least let us go into those swine." Jesus agreed, the unclean spirits entered the hogs, and the hogs rushed straight off a cliff and plunged into a lake. Hearing the story in Sunday school, my friends thought mainly of the pigs. (How big a splash did they make? Who paid for the lost pork?) But I thought of the redeemed lunatic, who bathed himself and put on clothes and calmly sat at the feet of Jesus, restored—so the Bible said—to "his right mind."

When drunk, our father was clearly in his wrong mind. He became a stranger, as fearful to us as any graveyard lunatic, not quite frothing at the mouth but fierce enough, quick-tempered, explosive; or else he grew maudlin and weepy, which frightened us nearly as much. In my boyhood despair, I reasoned that maybe he wasn't to blame for turning into an ogre: Maybe, like the lunatic, he was possessed by demons. I found support for my theory when I heard liquor referred to as "spirits," when the newspapers reported that somebody had been arrested for "driving under the influence," and when church ladies railed against that "demon drink."

If my father was indeed possessed, who would exorcise him? If he was a sinner, who would save him? If he was ill, who would cure him? If he suffered, who would ease his pain? Not ministers or doctors, for we could not bring ourselves to confide in them; not the neighbors, for we pretended they had never seen him drunk; not Mother, who fussed and pleaded but could not budge him; not my brother and sister, who were only kids. That left me. It did not matter that I, too, was only a child, and a bewildered one at that. I could not excuse myself.

On first reading a description of delirium tremens—in a book on alcoholism I smuggled from the library—I thought immediately of the frothing lunatic and the frenzied swine. When I read stories or watched films about grisly meta-morphoses—Dr. Jekyll becoming Mr. Hyde, the mild husband changing into a werewolf, the kindly neighbor taken over by a brutal alien—I could not help seeing my own father's mutation from sober to drunk. Even today, knowing better, I am attracted by the demonic theory of drink, for when I recall my father's transformation, the emergence of his ugly second self, I find it easy to believe in possession by unclean spirits. We never knew which version of Father would come home from work, the true or the tainted, nor could we guess how far down the slope toward cruelty he would slide.

How far a man *could* slide we gauged by observing our back-road neigh-bors the out-of-work miners who had dragged their families to our corner of Ohio from the desolate hollows of Appalachia, the tightfisted farmers, the surly mechanics, the balked and broken men. There was, for example, whiskey-soaked Mr. Flynn, who beat his wife and kids so hard we could hear their screams from the road. There was Mr. Pinto the wino, who fell asleep smok-ing time and again, until one night his disgusted wife bundled up the children and went outside and left him in his easy chair to burn; he awoke on his own, staggered out coughing into the yard, and pounded her flat while the children looked on and the shack turned to ash. There was the truck driver, Mr. Samp-son, who tripped over his son's tricycle one night while drunk and got so mad that he jumped into his semi and drove away, shifting through the dozen gears, and never came back. We saw the bruised children of these fathers clump onto our school bus, we saw the abandoned children huddle in the pews at church, we saw the stunned and battered mothers begging for help at our doors.

Our own father never beat us, and I don't think he ever beat Mother, but he threatened often. The Old Testament Yahweh was not more terrible in his wrath. Eyes blazing, voice booming, Father would pull out his belt and swear to give us a whipping, but he never followed through, never needed to, because we could imagine it so vividly. He shoved us, pawed us with the back of his hand, as an irked bear might smack a cub, not to injure, just to clear a space. I can see him grabbing Mother by the hair as she cowers on a chair during a nightly quarrel. He twists her neck back until she gapes up at him, and then he lifts over her skull a glass quart bottle of milk, the milk running down his forearm, and he yells at her, "Say just one more word, one goddamn word, and I'll shut you up!" I fear she will prick him with her sharp tongue, but she is terrified into silence, and so am I, and the leaking bottle quivers in the air, and milk slithers through the red hair of my father's uplifted arm, and the entire scene is there to this moment, the head jerked back, the club raised.

When the drink made him weepy, Father would pack a bag and kiss each of us children on the head, and announce from the front door that he was moving out. "Where to?" we demanded, fearful each time that he would leave for good, as Mr. Sampson had roared away for good in his diesel truck. "Someplace where I won't get hounded every minute," Father would answer, his jaw quivering. He stabbed a look at Mother, who might say, "Don't run into the ditch before you get there," or "Good riddance," and then he would slink away. Mother watched him go with arms crossed over her chest, her face closed like the lid on a box of snakes. We children bawled. Where could he go? To the truck stop, that den of iniquity? To one of those dark, ratty flophouses in town? Would he wind up sleeping under a railroad bridge or on a park bench or in a cardboard box, mummied in rags, like the bums we had seen on our trips to Cleveland and Chicago? We bawled and bawled, wondering if he would ever come back.

He always did come back, a day or a week later, but each time there was a sliver less of him.

In Kafka's *The Metamorphosis*, which opens famously with Gregor Samsa waking up from uneasy dreams to find himself transformed into an insect, Gregor's family keep reassuring themselves that things will be just fine again, "when he comes back to us." Each time alcohol transformed our father, we held out the same hope, that he would really and truly come back to us, our authentic father, the tender and playful and competent man, and then all things would be fine. We had grounds for such hope. After his weepy departures and chapfallen returns, he would sometimes go weeks, even months without drinking. Those were glad times. Joy banged inside my ribs. Every day without the furtive glint of bottles, every meal without a fight, every bedtime without sobs encouraged us to believe that such bliss might go on forever.

Mother was fooled by just such a hope all during the forty-odd years she knew this Greeley Ray Sanders. Soon after she met him in a Chicago delicatessen on the eve of World War II, and fell for his butter-melting Mississippi drawl and his wavy red hair, she learned that he drank heavily. But then so did a lot of men. She would soon coax or scold him into breaking the nasty habit. She would point out to him how ugly and foolish it was, this bleary drinking, and then he would quit. He refused to quit during their engagement, however, still refused during the first years of marriage, refused until my sister came along. The shock of fatherhood sobered him, and he remained sober through my birth at the end of the war and right on through until we moved in 1951 to the Ohio arsenal, that paradise of bombs. Like all places that make a business of death, the Arsenal had more than its share of alcoholics and drug addicts and other varieties of escape artists. There I turned six and started school and woke into a child's flickering awareness, just in time to see my father begin sneaking swigs in the garage.

He sobered up again for most of a year at the height of the Korean War, to celebrate the birth of my brother. But aside from that dry spell, his only breaks from drinking before I graduated from high school were just long enough to raise and then dash our hopes. Then during the fall of my senior year—the time of the Cuban missile crisis, when it seemed that the nightly explosions at the munitions dump and the nightly rages in our household might spread to engulf the globe—Father collapsed. His liver, kidneys, and heart all conked out. The doctors saved him, but only by a hair. He stayed in the hospital for weeks, going through a withdrawal so terrible that Mother would not let us visit him. If he wanted to kill himself, the doctors solemnly warned him, all he had to do was hit the bottle again. One binge would finish him.

Father must have believed them, for he stayed dry the next fifteen years. It was an answer to prayer, Mother said, it was a miracle. I believe it was a reflex of fear, which he sustained over the years through courage and pride. He knew a man could die from drink, for one of his brothers had done so. We children never laid eyes on that doomed uncle, but in the stories Mother told us he became a fairy-tale figure, like a boy who took the wrong turning in the woods and was gobbled up by the wolf.

The fifteen-year dry spell came to an end with Father's retirement in the spring of 1978. Like many men, he gave up his identity along with his job. One day he was a boss at the factory, with a brass plate on his door and a reputation to uphold; the next day he was a nobody at home. He and Mother were leaving Ontario, the last of the many places to which his job had carried them, and they were moving to a new house in Mississippi, his childhood stomping grounds. As a boy in Mississippi, Father sold Coca-Cola during dances while the moonshiners peddled their brew in the parking lot; as a young blade, he fought in bars and in the ring, seeking a state Golden Gloves championship; he gambled at poker, hunted pheasants, raced motorcycles and cars, played semiprofessional baseball, and, along with all his buddies—in the Black Cat Saloon, behind the cotton gin, in the woods—he drank. It was a perilous youth to dream of recovering.

After his final day of work, Mother drove on ahead with a car full of begonias and violets, while Father stayed behind to oversee the packing. When the van was loaded, the sweaty movers broke open a six-pack and offered him a beer.

"Let's drink to retirement!" they crowed. "Let's drink to freedom! to fishing! hunting! loafing! Let's drink to a guy who's going home!"

At least I imagine some such words, for that is all I can do, imagine, and I see Father's hand trembling in midair as he thinks about the fifteen sober years and about the doctors' warning, and he tells himself, *Goddamnit, I am a free man,* and *Why can't a free man drink one beer after a lifetime of hard work?* and I see his arm reaching, his fingers closing, the can tilting to his lips. I even supply a label for the beer, a swaggering brand that promises on television to deliver the essence of life. I watch the amber liquid pour down his throat, the alcohol steal into his blood, the key turn in his brain.

Soon after my parents moved back to Father's treacherous stomping ground, my wife and I visited them in Mississippi with our five-year-old daughter and seven-month-old son. Mother had been too distraught to warn me about the return of the demons. So when I climbed out of the car that bright July morning and saw my father napping in the hammock, I felt uneasy, for in all his sober years I had never known him to sleep in daylight. Then he lurched upright, blinked his bloodshot eyes, and greeted us in a syrupy voice. I was hurled back helpless into childhood.

"What's the matter with Papaw?" our daughter asked.

"Nothing," I said. "Nothing!"

Like a child again, I pretended not to see him in his stupor, and behind my phony smile I grieved. On that visit and on the few that remained before his death, once again I found bottles in the workbench, bottles in the woods. Again his hands shook too much for him to run a saw, to make his precious miniature furniture, to drive straight down back roads. Again he wound up in the ditch, in the hospital, in jail, in treatment centers. Again he shouted and wept. Again he lied. "I never touched a drop," he swore. "Your mother's making it up."

I no longer fancied I could reason with the men whose names I found on the bottles—Jim Beam, Jack Daniels—nor did I hope to save my father by burning down a store. I was able now to press the cold statistics about alcoholism against the ache of memory: ten million victims, fifteen million, twenty. And yet, in spite of my age, I reacted in the same blind way as I had in childhood, ignoring biology, forgetting numbers, vainly seeking to erase through my efforts whatever drove him to drink. I worked on their place twelve and sixteen hours a day, in the swelter of Mississippi summers, digging ditches, running electrical wires, planting trees, mowing grass, building sheds, as though what nagged at him was some list of chores, as though by taking his worries on my shoulders I could redeem him. I was flung back into boyhood, acting as though my father would not drink himself to death if only I were perfect.

I failed of perfection; he succeeded in dying. To the end, he considered himself not sick but sinful. "Do you want to kill yourself?" I asked him. "Why not?" he answered. "Why the hell not? What's there to save?" To the end, he would not speak about his feelings, would not or could not name the beast that was devouring him.

In silence, he went rushing off the cliff. Unlike the biblical swine, however, he left behind a few of the demons to haunt his children. Life with him and the loss of him twisted us into shapes that will be familiar to other sons and daughters of alcoholics. My brother became a rebel, my sister retreated into shyness, I played the stalwart and dutiful son who would hold the family together. If my father was unstable, I would be a rock. If he squandered money on drink, I would pinch every penny. If he wept when drunk—and only when drunk—I would not let myself weep at all. If he roared at the Little League umpire for calling my pitches balls, I would throw nothing but strikes. Watching him flounder and rage, I came to dread the loss of control. I would go through life without making anyone mad. I vowed never to put in my mouth or veins any chemical that would banish my everyday self. I would never make a scene, never lash out at the ones I loved, never hurt a soul. Through hard work, relentless work, I would achieve something dazzling—in the classroom, on the basketball floor, in the science lab, in the pages of books—and my achievement would distract the world's eyes from his humiliation. I would become a worthy sacrifice, and the smoke of my burning would please God.

It is far easier to recognize these twists in my character than to undo them. Work has become an addiction for me, as drink was an addiction for my father. Knowing this, my daughter gave me a placard for the wall: WORKAHOLIC. The labor is endless and futile, for I can no more redeem myself through work than I could redeem my father. I still panic in the face of other people's anger, because his drunken temper was so terrible. I shrink from causing sadness or disappointment even to strangers, as though I were still concealing the family shame. I still notice every twitch of emotion in the faces around me, having learned as a child to read the weather in faces, and I blame myself for their least pang of unhappiness or anger. In certain moods I blame myself for everything. Guilt burns like acid in my veins.

I am moved to write these pages now because my own son, at the age of ten, is taking on himself the griefs of the world, and in particular the griefs of his father. He tells me that when I am gripped by sadness he feels responsible; he feels there must be something he can do to spring me from depression, to fix my life. And that crushing sense of responsibility is exactly what I felt at the age of ten in the face of my father's drinking. My son wonders if I, too, am possessed. I write, therefore, to drag into the light what eats at me—the fear, the guilt, the shame—so that my own children may be spared.

I still shy away from nightclubs, from bars, from parties where the solvent is alcohol. My friends puzzle over this, but it is no more peculiar than for a man to shy away from the lions' den after seeing his father torn apart. I took my own first drink at the age of twenty-one, half a glass of burgundy. I knew the odds of my becoming an alcoholic were four times higher than for the sons of non-alcoholic fathers. So I sipped warily.

I still do—once a week, perhaps, a glass of wine, a can of beer, nothing stronger, nothing more. I listen for the turning of a key in my brain.

# Looking at Women

On that sizzling July afternoon, the girl who crossed at the stoplight in front of our car looked, as my mother would say, as though she had been poured into her pink shorts. The girl's matching pink halter bared her stomach and clung to her nubbin breasts, leaving little to the imagination, as my mother would also say. Until that moment, it had never made any difference to me how much or little a girl's clothing revealed, for my imagination had been entirely devoted to other mysteries. I was eleven. The girl was about fourteen, the age of my buddy Norman who lounged in the back seat with me. Staring after her, Norman elbowed me in the ribs and murmured, "Check out that chassis."

His mother glared around from the driver's seat. "Hush your mouth."

"I was talking about that sweet Chevy," said Norman, pointing out a souped-up jalopy at the curb.

"I know what you were talking about," his mother snapped.

No doubt she did know, since mothers could read minds, but at first I myself did not have a clue. Chassis? I knew what it meant for a car, an airplane, a radio, or even a cannon to have a chassis. But could a girl have one as well? I glanced after the retreating figure, and suddenly noticed with a sympathetic twitching in my belly the way her long raven ponytail swayed in rhythm to her walk and the way her fanny jostled in those pink shorts. In July's dazzle of sun, her swinging legs and arms beamed at me a semaphore I could almost read.

As the light turned green and our car pulled away, Norman's mother cast one more scowl at her son in the rearview mirror, saying, "Just think how it makes her feel to have you two boys gawking at her."

How? I wondered.

"Makes her feel like hot stuff," said Norman, owner of a bold mouth.

"If you don't get your mind out of the gutter, you're going to wind up in the state reformatory," said his mother.

Norman gave a snort. I sank into the seat, and tried to figure out what power had sprung from that sashaying girl to zap me in the belly.

Only after much puzzling did it dawn on me that I must finally have drifted into the force field of sex, as a space traveler who has lived all his years in free fall might rocket for the first time within gravitational reach of a star. Even as a bashful eleven-year-old I knew the word *sex,* of course, and I could paste that name across my image of the tantalizing girl. But a label for a mystery no more explains a mystery than the word *gravity* explains gravity. As I grew a beard and my taste shifted from girls to women, I acquired a more cagey language for speaking of desire. I picked up disarming theories. First by hearsay and then by experiment, I learned the delicious details of making babies. I came to appreciate the urgency for propagation that litters the road with maple seeds and drives salmon up waterfalls and yokes the newest crop of boys to the newest crop of girls. Books in their killjoy wisdom taught me that all the valentines and violins, the waltzes and glances, the long fever and ache of romance were merely embellishments on biology's instructions that we multiply our kind. And yet, the fraction of desire that actually leads to procreation is so vanishingly small as to seem irrelevant. In his lifetime a man sways to a million longings, only a few of which, or perhaps none at all, ever lead to the fathering of children.

Now, thirty years away from that July afternoon, firmly married, twice a father, I am still humming from the power unleashed by the girl in pink shorts, still wondering how it made her feel to have two boys gawk at her, still puzzling over how to dwell in the force field of desire.

How should a man look at women? It is a peculiarly and perhaps neurotically human question. Billy goats do not fret over how they should look at nanny goats. They look or don't look, as seasons and hormones dictate, and feel what they feel without benefit of theory. There is more billy goat in most men than we care to admit. None of us, however, is pure goat. To live utterly as an animal would make the business of sex far tidier but also drearier. If we tried, like Rousseau, to peel off the layers of civilization and imagine our way back to some pristine man and woman who have not yet been corrupted by hand-me-down notions of sexuality, my hunch is that we would find, in our speculative state of nature, that men regarded women with appalling simplicity. In any case, unlike goats, we dwell in history. What attracts our eyes and rouses our blood is only partly instinctual. Other forces contend in us as well, the voices of books and religions, the images of art and film and advertising, the entire chorus of culture. Norman's telling me to relish the sight of females and his mother's telling me to keep my eyes to myself are only two of the many voices quarreling in my head.

If there were a rule book for sex, it would be longer than the one for baseball (that byzantine sport), more intricate and obscure than tax instructions from the Internal Revenue Service. What I present here are a few images and reflections that cling, for me, to this one item in such a compendium of rules: How should a man look at women?

Well before I was to see any women naked in the flesh, I saw a bevy of them naked in photographs, hung in a gallery around the bed of my freshman roommate at college. A *Playboy* subscriber, he would pluck the centerfold from its staples each month and tape another airbrushed lovely to the wall. The gallery was in place when I moved in, and for an instant before I realized what I was looking at, all that expanse of skin reminded me of a meat locker back in Newton Falls, Ohio. I never quite shook that first impression, even after I had inspected the pinups at my leisure on subsequent days. Every curve of buttock and breast was news to me, an innocent kid from the puritan back roads. Today you would be hard-pressed to find a college freshman as ignorant as I was of female anatomy, if only because teenagers now routinely watch movies at home that would have been shown, during my teen years, exclusively on the fly-speckled screens of honky-tonk cinemas or in the basement of the Kinsey Institute. I studied those alien shapes on the wall with a curiosity that was not wholly sexual, a curiosity tinged with the wonder that astronomers must have felt when they pored over the early photographs of the far side of the moon.

The paper women seemed to gaze back at me, enticing or mocking, yet even in my adolescent dither I was troubled by the phony stare, for I knew this was no true exchange of looks. Those mascaraed eyes were not fixed on me but on a camera. What the models felt as they posed I could only guess—perhaps the boredom of any numbskull job, perhaps the weight of dollar bills, perhaps the sweltering lights of fame, perhaps a tingle of the power that launched a thousand ships.

Whatever their motives, these women had chosen to put themselves on display. For the instant of the photograph, they had become their bodies, as a prizefighter does in the moment of landing a punch, as a weightlifter does in the moment of hoisting a barbell, as a ballerina does in the whirl of a pirouette, as we all do in the crisis of making love or dying. It is supposed that men, ogling such photographs, feel that where so much surface is revealed there can be no depths. Yet I never doubted that behind the makeup and the plump curves and the two dimensions of the image there was an inwardness, a feeling self as mysterious as my own. In fact, during moments when I should have been studying French or thermodynamics, I would glance at my roommate's wall and invent mythical lives for those goddesses. The lives I made up were adolescent ones, to be sure; but so was my own life. Without that saving aura of inwardness, these women in the glossy photographs would have become merely another category of objects for sale, alongside the sports cars and stereo systems and liquors advertised in the same pages. If not extinguished, however, their humanity was severely reduced. And if by simplifying themselves they had lost some human essence, then by gaping at them I had shared in the theft.

What did that gaping take from me? How did it affect my way of seeing other women, those who would never dream of lying nude on a fake tiger rug before the million-faceted eye of a camera? The bodies in the photographs were implausibly smooth and slick and inflated, like balloon caricatures that might be floated overhead in a parade. Free of sweat and scars and imperfections, sensual without being fertile, tempting yet impregnable, they were Platonic ideals of the female form, divorced from time and the fluster of living, excused from the perplexities of mind. No actual woman could rival their insipid perfection.

The swains who gathered to admire my roommate's gallery discussed the pinups in the same tones and in much the same language as the farmers back home in Ohio used for assessing cows. The relevant parts of male or female bodies are quickly named—and, the *Kamasutra* and Marquis de Sade notwithstanding, the number of ways in which those parts can be stimulated or conjoined is touchingly small—so these studly conversations were more tedious than chitchat about the weather. I would lie on my bunk pondering calculus or Aeschylus and unwillingly hear the same few nouns and fewer verbs issuing from one mouth after another, and I would feel smugly superior. Here I was, improving my mind, while theirs wallowed in the notorious gutter. Eventually the swains would depart, leaving me in peace, and from the intellectual heights of my bunk I would glance across at those photographs . . . and yield to the gravity of lust. Idiot flesh! How stupid that a counterfeit stare and artful curves, printed in millions of copies on glossy paper, could arouse me. But there it was, not the first proof of my body's automatism and not the last.

Nothing in men is more machinelike than the flipping of sexual switches. I have never been able to read with a straight face the claims made by D. H. Lawrence and lesser pundits that the penis is a god, a lurking dragon. It more nearly resembles a railroad crossing signal, which stirs into life at intervals to announce "Here comes a train." Or, if the penis must be likened to an animal, let it be an ill-trained circus dog, sitting up and playing dead and heeling whenever it takes a notion, oblivious of the trainer's commands. Meanwhile, heart, lungs, blood vessels, pupils, and eyelids all assert their independence like the members of a rebellious troupe. Reason stands helpless at the center of the ring, cracking its whip.

While he was president, Jimmy Carter raised a brouhaha by confessing in a *Playboy* interview, of all shady places, that he occasionally felt lust in his heart for women. What man hasn't, aside from those who feel lust in their hearts for men? The commentators flung their stones anyway. Naughty, naughty, they chirped. Wicked Jimmy. Perhaps Mr. Carter could derive some consolation from psychologist Allen Wheelis, who, in *Doctor of Desire,* blames male appetite on biology: "We have been selected for desiring. Nothing could have convinced us by argument that it would be worthwhile to chase endlessly and insatiably after women, but something has transformed us from within, a plasmid has invaded our DNA, has twisted our nature so that now this is exactly what we *want* to do." Certainly, by Darwinian logic, those males who were most avid in their pursuit of females were also the most likely to pass on their genes. Consoling it may be, yet it is finally no solution to blame biology. "I am extremely sexual in my desires: I carry them everywhere and at all times," William Carlos Williams tells us on the opening page of his *Autobiography*. "I think that from that arises the drive which empowers us all. Given that drive, a man does with it what his mind directs. In the manner in which he directs that power lies his secret." I agree with the honest doctor. Whatever the contents of my DNA, however potent the influence of my ancestors, I still must direct that rebellious power. I still must live with the consequences of my looking and my longing.

Aloof on their blankets like goddesses on clouds, the pinups did not belong to my funky world. I was invisible to them, and they were immune to my gaze.

Not so the women who passed me on the street, sat near me in classes, shared a table with me in the cafeteria: it was risky to stare at them. They could gaze back, and sometimes did, with looks both puzzling and exciting. It only complicated matters for me to realize that so many of these strangers had taken precautions that men should notice them. The girl in matching pink halter and shorts who set me humming in my eleventh year might only have wanted to keep cool in the sizzle of July. But these alluring college femmes had deeper designs. Perfume, eye shadow, uplift bras (about which I learned in the Sears catalogue), curled hair, stockings, jewelry, lipstick, lace—what were these if not hooks thrown out into male waters?

I recall being mystified in particular by spike heels. They looked painful to me, and dangerous. Danger may have been the point, since the spikes would have made good weapons—they were affectionately known, after all, as stilettos. Or danger may have been the point in another sense, because a woman teetering along on such heels is tipsy, vulnerable, broadcasting her need for support. And who better than a man to prop her up, some guy who clomps around in brogans wide enough for the cornerstones of flying buttresses? (For years after college, I felt certain that spike heels had been forever banished, like bustles and foot-binding, but lately they have come back in fashion, and once more one encounters women teetering along on knife points.)

Back in those days of my awakening to women, I was also baffled by lingerie. I do not mean underwear, the proletariat of clothing, and I do not mean foundation garments, pale and sensible. I mean what the woman who lives in the house behind ours—owner of a shop called Bare Essentials—refers to as "intimate apparel." Those two words announce that her merchandise is both sexy and expensive. These flimsy items cost more per ounce than truffles, more than frankincense and myrrh. They are put-ons whose only purpose is to be taken off. I have a friend who used to attend the men-only nights at Bare Essentials, during which he would invariably buy a slinky outfit or two, by way of proving his serious purpose, outfits that wound up in the attic because his wife would not be caught dead in them. Most of the customers at the shop are women, however, as the models are women, and the owner is a woman. What should one make of that? During my college days I knew about intimate apparel only by rumor, not being that intimate with anyone who would have tricked herself out in such finery, but I could see the spike heels and other female trappings everywhere I turned. Why, I wondered then and wonder still, do so many women decorate themselves like dolls? And does that mean they wish to be viewed as dolls?

*Looking at Women*

On this question as on many others, Simone de Beauvoir has clarified matters for me, writing in *The Second Sex*: "The 'feminine' woman in making herself prey tries to reduce man, also, to her carnal passivity; she occupies herself in catching him in her trap, in enchaining him by means of the desires she arouses in him in submissively making herself a thing." Those women who transform themselves into dolls, in other words, do so because that is the most potent identity available to them. "It must be admitted," Beauvoir concedes, "that the males find in woman more complicity than the oppressor usually finds in the oppressed. And in bad faith they take authorization from this to declare that she has *desired* the destiny they have imposed on her."

*Complicity, oppressor, bad faith:* such terms yank us into a moral realm unknown to goats. While I am saddled with enough male guilt to believe three-quarters of Beauvoir's claim, I still doubt that men are so entirely to blame for the turning of women into sexual dolls. I believe human history is more collaborative than her argument would suggest. It seems unlikely to me that one-half the species could have "imposed" a destiny on the other half, unless that other half were far more craven than the females I have known. Some women have expressed their own skepticism on this point. Thus Joan Didion, in *The White Album*: "That many women are victims of condescension and exploitation and sex-role stereotyping was scarcely news, but neither was it news that other women are not: nobody forces women to buy the package." Beauvoir herself recognized that many members of her sex refuse to buy the "feminine" package: "The emancipated woman, on the contrary, wants to be active, a taker, and refuses the passivity man means to impose on her."

Since my college years, back in the murky 1960s, emancipated women have been discouraging their unemancipated sisters from making spectacles of themselves. Don't paint your face like a clown's or drape your body like a mannequin's, they say. Don't bounce on the sidelines in skimpy outfits, screaming your fool head off, while men compete in the limelight for victories. Don't present yourself to the world as a fluff pastry, delicate and edible. Don't waddle across the stage in a bathing suit in hopes of being named Miss This or That.

A great many women still ignore the exhortations. Wherever a crown for beauty is to be handed out, many still line up to stake their claims. Recently, Miss Indiana Persimmon Festival was quoted in our newspaper about the burdens of possessing the sort of looks that snag men's eyes. "Most of the time I enjoy having guys stare at me," she said, "but every once in a while it makes me feel like a piece of meat." The news photograph showed a cheerleader's perky face, heavily made-up, with starched hair teased into a blond cumulus. She put me in mind not of meat but of a plastic figurine, something you might buy from a booth outside a shrine. Nobody should ever be seen as meat, mere juicy stuff to satisfy an appetite. Better to appear as a plastic figurine, which is not meant for eating, and which is a gesture, however crude, toward art. Joyce described the aesthetic response as a contemplation of form without the impulse to action. Perhaps that is what Miss Indiana Persimmon Festival wishes to inspire in those who look at her, perhaps that is what many women who paint and primp themselves desire: to withdraw from the touch of hands and dwell in the eye alone, to achieve the status of art.

By turning herself (or allowing herself to be turned) into a work of art, does a woman truly escape men's proprietary stare? Not often, says the British critic John Berger in *Ways of Seeing*. Summarizing the treatment of women in Western painting, he concludes that—with a few notable exceptions, such as works by Rubens and Rembrandt—the woman on canvas is a passive object displayed for the pleasure of the male viewer, especially for the owner of the painting, who is, by extension, owner of the woman herself. Berger concludes: "Men look at women. Women watch themselves being looked at. This determines not only most relations between men and women but also the relation of women to themselves. The surveyor of woman in herself is male: the surveyed female. Thus she turns herself into an object—and most particularly an object of vision: a sight."

That sweeping claim, like the one quoted earlier from Beauvoir, also seems to me about three-quarters truth and one-quarter exaggeration. I know men who outdo the peacock for show, and I know women who are so fully possessed of themselves that they do not give a hang whether anybody notices them or not. The flamboyant gentlemen portrayed by Van Dyck are no less aware of being *seen* than are the languid ladies portrayed by Ingres. With or without clothes, both gentlemen and ladies may conceive of themselves as objects of vision, targets of envy or admiration or desire. Where they differ is in their potential for action: the men are caught in the midst of a decisive gesture or on the verge of making one; the women wait like fuel for someone else to strike a match.

I am not sure the abstract nudes favored in modern art are much of an advance over the inert and voluptuous ones of the old school. Think of two famous examples: Duchamp's *Nude Descending a Staircase* (1912), where the faceless woman has blurred into a waterfall of jagged shards, or Picasso's *Les Demoiselles d'Avignon* (1907), where the five angular damsels have been hammered as flat as cookie sheets and fitted with African masks. Neither painting invites us to behold a woman, but instead to behold what Picasso or Duchamp can make of one.

*Looking at Women*

The naked women in Rubens, far from being passive, are gleefully active, exuberant, their sumptuous pink bodies like rainclouds or plump nebulae. "His nudes are the first ones that ever made me feel happy about my own body," a woman friend told me in one of the Rubens galleries of the Prado Museum. I do not imagine any pinup or store-window mannequin or bathing-suited Miss Whatsit could have made her feel that way. The naked women in Rembrandt, emerging from the bath or rising from bed, are so private, so cherished in the painter's gaze, that we as viewers see them not as sexual playthings but as beloved persons. A man would do well to emulate that gaze.

⁂

I have never thought of myself as a sight. How much that has to do with being male and how much with having grown up on back roads where money was scarce and eyes were few, I cannot say. As a boy, apart from combing my hair when I was compelled to do so and regretting the patches on my jeans (only the poor wore patches), I took no trouble over my appearance. It never occurred to me that anybody outside my family, least of all a girl, would look at me twice. As a young man, when young women did occasionally glance my way, without any prospect of appearing handsome I tried at least to avoid appearing odd. A standard haircut and the cheapest versions of the standard clothes were camouflage enough. Now over the frontier of forty, I have achieved once more that boyhood condition of invisibility, with less hair to comb and fewer patches to humble me.

Many women clearly pass through the world aspiring to invisibility. Many others just as clearly aspire to be conspicuous. Women need not make spectacles of themselves in order to draw the attention of men. Indeed, for my taste, the less paint and fewer bangles the better. I am as helpless in the presence of subtle lures as a male moth catching a whiff of pheromones. I am a sucker for hair ribbons, a scarf at the throat, toes leaking from sandals, teeth bared in a smile. By contrast, I have always been more amused than attracted by the enameled exhibitionists whom our biblical mothers would identify as brazen hussies or painted Jezebels or, in the extreme cases, as whores of Babylon.

To encounter female exhibitionists in their full glory and variety, you need to go to a city. I never encountered ogling as a full-blown sport until I visited Rome, where bands of Italian men joined with gusto in appraising the charms of every passing female, and the passing females vied with one another in demonstrating their charms. In our own cities the most notorious bands of oglers tend to be construction gangs or street crews, men who spend much of their day leaning on the handles of shovels or pausing between bursts of riveting guns, their eyes tracing the curves of passersby. The first time my wife and kids and I drove into Boston we followed the signs to Chinatown, only to discover that Chinatown's miserably congested main street was undergoing repairs. That street also proved to be the city's home for X-rated cinemas and girlie shows and skin shops. LIVE SEX ACTS ON STAGE. PEEP SHOWS. PRIVATE BOOTHS. Caught in a traffic jam, we spent an hour listening to jackhammers and wolf whistles as we crept through the few blocks of pleasure palaces, my son and daughter with their noses hanging out the windows, my wife and I steaming. Lighted marquees peppered by burnt-out bulbs announced the titles of sleazy flicks; life-size posters of naked women flanked the doorways of clubs; leggy strippers in miniskirts, the originals for some of the posters, smoked on the curb between numbers.

After we had finally emerged from the zone of Eros, eight-year-old Jesse inquired, "What was *that* place all about?"

"Sex for sale," my wife Ruth explained.

That might carry us some way toward a definition of pornography: making flesh into a commodity, flaunting it like any other merchandise, divorcing bodies from selves. By this reckoning, there is a pornographic dimension to much advertising, where a charge of sex is added to products ranging from cars to shaving cream. In fact, the calculated imagery of advertising may be more harmful than the blatant imagery of the pleasure palaces, that frank raunchiness which Kate Millett in *Sexual Politics* refers to as the "truthful explicitness of pornography." One can leave the X-rated zone of the city, but one cannot escape the sticky reach of commerce, which summons girls to the high calling of cosmetic glamour, fashion, and sexual display, while it summons boys to the panting chase.

You can recognize pornography, according to D. H. Lawrence, "by the insult it offers, invariably, to sex, and to the human spirit" ("Pornography and Obscenity"). He should know, according to Millett, for in her view Lawrence himself was a purveyor of patriarchal and often sadistic pornography. I think she is correct about the worst of Lawrence, and that she identifies a misogynist streak in his work; but she ignores his career-long struggle to achieve a more public, tolerant vision of sexuality as an exchange between equals. In *Language and Silence,* George Steiner reminds us that "the list of writers who have had the genius to enlarge our actual compass of sexual awareness, who have given the erotic play of the mind a novel focus, an area of recognition previously unknown or fallow, is very small." Lawrence belongs on that brief list. The chief insult to the human spirit is to deny it, to pretend that we are merely conglomerations of molecules, to pretend that we exist purely as bundles of appetites or as food for the appetites of others.

All the hurtful ways for men to look at women are variations on this betrayal. "Thus she turns herself into an object," writes Berger. A woman's ultimate degradation is in "submissively making herself a thing," writes Beauvoir. To be turned into an object—whether by the brush of a painter or the lens of a photographer or the eye of a voyeur, whether by hunger or poverty or enslavement, by mugging or rape, bullets or bombs, by hatred, racism, car crashes, fires, or falls—is for each of us the deepest dread; and to reduce another person to an object is the primal wrong.

Caught in the vortex of desire, we have to struggle to recall the wholeness of persons, including ourselves. Beauvoir speaks of the temptation we all occasionally feel to give up the struggle for a self and lapse into the inertia of matter: "Along with the ethical urge of each individual to affirm his subjective existence, there is also the temptation to forgo liberty and become a thing." A woman in particular, given so much encouragement to lapse into thinghood, "is often very well pleased with her role as the *Other*."

Yet one need not forgo liberty and become a thing, without a center or a self, in order to become the Other. In our mutual strangeness, men and women can be doorways one for another, openings into the creative mystery that we share by virtue of our existence in the flesh. The effort of loving is reciprocal, not only in act but in desire, an *I* addressing a *Thou*, a meeting in that vivid presence. The distance a man stares across at a woman, or a woman at a man, is a gulf in the soul, out of which a voice cries: *Leap, leap.* One day all men may cease to look on themselves as prototypically human and on women as lesser miracles; women may cease to feel themselves the targets for desire; men and women both may come to realize that we are all mere flickerings in the universal fire; and then none of us, male or female, need give up humanity in order to become the Other.

Ever since I gawked at the girl in pink shorts, I have dwelt knowingly in the force field of sex. Knowingly or not, it is where we all dwell. Like the masses of planets and stars, our bodies curve the space around us. We radiate signals constantly, radio sources that never go off the air. We cannot help being centers of attraction and repulsion for one another. That is not all we are by a long shot, nor all we are capable of feeling, and yet, even after our much-needed revolution in sexual consciousness, the power of Eros will still turn our heads and hearts. In a world without beauty pageants, there will still be beauty, however its definition may have changed. As long as men have eyes, they will gaze with yearning and confusion at women.

When I return to the street with the ancient legacy of longing coiled in my DNA, and the residues from a thousand generations of patriarchs silting my brain, I encounter women whose presence strikes me like a slap of wind in the face. I must prepare a gaze that is worthy of their splendor.

# Reasons of the Body

My son has never met a sport he did not like. I have met a few that left an ugly tingle—boxing and rodeo and pistol shooting, among others—but, then, I have been meeting them for forty-four years, Jesse only for twelve. Our ages are relevant to the discussion, because, on the hill of the sporting life, Jesse is midway up the slope and climbing rapidly, while I am over the crest and digging in my heels as I slip down.

"You still get around pretty well for an old guy," he told me last night after we had played catch in the park.

The catch we play has changed subtly in recent months, a change that dramatizes a shift in the force field binding father and son. Early on, when I was a decade younger and Jesse a toddler, I was the agile one, leaping to snare his wild throws. The ball we tossed in those days was rubbery and light, a bubble of air as big around as a soup bowl, easy for small hands to grab. By the time he started school, we were using a tennis ball, then we graduated to a softball, then to gloves and a baseball. His repertoire of catches and throws increased along with his vocabulary.

Over the years, as Jesse put on inches and pounds and grace, I still had to be careful how far and hard I threw, to avoid bruising his ribs or his pride. But this spring, when we began limbering up our arms, his throws came whistling at me with a force that hurt my hand, and he caught effortlessly anything I could hurl back at him. It was as though the food he wolfed down all winter had turned into spring steel. I no longer needed to hold back. Now Jesse is the one, when he is feeling charitable, who pulls his pitches.

Yesterday in the park, he was feeling frisky rather than charitable. We looped the ball lazily back and forth awhile. Then he started backing away, backing away, until my shoulder twinged from the length of throws. Unsatisfied, he yelled, "Make me run for it!" So I flung the ball high and deep, low and wide, driving him over the grass, yet he loped easily wherever it flew, gathered it in, then whipped it back to me with stinging speed.

"Come on," he yelled, "put it where I can't reach it." I tried, ignoring the ache in my arm, and still he ran under the ball. He might have been gliding on a cushion of air, he moved so lightly. I was feeling heavy, and felt heavier by the minute as his return throws, grown suddenly and unaccountably wild, forced me to hustle back and forth, jump and dive.

"Hey," I yelled, waving my glove at him. "Look where I'm standing!"

"Standing is right," he yelled back. "Let's see those legs move!" His next throw sailed over my head, and the ones after that sailed farther still, now left now right, out of my range, until I gave up even trying for them, and the ball thudded accusingly to the ground. By the time we quit, I was sucking air, my knees were stiffening, and a fire was blazing in my arm. Jesse trotted up, his T-shirt dry, his breathing casual. This was the moment he chose to clap me on the back and say, "You still get around pretty well for an old guy."

It was a line I might have delivered, as a cocky teenager, to my own father. He would have laughed, and then challenged me to a round of golf or a bout of arm wrestling, contests he could still easily have won.

Whatever else these games may be, they are always contests. For many a boy, some playing field, some court or gym is the first arena in which he can outstrip his old man. For me, the arena was a concrete driveway where I played basketball against my father, shooting at a rusty hoop that was mounted over the garage. He had taught me how to dribble, how to time my jump, how to follow through on my shots. To begin with, I could barely heave the ball to the basket, and he would applaud if I so much as banged the rim. I banged away, year by year, my bones lengthening, muscles thickening. I shuffled over the concrete to the jazz of birdsong and the opera of thunderstorms. I practiced fervently, as though my life depended on putting the ball through the hoop, practiced when the driveway was dusted with pollen and when it was drifted with snow. From first light to twilight, while the chimney swifts spiraled out to feed on mosquitoes and the mosquitoes fed on me, I kept shooting, hour after hour. Many of those hours, Father was tinkering in the garage, which reverberated with the slap of my feet and the slam of the ball. There came a day when I realized that I could outleap him, outhustle and outshoot him. I began to notice his terrible breathing—terrible because I had not realized he could run short of air. I had not realized he could run short of anything. When he bent over and grabbed his knees, huffing, "You're too much for me," I felt at once triumphant and dismayed.

I still have to hold back when playing basketball with Jesse. But the day will come, and soon, when he grows taller and stronger, and he will be the one to show mercy. The only dessert I will be able to eat, if I am to avoid growing fat, will be humble pie. Even now my shots appear old-fashioned to him, as my father's arching two-handed heaves seemed antique to me. "Show me some of those Neanderthal moves," Jesse cries, as we shoot around at a basket in the park. "Show me how they did it in the Stone Age!" I do show him, clowning and hotdogging, wishing by turns to amuse and impress him. As I fake and spin, I am simultaneously father and son, playing games forward and backward in time.

The game of catch, like other sports where body faces body, is a dialogue carried on with muscle and bone. One body speaks by throwing a ball or a punch, by lunging with a foil, smashing a backhand, sinking a putt, rolling a strike, kicking a shot toward the corner of the net; the other replies by swinging, leaping, dodging, tackling, parrying, balancing. As in lovemaking, this exchange may be a struggle for power or a sharing of pleasure. The call and response may be in the spirit of antiphonal singing, a making of music that neither person could have achieved alone, or it may be in the spirit of insults bellowed across a table.

When a father and son play sports, especially a game the son has learned from the father, every motive from bitter rivalry to mutual delight may enter in. At first eagerly, and then grudgingly, and at last unconsciously, the son watches how his father grips the ball, handles the glove, swings the bat. In just the same way, the son has watched how the father swings a hammer, how the father walks, jokes, digs, starts a car, gentles a horse, pays a bill, shakes hands, shaves. There is a season in one's growing up, beginning at about the age Jesse is now, when a son comes to feel his old man's example as a smothering weight. You must shrug free of it, or die. And so, if your father carries himself soldier straight, you begin to slouch; if he strides along with a swagger, you slink; if he talks in joshing Mississippi accents to anybody with ears, you shun strangers and swallow your drawl. With luck and time, you may come to accept that you bear in your own voice overtones of your father's. You may come to rejoice that your own least motion—kissing a baby or opening a jar—is informed by memories of how your father would have done it. Between the early delight and the late reconciliation, however, you must pass through that season of rivalry, the son striving to undo or outdo his father's example, the father chewing on the bitter rind of rejection.

Why do I speak only of boys and men? Because, while there are females aplenty who relish any sport you can name, I have never shared a roof with one. In her seventies, my mother still dances and swims, even leads classes in aerobics, but she's never had much use for games played with balls, and neither has my wife or daughter. When Ruth, my wife, was a child, a bout of rheumatic fever confined her to bed and then to a wheelchair for several years. Until she was old enough for university, a heart rendered tricky by the illness kept her from doing anything that would raise her pulse, and by then she had invested her energies elsewhere, in music and science. To this day, Ruth sees no point in moving faster than a walk, or in defying gravity with exuberant leaps, or in puzzling over the trajectory of a ball.

And what of our daughter, sprightly Eva, firstborn? Surely I could have brought her up to become a partner for catch? Let me assure you that I tried. I put a sponge ball in her crib, as Father had put a baseball in mine. (I was going to follow tradition exactly and teethe her on a baseball, but Ruth, sensible of a baby's delicacy, said nothing doing.) From the moment the nurse handed Eva to me in the hospital, a quivering bundle, ours to keep, I coached my spunky girl, I coaxed and exhorted her, but she would not be persuaded that throwing or shooting or kicking a ball was a sensible way to spend an hour or an afternoon. After seventeen years of all the encouragement that love can buy, the one sport she will deign to play with me is volleyball, in which she hurtles over the grass, leaping and cavorting, as only a dancer could.

A gymnast and ballerina, Eva has always been on good terms with her body, and yet, along with her mother and my mother, she rolls her eyes when Jesse and I begin rummaging in the battered box on the porch for a baseball, basketball, or soccer ball. "So Dad," she calls, "it's off to recover past glories, is it? You show 'em, tiger. But don't break any bones."

Eva's amusement has made the opinion of the women in my life unanimous. Their baffled indulgence, bordering at times on mockery, has given to sports a tang of the mildly illicit.

Like many other women (not all, not all), those in my family take even less interest in talking about sports than in playing them. They pride themselves on being above such idle gab. They shake their heads when my son and I check the scores in the newspaper. They are astounded that we can spend longer rehashing a game than we spent in playing it. When Jesse and I compare aches after a session on field or court, the women observe mildly that it sounds as though we had been mugged. Surely we would not inflict such damage on ourselves? Perhaps we have gotten banged up from wrestling bears? We kid along and say, "Yes, we ran into the Chicago Bears," and my daughter or mother or wife will reply, "You mean the hockey team?"

In many households and offices, gossip about games and athletes breaks down along gender lines, the men indulging in it and the women scoffing. Those on each side of the line may exaggerate their feelings, the men pumping up their enthusiasm, the women their indifference, until sport becomes a male mystery. No locker room, no sweat lodge is needed to shut women out; mere talk will do it. Men are capable of muttering about wins and losses, batting averages and slam dunks, until the flowers on the wallpaper begin to wilt and every woman in the vicinity begins to yearn for a supply of gags. A woman friend of mine, an executive in a computing firm, has been driven in self-defense to scan the headlines of the sports pages before going to work, so that she can toss out references to the day's contests and stars, like chunks of meat, to feed the appetites of her male colleagues. After gnawing on this bait, the men may consent to speak with her of things more in keeping with her taste, such as books, birds, and the human condition.

My daughter has never allowed me to buy her a single item of sports paraphernalia. My son, on the other hand, has never said no to such an offer. Day and night, visions of athletic gear dance in his head. With religious zeal, he pores over magazine ads for sneakers, examining the stripes and insignia as if they were hieroglyphs of ultimate truth. Between us, Jesse and I are responsible for the hoard of equipment on our back porch, which contains at present the following items: one bicycle helmet and two bicycles; a volleyball set, badminton set, and a bag of golf clubs; three racquets for tennis, two for squash, one for paddleball; roller skates and ice skates, together with a pair of hockey sticks; goalie gloves, batting gloves, three baseball gloves and one catcher's mitt; numerous yo-yos; ten pairs of cleated or waffle-soled shoes; a drying rack festooned with shorts and socks and shirts and sweat suits; and a cardboard box heaped with (I counted) forty-nine balls, including ones for all the sports implicated above, as well as for Ping-Pong, lacrosse, juggling, and jacks.

Excavated by some future archaeologist, this porch full of gear would tell as much about how we passed our lives as would the shells and seeds and bones of a kitchen midden. An excavation of the word *sport* also yields evidence of breaks, bruises, and ambiguities. A sport is a game, an orderly zone marked off from the prevailing disorder, but it can also be a mutation, a violation of rules. To be good at sports is to be a winner, and yet a good sport is one who loses amiably, a bad sport one who kicks and screams at every setback. A flashy dresser might be called a sport, and so might a gambler, an idler, an easygoing companion, one who dines high on the hog of pleasure. But the same label may be attached to one who is the butt of jokes, a laughingstock, a goat. As a verb, to sport can mean to wear jewelry or clothes in a showy manner, to poke fun, to trifle, or to roll promiscuously in the hay. It is a word spiced with unsavory meanings, rather tacky and cheap, with hints of brothels, speakeasies, and malodorous dives. And yet it bears also the wholesome flavor of fairness, vigor, and ease.

The lore of sports may be all that some fathers have to pass down to their sons in place of lore about hunting animals, planting seeds, killing enemies, or placating the gods. Instead of telling him how to shoot a buffalo, the father whispers in the son's ear how to shoot a layup. Instead of consulting the stars or the entrails of birds, father and son consult the smudged print of newspapers to see how their chosen spirits are faring. They fiddle with the dials of radios, hoping to catch the oracular murmur of a distant game. The father recounts heroic deeds, not from the field of battle, but from the field of play. The seasons about which he speaks lead not to harvests but to championships. No longer intimate with the wilderness, no longer familiar even with the tamed land of farms, we create artificial landscapes bounded by lines of paint or lime. Within those boundaries, as within the frame of a chessboard or a painting, life achieves a memorable, seductive clarity. The lore of sports is a step down from that of nature, perhaps even a tragic step, but it is lore nonetheless, with its own demigods and demons, magic and myths.

The sporting legends I carry from my father are private rather than public. I am haunted by scenes that no journalist recorded, no camera filmed. Father is playing a solo round of golf, for example, early one morning in April. The fairways glisten with dew. Crows rasp and fluster in the pines that border the course. Father lofts a shot toward a par-three hole, and the white ball arcs over the pond, over the sand trap, over the shaggy apron of grass onto the green, where it bounces, settles down, then rolls toward the flag, rolls unerringly, inevitably, until it falls with a scarcely audible click into the hole. The only eyes within sight besides his own are the crows'. For once, the ball has obeyed him perfectly, harmonizing wind and gravity and the revolution of the spheres, one shot has gone where all are meant to go, and there is nobody else to watch. He stands on the tee, gazing at the distant hole, knowing what he has done and that he will never do it again. The privacy of this moment appeals to me more than all the clamor and fame of a shot heard round the world.

Here is another story I live by: The man who will become my father is twenty-two, a catcher for a bush-league baseball team in Tennessee. He will never make it to the majors, but on weekends he earns a few dollars for squatting behind the plate and nailing runners foolish enough to try stealing second base. From all those bus rides, all those red-dirt diamonds, the event he will describe for his son with deepest emotion is an exhibition game. Father's team of whites, most of them fresh from two-mule farms, is playing a touring black team, a rare event for that day and place. To make it even rarer, and the sides fairer, the coaches agree to mix the teams. And so my father, son of a Mississippi cotton farmer, bruised by racial notions that will take a lifetime to heal, crouches behind the plate and for nine innings catches fastballs and curves, changeups and screwballs from a whirling, muttering wizard of the Negro Baseball League, one Leroy Robert Paige, known to the world as Satchel. Afterward, Satchel Paige tells the farm boy, "You catch a good game," and the farm boy answers, "You've got the stuff, mister." And for the rest of my father's life, this man's pitching serves as a measure of mastery.

And here is a third myth I carry: One evening when the boy who will become my father is eighteen, he walks into the Black Cat Saloon in Tupelo, Mississippi. He is looking for a fight. Weary of plowing, sick of red dirt, baffled by his own turbulent energy, he often picks fights. This evening the man he picks on is a stranger who occupies a nearby stool at the bar, a husky man in his thirties, wearing a snap-brim hat, dark suit with wide lapels, narrow tie, and infuriatingly white shirt. The stranger is slow to anger. The red-headed Sanders boy keeps at him, keeps at him, mocking the Yankee accent, the hat worn indoors, the monkey suit, the starched shirt, until at last the man stands up and backs away from the bar, fists raised. The Sanders boy lands three punches, he remembers that much, but the next thing he remembers is waking up on the sidewalk, the stranger bending over him to ask if he is all right, and to ask, besides, if he would like a boxing scholarship to Mississippi State. The man is headed there to become the new coach. The boy who will become my father goes to Mississippi State for two years, loses some bouts and wins more, then quits to pursue a Golden Gloves title, and when he fails at that he keeps on fighting in bars and streets, and at last he quits boxing, his nose broken so many times there is no bone left in it, only a bulb of flesh which a boy sitting in his lap will later squeeze and mash like dough. From all those bouts, the one he will describe to his son with the greatest passion is that brawl from the Black Cat Saloon, when the stranger in the white shirt, a good judge of fighters, found him worthy.

Father tried, with scant success, to make a boxer of me. Not for a career in the ring, he explained, but for defense against the roughs and rowdies who would cross my path in life. If I ran into a mean customer, I told him, I could always get off the path. No, Father said, a man never backs away. A man stands his ground and fights. This advice rubbed against my grain, which inclined toward quickness of wits rather than fists, yet for years I strove to become the tough guy he envisioned. Without looking for fights, I stumbled into them at every turn, in schoolyard and backyard and in the shadows of barns. Even at my most belligerent, I still tried cajolery and oratory first. Only when that failed did I dig in my heels and start swinging. I gave bruises and received them, gave and received bloody noses, leading with my left, as Father had taught me, protecting my head with forearms, keeping my thumbs outside my balled fists to avoid breaking them when I landed a punch.

Some bullies saw my feistiness as a red flag. One boy who kept hounding me was Olaf Magnuson, a neighbor whose surname I would later translate with my primitive Latin as Son of Big. The name was appropriate, for Olaf was two years older and a foot taller and forty pounds heavier than I was. He pestered me, cursed me, irked and insulted me. When I stood my ground, he pounded me into it. One evening in my twelfth summer, after I had staggered home several times from these frays bloodied and bowed, Father decided it was time for serious boxing lessons. We would train for two months, he told me, then challenge Olaf Magnuson to a fight, complete with gloves and ropes and bell. This did not sound like a healthy idea to me; but Father insisted. "Do you want to keep getting pushed around," he demanded, "or are you going to lick the tar out of him?"

Every day for two months I ran, skipped rope, did chin-ups and push-ups. Father hung his old punching bag from a rafter in the basement, and I flailed at it until my arms filled with sand. He wrapped an old mattress around a tree and told me to imagine Olaf Magnuson's belly as I pounded the cotton ticking. I sparred with my grizzly old man, who showed me how to jab and hook, duck and weave, how to keep my balance and work out of corners. Even though his feet had slowed, his hands were still so quick that I sometimes dropped my own gloves to watch him, dazzled. "Keep up those dukes," he warned. "Never lower your guard." For two months I trained as though I had a boxer's heart.

Father issued our challenge by way of Olaf Magnuson's father, a strapping man with a voice like a roar in a barrel. Hell yes, my boy'll fight, the elder Magnuson boomed.

On the morning appointed for our bout, Father strung rope from tree to tree in the yard, fashioning a ring that was shaped like a lozenge. My mother, who had been kept in the dark about the grudge match until that morning, raised sand for a while; failing to make us see what fools we were, disgusted with the ways of men, she drove off to buy groceries. My sister carried word through the neighborhood, and within minutes a gaggle of kids and a scattering of bemused adults pressed against the ropes.

"You're going to make that lunkhead bawl in front of the whole world," Father told me in the kitchen while lacing my gloves. "You're going to make him call for his mama. Before you're done with him, he's going to swallow so many teeth that he'll never mess with you again."

So long as Father was talking, I believed him. I was a mean hombre. I was bad news, one fist of iron and the other one steel. When he finished his pep talk, however, and we stepped out into the sunshine, and I saw the crowd buzzing against the ropes, and I spied enormous Olaf slouching from his own kitchen door, my confidence hissed away like water on a hot griddle. In the seconds it took me to reach the ring, I ceased to feel like the bringer of bad news and began to feel like the imminent victim. I danced in my corner, eyeing Olaf. His torso, hulking above jeans and clodhopper boots, made my own scrawny frame look like a preliminary sketch for a body. I glanced down at my ropy arms, at my twiggy legs exposed below red gym shorts, at my high-topped basketball shoes, at the grass.

"He'll be slow," Father growled in my ear, "slow and clumsy. Keep moving. Bob and weave. Give him that left jab, watch for an opening, and then *bam*, unload with the right."

Not trusting my voice, I nodded, and kept shuffling my sneakers to hide the shivers.

Father put his palms to my cheeks and drew my face close to his and looked hard at me. Above that smushed, boneless nose, his brown eyes were as dark and shiny as those of a deer. "You okay, big guy?" he asked. "You ready for this?" I nodded again. "Then go get him," he said, turning me around and giving me a light shove toward the center of the ring.

I met Olaf there for instructions from the referee, a welder who lived down the road from us, a wiry man with scorched forearms who had just fixed our trailer hitch. I lifted my eyes reluctantly from Olaf's boots, along the trunks of his jean-clad legs, over the expanse of brawny chest and palooka jaw to his ice-blue eyes. They seemed less angry than amused.

A cowbell clattered. Olaf and I touched gloves, backed apart and lifted our mitts. The crowd sizzled against the ropes. Blood banged in my ears, yet I could hear Father yelling. I hear him still. And in memory I follow his advice. I bob, I weave, I guard my face with curled gloves, I feint and jab within the roped diamond, I begin to believe in myself, I circle my lummoxy rival and pepper him with punches, I feel a grin rising to my lips, and then Olaf tires of the game and rears back and knocks me flat. He also knocks me out. He also breaks my nose, which will remain crooked forever after.

That ended my boxing career. Olaf quit bullying me, perhaps because my blackout had given him a scare, perhaps because he had proved whatever he needed to prove. What I had shown my father was less clear. He may have seen weakness, may have seen a doomed and reckless bravery, may have seen a clown's pratfall. In any case, he never again urged me to clear the path with my fists.

And I have not offered boxing lessons to my son. Instead, I offered him the story of my defeat. When Jesse would still fit in my lap, I cuddled him there and told of my fight with Olaf, and he ran his delicate finger against the crook in my nose, as I had fingered the boneless pulp of Father's nose. I told Jesse about learning to play catch, the ball passing back and forth like a thread between my father and me, stitching us together. I told him about the time one of my pitches sailed over Father's head and shattered the windshield of our 1956 Ford, a car just three days old, and Father only shook his head and said, "Shoot, boy, you get that fastball down, and the batters won't see a thing but smoke." And I told Jesse about sitting on a feather tick in a Mississippi farmhouse, wedged between my father and grandfather, shaking with their excitement while before us on a tiny black-and-white television two boxers slammed and hugged each other. Cradling my boy, I felt how difficult it is for men to embrace without the liquor of violence, the tonic of pain.

Why do we play these games so avidly? All sports, viewed dispassionately, are dumb. The rules are arbitrary, the behaviors absurd. For boxing and running, perhaps, you could figure out evolutionary advantages. But what earthly use is it to become expert at swatting a ball with a length of wood or at lugging an inflated pigskin through a mob? Freudians might say that in playing with balls we men are simply toying with the prize portion of our anatomies. Darwinians might claim that we are competing for the attention of females, like so many preening peacocks or head-butting rams. Physicians might attribute the sporting frenzy to testosterone, economists might point to our dreams of professional paychecks, feminists might appeal to our machismo, philosophers to our fear of death.

No doubt all of those explanations, like buckets put out in the rain, catch some of the truth. But none of them catches all of the truth. None of them explains, for example, what moves a boy to bang a rubber ball against a wall for hours, for entire summers, as my father did in his youth, as I did in mine, as Jesse still does. That boy, throwing and catching in the lee of garage or barn, dwells for a time wholly in his body, and that is reward enough. He aims the ball at a knothole, at a crack, and then leaps to snag the rebound, mastering a skill, working himself into a trance. How different is his rapture from the dancing and drumming of a young brave? How different is his solitude from that of any boy seeking visions?

The less use we have for our bodies, the more we need reminding that the body possesses its own way of knowing. To steal a line from Pascal: The body has its reasons that reason knows nothing of. Although we struggle lifelong to dwell in the flesh without rancor, without division between act and desire, we succeed only for moments at a time. We treasure whatever brings us those moments, whether it be playing cello or playing pool, making love or making baskets, kneading bread or nursing a baby or kicking a ball. Whoever teaches us an art or a skill, whoever shows us a path to momentary wholeness, deserves our love.

I am conscious of my father's example whenever I teach a game to my son. Demonstrating a stroke in tennis or golf, I amplify my gestures, like a ham actor playing to the balcony. My pleasure in the part is increased by the knowledge that others, and especially Father, have played it before me. What I know about hitting a curve or shooting a hook shot or throwing a left jab, I know less by words than by feel. When I take Jesse's hand and curl his fingers over the baseball's red stitches, explaining how to make it deviously spin, I feel my father's hands slip over mine like gloves. Move like so, like so. I feel the same ghostly guidance when I hammer nails or fix a faucet or pluck a banjo. Working on the house or garden or car, I find myself wearing more than my father's hands, find myself clad entirely in his skin.

One blistering afternoon when I was a year younger than Jesse is now, a fly ball arched toward me in center field. I ran under it, lifted my face and glove, and lost the ball in the sun. The ball found me, however, crashing into my eye. In the split second before blacking out I saw nothing but light. We need not go hunting pain, for pain will find us. It hurts me more to see Jesse ache than to break one of my own bones. I cry out as the ground ball bangs into his throat. I wince as he comes down crookedly with a rebound and turns his ankle. I wish to spare him injury as I wish to spare him defeat, but I could not do so even if I had never lobbed him that first fat pitch.

As Jesse nears thirteen, his estimate of my knowledge and my power declines rapidly. He sees me slipping down the far slope. If I were a potter, say, or a carpenter, my skills would outreach his for decades to come. But where speed and stamina are the essence, a father in his forties will be overtaken by a son in his teens. Training for soccer, Jesse carries a stopwatch as he jogs around the park. I am not training for anything, only knocking rust from my joints and beguiling my heart, but I run along with him, puffing to keep up. I know that his times will keep going down, while I will never run faster than I do now. This is as it should be, for his turn has come. Slow as I am, and doomed to be slower, I relish his company.

In the game of catch, this dialogue of throw and grab we have been carrying on since he was old enough to crawl, Jesse has finally begun to put questions that I cannot answer. I know the answers; I can see how my back should twist, my legs should pump; but legs and back will no longer match my vision. This faltering is the condition of our lives, of course, a condition that will grow more acute with each passing year. I mean to live the present year before rushing off to any future ones. I mean to keep playing games with my son, so long as flesh will permit, as my father played games with me well past his own physical prime. Now that sports have begun to give me lessons in mortality, I realize they have also been giving me, all the while, lessons in immortality. These games, these contests, these grunting conversations of body to body, father to son, are not substitutes for some other way of being alive, but are the sweet and sweaty thing itself.

# After the Flood

*A* river poured through the landscape I knew as a child. It was the power of the place, gathering rain and snowmelt, surging through the valley under sun, under ice, under the bellies of fish and the curled brown boats of sycamore leaves. You will need a good map of Ohio to find the river I am talking about, the West Branch of the Mahoning. The stretch of it I knew best no longer shows on maps, a stretch that ran between wooded slopes and along the flanks of cornfields and pastures in the township of Charlestown, in Portage County, a rural enclave surrounded by the smokestacks and concrete of Akron, Youngstown, and Cleveland in the northeastern corner of the state.

Along that river bottom I gathered blackberries and hickory nuts, trapped muskrats, rode horses, followed baying hounds on the scent of raccoons. Spring and fall, I walked barefoot over the tilled fields, alert for arrowheads. Along those slopes I helped a family of Swedish farmers collect buckets of maple sap. On the river itself I skated in winter and paddled in summer, I pawed through gravel bars in search of fossils, I watched hawks preen and pounce, I courted and canoed and idled. This remains for me a primal landscape, imprinted on my senses, a place by which I measure every other place.

It is also, now, a drowned landscape. In the early 1960s, when I was in high school, politicians and bankers and realtors ordained that the Mahoning should be snared. A dam was built, the river died, and water backed up over most of the land I knew. No city needed the water for drinking. The reservoir, named after a man who had never lived in that valley, provided owners of loud boats with another playground for racing and waterskiing, and provided me with a lesson in loss. If the loss were mine alone, the story would not be worth telling. My grieving for a drowned landscape is private, a small ache in a bruised world. But the building of the dam, the obliteration of that valley, the displacement of people and beasts, these were public acts, the sort of acts we have been repeating from coast to coast as we devour the continent.

Like many townships in farm country, remote from the offices where the fate of land is decided, Charlestown has suffered more than one erasure. Long before the building of the reservoir, the government had already sliced away the northern third of the township for an arsenal, a wild, murderous place I have written about elsewhere as a paradise of bombs. On current maps of the township that upper third is blank white, and most of the remaining two-thirds, flooded by the reservoir, is vacant blue. Merely by looking at the map, one can tell that here is a sacrificial zone.

Returning to one's native ground, always tricky, becomes downright treacherous when the ground is at the bottom of a lake. Unwilling to dive through so much water, I can return to that drowned landscape, as I can return to childhood, only by diving through memory.

I had just become a teenager when the government began purchasing the farms and trailers and shacks that would be in the path of the reservoir. (If there had been mansions and factories in the way, the politicians would have doomed a different valley.) Among the first to be unhoused was the Swedish family, old Mr. Sivy and his two unmarried children, who had farmed that bottom land with big-shouldered horses, whose silage I had pitchforked in the steaming silo, whose cows I had fed, whose maple syrup I had savored hot from the vat. Uprooted, the old man soon died. The children bought a new farm on high ground, trying to start over, but it was no good, the soil too thin, worn out, no black bottom land, no fat maples, no river pouring through it. All down the valley it was the same, people forced to move by a blizzard of government paper, occasionally by the sheriff, in a few instances by the arrival of bulldozers at their front door.

While gangs of men with dynamite and dump trucks tore down the condemned buildings, other gangs with earthmovers and cement mixers slowly raised a wall across the river. For a year I watched it rise, while I wooed a girl who lived on a ridge overlooking the dam site. Crooners purred love songs from the stereo in her parlor, against an accompaniment of chuffs and shouts and whistles from the valley below. I studied the contours of that girl's face while the river's contours were bullied into the shape of blueprints. The huge concrete forms, the Tinkertoy scaffolds, the blasting, the snort of compressors, the lurch of heavy machines are confused in me now with the memory of damp hands and lingering kisses. The girl and I broke up, but the concrete held. Thereafter, I avoided that ridge, and did not see the laying of the dam's final tier, did not see the steel gates close. By the time I graduated from high school, water was beginning to lap over the banks of the Mahoning, but I could not bear to go down to the river and look.

When I left Ohio for college, my family left as well, trailing my father's work to Louisiana. My childhood friends dispersed—to war, to jail, to distant marriages and jobs, to cities where lights glittered and dollars sang. I had scant reason to visit that flooded township, and good reason to keep my distance. Why rush to see a muddy expanse of annihilating water?

Some years later, however, duties carried me through the northeastern corner of Ohio, within an hour's drive of my old neighborhood. I had not planned to make a detour. Yet the names of towns emblazoned on huge green signs along the highway tugged at me. The shapes of chimneys and roofs, the colors of barns, the accents in fast-food booths and gas stations, all drew me off the interstate onto the roads of Portage County, up the stream of recollection toward that childhood place.

The season of my return was late winter, after the last snow and before the first plowing, before grass resumed its green sizzle, before trees blurred with leaves. The shape of the land lay exposed. It was a gray day, a day to immunize one against nostalgia, a day safe, I supposed, for facing up to what I had lost. Surely I was prepared by now to see the great erasure. I was a man, and had put behind me a boy's affection for a stretch of river and a patch of dirt. New places had claimed me, thereby loosening the grip of that old landscape. Still, to ease my way back, before going to the reservoir I drove through the county seat, Ravenna, which had scarcely changed, and then through Edinburgh, Atwater, Deerfield, Palmyra, Paris, Wayland—tiny crossroad settlements where I had played baseball and eaten pie and danced—and these, too, had scarcely changed. Circling, I drew closer and closer to the blue splotch on the map.

The best way to approach the water, I decided, was along the road where, for half our years in Charlestown, my family had lived on five acres with horses and rabbits and dogs. Surely our gray-shingled house would still be there, safe on its ridge above the lake, even if most of the land I had known was drowned. So I turned from the highway onto that curving, cracked, tar-slick road, looking for the familiar. But at the corner, where there should have been a farmhouse, a silo, a barn, there was only a billboard marking the entrance to the West Branch Reservation. The fields where I had baled hay now bristled with a young woods. There was no house in the hollow where the road dipped down, where the family of Seventh-day Adventists used to live with their stacks of apocalyptic pamphlets and their sad-eyed children. The spinster's white bungalow was gone, along with the battered bus in the side yard which had served her for a chicken coop. Yard after yard had grown up in brush, and the shade trees spread darkness over their own seedlings. No mail boxes leaned on posts beside the road, no driveways broke the fringe of weeds. The trailer park was gone, the haunted house was gone, the tar-paper shanty where the drunk mechanic beat his wife and the wife beat her kids and the kids wailed, that was gone, and so was every last trailer and cottage and privy and shack, all down the blacktopped mile to our place.

I recognized our place by the two weeping willows out front. My father and I had planted those willows from slips, had fenced them round to protect the tender bark from deer, had watered and weeded and nursed them along. By the day of my visit those twigs had burgeoned into yellow fountains some fifty feet high, brimming over the woods that used to be our cleared land, woods that flourished where our house and barn had stood. I did not get out of the car. I could see from the road all that I was ready to see. The dense thicket, bare of leaves, was the color of rusty iron. Aside from the willows, no hint of our work or ownership survived.

I felt a fool. During the years of my absence, while my mind had suffered the waters to rise through the forest and up the ravines onto the margins of our land, I had preserved the gray-shingled house, the low white barn, the lilacs and forsythia, the orchard and pasture, the garden, the lawn. And yet, all the while, cedar and sumac and brambles, like the Earth's dark fur, had been pushing up through my past.

Sight of the reservoir, surely, could not be worse. I continued down the road through the vigorous woods. Not a house, not a barn, not a plowed field. The first clearing I came to was half a mile farther on, at the spot where a man named Ferry had lived. He used to let the neighborhood kids swim in his pond, even after a boastful boy dived into a rock and drowned. We knew that when we knocked at Mr. Ferry's door, raising money for school or Scouts, he would buy whatever we had to sell. He was a tender man. He loved his wife so much that when she died he planted a thousand white pines in her memory. The pines, spindly in my recollection, had grown into a forest by the day of my return.

In place of Mr. Ferry's house and yard there was a state campground now, encircled by the spiky green palisade of pines. The entrance booth was boarded up. A placard outside instructed campers to deposit their fees—so much for trailers, so much for tents—in the box below. There was no box below, only a slab of plywood with ragged holes from which the screws had been ripped. Nor were there any campers on this wintry afternoon. As I drove through the vacant lot, the only sounds were the crunch of gravel beneath my tires and the yawp of blue jays overhead and the shoosh of wind through the pines.

I pulled away from the campground and drove on. My mind raced ahead along the road as I remembered it, steeply downhill between fat maples and patchy sycamores to the river and the steel-girdered bridge. I had rolled down that hill in a school bus, swayed down on horseback, hurtled down on bicycle and sled, run down on foot. The slope and feel of it, fixed inside me, became my standard for all hills. From the bridge I had watched the river's current raveling over sandbars, minnows flickering in the shallows, water-striders dimpling the surface. Now and again, when the sun was right, I had spied my own face peering up from the stream. In memory, the road stretched on beyond the bridge, passing the tin-roofed shed where the maple syrup boiled, passing the Sivy farm, rising up the far slope to a T-junction with a ridgeline road. Turn left from there, and I would go to the high school. Turn right, and I would go to the barbershop and feed store. As my thoughts raced ahead of the car, inside me the valley opened and the river flexed its long sleek muscle.

Rounding the curve, however, I had to slam on the brakes to avoid running into a guardrail that blocked the road. Beyond the railing, where valley and bridge and river should have been, flat gray water spread away toward distant hills. You know this moment from dream: you are in a familiar room, but when you turn to leave, where a door should be there is a wall; or you come up behind someone you love, speak her name, yet when she turns around her face is blank; or you find the story of the universe written on a page, but when you draw close to read it, the letters dissolve. Waters of separation, waters of oblivion, waters of death.

I got out of the car and pressed my thighs against the cold steel barricade and stared. Gray, flat, empty lake. Not even a boat to redeem the emptiness. A lone crow slowly pumped toward the horizon on glossy black wings. Along the shore, a few sycamores still thrust up their mottled branches. Except for those trees, the pavement beneath my boots, and hills too high for water to claim, everything I knew had been swept away.

My worst imaginings had failed to prepare me for this. I stood there dazed. I could not take it in, so much had been taken away. For a long spell I leaned against the guardrail and dredged up everything I could remember of what lay beneath the reservoir. But memory was at last defeated by the blank gray water. No effort of mind could restore the river or drain the valley. I surrendered to what my eyes were telling me. Only then was I truly exiled.

Those who built the dam had their reasons. You have heard the litany: flood control, recreation, development. I very much doubt that more human good has come from that muddy, silting, rarely frequented lake than came from the cultivated valley and wild woods and free-flowing river. I am suspicious of the logic that would forestall occasional floods by creating a permanent one. But I do not wish to debate the merits of dams. I mean only to speak of how casually, how relentlessly we sever the bonds between person and place.

One's native ground is the place where, since before you had words for such knowledge, you have known the smells, the seasons, the birds and beasts, the human voices, the houses, the ways of working, the lay of the land and the quality of light. It is the landscape you learn before you retreat inside the illusion of your skin. You may love the place if you flourished there, or hate the place if you suffered there. But love it or hate it, you cannot shake free. Even if you move to the antipodes, even if you become intimate with new landscapes, you still bear the impression of that first ground.

I am all the more committed to know and care for the place I have come to as an adult because I have lost irretrievably the childhood landscapes that gave shape to my love of the Earth. The farm outside Memphis where I was born has vanished beneath parking lots and the poison-perfect lawns of suburbs. The Arsenal, with its herds of deer grazing on the grassy roofs of ammunition bunkers, is locked away behind chain-link fences, barbed wire, and guns. And the Mahoning Valley has been drowned. In our century, in our country, no fate could be more ordinary.

Of course, in mourning the drowned valley I also mourn my drowned childhood. The dry land preserved the traces of my comings and goings, the river carried the reflection of my beardless face. Yet even as a boy I knew the landscape was incomparably older than I, and richer, and finer. Some of the trees along the Mahoning had been rooted there when the first white settlers arrived from New England. Hawks had been hunting and deer had been drinking there since before our kind harnessed oxen. The gravels, laden with fossils, had been shoved there ten thousand years ago by glaciers. The river itself was the offspring of glaciers, a channel for meltwater to follow toward the Ohio, and thence to the Mississippi and the Gulf of Mexico. What I knew of the land's own history made me see that expanse of water as a wound.

Loyalty to place arises from sources deeper than narcissism. It arises from our need to be at home on the Earth. We marry ourselves to the creation by knowing and cherishing a particular place, just as we join ourselves to the human family by marrying a particular man or woman. If the marriage is deep, divorce is painful. My drive down that unpeopled road and my desolate watch beside the reservoir gave me a hint of what others must feel when they are wrenched from their place. I say a *hint,* because my loss is mild compared to what others have lost.

I think of the farmers who saw their wood lots and fields go under the flood. I think of the Miami and Shawnee who spoke of belonging to that land as a child belongs to a mother, and who were driven out by white soldiers. I think of the hundred other tribes that were herded onto reservations far from the graves of their ancestors. I think of the Africans who were yanked from their homes and bound in chains and shipped to this New World. I think about refugees, set in motion by hunger or tyranny or war. I think about children pushed onto the streets by cruelty or indifference. I think about migrant workers, Dust Bowl émigrés, all the homeless wanderers. I think about the poor everywhere—and it is overwhelmingly the poor—whose land is gobbled by strip mines, whose neighborhoods are wiped out by highways and shopping malls, whose villages are destroyed by bombs, whose forests are despoiled by chain saws and executive fountain pens.

The word *nostalgia* was coined in 1688 as a medical term, to provide an equivalent for the German word meaning homesickness. We commonly treat homesickness as an ailment of childhood, like mumps or chickenpox, and we treat nostalgia as an affliction of age. On our lips, nostalgia usually means a sentimental regard for the trinkets and fashions of an earlier time, for an idealized past, for a vanished youth. We speak of nostalgia for 1930s movies, say, or 1950s haircuts. It is a shallow use of the word. The two Greek roots of *nostalgia* literally mean *return pain.* The pain comes not from returning home but from longing to return. Perhaps it is inevitable that a nation of immigrants—who shoved aside the native tribes of this continent, who enslaved and transported

Africans, who still celebrate motion as if humans were dust motes—that such a nation should lose the deeper meaning of this word. A footloose people, we find it difficult to honor the lifelong, bone-deep attachment to place. We are slow to acknowledge the pain in yearning for one's native ground, the deep anguish in not being able, ever, to return.

On a warmer day I might have taken off my clothes and stepped over the guard-rail and waded on down that road under the lake. Where the water was too deep, I could have continued in a boat, letting down a line to plumb the bottom. I would not be angling for death, which is far too easy to catch, but for life. To touch the ground even through a length of rope would be some consolation. The day was cold, however, and I was far from anyone who knew my face. So I climbed into the car and turned away and drove back through the resurgent woods.

# House and Home

*W*hen our first child was born, a rosy wriggle of a girl we named Eva, my wife and I were living in a second-floor apartment on the noisiest avenue leading east and west through Bloomington, Indiana. Trucks grinding their gears, belching buses, howling ambulances and squad cars, unmuffled pickups and juiced-up jalopies roared past our windows, morning, noon, and night. What little dirt we could find between pavement and weeds in our tiny yard was slimed with engine oil.

To begin with, Eva weighed only six and a half pounds, all of them fidgety. Like any newborn she was pure appetite. With a stomach so small, she hardly seemed to close her eyes between feedings. Even when those brown eyes did fit fully close, they would snap open again at the least sound. Ruth nursed her to sleep, or I rocked her to sleep, and we'd lay her in the crib as gingerly as a bomb. Then some loud machine would come blaring down the street and Eva would twitch and wail.

Once an engine had frightened her, mere milk would not soothe this child, nor would a cradle endlessly rocking. Only songs would do, a rivery murmur while she snuggled against a warm chest, and the chest had to be swaying in rhythm to a steady walk. Fall silent or stop moving and you had a ruckus on your hands. Night after night, I worked my way through *The Folk Songs of North America,* cover to cover and back again, while carrying Eva in circles over the crickety floorboards. It took hours of singing and miles of walking to lull her to stillness in my arms, and then a siren or diesel could undo the spell in seconds.

After seven nearly sleepless months, Ruth and I exchanged bleary stares over the breakfast table one morning and muttered, as in a single breath, "We've got to move."

That day we set out looking for a house. Not just any house, but the right one, the inevitable one, the one made in carpenter's heaven to fit our family. But how to find this perfect place among the countless ones available? Even allowing for the fact that we had no money to speak of, there were still hundreds of possibilities. How to choose? It was a problem as difficult, and nearly as consequential, as finding a mate to marry.

To compound the difficulty, Ruth and I carried in our heads quite different postcards of the ideal house, for she had grown up in a city and I had grown up in the country. She wanted a sturdy old box shaded by sturdy old trees, within a few steps of the place next door, in a neighborhood of sidewalks and flower beds where folks traded recipes and sat on their porches and pushed babies in buggies at dusk. I wanted a log cabin beside a pond in three hundred acres of woods bordering on a wilderness. Failing that, I would settle for a run-down farmhouse on a dirt road unknown to maps.

We compromised by buying a house in town that was as badly in need of repair as any cabin in the country. Five lines in the For Sale by Owner section of the newspaper led us there:

CHARMING 2-story brick, walk
to work, Bryan Park & Elm
Heights. 3 bedrms., bath, liv.
rm. with fireplace. 1113 East
Wylie. $25,000.

Now that was cheap, even in 1974—not so cheap that I ever supposed we would live long enough to pay it off; nor so cheap that the loan officers at Workingmen's Federal didn't stare at us hard with their fiduciary gaze—but still, we could cover a monthly note on $25,000 without going naked or hungry.

More alluring than the price, however, was the location. That section of Wylie proved to be a two-block sanctuary of silence, cut off at one end by a cross street, at the other end by woods. No trucks, no sirens, no hustling jalopies. You could hear birds in the big trees, crickets in the grass, children on screened porches. At night, in the hush of a bedroom, you could hear a baby breathe. The houses were old and sturdy enough to please Ruth; the park just around the corner gave me a taste of country, with its green swells, sunsets, and star-spangled skies.

We had already toured more houses than Washington slept in, before we set our hearts on 1113 East Wylie. Whether it was charming, as the ad promised, the eye of the beholder would have to decide; but no one could doubt that it needed work. Realtors, in their cheery lingo, would have called it a fixer-upper or a handyman's dream. On our initial visit we made a list of items that would require swift attention, from roof to foundation. Of course we'd patch up that plaster, Ruth and I assured one another. We'd tear out that threadbare carpet and refinish the floors. We'd mend the chimney, ventilate the attic, dry up the basement, enclose the front porch, hang new doors, make over the kitchen, patch and paint and seal.

We moved in almost twenty years ago, and we are still working on that list. The list, in fact, has grown, season by season, like adult grief or the national debt. For every job completed, two new jobs arise. Reglaze a broken window, and before you've put away your tools a gutter sags or a switch burns out. In an old house, when handyman or handywoman takes on entropy, entropy always wins. Things fall apart—and not only in politics and religion. Pipes rust, nails work loose, shingles crumble, wood warps. The smooth turns rough and the straight grows crooked. A house is a shell caught in a surf that never stops grinding.

Over those same twenty years, our girl grew up. No longer a light sleeper, Eva went off to college last fall, having lived up to every beautiful promise in those original six and a half pounds. The vague bundle of possibilities that lay in the crib, suckled on milk and swaddled in song, has become a definite person. How to explain the continuity from baby to young woman, when every molecule in her body has been replaced and her mind has filled up with the world?

Unable to answer that, and more than a little blue about Eva's going away, I work on the house and consider how it holds me. Of course there is no single right place to live, any more than there is a single right man or woman to marry. And yet, having made my choice, I feel wedded to this house, as I do to my wife and my neighborhood and my region. To become attached to a woman, sure, and to neighbors, fair enough, and maybe even to the local terrain—but to a pile of brick and wood? How has this box, this frame of possibilities, come to fit me so exactly? By what alchemy does a house become a home?

\\\|//

The short answer is that these walls and floors and scruffy flower beds are saturated with our memories and sweat. Everywhere I look I see the imprint of hands, everywhere I turn I hear the babble of voices, I smell sawdust or bread, I recall bruises and laughter. After nearly two decades of intimacy, the house dwells in us as surely as we dwell in the house.

By American standards it's small, plain, old-fashioned: a cube roughly twenty-five feet on a side, encased in taffy-colored brick, with a low porch across the front, a wet basement below, and on top a roof in the shape of a pyramid. I have touched every one of those bricks, scraping ivy or pointing up the joints with fresh mortar. I have banged every joist and rafter, brushed every foundation stone. I know its crooks and crannies, its faults and fillings, as well as my dentist knows my teeth.

I could blame or thank my father and mother for the itch that keeps me tinkering. During my childhood, they fixed up their own series of dilapidated houses, turning sows' ears into silk purses, thereby convincing me that a place isn't truly yours until you rebuild it with your own hands. Thoreau, who cobbled together the most famous cabin in our literature, complained in *Walden* that "I never in all my walks came across a man engaged in so simple and natural an occupation as building his house." Had he been a contemporary of my father or me, he could have walked by our doors most weekends and found us hammering.

A month after we moved in, my parents came from Oklahoma to inspect the house and dandle Eva. As soon as my father could bear to put the baby down, he walked to the basement and opened the fuse box, hummed darkly, then came back upstairs and removed the faceplate from a light switch and peered inside. Turning to me with a frown, he said, "Son, you've got to rewire this house. I won't have my granddaughter sleeping in a firetrap."

"I've been meaning to get to that," I told him.

"We'll get to it starting this afternoon," he said. "Now where would you buy electrical supplies?"

We did start that afternoon, and Ruth and I kept on for months after my parents had gone back to Oklahoma. Room by room, we replaced every outlet, every switch, every wire, fishing new three-strand cable down from the attic or up from the basement, driving copper stakes into the soil to drain away any loose amps, until the juice from Public Service Indiana flowed innocuously.

During their visit the following winter, my father ran his hands over the walls in Eva's room. More dark humming. He lit a match, blew it out, then held the smoking stub near the window beside her crib. I knew what was coming. "Son," he announced, "you've got to insulate and weatherstrip and caulk, or my baby's going to catch pneumonia."

That job took two years, because Ruth and I decided not just to dribble loose fill into the wall cavities but to rip them open and do it right, with fiberglass batts and polyethylene vapor barrier and new Sheetrock. Eva slept in our room while we tore hers apart. When I pried away the lath and plaster next to where her crib had stood, I found a message scrawled in carpenter's chalk on the pine sheathing: BILLY WALES IS A STINKER! JUNE 12, 1920. The taunt was so mild, I thought about leaving that part of the cavity exposed, with a frame around it; but that would have allowed a draft to blow on my girl, and so I closed it up tight.

Inch by inch, as though the house were a ship in dry dock, we overhauled the place, driven by concerns about Eva and then later, when our second child came along, by concerns about Jesse. Who knew what corrosion lurked in the heart of those old iron pipes? Re-plumb with copper. Sparks from the fireplace might leap through cracks in the chimney, so line it with stainless steel and re-lay the bricks. Sand those oak floors to protect small toes from splinters. And what if there was lead in that peeling paint on the woodwork? Better pry loose the base-boards and trim, the moldings and sills, the mullioned windows; better carry it all outdoors, then scrape and sand and strip everything down to the bare wood, seal it anew with harmless finishes, and put every piece back where it belonged.

Like sap in maples, the urge to mend the house rises in me with special force in spring. So it happens that I am often hauling supplies up the front steps while birds in our yard are gathering twigs and grass and leaves. As I stagger to the door with a clutch of two-by-fours on my shoulder, I see catbirds or cardinals or robins laboring to their nests with loaded beaks. Whenever I stop sawing or drilling, I am likely to hear a chatter of construction from the trees. The link between their labor and mine is neither whimsical nor quaint, but a matter of life and death. The river that carries us along is wild, and we must caulk our boats to keep afloat.

※

Unlike the birds, of course, we fetch our sticks from the lumberyard, we get our mud ready-baked into bricks, we buy fibers that have been woven into blankets, curtains, carpets, mats. But for all that artifice, the house is still entirely derived from the land. The foundation is laid up with chunks of limestone from nearby quarries. The frame is a skeleton of pines. The chairs once grew as hickory, their seats as cane and rush. The white walls are gypsum from the bed of a primeval sea. The iron in the nails has been refined from ore, the glass in the windows from sand, even the unavoidable plastic has been distilled from the oil of ancient swamps. When I walk up the stairs and notice the oak treads, I feel their grain curving through me.

Because so few of us build our own homes, we forget that our dwellings, like our bodies, are made from the Earth. The first humans who settled in this part of the country fashioned their huts from bark, their tepees from tanned hides draped over poles. They warmed themselves at fires of buffalo chips and brush. How could they forget that they had wrapped themselves in the land? When white pioneers came to this region, a family would sometimes camp inside a hollow sycamore while they built a log cabin; so when at length they moved into the cabin, they merely exchanged life inside a single tree for life inside a stack of them. The bark on the walls and the clay in the chinks and the fieldstone in the chimney reminded them whence their shelter had come. Our technology has changed, but not our ultimate source. Even the newest ticky-tacky box in the suburbs, even the glitziest high-tech mansion, even an aluminum trailer is only a nest in disguise.

Nature does not halt at the property line, but runs right through our yard and walls and bones. Possums and raccoons browse among kitchen scraps in the compost bin. Moss grows on the shady side of the roof, mildew in the bathtub, mold in the fridge. Roots from our front yard elm invade the drains. Mice invade the cupboards. (The best bait, we've found, is peanut butter.) Male woodpeckers, advertising for mates, rap on the cedar siding of the porch. Wrens nest in our kitchen exhaust fan, the racket of their hungry chicks spicing up our meals. Blue jays clack noisily in the gutters, turning over leaves in a search for bugs. Thousands of maples sprout from those gutters each spring. Water finds its way through the foundation year-round. For all our efforts to seal the joints, rain and snowmelt still treat the basement like any other hole in the ground.

When we bought the house, it was covered with English ivy. "That's got to come off," Ruth said. "Think of all the spiders breeding outside Eva's window!"

Under assault from crowbar, shears, and wire brush, the ivy came off. But there has been no perceptible decline in the spider population, indoors or out. Clean a corner, and by the time you've put away the broom, new threads are gleaming. The spiders thrive because they have plenty of game to snare. Poison has discouraged the termites, but carpenter ants still look upon the house as a convenient heap of dead wood. (When Eva first heard us talk about carpenter ants, she imagined they would be dressed as her daddy was on weekends, with sweatband across the forehead, tool belt around the waist, and dangling hammer on the hip.) Summer and fall, we play host to grasshoppers, crickets, moths, flies, mosquitoes, and frogs, along with no-see-ums too obscure to name.

Piled up foursquare and plumb, the house is not only composed from the land but is itself a part of the landscape. Weather buffets it, wind sifts through. Leaves collect on the roof, hemlock needles gather on the sills, ice and thaw nudge the foundation, seeds lodge in every crack. Like anything born, it is mortal. If you doubt that, drive the back roads of the Ohio Valley and look at the forsaken farms. Abandon a house, even a brick one such as ours, and it will soon be reclaimed by forest. Left to itself, the land says bloodroot, chickadee, beech. Our shelter is on loan; it needs perpetual care.

The word *house* derives from an Indo-European root meaning to cover or conceal. I hear in that etymology furtive, queasy undertones. Conceal from what? From storms? beasts? enemies? From the eye of God? *Home* comes from a different root meaning "the place where one lies." That sounds less fearful to me. A weak, slow, clawless animal, without fur or fangs, can risk lying down and closing its eyes only where it feels utterly secure. Since the universe is going to kill us, in the short run or the long, no wonder we crave a place to lie in safety, a place to conceive our young and raise them, a place to shut our eyes without shivering or dread.

Married seven years already at the time we bought our house, I forgot to carry Ruth over the threshold, but I did carry Eva, and when newborn Jesse came home from the hospital, I carried him as well. Whatever else crossing the threshold might symbolize—about property or patriarchy—it should mean that you have entered a place of refuge. Not a perfect refuge, for there is no such thing: disease can steal in, so can poison or thugs, hunger and pain. If the people who cross the threshold are bent or cruel, the rooms will fill with misery. No locks will keep armies out, no roof will hold against a tornado. No, not perfectly safe, yet home is where we go to hide from harm, or, having been hurt, to lick our wounds.

At 1113 East Wylie, we have no shrine in the yard, no hex sign on the gable, no horseshoe nailed over the door. But I sympathize with those who mark their houses with talismans to ward off evil. Our neighbors across the street have a small box mounted on their doorpost, a mezuza, which contains a slip of paper bearing words from Deuteronomy (6:4–5): "Hear, O Israel: The Lord our God is one Lord; and you shall love the Lord your God with all your heart, and with all your soul, and with all your might." The words announce their faith, and honor their God, and turn away the wicked. Each family, in its own manner, inscribes a visible or invisible message on its doorway, a message contrary to the one that Dante found over the gateway to Hell. Take hope, we say, rest easy, ye who enter here.

However leaky or firm, whether tar paper or brick, the shell of a house gives only shelter; a home gives sanctuary. Perhaps the most familiar definition of *home* in the American language comes from Robert Frost's "The Death of the Hired Man," in lines spoken by a Yankee farmer: "Home is the place where, when you have to go there, / They have to take you in." Less familiar is the wife's reply: "I should have called it / Something you somehow haven't to deserve." The husband's remark is pure Yankee, grudging and grim. I side with the wife. Home is not where you *have* to go but where you *want* to go; nor is it a place where you are sullenly admitted, but rather where you are welcomed—by the people, the walls, the tiles on the floor, the flowers beside the door, the play of light, the very grass.

While I work on these pages, tucking in lines to make them tight, our newspaper carries an article with a grisly headline: HOMELESS WOMAN CRUSHED WITH TRASH. No one knows the woman's name, only that she crawled into a Dumpster to sleep, was loaded into a truck, was compressed with the trash, and arrived dead at the incinerator. She wore white tennis shoes, gray sweatpants, a red windbreaker, and, on her left hand, "a silver Indian Thunderbird ring." Nearby residents had seen her climb into the Dumpster, and later they heard the truck begin to grind, but they did not warn the driver soon enough, and so the woman died. Being homeless meant that she had already been discarded by family, neighbors, and community, and now she was gathered with the trash. This happened in Indianapolis, just up the road from my snug house. I read the article twice; I read it a dozen times. I pinned the clipping to the wall beside my desk, and keep returning to it as to a sore.

It *is* a sore, an affront, an outrage that thousands upon thousands of people in our country have nowhere to live. Like anyone who walks the streets of

America, I grieve over the bodies wrapped in newspapers or huddled in cardboard boxes, the sleepers curled on steam grates, the futureless faces. This is cause for shame and remedy, not only because the homeless suffer, but because they have no place to lay their heads in safety, no one except dutiful strangers to welcome them. Thank God for dutiful strangers; yet they can never take the place of friends. The more deeply I feel my own connection to home, the more acutely I feel the hurt of those who belong to no place and no one.

The longing for a safe place to lie down echoes through our holy songs and scriptures. Abused and scorned, we look over Jordan, and what do we see? A band of angels coming for to carry us home. If Earth has no room for us, we are promised, then heaven will. The string of assurances in the Twenty-third Psalm ends with the most comforting one of all:

> Surely goodness and mercy shall follow me
>> all the days of my life;
> and I shall dwell in the house of the Lord
>> for ever.

If we are ever going to dwell in the house of the Lord, I believe, we do so now. If any house is divinely made, it is this one here, this great whirling mansion of planets and stars.

Each constellation of the zodiac is said to live in its own house, Leo and Libra and Aquarius, and so on through all the twelve that ride the merry-go-round of our year. I do not believe that our future is written in the sky. And yet there is some truth in sketching houses around the stars. Viewed from chancy Earth, they appear to be stay-at-homes, abiding in place from generation to generation, secure beyond our imagining. And if the constellations belong in their houses so beautifully and faithfully, then so might we.

In baseball, home plate is where you begin your journey and also your destination. You venture out onto the bases, to first and second and third, always striving to return to the spot from which you began. There is danger on the basepath—pick-offs, rundowns, force-outs, double plays—and safety only back at home. I am not saying, as a true fan would, that baseball is the key to life; rather, life is the key to baseball. We play or watch this game because it draws pictures of our desires.

The homing pigeon is not merely able to find the roost from astounding distances; the pigeon *seeks* its home. I am a homing man. Away on solo trips, I am never quite whole. I miss family, of course, and neighbors and friends; but I also miss the house, which is planted in the yard, which is embraced by a city, which is cradled in familiar woods and fields, which gather snow and rain for the Ohio River. The house has worked on me as steadily as I have worked on the house. I carry slivers of wood under my fingernails, dust from demolition in the corners of my eyes, aches from hammering and heaving in all my joints.

During my lifetime the labels *homemaker* and *housewife* have come to seem belittling, as though a woman who wears them lacks the gumption to be anything else. A similar devaluation hit the word *homely* itself, which originally meant plain, simple, durable, worthy of use in the home, and gradually came to mean drab, graceless, ugly. Men can now be called househusbands, but the male variant, like the female, is used apologetically, as though qualified by the word *only*.

In a recent letter, a friend wrote me, "I'm still just a househusband; but I'm looking for work." I'd be surprised if there wasn't plenty of work to do in his own house. It's a rare home that couldn't do with more care. Wendell Berry warns us about that need in his poem, "The Design of a House":

Except in idea, perfection is as wild
as light; there is no hand laid on it.
But the house is a shambles
unless the vision of its perfection
    upholds it like stone.

Our rooms will only be as generous and nurturing as the spirit we invest in them. The Bible gives us the same warning, more sternly: Unless God builds the house, it will not stand. The one I live in has been standing for just over seventy years, a mere eyeblink, not long enough to prove there was divinity in the mortar. I do know, however, that mortar and nails alone would not have held the house together even for seventy years. It has also needed the work of many hands, the wishes of many hearts, vision upon vision, through a succession of families.

Real estate ads offer houses for sale, not homes. A house is a garment, easily put off or on, casually bought and sold; a home is skin. Merely change houses and you will be disoriented; change homes and you bleed. When the shell you live in has taken on the savor of your love, when your dwelling has become a taproot, then your house is a home.

\|///

I heard more than hunger in Eva's infant cry. I heard a plea for shelter from the terror of things. I felt called on to enfold her, in arms and walls and voice. No doubt it is only a musical accident that *home* and *womb* share the holy sound of *om,* which Hindu mystics chant to put themselves in harmony with the ultimate power. But I accept all gifts of language. There is in the word a hum of yearning.

Since Eva went off to college, I find it hard not to think of our home as a cocoon from which the butterfly has flown. I miss my daughter. The rug bristles with the absence of her dancing feet. The windows glint with the history of her looking. Water rings on the sills recall where her teacup should be. The air lacks a sweet buzz.

Unlike a butterfly, a daughter blessedly returns now and again, as Eva comes home soon for summer vacation. Ruth and I have been preparing the house to receive her. Before leaving in August, Eva bet me that I would not have finished remodeling the sun porch by the time of her return in May. I stole hours to work on it all the autumn and winter. Now I must go and put on the last coat of varnish, so that, when she enters, the room will shine.

# Staying Put

Two friends arrived at our house for supper one May evening along with the first rumblings of thunder. As my wife, Ruth, and I sat talking with them on our front porch, we had to keep raising our voices a notch to make ourselves heard above the gathering storm. The birds, more discreet, had already hushed. The huge elm beside our door began to sway, limbs creaking, leaves hissing. Black sponges of clouds blotted up the light, fooling the street lamps into coming on early. Above the trees and rooftops, the murky southern sky crackled with lightning. Now and again we heard the pop of a transformer as a bolt struck the power lines in our neighborhood. The pulses of thunder came faster and faster, until they merged into a continuous roar.

We gave up on talking. The four of us, all midwesterners teethed on thunderstorms, sat down there on the porch to our meal of lentil soup, cheddar cheese, bread warm from the oven, sliced apples and strawberries. We were lifting the first spoonfuls to our mouths when a stroke of lightning burst so nearby that it seemed to suck away the air, and the lights flickered out, plunging the whole street into darkness.

After we had caught our breath, we laughed—respectfully, as one might laugh at the joke of a giant. The sharp smell of ozone and the musty smell of damp earth mingled with the aroma of bread. A chill of pleasure ran up my spine. I lit a pair of candles on the table, and the flames rocked in the gusts of wind. In the time it took for butter to melt on a slice of bread, the wind fell away, the elm stopped thrashing, the lightning let up, and the thunder ceased. The sudden stillness was more exciting than the earlier racket. A smoldering yellow light came into the sky, as though the humid air had caught fire. We gazed at one another over the steady candle flames and knew without exchanging a word what this eerie lull could mean.

"Maybe we should go into the basement," Ruth suggested.

"And leave this good meal?" one of our friends replied.

The wail of a siren broke the stillness, not the lesser cry of ambulance or fire engine or squad car, but the banshee howl of the civil defense siren at the park a few blocks away.

"They must have sighted one," I said.

"We could take the food down with us on a tray," Ruth told our guests.

"It's up to you," I told them. "We can go to the basement like sensible people, or we can sit here like fools and risk our necks."

"What do you want to do?" one of them asked me.

"You're the guests."

"You're the hosts."

"I'd like to stay here and see what comes," I told them. Ruth frowned at me, but there we stayed, savoring our food and the sulfurous light. Eventually the siren quit. When my ears stopped ringing, I could hear the rushing of a great wind, like the growl of a waterfall. An utter calm stole over me. The hair on my neck bristled. My nostrils flared. Heat rose in my face as though the tip of a wing had raked over it.

Although I found myself, minutes later, still in the chair, the faces of my wife and friends gleaming in the candlelight, for a spell I rode the wind, dissolved into it, and there was only the great wind, rushing.

The tornado missed us by half a mile. It did not kill anyone in our vicinity, but it ripped off chimneys, toyed with cars, and plucked up a fat old maple by the roots. Prudent folks would have gone to the basement. I do not recommend our decision; I merely report it. Why the others tarried on the porch I cannot say, but what kept me there was a mixture of curiosity and awe. I had never seen the whirling black funnel except in cautionary films, where it left a wake of havoc and tears. And now here was that tremendous power, paying us a visit. When a god comes calling, no matter how bad its reputation, would you go hide? If the siren had announced the sighting of a dragon, I might have sat there just the same, hoping to catch a glimpse of the spiked tail or fiery breath.

As a boy in Ohio I knew a farm family, the Millers, who not only saw but suffered from three tornadoes. The father, mother, and two sons were pulling into their driveway after church when the first tornado hoisted up their mobile home, spun it around, and carried it off. With the insurance money, they built a small frame house on the same spot. Several years later, a second tornado peeled off the roof, splintered the garage, and rustled two cows. The younger of the sons, who was in my class at school, told me that he had watched from the barn as the twister passed through, "And it never even mussed up my hair." The Millers rebuilt again, raising a new garage on the old foundation and adding another story to the house. That upper floor was reduced to kindling by a third tornado, which also pulled out half the apple trees and slurped water from the stock pond. Soon after that I left Ohio, snatched away by college as forcefully as by any cyclone. Last thing I heard, the family was preparing to rebuild yet again.

Why did the Millers refuse to budge? I knew them well enough to say they were neither stupid nor crazy. After the garage disappeared, the father hung a sign from the mailbox that read: TORNADO ALLEY. He figured the local terrain would coax future whirlwinds in their direction. Then why not move? Plain stubbornness was a factor. These were people who, once settled, might have remained at the foot of a volcano or on the bank of a flood-prone river or beside an earthquake fault. They had relatives nearby, helpful neighbors, jobs and stores and school within a short drive, and those were all good reasons to stay. But the main reason, I believe, was because the Millers had invested so much of their lives in the land, planting orchards and gardens, spreading manure on the fields, digging ponds, building sheds, seeding pastures. Out back of the house were groves of walnuts, hickories, and oaks, all started by hand from acorns and nuts. Honeybees zipped out from a row of white hives to nuzzle clover in the pasture. April through October, perennial flowers in the yard pumped out a fountain of blossoms. This farm was not just so many acres of dirt, easily exchanged for an equal amount elsewhere; it was a particular place, intimately known, worked on, dreamed over, cherished.

Psychologists tell us that we answer trouble with one of two impulses, either fight or flight. I believe that the Millers' response to tornadoes and my own keen expectancy on the porch arose from a third instinct, that of staying put. When the pain of leaving behind what we know outweighs the pain of embracing it, or when the power we face is overwhelming and neither fight nor flight will save us, there may be salvation in sitting still. And if salvation is impossible, then at least before perishing we may gain a clearer vision of where we are. By sitting still I do not mean the paralysis of dread, like that of a rabbit frozen beneath the dive of a hawk. I mean something like reverence, a respectful waiting, a deep attentiveness to forces much greater than our own. If indulged only for a moment, as in my case on the porch, this reverent impulse may amount to little; but if sustained for months and years, as by the Millers on their farm, it may yield marvels. The Millers knew better than to fight a tornado, and they chose not to flee. Instead they devoted themselves, season after season, to patient labor. Instead of withdrawing, they gave themselves more fully. Their commitment to the place may have been foolhardy, but it was also grand. I suspect that most human achievements worth admiring are the result of such devotion.

These tornado memories dramatize a choice we are faced with constantly: whether to go or stay, whether to move to a situation that is safer, richer, easier, more attractive, or to stick where we are and make what we can of it. If the shine goes off our marriage, our house, our car, do we trade it for a new one? If the fertility leaches out of our soil, the creativity out of our job, the money out of our pocket, do we start over somewhere else? There are voices enough, both inner and outer, urging us to deal with difficulties by pulling up stakes and heading for new territory. I know them well, for they have been calling to me all my days. I wish to raise here a contrary voice, to say a few words on behalf of staying put, confronting the powers, learning the ground, going deeper.

In a poem entitled "Roots," composed not long before he leapt from a bridge over the Mississippi River, John Berryman ridiculed those who asked about his "roots" ("as if I were a *plant*"), and he articulated something like a credo for the dogma of rootlessness:

> Exile is in our time like blood. Depend on
> interior journeys taken anywhere.
>
> I'd rather live in Venice or Kyoto,
> except for the languages, but
> O really I don't care where I live or have lived.
> Wherever I am, young Sir, my wits about me,
>
> memory blazing, I'll cope & make do.

It is a bold claim, but also a hazardous one. For all his wits, Berryman in the end failed to cope well enough to stave off suicide. The truth is, none of us can live by wits alone. For even the barest existence, we depend on the labors of other people, the fruits of the Earth, the inherited goods of our given place. If our interior journeys are cut loose entirely from that place, then both we and the neighborhood will suffer.

Exile usually suggests banishment, a forced departure from one's homeland. Famines and tyrants and wars do indeed force entire populations to flee; but most people who move, especially within the industrialized world, do so by choice. Salman Rushdie chose to leave his native India for England, where he has written a series of brilliant books from the perspective of a cultural immigrant. Like many writers, he has taken his own condition to represent not merely a possibility but a norm. In the essays of *Imaginary Homelands* he celebrates "the migrant sensibility," whose development he regards as "one of the central themes of this century of displaced persons." Rushdie has also taken this condition to represent something novel in history:

> The effect of mass migrations has been the creation of radically new types of human being: people who root themselves in ideas rather than places, in memories as much as in material things; people who have been obliged to define themselves—because they are so defined by others—by their otherness; people in whose deepest selves strange fusions occur, unprecedented unions between what they were and where they find themselves.

In the history of my own country, that description applies just as well to the Pilgrims in Plymouth, say, or to Swiss homesteading in Indiana, or to Chinese trading in California, or to former slaves crowding into cities on the Great Lakes, or to Seminoles driven onto reservations a thousand miles from their traditional land. Displaced persons are abundant in our century, but hardly a novelty.

Claims for the virtues of shifting ground are familiar and seductive to Americans, this nation of restless movers. From the beginning, our heroes have been sailors, explorers, cowboys, prospectors, speculators, backwoods ramblers, rainbow-chasers, vagabonds of every stripe. Our Promised Land has always been over the next ridge or at the end of the trail, never under our feet. One hundred years after the official closing of the frontier, we still have not shaken off the romance of unlimited space. If we fish out a stream or wear out a field, or if the smoke from a neighbor's chimney begins to crowd the sky, why, off we go to a new stream, a fresh field, a clean sky. In our national mythology, the worst fate is to be trapped on a farm, in a village, in the sticks, in some dead-end job or unglamorous marriage or played-out game. Stand still, we are warned, and you die. Americans have dug the most canals, laid the most rails, built the most roads and airports of any nation. In today's newspaper I read that, even though our sprawling system of interstate highways is crumbling, the president has decided that we should triple it in size, and all without raising our taxes a nickel. Only a populace drunk on driving, a populace infatuated with the myth of the open road, could hear such a proposal without hooting.

So we Americans are likely to share Rushdie's enthusiasm for migration, for the "hybridity, impurity, intermingling, the transformation that comes of new and unexpected combinations of human beings, cultures, ideas, politics, movies, songs." Everything about us is mongrel, from race to language, and we are stronger for it. Yet we might respond more skeptically when Rushdie says that "to be a migrant is, perhaps, to be the only species of human being free of the shackles of nationalism (to say nothing of its ugly sister, patriotism)." Lord knows we could do with less nationalism (to say nothing of its ugly siblings, racism, religious sectarianism, or class snobbery). But who would pretend that a history of migration has immunized the United States against bigotry? And even if, by uprooting ourselves, we shed our chauvinism, is that all we lose?

In this hemisphere, many of the worst abuses—of land, forests, animals, and communities—have been carried out by "people who root themselves in ideas rather than places." Rushdie claims that "migrants must, of necessity, make a new imaginative relationship with the world, because of the loss of familiar habitats." But migrants often pack up their visions and values with the rest of their baggage and carry them along. The Spaniards devastated Central and South America by imposing on this New World the religion, economics, and politics of the Old. Colonists brought slavery with them to North America, along with smallpox and Norway rats. The Dust Bowl of the 1930s was caused not by drought, which the unplowed prairie had evolved to endure, but by the transfer onto the Great Plains of farming methods that were suitable to wetter regions. The habit of our industry and commerce has been to force identical schemes onto differing locales, as though the mind were a cookie cutter and the land were dough.

I quarrel with Rushdie because he articulates as eloquently as anyone the orthodoxy that I wish to counter: the belief that movement is inherently good, staying put is bad; that uprooting brings tolerance, while rootedness breeds intolerance; that imaginary homelands are preferable to geographical ones; that to be modern, enlightened, fully of our time, is to be displaced. Whole-sale *dis*placement may be inevitable; but we should not suppose that it occurs without disastrous consequences for the Earth and for ourselves. People who root themselves in places are likelier to know and care for those places than are people who root themselves in ideas. When we cease to be migrants and become inhabitants, we might begin to pay enough heed and respect to where we are. By settling in, we have a chance of making a durable home for ourselves, our fellow creatures, and our descendants.

What are we up against, those of us who aspire to become inhabitants, who wish to commit ourselves to a place? How strong, how old, is the impulse we are resisting?

Although our machines enable us to move faster and farther, humans have been on the move for a long time. Within a few ticks on the evolutionary clock, our ancestors roamed out of their native valleys in Africa and spread over the Eurasian continent. They invaded the deserts, the swamps, the mountains and valleys, the jungle and tundra. Drifting on boats and rafts, they pushed on to island after island around the globe. When glaciers locked up enough seawater to expose a land bridge from Asia to North America, migrants crossed into this unknown region, and within a few thousand years their descendants had scattered from the Bering Straits to Tierra del Fuego.

The mythology of those first Americans often claimed that a tribe had been attached to a given spot since the beginning of time, and we in our craving for rootedness may be inclined to believe in this eternal bond between people and place; but archaeology suggests that ideas, goods, and populations were in motion for millennia before the first Europeans reached these shores, hunters and traders and whole tribes roving about, boundaries shifting, homelands changing hands. Even agricultural settlements, such as those associated with the mound-building cultures in the Mississippi and Ohio Valleys, reveal a history of arrivals and departures, sites used for decades or centuries and then abandoned. By comparison to our own hectic movements, an association between people and place lasting decades or centuries may seem durable and enviable; but it is not eternal.

What I am saying is that we are a wandering species, and have been since we reared up on our hind legs and stared at the horizon. Our impulse to wander, to pick up and move when things no longer suit us in our present place, is not an ailment brought on suddenly by industrialization, by science, or by the European hegemony over dark-skinned peoples. It would be naive to think that Spanish horses corrupted the Plains Indians, tempting a sedentary people to rush about, or that snowmobiles corrupted the Inuit, or that jeeps corrupted the Aborigines. It would be just as naive to say that the automobile gave rise to our own restlessness; on the contrary, our restlessness gave rise to the automobile, as it led earlier to the bicycle, steamboat, and clipper ship, as it led to the taming of horses, lacing of snowshoes, and carving of dugout canoes. With each invention, a means of moving farther, faster, has answered to a desire that coils in our genes. Mobility is the rule in human history, rootedness the exception.

Our itch to wander was the great theme of the English writer Bruce Chatwin, who disguised the fact that he was dying of AIDS by claiming that he suffered from a rare disease contracted in the course of his own incessant travels. For Chatwin, "the nature of human restlessness" was "the question of questions." One hundred pages of *The Songlines,* his best-known work, are filled with notebook entries supporting the view that "man is a migratory species." In a posthumous collection of essays entitled *What Am I Doing Here,* he summed up his observations:

> We should perhaps allow human nature an appetitive drive for movement in the widest sense. The act of journeying contributes towards a sense of physical and mental well-being, while the monotony of prolonged settlement or regular work weaves patterns in the brain that engender fatigue and a sense of personal inadequacy. Much of what the ethologists have designated "aggression" is simply an angered response to the frustrations of confinement.

I am dubious about the psychology here, for I notice Chatwin's own frustrations in the passage, especially in that irritable phrase about "the monotony of prolonged settlement or regular work"; but I agree with his speculation that deep in us there is "an appetitive drive for movement."

The movement chronicled in *The Songlines*—the purposeful wandering of the Australian Aborigines—may suggest a way for us to harness our restlessness, a way to reconcile our need to rove with our need to stay put. As hunter-gatherers in a harsh continent, the Aborigines must know their land thoroughly and travel it widely in order to survive. According to their belief, the land and all living things were created in a mythic time called the Dreaming, and the creative spirits are still at work, sustaining the world. Humans keep the world in touch with the power of the Dreaming by telling stories and singing songs. The whole of Australia is crisscrossed by pathways known to the Aborigines, who must walk them at intervals, performing the songs that belong to each path. Every tribe is responsible for the tracks within its own territory, and for passing down the appropriate songs from generation to generation. "There was hardly a rock or creek in the country," Chatwin remarks, "that could not or had not been sung." The movement of the Aborigines is not random, therefore, but deliberate, guided by hunger and thirst, but also by the need to participate in the renewal of the world. The land supplies the necessities of life, and in return humans offer knowledge, memory, and voice.

The Aboriginal walkabout illustrates "the once universal concept," in Chatwin's words, "that wandering re-establishes the original harmony . . . between man and the universe." Unlike vagabonds, who use up place after place without returning on their tracks, the Aborigines wed themselves to one place, and range over it with gratitude and care. So that they might continue as residents, they become stewards. Like the rest of nature, they move in circles, walking again and again over sacred ground.

The Australian Aborigines are among the "inhabitory peoples" whom Gary Snyder has studied in his search for wisdom about living in place, a wisdom he described in *The Old Ways:*

> People developed specific ways to *be* in each of those niches: plant knowledge, boats, dogs, traps, nets, fishing—the smaller animals, and smaller tools. From steep jungle slopes of Southwest China to coral atolls to barren arctic deserts—*a spirit of what it was to be there* evolved, that spoke of a direct sense of relation to the "land"—which really means, the totality of the local bio-region system, from cirrus clouds to leaf-mold.

Such knowledge does not come all at once; it accumulates bit by bit over generations, each person adding to the common lore.

Even nomads, whose name implies motion, must be scholars of their bioregion. As they follow herds from pasture to pasture through the cycle of the year, they trace a loop that is dictated by what the land provides. For inhabitory peoples, listening to the land is a spiritual discipline as well as a practical one. The alertness that feeds the body also feeds the soul. In Native American culture, "medicine" is understood not as a human invention, but as a channeling of the power by which all things live. Whether you are a hunter-gatherer, a nomad, a farmer, or a suburbanite, to be at home in the land is to be sane and whole. Your own health and that of your community derive from the health of the soil, the waters, the air, the plants, and the beasts.

The Aborigines worked out an accommodation with their land over forty thousand years, no doubt through trial and error. They would not have survived if their mythology had not soon come to terms with their ecology. Even so, their population was never more than about one hundredth as large as that of modern Australia. We who live in North America are engaged in our own trials and errors, which are greatly magnified by the size of our population and the power of our technology. A man with a bulldozer can make a graver mistake in one day than a whole tribe with digging sticks can make in a year. In my home region, mistakes are being made seven days a week—with machinery, chemicals, guns, plows, fountain pens, and bare hands. I suspect the same is true in every region. But who is keeping track? Who speaks for the wordless creatures? Who supplies memory and conscience for the land?

Half a century ago, in *A Sand County Almanac,* Aldo Leopold gave us an ecological standard for judging our actions: "A thing is right when it tends to preserve the integrity, stability, and beauty of the biotic community. It is wrong when it tends otherwise." We can only apply that standard if, in every biotic community, there are residents who keep watch over what is preserved and what is lost, who see the beauty that escapes the frame of the tourist's windshield or the investor's spreadsheet. "The problem," Leopold observed, "is how to bring about a striving for harmony with land among a people many of whom have forgotten there is any such thing as land, among whom education and culture have become almost synonymous with landlessness."

The question is not whether land belongs to us, through titles registered in a courthouse, but whether we belong to the land, through our loyalty and awareness. In the preface to his *Natural History of Selborne,* the eighteenth-century English vicar Gilbert White notes that a comprehensive survey of England might be compiled if only "stationary men would pay some attention to the districts on which they reside." Every township, every field and creek, every mountain and forest on Earth would benefit from the attention of stationary men and women. No one has understood this need better than Gary Snyder (speaking here in an interview from *The Real Work*):

> One of the key problems in American society now, it seems to me, is
> people's lack of commitment to any given place—which, again, is totally
> unnatural and outside of history. Neighborhoods are allowed to deterio-

rate, landscapes are allowed to be strip-mined, because there is nobody who will live there and take responsibility; they'll just move on. The reconstruction of a people and of a life in the United States depends in part on people, neighborhood by neighborhood, county by county, deciding to stick it out and make it work where they are, rather than flee.

We may not have forty years, let alone forty thousand, to reconcile our mythology with our ecology. If we are to reshape our way of thinking to fit the way of things, as the songs of the Aborigines follow their terrain, many more of us need to *know* our local ground, walk over it, care for it, fight for it, bear it steadily in mind.

But if you stick in one place, won't you become a stick-in-the-mud? If you stay put, won't you be narrow, backward, dull? You might. I have met ignorant people who never moved; and I have also met ignorant people who never stood still. Committing yourself to a place does not guarantee that you will become wise, but neither does it guarantee that you will become parochial. Who knows better the limitations of a province or a culture than the person who has bumped into them time and again? The history of settlement in my own district and the continuing abuse of land hereabouts provoke me to rage and grief. I know the human legacy here too well to glamorize it.

To become intimate with your home region, to know the territory as well as you can, to understand your life as woven into the local life does not prevent you from recognizing and honoring the diversity of other places, cultures, and ways. On the contrary, how can you value other places if you do not have one of your own? If you are not yourself *placed,* then you wander the world like a sightseer, a collector of sensations, with no gauge for measuring what you see. Local knowledge is the grounding for global knowledge. Those who care about nothing beyond the confines of their parish are in truth parochial, and are at least mildly dangerous to their parish; on the other hand, those who *have* no parish, those who navigate ceaselessly among postal zones and area codes, those for whom the world is only a smear of highways and bank accounts and stores, are a danger not just to their parish but to the planet.

Since birth, my children have been surrounded by images of Earth as viewed from space, images that I first encountered when I was in my twenties. Those photographs show vividly what in our sanest moments we have always known—that our planet is a closed circle, lovely and rare. On the wall beside me as I write there is a poster of the big blue marble encased in its white swirl of clouds. That is one pole of my awareness; the other pole is what I see through my window. I try to keep both in sight at once.

For all my convictions, I still have to wrestle with the fear—in myself, in my children, and in some of my neighbors—that our place is too remote from the action. This fear drives many people to pack their bags and move to some resort or burg they have seen on television, leaving behind what they learn to think of as the boondocks. I deal with my own unease by asking just what action I am remote *from*—a stock market? a debating chamber? a drive-in mortuary? The action that matters, the work of nature and community, goes on everywhere.

Since Copernicus we have known better than to see the Earth as the center of the universe. Since Einstein, we have learned that there is no center; or alternatively, that any point is as good as any other for observing the world. I take this to be roughly what medieval theologians meant when they defined God as a circle whose circumference is nowhere and whose center is everywhere. If you stay put, your place may become a holy center, not because it gives you special access to the divine, but because in your stillness you hear what might be heard anywhere.

The Lakota medicine man whose story is told by John Neihardt in *Black Elk Speaks* explained that in a vision he saw "the whole hoop of the world" encircling his own sacred mountain peak in the Black Hills of South Dakota. Although he gazed into the heart of creation, this did not mean that he was standing in a privileged location, Black Elk went on to say, because "anywhere is the center of the world." There are no privileged locations. No place has a corner on the truth. All there is to see can be seen from anywhere in the universe, if you know how to look; and the influence of the entire universe converges on every spot.

Except for the rare patches of wilderness, every place on Earth has been transformed by human presence. "Ecology becomes a more complex but far more interesting science," René Dubos observes in *The Wooing of Earth*, "when human aspirations are regarded as an integral part of the landscape." Through "long periods of intimate association between human beings and nature," Dubos argues, landscape may take on a "quality of blessedness." The understanding of how to dwell in a place arises out of the sustained conversation between people and land.

If our fidelity to place is to help renew and preserve our neighborhoods, it will have to be informed by what Wendell Berry in *Standing by Words* calls "an ecological intelligence: a sense of the impossibility of acting or living alone or solely in one's own behalf, and this rests in turn upon a sense of the order upon which any life depends and of the proprieties of place within that order." Proprieties of place: actions, words, and values that are *proper* to your home ground. I think of my home ground as a series of nested rings, with house and family and marriage at the center, surrounded by the wider and wider hoops of neighborhood and community, the bioregion within walking distance of my door, the wooded hills and karst landscape of southern Indiana, the watershed of the Ohio Valley, and so on outward—and inward—to the ultimate source.

The longing to become an inhabitant rather than a drifter sets me against the current of my culture, which nudges everyone into motion. Newton taught us that a body at rest tends to stay at rest, unless acted on by an outside force. We are acted on ceaselessly by outside forces—advertising, movies, magazines, speeches—and also by the inner force of biology. I am not immune to their pressure. Before settling in my present home, I lived in seven states and two countries, tugged from place to place in childhood by my father's work and in early adulthood by my own. This itinerant life is so common among the people I know that I have been slow to conceive of an alternative. Only by knocking against the golden calf of mobility, which looms so large and shines so brightly, have I come to realize that it is hollow. Like all idols, it distracts us from the true divinity.

The ecological argument for staying put may be easier for us to see than the spiritual one, worried as we are about saving our skins. Few of us worry about saving our souls, and fewer still imagine that the condition of our souls has anything to do with the condition of our neighborhoods. Talk about enlightenment makes us nervous, because it implies that we pass our ordinary days in darkness. You recall the scene in *King Lear* when blind and wretched old Gloucester, wishing to commit suicide, begs a young man to lead him to the edge of a cliff. The young man is Gloucester's son, Edgar, who fools the old man into thinking they have come to a high bluff at the edge of the sea. Gloucester kneels, and then tumbles forward onto the level ground; on landing, he is amazed to find himself alive. He is transformed by the fall. Blind, at last he is able to see his life clearly; despairing, he discovers hope. To be enlightened, he did not have to leap to someplace else; he only had to come hard against the ground where he already stood.

I am encouraged by the words of a Crow elder, quoted by Gary Snyder in *The Practice of the Wild:* "You know, I think if people stay somewhere long enough—even white people—the spirits will begin to speak to them. It's the power of the spirits coming up from the land. The spirits and the old powers aren't lost, they just need people to be around long enough and the spirits will begin to influence them." No need to put out your eyes like Gloucester in order to see. No need to be grim. I embrace the Buddhist advice: Learn what you can, live as mindfully as you can, treat with loving kindness all the creatures that share the sunlight with you, and be joyful.

My friend Richard, who wears a white collar to his job, recently bought forty acres of land that had been worn out by the standard local regimen of chemicals and corn. Evenings and weekends, he has set about restoring the soil by spreading manure, planting clover and rye, and filling the eroded gullies with brush. His pond has gathered geese, his young orchard has tempted deer, and his nesting boxes have attracted swallows and bluebirds. Now he is preparing a field for the wildflowers and prairie grasses that once flourished here. Having contemplated this work since he was a boy, Richard will not be chased away by fashions or dollars or tornadoes. On a recent airplane trip he was distracted from the book he was reading by thoughts of renewing the land. So he sketched on the flyleaf a plan of labor for the next ten years. Most of us do not have forty acres to care for, but that should not keep us from sowing and tending local crops.

I think about Richard's ten-year vision when I read a report that shows computer users grow impatient if they have to wait more than a second to see the results of their actions. If a machine or a program takes longer than a second to respond, customers will shun it. I use a computer, but I am wary of the haste it encourages. Few answers that matter will come to us in a second; some of the most vital answers will not come in ten years, or a hundred.

When the chiefs of the Iroquois nation sit in council, they are sworn to consider how their decisions will affect their descendants seven generations into the future. Seven generations! Imagine our politicians thinking beyond the next opinion poll, beyond the next election, beyond their own lifetimes, two centuries ahead. Imagine our bankers, our corporate executives, our advertising moguls weighing their judgments on that scale. Looking seven generations into the future, could a developer pave another farm? Could a farmer spray another pound of poison? Could the captain of an oil tanker flush his tanks at sea? Could you or I write checks and throw switches without a much greater concern for what is bought and sold, what is burned?

As I write this, I hear the snarl of earthmovers and chain saws a mile away destroying a farm to make way for another shopping strip. I would rather hear a tornado, whose damage can be undone. The elderly woman who owned the farm had it listed in the National Register, then willed it to her daughters on condition they preserve it. After her death, the daughters, who live out of state, had the will broken, so the land could be turned over to the chain saws and earthmovers. The machines work around the clock. Their noise wakes me at midnight, at three in the morning, at dawn. The roaring abrades my dreams. The sound is a reminder that we are living in the midst of a holocaust. I do not use the word lightly. Earth is being pillaged, and every one of us, willingly or grudgingly, is taking part. We ask how sensible, educated, supposedly moral people could have tolerated slavery or the slaughter of Jews. Similar questions will be asked about us by our descendants, to whom we bequeath an impoverished planet. They will demand to know how we could have been party to such waste and ruin. They will have good reason to curse our memory.

What does it mean to be alive in an era when the Earth is being devoured, and in a country which has set the pattern for that devouring? What are we called to do? I think we are called to the work of healing, both inner and outer: healing of the mind through a change in consciousness, healing of the Earth through a change in our lives. We can begin that work by learning how to abide in a place. I am talking about an active commitment, not a passive lingering. If you stay with a husband or wife out of laziness rather than love, that is inertia, not marriage. If you stay put through cowardice rather than conviction, you will have no strength to act. Strength comes, healing comes, from aligning yourself with the grain of your place and answering to its needs.

"The man who is often thinking that it is better to be somewhere else than where he is excommunicates himself," we are cautioned by Thoreau, that notorious stay-at-home (*Journal*, November 20, 1857). The metaphor is religious: to withhold yourself from where you are is to be cut off from communion with the source. It has taken me half a lifetime of searching to realize that the likeliest path to the ultimate ground leads through my local ground. I mean the land itself, with its creeks and rivers, its weather, seasons, stone outcroppings, and all the plants and animals that share it. I cannot have a spiritual center without having a geographical one; I cannot live a grounded life without being grounded in a *place*.

In belonging to a landscape, one feels a rightness, at-homeness, a knitting of self and world. This condition of clarity and focus, this being fully present, is akin to what the Buddhists call mindfulness, what Christian contemplatives refer to as recollection, what Quakers call centering down. I am suspicious of any philosophy that would separate this-worldly from other-worldly commitment. There is only one world, and we participate in it here and now, in our flesh and our place.

# Wayland

wo blacktop roads, broken by frost and mended with tar, running from nowhere to nowhere, cross at right angles in the rumpled farm country of northeastern Ohio. The neighborhood where they intersect is called Wayland—not a village, not even a hamlet, only a cluster of barns and silos and frame houses and a white steepled Methodist church. Just north of Wayland, the army fenced in thirty square miles of ground for their bomb factory, and just to the south the Corps of Engineers built their reservoir. I grew up behind those government fences in the shadows of bunkers, and on farms that have since vanished beneath those imprisoned waters. Family visits to church began carrying me to Wayland when I was five, romance was carrying me there still at seventeen, and in the years between I was drawn there often by duty or desire. Thus it happened that within shouting distance of the Wayland crossroads I met seven of the great mysteries.

Even as a boy, oblivious much of the time to all save my own sensations, I knew by the tingle in my spine when I had bumped into something utterly new. I groped for words to describe what I had felt, as I grope still. Since we give labels to all that puzzles us, as we name every blank space on the map, I could say that what I stumbled into in Wayland were the mysteries of death, life, beasts, food, mind, sex, and God. But these seven words are only tokens, worn coins that I shove onto the page, hoping to bribe you, coins I finger as reminders of those awful encounters.

The roads that cross at Wayland are too humble to show on the Ohio map, too small even to wear numbers. And yet, without maps or mistakes, without quite meaning to, I recently found my way back there from several hundred miles away, after an absence of twenty-five years, led along the grooves of memory.

The grooves are deep, and they set me vibrating well before I reached the place, as the spiral cuts in phonograph records will shake music from a needle. I was heading toward Cleveland when I took a notion to veer off the interstate and see what had become of Akron, which led me to see what had become of Kent, which led me to Ravenna, the seat of Portage County. Nothing aside from stoplights made me pause. Not sure what I was looking for, I drove east from the county seat along a highway hurtling with trucks. Soon the rusted chain-link fence of the Ravenna Arsenal came whipping by on my left and the raised bed of the Baltimore & Ohio tracks surged by on the right. Then I realized where I was going. My knuckles whitened on the steering wheel as I turned from the highway, put my back toward the trucks and bombs, and passed under the railroad through a concrete arch. Beyond the arch, the woods and fields and houses of Wayland shimmered in the October sunlight, appearing to my jealous eye scarcely changed after a quarter of a century.

I knew the place had changed, of course, if only because in the years since I had come here last—drawn in those days like a moth to the flame of a girl—the population of the Earth had nearly doubled. Every crossroads, every woods, every field on the planet was warping under the pressure of our terrible hunger. So I knew that Wayland had changed, for all its pastoral shimmer in the autumn light. Yet I was grateful that on the surface it so much resembled my childhood memories, for, in my effort to live adequately in the present, I had come here to conduct some business with the past. What had brought me back to Wayland was a need to dig through the fluff and debris of ordinary life, down to some bedrock of feeling and belief.

I left my car in the graveled parking lot of the church and set out walking. Without planning my steps, I meandered where memory led, and where it led was from station to station of my childhood astonishment. Not yet ready for the church, I went next door to the parsonage, where I had first caught a whiff of death. The two-story house—covered in white asbestos siding and plain as a box of salt, with a porch across the front and a green gabled roof—could have belonged to any of the neighboring farms. That was appropriate, for the ministers who succeeded one another in the house often preached as though they were farmers, weeding out sins, harvesting souls.

The minister whom I knew first was the Reverend Mr. Kline, a bulky man sunken with age, his hair as white as the siding on the parsonage, his voice like the cooing of pigeons in the barn. Much in life amused him. Whenever he told you something that struck him as funny, he would cover his mouth with a hand to hide his smile. Despite the raised hand, often his laugh burst free and rolled over you. I began listening to him preach and pray and lead hymns when I was five, and for the next two years I heard Reverend Kline every Sunday, until his voice became for me that of the Bible itself, even the voice of God. Then one Sunday when I was seven, I shook his great hand after the service as usual, suffering him to bend down and pat my head, and I went home to my dinner and he went home to his. While his wife set the table in the parsonage, Reverend Kline rested on the front porch in his caned rocking chair, drifted off to sleep, and never woke up.

When Mother told me of this, the skin prickled on my neck. To sleep and never wake! To be a white-haired man with a voice like a barn full of pigeons, and the next minute to be nothing at all! Since my parents considered me too young to attend the funeral, I could only imagine what had become of his body, and I imagined not decay but evaporation—the flesh dispersing into thin air like morning mist from a pond.

The following Sunday, while a visitor preached, I stole away from church and crept over to the parsonage. I drew to the edge of the porch, rested my chin on the railing, and stared at the empty rocker. Reverend Kline will never sit in that chair again, I told myself. Never, never, never. I tried to imagine how long forever would last. I tried to imagine how it would feel to be nothing. No thing. Suddenly chair and house and daylight vanished, and I was gazing into a dark hole, I was falling, I was gone. Falling, I caught a whiff of death, the damp earthy smell seeping from beneath the porch. It was also the smell of mud, of leaping grass, of spring. Clinging to that sensation, I pulled myself up out of the hole. There was the house again, the chair. I lifted my chin from the railing, swung away, and ran back to the church, chanting to myself: He was old and I am young, he was old and I am young.

Nights, often, and sometimes in the broad light of day, I still have to scrabble up out of that hole. We all do. In childhood, early or late, each of us bangs head-on into the blank fact we call death. Once that collision takes place, the shock of it never wears off. We may find ourselves returning to the spot where it occurred as to the scene of an accident, the way I found myself drawn, half a lifetime later, to the front steps of this parsonage. I was a stranger to the family who lived there now. Not wishing to intrude on them, I paused by the steps and surveyed the porch. An aluminum folding chair had replaced the rocker. I squatted by the railing, lowering my face to the height of a seven-year-old, closed my eyes against the shadows, and sniffed. From below the sill of the porch came the Earth's dank perennial breath, fetid and fertile. Yes, I thought, filling myself with the smell: This abides, this is real; no matter the name we give it, life or death, it is a fact as rough and solid as a stone squeezed in the palm of the hand.

A dog yapped inside the parsonage. I stood up hurriedly and backed away, before anyone could appear at the door to ask me what in tarnation I was looking for under that porch.

Still following the grooves of memory, I crossed the road to stand in the driveway of another house, this one a bungalow encased in stone and aluminum. It was not so much the house that drew me as it was the side yard, where, about this time each fall, we brought our apples for pressing. The old press with its wooden vat and iron gears used to balance on concrete blocks in the shade of a weeping willow. We would pick apples in the Arsenal, from orchards which had been allowed to go wild after the government bulldozed the farmsteads. Unsprayed, blotched and wormy, these apples were also wonderfully sweet. We kept them in bushel baskets and cardboard boxes in the cellar, their fragrance filling the house, until we had accumulated enough to load our station wagon. Then we drove here, parked beside the willow, and fed our fruit into the press. On this mild October day, the willow looked as I remembered it, thick in the trunk and gold in the leaves. There was no sign of a press, but that did not keep me from remembering what it was like to squeeze apples. First we pulped them in a mill, then we wrapped them in cheesecloth and tamped them down, layer by layer, into the slotted wooden vat. To mash them, we spun a cast-iron wheel. It was easy to begin with, so easy that my brother and sister and I could make the spokes whirl. Later, the cranking would become too hard for us, and our mother would take her turn, then our father, then both of them together. The moment that set me trembling, however, came early on, while my hand was still on the iron wheel, the moment when cider began to ooze through the cheesecloth, between the slats, and down the spout into a waiting bucket. Out of the dirt, out of the gnarled trunks and wide-flung branches, out of the ripe red fruit, had come this tawny juice. When my arms grew tired, I held a Mason jar under the spout, caught a glassful, and drank it down. It was as though we had squeezed the planet and out had poured sweetness.

What came back to me, musing there by the willow all these years later, was the sound of cider trickling into the bucket, the honeyed taste of it, and my bewilderment that rain and wood and dirt and sun had yielded this juice. Amazing, that we can drink the Earth! Amazing, that it quenches our thirst, answers our hunger! Who would have predicted such an outlandish thing? Who, having sipped, can forget that it is the Earth we swallow?

Well, I had forgotten; or at least I had buried under the habits of casual eating that primal awareness of the meaning of food. And so here was another fundamental perception, renewed for me by my sojourn in Wayland. This image of cider gushing from a spout was my cornucopia, proof of the dazzling abundance that sustains us.

From the cider house I walked downhill to the crossroads. One corner was still a pasture, grazed by three horses; another was a scrubby field grown up in brush and weeds; and the other two corners were expansive lawns. Through the brushy field meandered a creek where I used to hunt frogs with a flashlight and bucket. As in all the Octobers I could remember, the maples in the yards were scarlet, the pasture oaks were butterscotch, and the sycamores along the creek were stripped down to their voluptuous white limbs. Yellow mums and bright red pokers of salvia were still thriving in flowerbeds. A portly older man on a riding mower was cutting one of the lawns, while from a stump beside the driveway an older woman observed his progress, a hand shading her eyes. I knew them from childhood, but their names would not come. I waved, and they waved back. That was conversation enough. I had no wish to speak with them or with anyone in Wayland, since I would have been hard put to explain who I was or why I had come back. Maybe I also wanted to keep the past pure, unmixed with the present.

Because the crossroads are laid out on the grid of survey lines, the blacktop runs due north and south, east and west. The roads were so little traveled that I could stand in the intersection, gummy tar beneath my boots, and gaze along the pavement in each of the cardinal directions. I had just come from the south, where the church gleamed on its hill. My view to the north was cut off by the railroad, except for the arched opening of the underpass, through which

I could see the rusted fence of the Arsenal. Memories of a girl I had courted were beckoning from the west; but less fervent memories beckoned from the opposite direction, and that is where I chose to go next.

A quarter mile east of the crossroads I came to a farm where the Richards family used to breed and board and train horses. Although the name on the mailbox had changed, ten or twelve horses were grazing, as before, in a paddock beside the barn. I leaned against the slat fence and admired them.

In boyhood I had raised and ridden horses of my own, a stocky mixture of Shetland pony and the high-stepping carriage breed known as Hackney. They all came out of a single ornery mare called Belle, and they all had her color, a sorrel coat that grew sleek in summer and shaggy in winter. We used to bring Belle here to the Richards' place for mating with a Hackney stallion. Years before the voltage of sex began to make my own limbs jerk, I had been amazed by the stallion's fervor and the mare's skittishness. He nipped and nuzzled and pursued her; she danced and wheeled. Their energy seemed too great for the paddock to hold. Surely the fence would give way, the barn itself would fall! Then at length Belle shivered to a standstill and allowed the stallion to lift his forelegs onto her rump, his back legs jigging, hoofs scrabbling for purchase, her legs opening to his dark pizzle, the two of them momentarily one great plunging beast. And then, if luck held, eleven or twelve months later Belle would open her legs once more and drop a foal. Within minutes of entering the world, the foal would be tottering about on its wobbly stilts, drunk on air, and it would be ramming its muzzle into Belle's belly in search of milk. What a world, that the shivering union of mare and stallion in the barnyard should lead to this new urgency!

Musing there by the paddock on this October afternoon, I felt toward the grazing horses a huge affection. Each filled its hide so gloriously. I gave a low whistle. Several massive heads bobbed up and swung toward me, jaws working on grass, ears pricked forward. Their black eyes regarded me soberly, and then all but one of the heads returned to grazing. The exception was a palomino gelding, who tossed his white mane, switched his white tail, and started ambling in my direction. As he drew near, I stretched my right arm toward him, palm open. Had I known I would be coming here, I would have brought apples or sugar cubes. My father would have pulled a cigarette from his pocket and offered that. But all I had to offer was the salt on my skin. The palomino lowered his muzzle to my palm, sniffed cautiously, then curled out his rasping red tongue and licked.

I knew that sandpapery stroke on my hand as I knew few other sensations. Just so, my own horses had scrabbled up oats and sugar and sweat from my palm. The pressure of their tongues made my whole body sway. There by the fence, past and present merged, and I was boy and man, swaying. I reveled in the muscular touch, animal to animal. Contact! It assured me that I was not alone in the world. I was a creature among creatures.

When the palomino lost interest in my right hand, I offered my left. He sniffed idly, and, finding it empty, turned back to the greater temptation of grass. But the rasp of his tongue on my palm stayed with me, another clean, hard fact, another piece of bedrock on which to build a life.

The field across the road from the Richards place was grown up into a young woods, mostly staghorn sumac and cedar and oak. When I had seen it last, twenty-five years earlier, this had been a meadow luxuriant with grasses and wildflowers. Back where the far edge of the field ran up against the sinuous line of willows bordering the creek, there had been a cottage, low and brown, moss growing on the roof, weeds lapping at the windows, a place that looked from a distance more like a forgotten woodpile than a house. Today, no cottage showed above the vigorous trees. But near my feet I could see the twin ruts of the dirt track that led back to the place. I followed them, my boots knocking seeds from thistle and wild rye.

I knew the meadow and the cottage because the woman who used to live here was my science teacher in high school. Fay Given must have been in her early sixties when I met her in my freshman year. Many students mocked her for being so unthinkably old, for looking like a schoolmarm, for loving science, for trembling when she spoke about nature. She would gaze fervently into a beaker as though an entire galaxy spun before her. She grew so excited while recounting the habits of molecules that she would skip about the lab and clap her spotted hands. She would weep for joy over what swam before her in a microscope. Mrs. Given wept easily, more often than not because of a wisecrack or prank from one of the students. Our cruelty was a defense against the claim she made on us. For she was inviting us to share her passionate curiosity. She called us to hunger and thirst after knowledge of the universe.

I would not join the others in mocking her. I supposed it was pity that held me back, or an ingrained respect for my elders. Only in the fall of my freshman year, on a day when Mrs. Given brought us here to this field for a botany class, did I realize that I could not mock her because I loved her. She led us through her meadow, naming the plants, twirling the bright fallen leaves, telling which birds ate which berries, opening milkweed pods, disclosing the burrows of groundhogs, parting the weeds to reveal caterpillars and crickets, showing where mice had severed blades of grass. Much of the meadow she had planted, with seeds carried in her pockets from the neighboring countryside. Every few years she burned it, as the Indians had burned the prairies, to keep the woods from reclaiming it.

While Mrs. Given told us these things in her quavery voice, students kept sidling away to smoke or joke or dabble their hands in the creek, until there were only three of us following her. I stayed with her not from a sense of obedience but from wonder. To know this patch of land, I dimly realized, would be the work of a lifetime. But in knowing it deeply, right down to the foundations, you would comprehend a great deal more, perhaps everything. As she touched the feathery plants of her meadow, as she murmured the names and histories of the creatures who shared the place with her, I came to feel that this was holy ground. And if the meadow was holy, maybe other fields and woods and crossroads and backyards were also holy.

At one point, Mrs. Given knelt amid the bristly spikes of a tall russet grass. "You see why it's called foxtail, don't you?" she said. "Livestock won't eat it, but you can twist the stalks together and make a fair rope. Farmers used to bind up corn fodder with hanks of foxtail." She grasped one of the spikes, and, with a rake of her thumb, brushed seeds into her palm. She poured a few seeds into my hand and a few into the hands of the other two students who had remained with her. "Now what do you have there?" she asked us.

We stared at the barbed grains in our palms. "Seeds," one of us replied.

"That's the universe unfolding," she told us, "right there in your hands. The same as in every cell of our bodies. Now *why*? That's the question I can't ever get behind. Why should the universe be alive? Why does it obey laws? And why these particular laws? For that matter, why is there a universe at all?" She gave a rollicking laugh. "And isn't it curious that there should be creatures like us who can walk in this beautiful field and puzzle over things?"

She asked her questions gaily, and I have carried them with me all these years in the same spirit. They rose in me again on this October afternoon as I followed the dirt track to the spot where her cottage used to be. Stones marked the cellar hole and the front stoop. Brush grew up through the space left by her death. The woods had reclaimed her meadow. Yet the ground still felt holy. Her marveling gaze had disclosed for me the force and shapeliness of things, and that power survived her passing. She taught me that if only we could be adequate to the given world, we need not dream of paradise.

Reversing my steps, I walked back to the crossroads and kept going west for a hundred yards or so, until I fetched up before the house where, as a simmering teenager, I had wooed a girl. Let me call her Veronica. She and her family moved from Wayland soon after the Army Corps of Engineers built that needless dam, and so on this October day her house was for me another shell filled only with memory. The present kept abrading the past, however, because during the few minutes while I stood there a grown man in a go-kart kept zooming around the yard, following a deeply gouged path. Every time he roared past, he peered at me from beneath his crash helmet. I nodded, assuming the look of one who is infatuated with loud machines, and that appeared to satisfy him.

Veronica had the face of a queen on the deck of cards with which I learned to play poker, a face I considered perfect. Words tumbled from her lush lips, impulsively, like rabbits fleeing a burrow. Black wavy hair tumbled down her back, twitching nearly to her slender hips. Having learned in marriage what it means to love a woman, I cannot say that what I felt for Veronica was quite love. Nor was it simply lust, although for much of my seventeenth year the mere thought of her set me aching. At that age, I would have been reluctant to see myself as the urgent stallion and Veronica as the skittish mare.

In her backyard there was a sycamore tree that loomed high over the house, its fat trunk a patchwork of peeling bark and its crooked upper branches as creamy as whole milk. Wooden crossbars nailed to the trunk formed a ladder up to a treehouse. Veronica and I often sat beneath the sycamore on a stone bench, talking and falling silent, aware of parental eyes watching us from the kitchen. With our backs to the house, our sides pressed together, I could risk brushing a hand over her knee, she could run a fingernail under my chin. But even a kiss, our mouths so visibly meeting, would have prompted a visit from the kitchen.

One October day, a day very like this one of my return to Wayland, Veronica and I were sitting on the bench, hunting for words to shape our confusion, when suddenly she leapt to her feet and said, "Let's go up to the treehouse."

"We'll get filthy," I said. I glanced with misgiving at my white knit shirt and chino pants, so carefully pressed. Her lemony blouse was protected by a green corduroy jumper.

"It'll wash out," she said, tugging me by the hand.

I stood. Without waiting for me, she kicked off her shoes and clambered up the wooden rungs, but instead of halting at the rickety platform of the treehouse, she kept on, swaying from limb to limb. I watched until the flashing of her bare legs made me look away. When she had gone as high as she dared, high enough to escape the view from the kitchen, she balanced on a branch and called to me, "Come on up! Are you afraid?"

I was afraid—but not of the tree. I stepped onto a cross brace and started climbing, and as I climbed there was nowhere else to look but up, and there was nothing else to see above me except those white legs parted within the green hoop of her skirt. Her creamy forked limbs and the creamy forked limbs of the sycamore merged in my sight, as they merge now in memory, and I was drawn upward into the pale shadows between her thighs. My knowledge of what I was climbing toward would remain abstract for a number of years. I understood only that where her legs joined there was an opening, a gateway for life coming and going. When I reached Veronica I put my hand, briefly, where my gaze had gone, just far enough to feel the surprising warmth of that secret, satiny place. Then I withdrew my hand and she smoothed her skirt, neither of us risking a word, and we teetered there for a hundred heartbeats on those swaying branches, shaken by inner as well as outer winds. Then the kitchen door creaked open and her mother's voice inquired as to our sanity, and we climbed down. I went first, as though to catch Veronica should she fall, my gaze toward the ground.

The buzzing of the go-kart eventually wore through the husk of memory, and my lungs filled with the present. I became again what I was, a man long married, a man with a daughter older than Veronica had been on that day of our climb into the tree. The sycamore still rose behind the house, twenty-five years taller, crisp brown leaves rattling in the wind, the upper limbs as pale and silky as ever.

I had a choice of returning to the church by the road or across the stubble of a cornfield. I chose the field. All the way, I could see the white steepled box gleaming on its rise. The only car in the graveled parking lot was mine. Beyond a tree line to the southwest, beyond the annihilating waters of the reservoir that I could not bear to look at, the sun wallowed down toward dusk. The church might already be locked, I thought, so late on a weekday afternoon. Still I did not hurry. My boots scuffed the ridges where corn had stood. Raccoons and crows would find little to feast on in this stubble, for the harvester had plucked it clean. I recalled the biblical injunction to farmers, that they leave the margins of their fields unpicked, for the poor and the beasts. I thought of the margins in a life, in my life, the untended zones beyond the borders of clarity, the encircling wilderness out of which new powers and visions come.

A cornfield is a good approach to a church, for you arrive with dirt on your boots, the smell of greenery in your nostrils, dust on your tongue. The door would be locked, I figured, and the main door was, the broad entrance through which the Methodist women carried their piety and their pies, through which men carried mortgages and mortality, through which children like myself carried their nagging questions. But the rear door was unlocked. I left my boots on the stoop and went inside.

The back room I entered had the familiarity of a place one returns to in dream: the squeaky pine boards of the floor, the dwarf tables where children would sit on Sundays to color pictures of Jesus, the brass hooks where the choir would hang their robes and the minister his hat, the folding chairs collapsed into a corner, the asthmatic furnace, and on a counter the stack of lathe-turned walnut plates for the offering.

Every few paces I halted, listening. The joints of the church cricked as the sun let it go. Birds fussed beyond the windows. But no one else was about; this relieved me, for here least of all was I prepared to explain myself. I had moved too long in circles where to confess an interest in religious things marked one as a charlatan, a sentimentalist, or a fool. No doubt I have all three qualities in my character. But I also have another quality, and that is an unshakable hunger to know who I am, where I am, and into what sort of cosmos I have been so briefly and astonishingly sprung. Whatever combination of shady motives might have led me here, the impulse that shook me right then was a craving to glimpse the very source of things.

I made my way out through the choir door into the sanctuary. Cushionless pews in somber ranks, uncarpeted floor, exposed beams in the vault overhead and whitewashed plaster on the walls: it was a room fashioned by men and women who knew barns, for preachers who lived out of saddlebags, in honor of a God who cares nothing for ornament. No tapestries, no shrines, no racks of candles, no gold on the altar, no bragging memorials to vanished patrons. The window glass, unstained, let in the plain light of day.

I sat in a pew midway along the central aisle and looked out through those clear windows. My reasons for coming here were entwined with that sky full of light. As a boy I had looked out, Sunday after Sunday, to see corn grow and clouds blow, to watch crows bustle among the tops of trees, to follow hawks, unmindful of the Sabbath, on their spiraling hunts, and to sense in all this radiant surge the same rush I felt under my fingers when I pressed a hand to my throat.

There was no gulf between outside and inside. We gathered in this room not to withdraw, but more fully to enter the world.

On this day of my return I kept watching the sky as the light thinned and the darkness thickened. I became afraid. Afraid of dying, yes, but even more of not having lived, afraid of passing my days in a stupor, afraid of squandering my moment in the light. I gripped the pew in front of me to still my trembling. I wanted to dive down to the center of being, touch bedrock, open my eyes and truly, finally, unmistakably see. I shifted my gaze from the darkening window to the altar, to the wooden cross, to the black lip of the Bible showing from the pulpit. But those were only props for a play that was forever in rehearsal, the actors clumsy, the script obscure. I was myself one of the actors, sustained in my bumbling efforts by the hope that one day the performance would be perfect, and everything would at last come clear.

One cannot summon grace with a whistle. The pew beneath me, the air around me, and the darkening windows did not turn to fire. The clouds of unknowing did not part. I sat there for a long while, and then I rose and made my way down the aisle, past the organ, through the choir door and back room, out into the freshening night. On the stoop I drew on my boots and laced them up. The chrome latch of my car was already cool. I drove back through the crossroads with headlights glaring, alert for animals that might dash before me in the confusion of dusk.

\\||//

There is more to be seen at any crossroads than one can see in a lifetime of looking. My return visit to Wayland was less than two hours long. Once again several hundred miles distant from that place, back here in my home ground making this model from slippery words, I cannot be sure where the pressure of mind has warped the surface of things. If you were to go there, you would not find every detail exactly as I have described it. How could you, bearing as you do a past quite different from mine? No doubt my memory, welling up through these lines, has played tricks with time and space.

What memory is made of I cannot say; my body, at least, is made of atoms on loan from the Earth. How implausible, that these atoms should have gathered to form this I, this envelope of skin that walks about and strokes horses and tastes apples and trembles with desire in the branches of a sycamore and gazes through the windows of a church at the ordinary sky. Certain moments in one's life cast their influence forward over all the moments that follow. My encounters in Wayland shaped me first as I lived through them, then again as I recalled them during my visit, and now as I write them down. That is of course why I write them down. The self is a fiction. I make up the story of myself with scraps of memory, sensation, reading, and hearsay. It is a tale I whisper against the dark. Only in rare moments of luck or courage do I hush, forget myself entirely, and listen to the silence that precedes and surrounds and follows all speech.

If you were keeping count, you may have toted up seven mysteries, or maybe seven times seven, or maybe seven to the seventh power. My hunch is that, however we count, there is only one mystery. In our nearsightedness, we merely glimpse the light scintillating off the numberless scales of Leviathan, and we take each spark for a separate wonder.

Could we bear to see all the light at once? Could we bear the roar of infinite silence? I sympathize with science, where, in order to answer a question, you limit the variables. You draw a circle within which everything can be measured, and you shut out the rest of the universe. I draw my own circles with these narratives, telling of rivers and tornadoes, house and family, dirt and dreams. I lay out stories like fences to enclose for myself a home ground within the frightening infinities. Yet every enclosure is a makeshift, every boundary an illusion. With great ingenuity, we decipher some of the rules that govern this vast shining dance, but all our efforts could not change the least of them.

Nothing less than the undivided universe can be our true home. Yet how can one speak or even think about the whole of things? Language is of only modest help. Every sentence is a wispy net, capturing a few flecks of meaning. The sun shines without vocabulary. The salmon has no name for the urge that drives it upstream. The newborn groping for the nipple knows hunger long before it knows a single word. Even with an entire dictionary in one's head, one eventually comes to the end of words. Then what? Then drink deep like the baby, swim like the salmon, burn like any brief star.

# Letter to a Reader

Since you ask for an account of my writing, I will give you one. But I do so warily, because when writers speak about their work they often puff up like blowfish. Writing *is* work, and it can leave you gray with exhaustion, can devour your days, can break your heart. But the same is true of all the real work that humans do, the planting of crops and nursing of babies, the building of houses and baking of bread. Writing is neither holy nor mysterious, except insofar as everything we do with our gathered powers is holy and mysterious. Without trumpets, therefore, let me tell you how I began and how I have pursued this art. Along the way I must also tell you something of my life, for writing is to living as grass is to soil.

I did not set out to become a writer. I set out to become a scientist, for I wished to understand the universe, this vast and exquisite order that runs from the depths of our bodies to the depths of space. In studying biology, chemistry, and above all physics, I drew unwittingly on the passions of my parents. Although neither of them had graduated from college, my father was a wizard with tools, my mother with plants. My father could gaze at any structure—a barn or a music box—and see how it fit together. He could make from scratch a house or a hat, could mend a stalled watch or a silent radio. He possessed the tinkerer's genius that has flourished in the stables and cellars and shops of our nation for three hundred years. My mother's passion was for nature, the whole dazzling creation, from stones to birds, from cockleburs to constellations. Under her care, vegetables bore abundantly and flowers bloomed. The Great Depression forced her to give up the dream of becoming a doctor, but not before

141

she had acquired a lifelong yen for science. When I think of them, I see my father in his workshop sawing a piece of wood, my mother in her garden planting seeds. Their intelligence spoke through their hands. I learned from them to think of writing as manual labor, akin to carpentry and farming.

I was born to these parents in October 1945, two months after the bombing of Hiroshima and Nagasaki, so I have lived all my days under the sign of the mushroom cloud. My first home was a farm near Memphis, close enough to the Mississippi to give me an abiding love for rivers, far enough south to give me an abiding guilt over racism. Across the road from our house was a prison farm, where I helped the black inmates pick cotton under the shotgun eyes of guards. My sister, Sandra, three years older than I, taught me to read on the screened back porch of that house as we listened to the locusts and the billy goat and the cow. By the age of four I could turn the ink marks on paper into stories in my head, an alchemy I still find more marvelous than the turning of lead into gold.

My birth along the Mississippi, those forlorn black faces in the prison fields, and the country turn of my father's speech all prepared me to be spellbound when, at the age of eight, I climbed aboard the raft with Huckleberry Finn and Jim. That novel was the first big book I read from cover to cover. After finishing the last page, I returned immediately to page one and started over. From that day onward, I have known that the speech of back roads and fields and small towns—*my* speech—is a language worthy of literature. Nor have I forgotten how close laughter is to pain. Nor have I doubted that stories can bear us along on their current as powerfully as any river.

The summer before I started school, my family moved from Tennessee to Ohio, where we lived for the next few years on a military reservation surrounded by soldiers and the machinery of war. This place, the Ravenna Arsenal, would later provide me with the title and central themes for my book of essays, *The Paradise of Bombs*. The move from South to North, from red dirt to concrete, from fields planted in cotton to fields planted in bombs, opened a fissure in me that I have tried to bridge, time and again, with words.

An army bus, olive drab to hide it from enemy planes, carried us children to a tiny school just outside the chain-link fence. There were thirteen in my class, the sons and daughters of truck drivers, mechanics, farmers, electricians. At recess I learned whose father had been laid off, whose mother had taken sick, whose brother had joined the marines. From our desks we could see armed guards cruising the Arsenal's perimeter, the long antennas on their camouflaged Chevrolets whipping the air. And in the opposite direction, beyond the playground, we could see horses grazing in a pasture and trees pushing against the sky.

Before I finished the eight grades of that school, my family moved from the Arsenal to a patch of land nearby, and there I resumed my country ways, raising ponies and hoeing beans and chasing dogs through the woods. On local farms I helped bale hay and boil maple syrup. Sputnik was launched in the month I turned twelve, adding to my adolescence the romance of space to go along with the romance of girls. I mixed black powder in the basement and fired model rockets from the pigpen, brooding on the curves of orbits and lips. Our neighbors were mostly poor, living in trailers or tarpaper shacks, often out of work, forever on the shady side of luck. Several of those aching people, their lives twisted by fanaticism or loss, would show up in my first book of stories, *Fetching the Dead*.

Many of the adults and some of the children in those trailers and shacks were alcoholic, as was my own good father. Throughout my childhood, but especially in my high school years, he drank with a fearful thirst. Instead of putting out the fire in his gut, the alcohol made it burn more fiercely. This man who was so gentle and jovial when sober would give in to sulks and rages when drunk. The house trembled. I feared that the windows would shatter, the floors buckle, the beds collapse. Above all I feared that neighbors or friends would learn our bitter secret. The pressure of that secret, always disguised, shows up in my early books, especially in *Fetching the Dead* and the novel *Bad Man Ballad*.

I was not able to write openly about my father's drinking until well after his death, in "Under the Influence," the lead essay in *Secrets of the Universe*. As a boy, I felt only bewilderment and shame. Craving order, I hurled myself into one lucid zone after another—the chessboard, the baseball diamond and basketball court, the periodic table, the wiring diagrams of electronics, the graphs of calculus, the formulas of physics. I pitched the baseball so hard I tore up my elbow; I rushed down the basketball court so recklessly I broke my foot against the gymnasium wall; I scrambled so far into mathematics that I could scarcely find my way back; I searched the teeming pool under the microscope for clues that would bind together the tatters of the world.

A scholarship to study physics paid my way to Brown University in Providence, where I spent four years feeling like a country duckling among swans. My classmates arrived with luggage bearing flight tags from the world's airports, wallets bulging with credit cards, voices buzzing with the voltage of cities. These polished men and women seemed to know already more than I could ever learn. My own pockets were empty. My voice betrayed the hills of Tennessee and the woods of Ohio. My devotion to the abstruse games of science marked me as odd. Fear of failing kept me so steadily at my books that I graduated first in my class. I mention the achievement because I am proud of it, but also because I have still not overcome that dread of failure, that sense of being an outsider, a hick among sophisticates. Standing on the margin, I formed the habit of looking and listening. On the margin, I was free to envision a way of life more desirable and durable than this one that excluded me.

The public turmoil of the 1960s and early 1970s deepened my private confusion. Even though I was not an especially political animal, during those college years I was gripped by one cause after another—securing full rights for women and blacks and Native Americans, saving the environment, ending the Vietnam War. All these causes seemed utterly removed from the bloodless abstractions of physics. I began to gasp for air among the crystalline formulas. I longed for the smell of dirt, the sound of voices, the weight of tools in my hands. I grew dizzy with the desire to heal—to heal my father and myself, to comfort the poor and despised, to speak for the mute, to care for the Earth.

In this time of great confusion I began keeping a journal. I strung out sentences like guy wires to hold myself upright in the winds of uncertainty. In those creamy pages, I wrote as though my life depended on it—and in a sense it did. Gradually I found words to address the inescapable questions: Who am I? What sense can I make of this inner tumult? How should I live? Does the universe have a purpose? Do we? What finally and deeply matters? What is true, and how can we know? I was too naive to realize that worldly men and women do not brood on such imponderable matters. I brooded. I pondered. I haunted the library, cross-examined the stars, and walked the grimy streets of Providence looking for answers. Here science failed me. These mysteries lay in shadow outside the bright circle of scientific method, beyond the reach of gauges or graphs. There were no diagrams for meaning, and I desired meaning with an unappeasable hunger.

Pushed by spiritual hungers and pulled by social concerns, I decided in my junior year at Brown that I could not become a physicist. Then what new path should I follow? I considered history, philosophy, religion, and psychology; but at length I settled on literature, which had been calling to me ever since my sister taught me to read on that porch in Tennessee. All those years I had been living within the curved space of books. I read as I breathed, incessantly. Books lined the walls of my room, they rested on the table beside my pillow as I slept, they rode with me everywhere in pockets or pack, they poured through me constantly their murmur of words. At the age of twenty I still did not imagine that I would make any books of my own, but I knew that I would live in their company.

⁂

Another scholarship enabled me to continue my study of literature at Cambridge University. I sailed to England in the fall of 1967 along with my new bride, Ruth Ann McClure. I had met her at a summer science camp when she was fifteen and I was sixteen, the fruity smells of organic chemistry lab in our hair, and for five years we had carried on an epistolary romance. At first we exchanged letters monthly, then weekly, and at last daily, through the rest of high school and all through college. Page by page, this girl turned into a woman before my eyes, and page by page I stumbled on from boy to man.

During those five years, Ruth and I saw one another in the flesh no more than a dozen times. And yet, after exchanging sheaves of letters, I knew this woman more thoroughly, understood more about her beliefs and desires, and loved her more deeply than I would have if I had been living next door to her all that while. Even more than the keeping of a journal, that epistolary courtship revealed to me the power in writing. It convinced me that language can be a showing forth rather than a hiding, a joining rather than a sundering. It persuaded me that we can discover who we are through the search for words. In composing those letters, I was moved by affection for my reader and my subject, as I am still moved by affection in all that I write.

Marriage to Ruth is the air I have breathed now for over half my life. From the richness of marriage, its depths and delights, I have learned the meaning of commitment—to a person, to a place, to a chosen work. Outside of this union I would have written quite different books, or perhaps none at all. To speak adequately of our shared life would require a much longer story; I have made a beginning, but only a beginning, in my fourth book of personal narratives, *Staying Put.*

At Cambridge, once more I was a duck among swans. Once more I felt raw and rough, like a backwoodsman trying to move in the parlors of the gentry without upsetting the tea cart or the vicar. Despite my good marriage, despite my success at Brown, despite the scholarship that had brought me to England, I still needed to prove myself. It seemed to me that all the other students were entering upon their rightful inheritance, while I had to earn, day by day, the privilege of being there.

For the subject of my dissertation I chose D. H. Lawrence. He was another outsider, another scholarship boy, with a father given to drink, a mother given to worry, a childhood divided between ugly industry and beautiful countryside. I was troubled by much of what Lawrence wrote about women, and I despised his authoritarian politics. I grew impatient when he played the shaman or crowed about blood. Yet he knew how it feels to emerge from the hinterland and fight to join the great conversation of culture. He honored the work of hands, whether of colliers or gamekeepers or cooks. He wrote about the Earth, about flowers and birds and beasts, with something close to the shimmer of life itself. He knew that we are bound through our flesh to the whole of nature, and that nature may be all we can glimpse of the sacred. The dissertation, much revised, became my first book, *D. H. Lawrence: The World of the Major Novels.* Whatever it may reveal about Lawrence, it says a great deal about me.

On the sly, while pursuing graduate studies, I began writing stories. The earliest of them were clumsy and gaudy efforts to speak of what I found troubling in my own life—the Arsenal, the bombs, the black prisoners on that Tennessee farm, the pinched lives of poor whites in Ohio, my father's drinking, my mother's discontent, the war that was devouring my generation. The stories were clumsy because I was a beginner. They were gaudy because I felt I had to dress up my scrawny experience in costumes borrowed from the great modernists—from Lawrence, of course, but also from Joyce, Woolf, Gide, Proust, Yeats, and Eliot. I fancied that the point of writing was to dazzle your readers, keep them off balance, show them what intricate knots you could tie with strings of words. I suspected that real life occurred only on foreign soil, usually in cities, and among bored expatriates.

I was saved from the worst of these illusions through reading another modernist, a Mississippian like my father, a man haunted by the legacy of racism and by the sound of American speech. Faulkner inspired me for a spell to even flashier verbal hotdogging, but, along with Lawrence and Mark Twain, he cured me of thinking that the life I knew on back roads was too obscure or too shabby for literature. Eventually I stopped showing off, accepted the material that my life had given me, and began learning to say as directly as I could what I had to say.

During those years in England I formed the habit of rising at five or six, to write for a couple of hours before breakfast, before looking at the calendar, before yielding to the demands of the day. The world's hush, broken only by birdsong or passing cars, the pool of light on the table encircled by darkness, the peck of the keyboard, the trail of ink on paper—these became the elements in a morning ritual that I have practiced ever since. I wake early in order to write, and I write in order to come more fully awake.

A few of those stories, written dawn after dawn, found their way into British magazines, the very first in *Cambridge Review* in 1968, when I was twenty-two, then others in *Transatlantic Review* and *Stand* the following year. I suspect that the editors overlooked my feverish style for the sake of my characters—the Mississippi sharecroppers and Ohio prophets and Greyhound bus riders—whom they would rarely if ever have met before through Her Majesty's mails. When I received my first check, I was amazed that a magazine would not only do me the honor of printing my work but would actually pay me for it. To celebrate, Ruth and I took these unexpected few pounds and went to see an exhibit of van Gogh's paintings in London. By 1969 I was reviewing fiction for *Cambridge Review,* and over the next two years I served as that magazine's literary editor. My association with this old, illustrious journal, and my friendship with the young, industrious editors, Eric Homberger and Iain Wright, were crucial in helping me see my way toward becoming a writer.

With the change left over from my scholarship and with money Ruth earned as a teacher's aide, we traveled during vacations all over Europe and the British Isles. For me, these were literary pilgrimages, so that in Ireland I was looking for Joyce and Yeats, in Wales for Dylan Thomas, in Scotland for Burns. Inevitably, I saw the Lake District through the lines of Wordsworth and Coleridge, London through Dickens and Orwell and Woolf, the industrial Midlands through Lawrence, the southern counties through Wells and James, the western counties through Austen and Hardy, all of England through Shakespeare. I read Balzac, Hugo, and Sartre in Paris, Cervantes in Madrid, Kafka in Prague, Günter Grass in Berlin, Thomas Mann in Venice, Calvino in Rome. Traveling with books, I came to understand that all enduring literature is local, rooted in place, in landscape or cityscape, in particular ways of speech and climates of mind.

In 1971, I brought back with me from England a fresh Ph.D. and a suitcase of manuscripts. The degree had earned me several offers of teaching jobs. (I never considered trying to write without holding a job. The unemployed men I had known while growing up were miserable, humiliated, broken.) I chose to come to Indiana University because it is in my home region, the Midwest, because it attracts students with backgrounds similar to my own, and because the people who interviewed me for the job had gone to the trouble of reading my fiction as well as my criticism. They wanted me to come, they assured me, even if I turned out to be a writer instead of a scholar. Here I came, and here I have stayed. Of course I travel; I spend months and even occasional years living elsewhere. I hear the call of cities and oceans, mountains and museums. But I keep returning to this terrain, this town, this house, this work. The why and how of that commitment became the subject of *Staying Put.*

Fidelity to place, not common for writers in any part of the United States, may be least common of all in the Midwest. This region is more famous for the writers who have left than for those who have stayed. Samuel Clemens, William Dean Howells, Willa Cather, Ernest Hemingway, F. Scott Fitzgerald, Theodore Dreiser, T. S. Eliot, Sherwood Anderson, Hart Crane, Langston Hughes, Kurt Vonnegut, Robert Coover, Toni Morrison: the list of departed midwesterners is long and luminous. You don't have to look hard for reasons to leave. The region has not been very hospitable to writers. Vachel Lindsay, who chose to stay and make his poems in Springfield, Illinois, complained of "the usual Middle West crucifixion of the artist." I think he had in mind the grudging, grinding legacy of puritanical religion and agrarian politics: art may shock Grandmother or corrupt the children; you cannot raise art in the fields or mass-produce it in factories, cannot sell it by the pound. Publishers and reviewers, most of whom live on the coasts, often regard the heart of the country as an emptiness one must fly over on the way between New York and California.

The message of all those departures from the Midwest is that life happens elsewhere, in Boston or Paris, in the suburbs of London or San Francisco. Some editors and fellow writers have asked me, directly or indirectly, how I can bear to live in a backwater. I tell them there are no backwaters. There is only one river, and we are all in it. Wave your arm, and the ripples will eventually reach me. For the writer, for anyone, where you live is less important than how devotedly and perceptively you inhabit that place. I stay here in the Midwest out of affection for the land, the people, the accents and foods, the look of towns and lay of farms, for the trees and flowers and beasts. I also stay from a sense of responsibility. Every acre of the planet could use some steady attention. I open my eyes on a place that has scarcely been written about. However great or small my talents, here is where they will do the most good.

Those talents did not bear much fruit during my first years in Indiana. I revised the Lawrence book, which appeared from a London publisher in 1973 and from Viking Press in 1974. On the strength of my few, feverish stories, two senior

## Letter to a Reader

Viking editors, Marshall Best and Malcolm Cowley, secured for me a modest advance on a first novel. I had been laboring on a novel called *Warchild* since returning from England, but I was at last able to complete it thanks to the generosity of Phillips Exeter Academy, in New Hampshire, where I spent the school year of 1974–75 as writer in residence. The hero was a young man suspiciously like myself: born under the sign of the mushroom cloud, reared on an army munitions base, conscientious objector during the Vietnam War. In passing, the novel also chronicled the decline of industrial civilization and the death of nature. Thomas Mann in his late years or Tolstoy in his prime might have done justice to my scheme; I could not. In all of its innumerable drafts, *Warchild* remained a sprawling, operatic, rambunctious book. Just before I mailed it to Cowley and Best, Viking was purchased by Penguin, and as a result the lesser contracts, including mine, soon became scrap paper. After the gloom cleared, I realized that the world was better off with *Warchild* in a box on my shelf.

While at Exeter, in mourning for my botched first novel, I chanced to read the account of a murder that had occurred in 1813 in the northeastern Ohio county of Portage, where I grew up. A roving peddler was killed in the woods near the county seat. Suspicion immediately fell on the muscular back of a gigantic foundryman who had been carrying the peddler's goods. Two local men volunteered to pursue the giant through the woods. They caught up with him, led him back for trial, and assisted at his hanging. After the burial, three separate groups tried to steal the huge corpse. All this transpired against the bloody backdrop of the War of 1812, amid skirmishes with the English and the Indians. The conjunction of war and wilderness, a fearful village and a mysterious fugitive, set me thinking. The fruit of that thinking, begun in Exeter and carried on intermittently for eight years, was *Bad Man Ballad*, a novel that opens with birdsong and closes with human song, veering from history toward myth. The concerns of the book are not so different from those of *Warchild*, for I was still trying to figure out how we Americans had become so violent—toward strangers and neighbors, toward animals and trees and the land itself.

Reading in my haphazard way about the frontier period in the Ohio Valley, hoping to get the feel of history into *Bad Man Ballad*, I kept turning up curious anecdotes about the settlers. An escaped slave, a philosophical cobbler, a savvy farmer, a love-struck carpenter would be preserved in the dusty chronicles on the strength of a single flamboyant gesture. A few of these worthies made their way into *Bad Man Ballad* as minor characters, but most of them would not fit. Unwilling to abandon them once more to the archives, yet unwilling to interrupt work on my novel long enough to write full stories, I began composing two-page summaries of what I found memorable in these frontier lives.

At first, I thought I would return to elaborate these compressed narratives later on; but I soon found them to be satisfying in all their brevity, with a flavor of ballads and folktales, forms that have always appealed to me because they cut to the heart of experience. Over the next few years I kept writing these miniature tales in batches, until I had accumulated fifty, spanning the period of settlement in the Ohio Valley, from the Revolution to the Civil War. These were gathered into *Wilderness Plots,* a slim volume for which I feel an ample fondness, in part because it came to me like an unexpected child, in part because, although it was the fourth book of fiction I wrote, it was the first one published.

By now you may have noticed, if you pay attention to dates, that long periods elapsed between the writing of my early books and their publication. This is a fate so common for young writers, and so discouraging, as to deserve a few words here. The latest of the stories in *Fetching the Dead* was completed seven years before that book appeared. *Bad Man Ballad* took five years to reach print and *Terrarium,* my next novel, took four. By the time William Morrow gave me a contract for *Wilderness Plots* in 1982, I had been writing seriously for a dozen years, with only a single book of criticism to show for it. Dawn after dawn I forced myself from bed, hid away in my cramped study, bent over the keyboard, and hammered lines across the blank pages, all the while struggling to ignore the voices of my young children, first Eva and then Jesse, who clamored at the door, struggling to forget the well-meaning questions of friends who asked me whatever had become of this book or that, fighting against my own doubts. Every writer must pass through such seasons of despondency, some for shorter periods, some for longer. Each of us must find reasons to keep on.

What kept me writing? Stubbornness, for one thing—a refusal to give up certain stories, questions, images, and characters. The pleasure of living among words, for another thing. When I was in the flow of work, I felt free and whole. I played the eighty-eight keys of language as a musician improvises on piano, my fingers and ears captured by it, my body swaying. Although it is unfashionable to say so, a good marriage also helped me to keep writing. I hid my gloom from everyone except Ruth, who stood by me in the dark, and who urged me to follow my talent, no matter how crooked it was, no matter if the world never took any notice.

In the late 1970s, even while my books languished, my short fiction continued to appear in magazines, mostly quarterlies and reviews. For me, as for many writers of my generation, the magazines—with their underpaid editors working on shoestring budgets—have provided a training ground and a community of readers. In the years when I could but dimly see my way forward, I was greatly encouraged by a handful of editors—Roger Mitchell at *Minnesota Review,* Wayne Dodd at *Ohio Review,* Stanley Lindberg at *Georgia Review,* Robley Wilson at *North American Review,* and Ellen Datlow at *Omni.*

The final item in that list may strike you as out of place. Unlike the others, *Omni* was a glossy production, paid handsomely, and published science fiction. After exploring the past in *Bad Man Ballad* and *Wilderness Plots,* I began pushing my questions into the future. Where might our fear of wildness and our infatuation with technology lead us? How far could we carry our divorce from nature? What might keep us from ravaging the Earth? According to the arbitrary divisions imposed by critics and publishers, to speculate about the future is to enter the realm of science fiction. And yet, whether set in past or future, all my fiction interrogates the present.

Beginning with a visit to Oregon in 1978–79, and continuing for the next ten years, I wrote a series of stories that appeared in *Omni, The Magazine of Fantasy and Science Fiction, Isaac Asimov's Science Fiction Magazine, New Dimensions,* and several anthologies; and I wrote three speculative novels. The first of these, *Terrarium,* arose from a nightmare image of domed cities afloat on the oceans, all bound into a global network by translucent tubes. Citizens of this Enclosure would pass their whole lives without going outside, without meeting anything except what humans had made. Set over against this claustrophobic image were the green mountains and rocky coast of Oregon, where *Terrarium* was conceived, and where my fictional renegades would try to make a new life. I returned to this Enclosure world in *The Engineer of Beasts,* a novel whose central figure builds robot animals for disneys, the successors to zoos in those denatured cities. The central figure in *The Invisible Company,* third of my future histories, is a physicist who must come to terms with the lethal consequences of his own early discoveries, while caught in a technological masquerade inspired by Thomas Mann's *Death in Venice.*

As though I had not already violated enough boundaries by writing science fiction, historical fiction, criticism, fables, and short stories, during the 1980s I added personal essays, documentary, biographical fiction, and children's books to my profusion of forms. And why not a profusion? The world is various. Nature itself is endlessly inventive. How dull, if birds had stopped with sparrows and not gone on to ospreys and owls. How dull, if plants had not spun on from ferns to lilacs and oaks. Why squeeze everything you have to say into one or two literary molds for the convenience of booksellers and critics? Anyone persistent enough to read my work from beginning to end will find, beneath the surface play of form, the same few themes: our place in nature, our murderous and ingenious technology, the possibilities of community, love and strife within families, the search for a spiritual ground.

The subject of my biographical fiction is John James Audubon, a virtuoso who combined a number of classic American roles: immigrant, entrepreneur, real estate speculator, salesman, artist, naturalist, frontiersman, and man of letters. He was also a neighbor of mine, in geography and spirit, because he lived for a dozen years in the Ohio Valley and he formed his vision of wilderness in contact with the birds, beasts, rivers, and woods of my region. Although I have sketched a novel about his entire life, from the illegitimate birth in Haiti to senile retirement on the Hudson River, I have thus far been able to imagine freely only his childhood and youth, about which the scholars know few facts. *Wonders Hidden* follows Audubon up to the age of eighteen, when he escaped from France to avoid Napoleon's draft and set out for America, where his name would eventually become a talisman for the protection of wildlife.

I began writing for children in response to an invitation from Richard Jackson, founder and longtime director of Bradbury Press. He liked the narrative flair of *Wilderness Plots* and wanted to know if I had considered telling stories for children. Yes indeed, I replied, for in those days I was making up stories nightly for my young son and daughter. Then propose something, he said. I offered to write my own versions of the tales that lay behind twenty American folk songs, like "Yankee Doodle" and "John Henry" and "Blue-Tailed Fly," songs my father had sung to me when I was a boy and that I now sang to Jesse and Eva. The result was *Hear the Wind Blow,* a book that runs the gamut from tragedy to farce, rejoicing all the while in our mongrel speech. Also for Bradbury Press, I adapted a pair of stories from *Wilderness Plots* to make two picture books, *Aurora Means Dawn* and *Warm as Wool;* and for Macmillan I composed a series of tales about the settlement of the Midwest, including *Here Comes the Mystery Man, The Floating House,* and *A Place Called Freedom.* Children are a tough audience, refusing to feign an interest they do not feel, and they are also an inspiring one, for they have not lost their delight in the play of words and the shapes of stories, nor their capacity for wonder.

I was lured into writing a documentary narrative by the quirks of my childhood and the accidents of geology. My home in southern Indiana happens to be surrounded by the largest outcropping of premium limestone in North America. Wherever you see gritty stone buildings the color of biscuits or gravy, from New York's Empire State skyscraper to San Francisco's City Hall, from the Pentagon to the Dallas Museum of Art and Chicago's Tribune Tower, you may well be looking at rock that was quarried and milled in my neighborhood. After a boyhood on farms and construction sites, near munitions load lines and factories and workshops, I am drawn to men and women who labor with their bodies, using heavy tools to wrestle with raw, stubborn matter. So how could I resist the quarries, with their bristling derricks, or the humpbacked mills with their perpetual grinding, or the stone cutters with their shrewd eyes and skilled hands? In its original version, my portrait of these people and their landscape appeared with photographs by Jeffrey Wolin in a volume entitled *Stone Country*, and then my revised text appeared later, without photos, as *In Limestone Country*.

Some years earlier, baffled in my work on a novel, I had begun writing another kind of nonfiction, the personal essays that would be collected in *The Paradise of Bombs, Secrets of the Universe, Staying Put*, and *Writing from the Center*. The earliest of these were straightforward accounts of experiences that had moved me— carrying my infant son up a mountain in Oregon, listening to owls beside an Indiana lake. Gradually I enlarged the scope of the essays until they began to disclose patterns in my life that I had never before seen, such as the confrontation between wilderness and technology in "At Play in the Paradise of Bombs," or the legacy of a rural childhood in "Coming from the Country," or the impact of my father's drinking in "Under the Influence," or the quest for the holy in "Wayland." Although grounded in the personal, all my essays push toward the impersonal; I reflect on my own experience in hopes of illuminating the experience of others.

The challenge for any writer is to be faithful at once to your vision and your place, to the truth you have laboriously found and the people whom this truth might serve. In order to work, I must withdraw into solitude, must close my door against the world and close my mind against the day's news. But unless the writing returns me to the life of family, friends, and neighbors with renewed energy and insight, then it has failed. My writing is an invitation to community, an exploration of what connects us to one another and to the Earth.

I love words, yet I love the world more. I do not think of language as thread for a private game of cat's cradle, but as a web flung out, attaching me to the creation. Of course the medium is constantly debased. Television, advertising, government, and schools have so cheapened or inflated language that many writers doubt whether it can still be used in the search for understanding. But knowledge has never been handed to us like pebbles or potatoes; we have always had to dig it up for ourselves. All of culture, writing included, is a struggle over how we should imagine our lives.

Stories are containers in which we carry some of those imaginings. They are the pots and bowls and baskets we use for preserving and sharing our discoveries. Whether in fiction, film, poetry, drama, or essays, stories tell about human character and action, and the consequences of character and action; by making stories and reading them, we are testing ways of being human. It seems idle to protest, as many critics do, that stories are artificial, since everything we make is shot through with artifice. To protest that experience is scattered, not gathered neatly as in stories, is no more than to say that seeds and berries are scattered, not gathered as in the bowl we have filled for supper.

Without venturing into metaphysics, where I would soon get lost, I need to declare that I believe literature is more than self-regarding play. It gestures beyond itself toward the universe, of which you and I are vanishingly small parts. The moves in writing are not abstract, like those in algebra or chess, for words cannot be unhooked from the world. They come freighted with memory and feeling. Linguists describe our ordinary speech as a "natural" language, to distinguish it from the formal codes of mathematics or computers or logic. The label is appropriate, a reminder that everyday language is *wild;* no one defines or controls it. You can never force words to mean only and exactly what you wish them to mean, for they escape every trap you lay for them.

Insofar as my writing is important, it gains that importance from what it witnesses to. I have written from the outset with a pressing awareness of the world's barbarities—the bombing of cities, oppression of the poor, extinction of species, exhaustion of soil, pollution of water and air, murder, genocide, racism, war. If I stubbornly believe that nature is resilient, that love is potent, that humankind may be truly kind, I do so in the face of this cruelty and waste. Without denying evil, literature ought to reduce the amount of suffering, in however small a degree, and not only human suffering but that of all creatures. Although we cannot live without causing harm, we could cause much less harm than we presently do.

The desire to articulate a shared world is the root impulse of literature as it is of science. Individual scientists, like writers, may be cutthroat competitors, out for their own glory; but science itself, the great cathedral of ideas slowly rising, is a common enterprise. Perhaps the symbol for literature should be a rambling library, to which each of us adds a line, a page, a few books. Whether one is a scientist or a writer, the universe outshines those of us who glimpse a bit of it and report what we see. Right now we urgently need to rethink our place on Earth, to discover ways of living that do not devour the planet, and this need is far more important than the accomplishments of all writers put together. The health of our land and our fellow creatures is the ultimate measure of the worth and sanity of our lives.

I am forty-eight as I compose this letter to you. I have been writing seriously for twenty-five years, skillfully for about fifteen. Given decent luck, I might continue making books for another twenty-five years. So I think of myself as being midway in my journey as a writer. My steady desire has been to wake up, not to sleepwalk through this brief, miraculous life. I wish to go about with mind and senses alert to the splendor of the world. I wish to see the burning bush.

Writing is hard labor, shot through with intervals of joy. If there were no pleasure in the sinewy turns of a sentence, the bubbling up of an idea, the finding of a path through the maze, who would keep going? I feel the need to tell you many things for which there is no room in a letter, even a long letter. Nothing I have told you here can replace my books, which live or die in the minds of readers like you, and which bear on their current of words more meanings than I know.

# Buckeye

Years after my father's heart quit, I keep in a wooden box on my desk the two buckeyes that were in his pocket when he died. Once the size of plums, the brown seeds are shriveled now, hollow, hard as pebbles, yet they still gleam from the polish of his hands. He used to reach for them in his overalls or suit pants and click them together, or he would draw them out, cupped in his palm, and twirl them with his blunt carpenter's fingers, all the while humming snatches of old tunes.

"Do you really believe buckeyes keep off arthritis?" I asked him more than once.

He would flex his hands and say, "I do so far."

My father never paid much heed to pain. Near the end, when his worn knee often slipped out of joint, he would pound it back in place with a rubber mallet. If a splinter worked into his flesh beyond the reach of tweezers, he would heat the blade of his knife over a cigarette lighter and slice through the skin. He sought to ward off arthritis not because he feared pain but because he lived through his hands, and he dreaded the swelling of knuckles, the stiffening of fingers. What use would he be if he could no longer hold a hammer or guide a plow? When he was a boy he had known farmers not yet forty years old whose hands had curled into claws, men so crippled up they could not tie their own shoes, could not sign their names.

"I mean to tickle my grandchildren when they come along," he told me, "and I mean to build dollhouses and turn spindles for tiny chairs on my lathe."

So he fondled those buckeyes as if they were charms, carrying them with him when our family moved from Ohio at the end of my childhood, bearing them to new homes in Louisiana, then Oklahoma, Ontario, and Mississippi, carrying them still on his final day when pain a thousand times fiercer than arthritis gripped his heart.

The box where I keep the buckeyes also comes from Ohio, made by my father from a walnut plank he bought at a farm auction. I remember the auction, remember the sagging face of the widow whose home was being sold, remember my father telling her he would prize that walnut as if he had watched the tree grow from a sapling on his own land. He did not care for pewter or silver or gold, but he cherished wood. On the rare occasions when my mother coaxed him into a museum, he ignored the paintings or porcelain and studied the exhibit cases, the banisters, the moldings, the parquet floors.

I remember him planing that walnut board, sawing it, sanding it, joining piece to piece to make footstools, picture frames, jewelry boxes. My own box, a bit larger than a soap dish, lined with red corduroy, was meant to hold earrings and pins, not buckeyes. The top is inlaid with pieces fitted so as to bring out the grain, four diagonal joints converging from the corners toward the center. If I stare long enough at those converging lines, they float free of the box and point to a center deeper than wood.

I learned to recognize buckeyes and beeches, sugar maples and shagbark hickories, wild cherries, walnuts, and dozens of other trees while tramping through the Ohio woods with my father. To his eyes, their shapes, their leaves, their bark, their winter buds were as distinctive as the set of a friend's shoulders. As with friends, he was partial to some, craving their company, so he would go out of his way to visit particular trees, walking in a circle around the splayed roots of a sycamore, laying his hand against the trunk of a white oak, ruffling the feathery green boughs of a cedar.

"Trees breathe," he told me. "Listen."

I listened, and heard the stir of breath.

He was no botanist; the names and uses he taught me were those he had learned from country folks, not from books. Latin never crossed his lips. Only much later would I discover that the tree he called ironwood, its branches like muscular arms, good for ax handles, is known in the books as hop hornbeam; what he called canoe wood, ideal for log cabins, is officially tulip tree; what he called hoop ash, good for barrels and fence posts, appears in books as hackberry.

When he introduced me to the buckeye, he broke off a chunk of the gray bark and held it to my nose. I gagged.

"That's why the old-timers called it stinking buckeye," he told me. "They used it for cradles and feed troughs and peg legs."

"Why for peg legs?" I asked.

"Because it's light and hard to split, so it won't shatter when you're clumping around."

He showed me this tree in late summer, when the fruits had fallen and the ground was littered with prickly brown pods. He picked up one, as fat as a lemon, and peeled away the husk to reveal the shiny seed. He laid it in my palm and closed my fist around it so the seed peeped out from the circle formed by my index finger and thumb. "You see where it got the name?" he asked.

I saw: what gleamed in my hand was the eye of a deer, bright with life. "It's beautiful," I said.

"It's beautiful," my father agreed, "but also poisonous. Nobody eats buckeyes, except maybe a fool squirrel."

I knew the gaze of deer from living in the Ravenna Arsenal, in Portage County, up in the northeastern corner of Ohio. After supper we often drove the Arsenal's gravel roads, past the munitions bunkers, past acres of rusting tanks and wrecked bombers, into the far fields where we counted deer. One June evening, while mist rose from the ponds, we counted three hundred and eleven, our family record. We found the deer in herds, in bunches, in amorous pairs. We came upon lone bucks, their antlers lifted against the sky like the bare branches of dogwood. If you were quiet, if your hands were empty, if you moved slowly, you could leave the car and steal to within a few paces of a grazing deer, close enough to see the delicate lips, the twitching nostrils, the glossy, fathomless eyes.

The wooden box on my desk holds these grazing deer, as it holds the buckeyes and the walnut plank and the farm auction and the munitions bunkers and the breathing forests and my father's hands. I could lose the box, I could lose the polished seeds, but if I were to lose the memories I would become a bush without roots, and every new breeze would toss me about. All those memories lead back to the northeastern corner of Ohio, the place where I came to consciousness, where I learned to connect feelings with words, where I fell in love with the Earth.

It was a troubled love, for much of the land I knew as a child had been ravaged. The ponds in the Arsenal teemed with bluegill and beaver, but they were also laced with TNT from the making of bombs. Because the wolves and coyotes had long since been killed, some of the deer, so plump in the June grass, collapsed on the January snow, whittled by hunger to racks of bones. Outside the Arsenal's high barbed fences, many of the farms had failed, their barns caving in, their topsoil gone. Ravines were choked with swollen couches and junked washing machines and cars. Crossing fields, you had to be careful not to slice your feet on tin cans or shards of glass. Most of the rivers had been dammed, turning fertile valleys into scummy playgrounds for boats.

One free-flowing river, the West Branch of the Mahoning, ran past the small farm near the Arsenal where our family lived during my later years in Ohio. We owned just enough land to pasture three ponies and grow vegetables for our table, but those few acres opened onto miles of woods and creeks and secret meadows. I walked that land in every season, every weather, following animal trails. But then the Mahoning, too, was doomed by the Army Corps; we were forced to sell our land, and a dam began to rise across the river.

If enough people had spoken for the river, we might have saved it. If enough people had believed that our scarred country was worth defending, we might have dug in our heels and fought. Our attachments to the land were all private. We had no shared lore, no literature, no art to root us there, to give us courage, to help us stand our ground. The only maps we had were those issued by the state, showing a maze of numbered lines stretched over emptiness. The Ohio landscape never showed up on postcards or posters, never unfurled like tapestry in films, rarely filled even a paragraph in books. There were no mountains in that place, no waterfalls, no rocky gorges, no vistas. It was a country of low hills, cut over woods, scoured fields, villages that had lost their purpose, roads that had lost their way.

"Let us love the country of here below," Simone Weil urged in *Waiting for God*. "It is real; it offers resistance to love. It is this country that God has given us to love. He has willed that it should be difficult yet possible to love it." Which is the deeper truth about buckeyes, their poison or their beauty? I hold with the beauty; or rather, I am held by the beauty, without forgetting the poison. In my corner of Ohio the gullies were choked with trash, yet cedars flickered up like green flames from cracks in stone; in the evening bombs exploded at the ammunition dump, yet from the darkness came the mating cries of owls. I was saved from despair by knowing a few men and women who cared enough about the land to clean up trash, who planted walnuts and oaks that would long outlive them, who imagined a world that would have no call for bombs.

How could our hearts be large enough for heaven if they are not large enough for Earth? The only country I am certain of is the one here below. The only paradise I know is the one lit by our everyday sun, this land of difficult love, shot through with shadow. The place where we learn this love, if we learn it at all, shimmers behind every new place we inhabit.

A family move carried me away from Ohio thirty years ago; my schooling and marriage and job have kept me away ever since, except for visits in memory and in flesh. I returned to the site of our farm one cold November day, when the trees were skeletons and the ground shone with the yellow of fallen leaves. From a previous trip I knew that our house had been bulldozed, our yard and pasture had grown up in thickets, and the reservoir had flooded the woods. On my earlier visit I had merely gazed from the car, too numb with loss to climb out. But on this November day, I parked the car, drew on my hat and gloves, opened the door, and walked.

I was looking for some sign that we had lived there, some token of our affection for the place. All that I recognized, aside from the contours of the land, were two weeping willows that my father and I had planted near the road. They had been slips the length of my forearm when we set them out, and now their crowns rose higher than the telephone poles. When I touched them last, their trunks had been smooth and supple, as thin as my wrist, and now they were furrowed and stout. I took off my gloves and laid my hands against the rough bark. Immediately I felt the wince of tears. Without knowing why, I said hello to my father, quietly at first, then louder and louder, as if only shouts could reach him through the bark and miles and years.

Surprised by sobs, I turned from the willows and stumbled away toward the drowned woods, calling to my father. I sensed that he was nearby. Even as I called, I was wary of grief's deceptions. I had never seen his body after he died. By the time I reached the place of his death, a furnace had reduced him to ashes. The need to see him, to let go of him, to let go of this land and time, was powerful enough to summon mirages; I knew that. But I also knew, stumbling toward the woods, that my father was here.

At the bottom of a slope where the creek used to run, I came to an expanse of gray stumps and withered grass. It was a bay of the reservoir from which the water had retreated, the level drawn down by engineers or drought. I stood at the edge of this desolate ground, willing it back to life, trying to recall the woods where my father had taught me the names of trees. No green shoots rose. I walked out among the stumps. The grass crackled under my boots, breath rasped in my throat, but otherwise the world was silent.

*Buckeye*

Then a cry broke overhead and I looked up to see a red-tailed hawk launching out from the top of an oak. I recognized the bird from its band of dark feathers across the creamy breast and the tail splayed like rosy fingers against the sun. It was a red-tailed hawk for sure; and it was also my father. Not a symbol of my father, not a reminder, not a ghost, but the man himself, right there, circling in the air above me. I knew this as clearly as I knew the sun burned in the sky. A calm poured through me. My chest quit heaving. My eyes dried.

Hawk and father wheeled above me, circle upon circle, wings barely moving, head still. My own head was still, looking up, knowing and being known. Time scattered like fog. At length, father and hawk stroked the air with those powerful wings, three beats, and then vanished over a ridge.

The voice of my education told me then and tells me now that I did not meet my father, that I merely projected my longing onto a bird. My education may well be right; yet nothing I heard in school, nothing I've read, no lesson reached by logic has ever convinced me as utterly or stirred me as deeply as did that red-tailed hawk. Nothing in my education prepared me to love a piece of the Earth, least of all a humble, battered country like northeastern Ohio; I learned from the land itself.

Before leaving the drowned woods, I looked around at the ashen stumps, the wilted grass, and for the first time since moving from this place I was able to let it go. This ground was lost; the flood would reclaim it. But other ground could be saved, must be saved, in every watershed, every neighborhood. For each home ground we need new maps, living maps, stories and poems, photographs and paintings, essays and songs. We need to know where we are, so that we may dwell in our place with a full heart.

# The Common Life

One delicious afternoon while my daughter, Eva, was home from college for spring vacation, she invited two neighbor girls to help her make bread. The girls are sisters, five-year-old Alexandra and ten-year-old Rachel, both frolicky, with eager dark eyes and shining faces. They live just down the street from us here in Bloomington, Indiana, and whenever they see me pass by, on bicycle or on foot, they ask about Eva, whom they adore.

I was in the yard that afternoon mulching flower beds with compost, and I could hear the girls chattering as Eva led them up the sidewalk to our door. I had plenty of other chores to do in the yard, where every living thing was urgent with April. But how could I stay outside, when so much beauty and laughter and spunk were gathered in the kitchen?

I kept looking in on the cooks, until Eva finally asked, "Daddy, you wouldn't like to knead some dough, would you?"

"I'd love to," I said. "You sure there's room for me?"

"There's room," Eva replied, "but you'll have to wash in the basement."

Hands washed, I took my place at the counter beside Rachel and Alexandra, who perched on a stool I had made for Eva when she was a toddler. Eva had still needed that stool when she learned to make bread on this counter; and my son, now six feet tall, had balanced there as well for his own first lessons in cooking. I never needed the stool, but I needed the same teacher—my wife Ruth, a woman with eloquent fingers.

Our kitchen is small; Ruth and I share that cramped space by moving in a kind of dance we have been practicing for years. When we bump one another, it is usually for the pleasure of bumping. But Eva and the girls and I jostled like

162

birds too numerous for a nest. We spattered flour everywhere. We told stories. We joked. All the while I bobbed on a current of bliss, delighting in the feel of live dough beneath my fingers, the smell of yeast, the piping of child-voices so much like the birdsong cascading through our open windows, the prospect of whole-wheat loaves hot from the oven.

An artist might paint this kitchen scene in pastels for a poster, with a tender motto below, as evidence that all is right with the world. All is manifestly *not* right with the world. The world, most of us would agree, is a mess: rife with murder and mayhem, abuse of land, extinction of species, lying and theft and greed. There are days when I can see nothing but a spectacle of cruelty and waste, and the weight of dismay pins me to my chair. On such days I need a boost merely to get up, uncurl my fists, and go about my work. The needed strength may come from family, from neighbors, from a friend's greeting in the mail, from the forked leaves of larkspur breaking ground, from rainstorms and music and wind, from the lines of a handmade table or the lines in a well-worn book, from the taste of an apple or the brash trill of finches in our backyard trees. Strength also comes to me from memories of times when I have felt a deep and complex joy, a sense of being exactly where I should be and doing exactly what I should do, as I felt on that bread-making afternoon.

I wish to reflect on the sources of that joy, that sense of being utterly in place, because I suspect they are the sources of all that I find authentic in my life. So much in life seems to me inauthentic, I cannot afford to let the genuine passages slip by without considering what makes them ring true. It is as though I spend my days wandering about, chasing false scents, lost, and then occasionally, for a few ticks of the heart, I stumble onto the path. While making bread with my daughter and her two young friends, I was on the path. So I recall that time now as a way of keeping company with Eva, who has gone back to college, but also as a way of discovering in our common life a reservoir of power and hope.

What is so powerful, so encouraging, in that kitchen scene? To begin with, I love my three fellow cooks; I relish every tilt of their heads and turn of their voices. In their presence I feel more alive and alert, as if the rust had been knocked off my nerves. The armor of self dissolves, ego relaxes its grip, and I am simply there, on the breeze of the moment.

Rachel and Alexandra belong to the Abed family, with whom we often share food and talk and festivities. We turn to the Abeds for advice, for starts of plants, for cheer, and they likewise turn to us. Not long ago they received troubling news that may force them to move away, and we have been sharing in their distress. So the Abed girls brought into our kitchen a history of neighborliness, a history all the more valuable because it might soon come to an end.

The girls also brought a readiness to learn what Eva had to teach. Eva, as I mentioned, had learned from Ruth how to make bread, and Ruth had learned from a Canadian friend, and our friend had learned from her grandmother. As Rachel and Alexandra shoved their hands into the dough, I could imagine the rope of knowledge stretching back and back through generations, to folks who ground their grain with stones and did their baking in woodstoves or fireplaces or in pits of glowing coals.

If you have made yeast bread, you know how at first the dough clings to your fingers, and then gradually, as you knead in more flour, it begins to pull away and take on a life of its own, becoming at last as resilient as a plump belly. If you have not made yeast bread, no amount of hearing or reading about it will give you that knowledge, because you have to learn through your body, through fingers and wrists and aching forearms, through shoulders and back. Much of what we know comes to us that way, passed on from person to person, age after age, surviving in muscle and bone. I learned from my mother how to transplant a seedling, how to sew on a button; I learned from my father how to saw a board square, how to curry a horse, how to change the oil in a car. The pleasure I take in sawing or currying, in planting or sewing, even in changing oil, like my pleasure in making bread, is bound up with the affection I feel for my teachers and the respect I feel for the long, slow accumulation of knowledge that informs our simplest acts.

Those simple acts come down to us because they serve real needs. You plant a tree or sweep a floor or rock a baby without asking the point of your labors. You patch the roof to stop a leak, patch a sweater to keep from having to throw it out. You pluck the banjo because it tickles your ears and rouses Grandpa to dance. None of us can live entirely by such meaningful acts; our jobs, if nothing else, often push us through empty motions. But unless at least some of what we do has a transparent purpose, answering not merely to duty or fashion but to actual needs, then the heart has gone out of our work. What art could be more plainly valuable than cooking? The reason for baking bread is as palpable as your tongue. After our loaves were finished, Eva and I delivered two of them to the Abeds, who showed in their faces a perfect understanding of the good of bread.

When I compare the dough to a plump belly, I hear the sexual overtones, of course. By making the comparison, I do not wish to say, with Freud, that every sensual act is a surrogate for sex; on the contrary, I believe sex comes closer to being a stand-in, rather brazen and obvious, like a ham actor pretending to be the whole show, when it is only one player in the drama of our sensual life. That life flows through us constantly, so long as we do not shut ourselves off. The sound of birds and the smell of April dirt and the brush of wind through the open door were all ingredients in the bread we baked.

Before baking, the yeast was alive, dozing in the refrigerator. Scooped out of its jar, stirred into warm water, fed on sugar, it soon bubbled out gas to leaven the loaves. You have to make sure the water for the yeast, like milk for a baby, is neither too hot nor too cold, and so, as for a baby's bottle, I test the temperature on my wrist. The flour, too, had been alive not long before as wheat thriving in sun and rain. Our nourishment is borrowed life. You need not be a Christian to feel, in a bite of bread, a sense of communion with the energy that courses through all things. The lump in your mouth is a chunk of Earth; there is nothing else to eat. In our house we say grace before meals, to remind ourselves of that gift and that dependence.

The elements of my kitchen scene—loving company, neighborliness, inherited knowledge and good work, shared purpose, sensual delight, and union with the creation—sum up for me what is vital in community. Here is the spring of hope I have been led to by my trail of bread. In our common life we may find the strength not merely to carry on in face of the world's bad news, but to resist cruelty and waste. I speak of it as common because it is ordinary, because we make it together, because it binds us through time to the rest of humanity and through our bodies to the rest of nature. By honoring this common life, nurturing it, carrying it steadily in mind, we might renew our households and neighborhoods and cities, and in doing so might redeem ourselves from the bleakness of private lives spent in frenzied pursuit of sensation and wealth.

Ever since the eclipse of our native cultures, the dominant American view has been more nearly the opposite: that we should cultivate the self rather than the community; that we should look to the individual as the source of hope and the center of value, while expecting hindrance and harm from society.

What other view could have emerged from our history? The first Europeans to reach America were daredevils and treasure seekers, as were most of those who mapped the interior. Many colonists were renegades of one stripe or another, some of them religious nonconformists, some political rebels, more than a few of them fugitives from the law. The trappers, hunters, traders, and free-booters who pushed the frontier westward seldom recognized any authority beyond the reach of their own hands. Coast to coast, our land has been settled and our cities have been filled by generations of immigrants more intent on leaving behind old tyrannies than on seeking new social bonds.

Our government was forged in rebellion against alien control. Our economy was founded on the sanctity of private property, and thus our corporations have taken on a sacred immunity through being defined under the law as persons. Our criminal justice system is so careful to protect the rights of individuals that it may require years to convict a bank robber who killed a bystander in front of a crowd, or a bank official who left a trail of embezzlement as wide as the Mississippi.

Our religion has been marked by an evangelical Protestantism that emphasizes personal salvation rather than social redemption. To "Get Right with God," as signs along the roads here in the Midwest gravely recommend, does not mean to reconcile your fellow citizens to the divine order, but to make a separate peace, to look after the eternal future of your own singular soul. True, we have a remarkable history of communal experiments, many of them religiously inspired—from Plymouth Colony, through the Shaker villages, Robert Owen's New Harmony, the settlements at Oneida, Amana, and countless other places, to the communes in our own day. But these are generally known to us, if they are known at all, as utopian failures.

For much of the present century, Americans have been fighting various forms of collectivism—senile empires during World War I, then Nazism, Communism, and now fundamentalist theocracies—and these wars, the shouting kind as well as the shooting kind, have only strengthened our commitment to individualism. We have understood freedom for the most part negatively rather than positively, as release from constraints rather than as the condition for making a decent life in common. Hands off, we say; give me elbow room; good fences make good neighbors; my home is my castle; don't tread on me. I'm looking out for number one, we say; I'm doing my own thing. We have a Bill of Rights, which protects each of us from a bullying society, but no Bill of Responsibilities, which would oblige us to answer the needs of others.

Even where America's founding documents clearly address the public good, they have often been turned to private ends. Consider just one notorious example, the Second Amendment to the Constitution: "A well regulated Militia, being necessary to the security of a free State, the right of the people to keep and bear Arms, shall not be infringed." It would be difficult to say more plainly that arms are to be kept for the sake of a militia, and a militia is to be kept for defense of the country. In our day, a reasonable person might judge that the Pentagon deploys quite enough weapons, without requiring any supplement from household arsenals. Yet this lucid passage has been construed to justify a domestic arms race, until we now have in America more gun shops than gas stations, we have nearly as many handguns as hands, and we have concentrated enough firepower in the average city to carry on a war—which is roughly what, in some cities, is going on. Thus, by reading the Second Amendment through the lens of individualism, we have turned a provision for public safety into a guarantee of public danger.

Observe how zealously we have carved up our cities and paved our land and polluted our air and burned up most of the Earth's petroleum within a single generation—all for the sake of the automobile, a symbol of personal autonomy even more potent than the gun. There is a contemptuous ring to the word "mass" in mass transportation, as if the only alternative to private cars were cattle cars. Motorcycles and snowmobiles and four-wheelers fill our public lands with the din of engines and tear up the terrain, yet any effort to restrict their use is denounced as an infringement of individual rights. Millions of motorists exercise those rights by hurling the husks of their pleasures onto the roadside, boxes and bottles and bags. Ravines and ditches in my part of the country are crammed with rusty cars and refrigerators, burst couches and stricken TVs, which their former owners would not bother to haul to the dump. Meanwhile, advertisers sell us everything from jeeps to jeans as tokens of freedom, and we are so infatuated with the sovereign self that we fall for the spiel, as if by purchasing one of a million identical products we could distinguish ourselves from the herd.

The cult of the individual shows up everywhere in American lore, which celebrates drifters, rebels, and loners, while pitying or reviling the pillars of the community. The backwoods explorer like Daniel Boone, the riverboat rowdy like Mike Fink, the lumberjack, the prospector, the rambler and gambler, the daring crook like Jesse James or the resourceful killer like Billy the Kid, along with countless lonesome cowboys, all wander, unattached, through the great spaces of our imagination. When society begins to close in, making demands and asking questions, our heroes hit the road. Like Huckleberry Finn, they are forever lighting out for the Territory, where nobody will tell them what to do. Huck Finn ran away from what he called civilization in order to leave behind the wickedness of slavery, and who can blame him, but he was also running away from church and school and neighbors, from aunts who made him wash before meals, from girls who cramped his style, from chores, from gossip, from the whole nuisance of living alongside other people.

In our literature, when community enters at all, it is likely to appear as a conspiracy against the free soul of a hero or heroine. Recall how restless Natty Bumppo becomes whenever Cooper drags him in from the woods to a settlement. Remember how strenuously Emerson preaches against conforming to society and in favor of self-reliance, how earnestly Hawthorne warns us about the tyranny of those Puritan villages. Think of Thoreau running errands in Concord, rushing in the front door of a house and out the back, then home to his cabin in the woods, never pausing, lest he be caught in the snares of the town. Think of the revulsion Edna Pontellier feels toward the Creole society of New Orleans in Kate Chopin's *The Awakening*. Think of Willa Cather's or Toni Morrison's or James Baldwin's high-spirited women and men who can thrive only by fleeing their home communities. Think of Spoon River, Winesburg, Gopher Prairie, Zenith, all those oppressive fictional places, the backward hamlets and stifling suburbs and heartless cities that are fit only for drones and drudges and mindless Babbitts.

In *The Invasion of the Body Snatchers,* a film from my childhood that still disturbs my dreams, an alien life form takes over one person after another in a small town, merging them into a single creature with a single will, until just one freethinking individual remains, and even he is clearly doomed. Along with dozens of other invasion tales, the film was a warning against Communism, I suppose, but it was also a caution against the perils of belonging, of losing your one sweet self in the group, and thus it projected a fear as old as America.

Of course you can find American books and films that speak as passionately for the virtues of our life together as for the virtues of our lives apart. To mention only a few novels from the past decade, I think of Gloria Naylor's *Mama Day,* Wendell Berry's *A Place on Earth,* Ursula Le Guin's *Always Coming Home,* and Ernest Gaines's *A Gathering of Old Men.* But they represent a minority opinion. The majority opinion fills best-seller lists and cinema screens and billboards with isolated, alienated, rebellious figures who are too potent or sensitive for membership in any group.

I have been shaped by this history, and I, too, am uneasy about groups, especially large ones, above all those that are glued together by hatred, those that use a color of skin or a cut of clothes for admission tickets, and those that wrap themselves in scriptures or flags. I have felt a chill from blundering into company where I was not wanted. I have known women and men who were scorned because they refused to fit the molds their neighbors had prepared for them. I have seen Klansmen parading in white hoods, their crosses burning on front lawns. I have seen a gang work its way through a subway car, picking on the old, the young, the weak. Through film I have watched the Nuremberg rallies, watched policemen bashing demonstrators in Chicago, missiles parading in Red Square, tanks crushing dissidents in Tiananmen Square. Like everyone born since World War II, I have grown up on television images of atrocities carried out, at home and abroad, with the blessing of governments or revolutionary armies or charismatic thugs.

In valuing community, therefore, I do not mean to approve of any and every association of people. Humans are drawn together by a variety of motives, some of them worthy, some of them ugly. Anyone who has spent recess on a school playground knows the terror of mob rule. Anyone who has lived through a war knows that mobs may pretend to speak for an entire nation. I recently saw, for the first time in a long while, a bumper sticker that recalled for me the angriest days of the Vietnam War: AMERICA—LOVE IT OR LEAVE IT. What loving America seemed to mean, for those who brandished that slogan back around 1970, was the approval of everything the government said or the army did in our name. "All those who seek to destroy the liberty of a democratic nation ought to know," Alexis de Tocqueville observed in *Democracy in America*, "that war is the surest and the shortest means to accomplish it." As a conscientious objector, with a sister who studied near my home in Ohio on a campus where National Guardsmen killed several protesters, I felt the force of despotism in that slogan.

Rather than give in to despotism, some of my friends went to jail and others into exile. My wife and I considered staying in England, where we had been studying for several years and where I had been offered a job. But instead we chose to come home, here to the Midwest where we had grown up, to work for change. In our idealism, we might have rephrased that bumper sticker to read AMERICA—LOVE IT AND REDEEM IT. For us, loving America had little to do with politicians and even less with soldiers, but very much to do with what I have been calling the common life: useful work, ordinary sights, family, neighbors, ancestors, our fellow creatures, and the rivers and woods and fields that make up our mutual home.

During the more than twenty years since returning to America, I have had some of the idealism knocked out of me, but I still believe that loving your country or city or neighborhood may require you to resist, to call for change, to speak on behalf of what you believe in, especially if what you believe in has been neglected or abused.

What we have too often neglected, in our revulsion against tyranny and our worship of the individual, is the common good. The results of that neglect are visible in the decay of our cities, the despoiling of our land, the fouling of our rivers and air, the haphazard commercial sprawl along our highways, the gluttonous feeding at the public trough, the mortgaging of our children's and grandchildren's future through our refusal to pay for current consumption. Only a people addicted to private pleasure would allow themselves to be defined as consumers—rather than as conservers or restorers—of the Earth's abundance.

In spite of the comforting assurances, from Adam Smith onwards, that the unfettered pursuit of private wealth should result in unlimited public good, we all know that to be mostly a lie. If we needed reminders of how great a lie that is, we could look at the savings and loan industry, where billions of dollars were stolen from small investors by rich managers who yearned to be richer; we could look at the Pentagon, where contracts are routinely encrusted with graft, or at Wall Street, where millionaires finagle to become billionaires through insider trading; we could look at our national forests, where logging companies buy timber for less than the cost to taxpayers of harvesting it; or we could look at our suburbs, where palaces multiply, while downtown more and more people are sleeping in cardboard boxes. Wealth does not precipitate like dew from the air; it comes out of the Earth and from the labor of many hands. When a few hands hold on to great wealth, using it only for personal ease and display, that is a betrayal of the common life, the sole source of riches.

Fortunately, while our tradition is heavily tilted in favor of private life, we also inherit a tradition of caring for the community. Although Tocqueville found much to fear and quite a bit to despise in this raw democracy, he praised Americans for having "carried to the highest perfection the art of pursuing in common the object of their common desires." Writing of what he had seen in the 1830s, Tocqueville judged Americans to be avaricious, self-serving, and aggressive; but he was also amazed by our eagerness to form clubs, to raise barns or town halls, to join together in one cause or another: "In no country in the world, do the citizens make such exertions for the common weal. I know of no people who have established schools so numerous and efficacious, places of public worship better suited to the wants of the inhabitants, or roads kept in better repair."

Today we might revise his estimate of our schools or roads, but we can still see all around us the fruits of that concern for the common weal—the libraries, museums, courthouses, hospitals, orphanages, universities, parks, on and on. Born as most of us are into places where such amenities already exist, we may take them for granted; but they would not be there for us to use had our forebears not cooperated in building them. No matter where we live, our home places have also benefited from the Granges and unions, the volunteer fire brigades, the art guilds and garden clubs, the charities, food kitchens, homeless shelters, soccer and baseball teams, the Scouts and 4-H, the Girls and Boys Clubs, the Lions and Elks and Rotarians, the countless gatherings of people who saw a need and responded to it.

This history of local care hardly ever makes it into our literature, for it is less glamorous than rebellion, yet it is a crucial part of our heritage. Any of us could cite examples of people who dug in and joined with others to make our home places better places. Women and men who invest themselves in their communities, fighting for good schools or green spaces, paying attention to where they are, seem to me as worthy of celebration as those adventurous loners who keep drifting on, prospecting for pleasure.

A few days after our bread-making, Eva and I went to a concert in Bloomington's newly opened arts center. The old limestone building had once been the town hall, then a fire station and jail, then for several years an abandoned shell. Volunteers bought the building from the city for a dollar, then renovated it with materials, labor, and money donated by local people. Now we have a handsome facility that is in constant use for pottery classes, theater productions, puppet shows, art exhibits, poetry readings, and every manner of musical event.

The music Eva and I heard was *Hymnody of Earth,* for hammer dulcimer, percussion, and children's choir. Composed by our next-door neighbor, Malcolm Dalglish, and featuring lyrics by our Ohio Valley neighbor Wendell Berry, it was performed that night by Malcolm, percussionist Glen Velez, and the Bloomington Youth Chorus. As I sat there with Eva in a sellout crowd—about a third of whom I knew by name, another third by face—I listened to music that had been elaborated within earshot of my house, and I heard my friend play his instrument, and I watched those children's faces shining with the colors of the human spectrum, and I felt the restored building clasping us all like the cupped hands of our community. I knew once more that I was in the right place, a place created and filled and inspired by our lives together.

A woman who recently moved from Los Angeles to Bloomington told me that she would not be able to stay here long, because she was already beginning to recognize people in the grocery stores, on the sidewalks, in the library. Being surrounded by familiar faces made her nervous, after years in a city where she could range about anonymously. Every traveler knows the sense of liberation that comes from journeying to a place where nobody expects anything of you. Everyone who has gone to college knows the exhilaration of slipping away from the watchful eyes of Mom and Dad. We all need seasons of withdrawal from responsibility. But if we make a career of being unaccountable, we have lost something essential to our humanity, and we may well become a burden or a threat to those around us. A community can support a number of people who are just passing through, or who care about no one's needs but their own; the greater the proportion of such people, however, the more vulnerable the community, until eventually it breaks down. That is true on any scale, from a household to a planet.

The words *community, communion,* and *communicate* all derive from *common,* and the two syllables of *common* grow from separate roots, the first meaning "together" or "next to," the second having to do with barter or exchange. Embodied in that word is a sense of our shared life as one of giving and receiving—music, touch, ideas, recipes, stories, medicine, tools, the whole range of artifacts and talents. After twenty-five years with Ruth, that is how I have come to understand marriage, as a constant exchange of labor and love. We do not calculate who gives how much; if we had to, the marriage would be in trouble. Looking outward from this community of two, I see my life embedded in ever larger exchanges—those of family and friendship, neighborhood and city, countryside and country—and on every scale there is giving and receiving, calling and answering.

Many people shy away from community out of a fear that it may become suffocating, confining, even vicious; and of course it may, if it grows rigid or exclusive. A healthy community is dynamic, stirred up by the energies of those who already belong, open to new members and fresh influences, kept in motion by the constant bartering of gifts. It is fashionable just now to speak of this open quality as "tolerance," but that word sounds too grudging to me—as though, to avoid strife, we must grit our teeth and ignore whatever is strange to us. The community I desire is not grudging; it is exuberant, joyful, grounded in affection, pleasure, and mutual aid. Such a community arises not from duty or money but from the free interchange of people who share a place, share work and food, sorrows and hope. Taking part in the common life means dwelling in a web of relationships, the many threads tugging at you while also holding you upright.

I have told elsewhere the story of a man who lived in the Ohio township where I grew up, a builder who refused to join the volunteer fire department. Why should he join, when his house was brick, properly wired, fitted out with new appliances? Well, one day that house caught fire. The wife dialed the emergency number, the siren wailed, and pretty soon the volunteer firemen, my father among them, showed up with the pumper truck. But they held back on the hoses, asking the builder if he still saw no reason to join, and the builder said he could see a pretty good reason to join right there and then, and the volunteers let the water loose.

I have also told before the story of a family from that township whose house burned down. The fire had been started accidentally by the father, who came home drunk and fell asleep smoking on the couch. While the place was still ablaze, the man took off, abandoning his wife and several young children. The local people sheltered the family, then built them a new house. This was a poor township. But nobody thought to call in the government or apply to a foundation. These were neighbors in a fix, and so you helped them, just as you would harvest corn for an ailing farmer or pull a flailing child from the creek or put your arm around a weeping friend.

I am not harking back to some idyllic past, like the one embalmed in the *Saturday Evening Post* covers by Norman Rockwell or the prints of Currier and Ives. The past was never golden. As a people, we still need to unlearn some of the bad habits formed during the long period of settlement. One good habit we might reclaim, however, is that of looking after those who live nearby. For much of our history, neighbors have kept one another going, kept one another sane. Still today, in town and country, in apartment buildings and barrios, even in suburban estates, you are certain to lead a narrower life without the steady presence of neighbors. It is neither quaint nor sentimental to advocate neighborliness; it is far more sentimental to suggest that we can do without such mutual aid.

Even Emerson, preaching self-reliance, knew the necessity of neighbors. He lived in a village, gave and received help, and delivered his essays as lectures for fellow citizens whom he hoped to sway. He could have left his ideas in his journals, where they first took shape, but he knew those ideas would only have effect when they were shared. I like to think he would have agreed with the words attributed to a Lakota shaman in *Black Elk Speaks,* that "a man who has a vision is not able to use the power of it until after he has performed the vision on earth for the people to see." If you visit Emerson's house in Concord, you will find leather buckets hanging near the door, for he belonged to the village fire brigade, and even in the seclusion of his study, in the depths of thought, he kept his ears open for the alarm bell.

We should not have to wait until our houses are burning before we see the wisdom of facing our local needs by joining in common work. We should not have to wait until gunfire breaks out in our schools, rashes break out on our skin, dead fish float in our streams, or beggars sleep on our streets before we act on behalf of the community. On a crowded planet, we had better learn how to live well together, or we will live miserably apart.

In cultural politics these days there is much talk of diversity and difference. This is all to the good, insofar as it encourages us to welcome the many distinctive traditions and visions that have flowed into America from around the world. But if, while respecting how we differ, we do not also recognize how much we have in common, we will have climbed out of the melting pot into the fire. Every day's newspaper brings word of people suffering and dying in the name of one distinction or another. We have never been slow to notice differences—of accent, race, dress, or habits. If we merely change how those differences are valued, celebrating what had formerly been despised or despising what had been celebrated, we continue to define ourselves and one another in the old divisive ways.

Ethnic labels are especially dangerous, for, while we pin them on as badges of pride, we may have difficulty taking them off when others decide to use them as targets. The larger the group identified by a label, the less likely it is to be a genuine community. Haste or laziness may lead us to speak of blacks and whites, of Christians and Muslims and Jews, of Armenians and Mexicans, yet the common life transcends such categories. Sharing a national anthem, a religion, or a skin color may be grounds for holding rallies or waging war, but community is more intimate than nationality, more subtle than race or creed, arising not from abstract qualities but from the daily give-and-take among particular people in a particular place.

It is also dangerous to separate a concern for human diversity from a concern for natural diversity. Since Europeans arrived in North America, we have been drawing recklessly on beaver and bison, trees and topsoil, petroleum, coal, iron and copper ore, clean air and water. Many of the achievements on which we pride ourselves are the result not of our supposed virtues but of this plundered bounty. We do not have another continent to use up; unless we learn to inhabit this one more conservingly, we will see our lives, as well as the land, swiftly degraded. There is no contradiction between caring for our fellow human beings and caring for the rest of nature; on the contrary, only by attending to the health of the land can we measure our true needs or secure a lasting home.

Just before Eva was to leave again for college, she and I went for a hike in a nature preserve along Clear Creek, near Bloomington, to look at the hepatica and bloodroot and listen to the spring-high water. At the edge of the preserve, a wooden sign declared that the riding of horses was prohibited. The trail had been freshly gouged by horseshoes and was eroding badly. Trash snagged in the roots of sycamores along the stream. Much of the soil and its cover of wildflowers had washed from the slopes where people scrambled up to picnic on the limestone bluff. Some of the cans they had left behind glinted among white stars of trillium.

I wondered what it would take to persuade the riders to get down off their horses and go on foot. What would it take to discourage people from dumping their worn-out washing machines in ditches? What would convince farmers to quit spraying poisons on their fields, suburbanites to quit spraying poisons on their lawns? What power in heaven or Earth could stop loggers from seeing every tree as lumber, stop developers from seeing every acre of land as real estate, stop oil company executives from seeing our last few scraps of wilderness as pay dirt waiting to be drilled? What would it take to persuade all of us to eat what we need, rather than what we can hold; to buy what we need, rather than what we can afford; to draw our pleasure from inexhaustible springs?

Signs will not work that change of mind, for in a battle of signs the billboards always win. Police cannot enforce it. Tongue lashings and sermons and earnest essays will not do it, nor will laws alone bring it about. The framers of the Constitution may have assumed that we did not need a Bill of Responsibilities because religion and reason and the benign impulses of our nature would lead us to care for one another and for our home. At the end of a bloody century, on the eve of a new millennium that threatens to be still bloodier, few of us now feel much confidence in those redeeming influences. Only a powerful ethic might restrain us, retrain us, restore us. Our survival is at stake, yet worrying about our survival alone is too selfish a motive to carry us as far as we need to go. Nothing short of reimagining where we are and what we are will be radical enough to transform how we live.

Aldo Leopold gave us the beginnings of this new ethic half a century ago, in *A Sand County Almanac,* where he described the land itself as a community made up of rock, water, soil, plants, and animals—including Homo sapiens, the only species clever enough to ignore, for a short while, the conditions of membership. "We abuse land because we see it as a commodity belonging to us," Leopold wrote. "When we see land as a community to which we belong, we may begin to use it with love and respect." To use our places with love and respect demands from us the same generosity and restraint that we show in our dealings with a wife or husband, a child or parent, a neighbor, or a stranger in trouble.

Once again this spring, the seventy-seventh of her life, my mother put out lint from her clothes dryer for the birds to use in building their nests. "I know how hard it is to make a home from scratch," she says. "I've done it often enough myself." That is not anthropomorphism; it is fellow feeling, the root of all kindness.

Doctors the world over study the same physiology, for we are one species, woven together by strands of DNA that stretch back to the beginnings of life. There is, in fact, only one life, one pulse animating the dust. Sycamores and snakes, grasshoppers and grass, hawks and humans all spring from the same source and all return to it. We need to make of this common life not merely a metaphor, although we live by metaphors, and not merely a story, although we live by stories; we need to make the common life a fact of the heart. That awareness, that concern, that love needs to go as deep in us as the feeling we have when a child dashes into the street and we hear a squeal of brakes, or when a piece of our home ground goes under concrete, or when a cat purrs against our palms or rain sends shivers through our bones or a smile floats back to us from another face.

With our own population booming, with frogs singing in the April ponds, with mushrooms cracking the pavement, life may seem the most ordinary of forces, like hunger or gravity; it may seem cheap, since we see it wasted every day. But in truth life is expensive, life is extraordinary, having required four billion years of struggle and luck on one stony, watery planet to reach its present precarious state. And so far as we have been able to discover from peering out into the great black spaces, the life that is common to all creatures here on Earth is exceedingly uncommon, perhaps unique, in the universe. How, grasping that, can we remain unchanged?

It may be that we will not change, that nothing can restrain us, that we are incapable of reimagining our relations to one another or our place in creation. So many alarm bells are ringing, we may be tempted to stuff our ears with cotton. Better that we should keep ears and eyes open, take courage as well as joy from our common life, and work for what we love. What I love is curled about a loaf of bread, a family, a musical neighbor, a building salvaged for art, a town of familiar faces, a creek and a limestone bluff and a sky full of birds. Those may seem like frail threads to hold anyone in place while history heaves us about, and yet, when they are braided together, I find them to be amazingly strong.

# Voyageurs

In morning mist on a northern river, a slab of stone tumbled from a boulder into the water, where it came to life and floated, turning into a sleek black head that swam in circles dragging a V of ripples behind it. A beaver, I thought, as I watched from shore. But no sooner had I named it than the creature bobbed up and then dove, exposing a long neck and humped back and pointed tail. Not a beaver, I realized, but an otter. I was pleased to find a label for this animate scrap, as though by pinning the right word on the shape-shifter I could hold it still.

Presently a second otter, then a third and fourth broke free of the boulder and slithered down into the mercury sheen of the river. They dove without a splash, their tails flipping up to gleam like wands in the early sunlight, and they surfaced so buoyantly that their forepaws and narrow shoulders lifted well out of the water. Then one after another they clambered back onto the rock and dove again, over and over, like tireless children taking turns on a playground slide.

My daughter, Eva, came to stand beside me, the hood of her parka drawn up against the cool of this July morning here in the north woods, on the boundary between Minnesota and Ontario. We passed her binoculars back and forth, marveling at these sleek, exuberant animals.

"Wouldn't you love to swim with them?" she whispered.

"I'd love to sit on that boulder and let them do the swimming," I answered.

"Oh, if only they'd let us!"

Always quick to notice the flicker of life, Eva had spent the past two summers studying birds with a research team, and now, halfway through college, she had become a disciplined as well as a passionate observer. Science had complicated her vision without lessening her delight in other creatures.

"What do you suppose they're doing?" I asked.

"The technical term for it," she said, "is goofing around."

"I suppose you've got some data to back that up."

"I'll show you the graphs when we get home."

Drawn by our whispers and watchfulness, the others from our camp soon joined us on the granite bluff, some bearing mugs of coffee, some with plates of steaming blueberry pancakes. We had been canoeing in the Boundary Waters Wilderness for several days, long enough for the men's faces to stubble with beards, for the women's faces to burnish from wind and sun. When all ten of us were gathered there beside the river, intently watching, suddenly the otters quit diving, swiveled their snouts in our direction, and then ducked into hiding beneath some lily pads. After a couple of minutes, as though having mulled over what to do about this intrusion, they sallied out again and resumed their romping, chasing one another, bobbing and plunging, but farther and farther away, until they disappeared around the next bend.

If our scent or voices did not spook them, then our upright silhouettes, breaking the glacier-smoothed outline of the shore, must have signaled danger to the otters. There was no way of knowing what else, if anything, we meant to them. What did the otters mean to us? What held us there while our pancakes cooled, while acres of mist rode the current past our feet, while the sun rose above a jagged fringe of trees and poured creamy light onto the river? What did we want from these elegant swimmers?

Or, to put the question in the only form I can hope to answer, what did *I* want? Not their hides, as the native people of this territory, the Chippewa, or the old French voyageurs might have wanted; not their souls or meat. I did not even want their photograph, although I found them surpassingly beautiful. I wanted their company. I desired their instruction, as if, by watching them, I might learn to belong somewhere as they so thoroughly belonged here. I yearned to slip out of my skin and into theirs, to feel the world for a spell through their senses, to think otter thoughts, and then to slide back into myself, a bit wiser for the journey.

In tales of shamans the world over, men and women make just such leaps, into hawks or snakes or bears, and then back into human shape, their vision enlarged, their sympathy deepened. I am a poor sort of shaman. My shape never changes, except, year by year, to wrinkle and sag. I did not become an otter, even for an instant. But the yearning to leap across the distance, the reaching out in imagination to a fellow creature, seems to me a worthy impulse, perhaps the most encouraging and distinctive one we have. It is the same impulse that moves us to reach out to one another across differences of race or gender, age or class. What I desired most keenly from the otters was also what I most wanted from my daughter and from the friends with whom we were canoeing, and it is what I have always desired from neighbors and strangers. I wanted their blessing. I wanted to dwell alongside them with understanding and grace. I wanted them to go about their lives in my presence as though I were kin to them, no matter how much I might differ from them outwardly.

The root of *wild* means shaggy hair, and *wilderness* means an unruly, disorderly place where shaggy creatures roam. I became shaggier during our stay in the Boundary Waters, for I left my razor at home in Indiana, as I left behind my watch, calendar, and books. Because of limited cargo space in the canoes, and because every item would have to be portaged many times, each of us was allotted for personal gear a bag the size of a grocery sack. Packing for the trip, Eva and I whittled away and whittled away, aiming to carry only the essentials.

Discovering what is essential, after all, was one of our prime reasons for going to the wilderness. When everything that you will use for a week, except water and air, must ride on your back or on the back of a friend, you think hard about what you truly need. If I had been allotted the cargo hold of a freighter for my gear, I still might not have carried a book—my favorite tool—and I certainly would not have carried a calendar or watch. I wished to unplug myself from all our ingenious grids. I wished to withdraw from print, from telephones, mailboxes, computer screens, from radio and television, in order to hear nonhuman voices. There were the Earth and sky to read, sun and belly for keeping time. As for the razor, my whiskers would grow without any tending.

I decided not to shave on the morning of our departure. By the next morning, when we reached our putting-in spot on Fall Lake near Ely, Minnesota, I already looked like a bum, according to Eva.

"If you wrapped yourself in a greasy blanket," she told me, "you could beg for spare change."

I raked a palm against my jaw to feel the bristles, but I would not see my grizzled beard until after returning home, for I avoided the mirrors in truck stop restrooms on the drive to and from the Boundary Waters. As we slid our canoes into Fall Lake shortly after dawn, the surface was calm enough to mirror the shore, and I could have studied my reflection by gazing straight down.

Yet I felt no desire to see my face, not then, not once all week. I meant to leave behind whatever I could that had the word *my* attached to it.

That first day, Eva and I paddled together, she in the bow and I in the stern. We were out of practice, and so, while the other four canoes in our party pulled straight across the water, we traced out a zigzag path familiar to all amateur canoeists. As the day wore on, however, and we wore down, shoulders and backs beginning to ache, we stopped trying so hard and eventually found our rhythm. For minutes at a stretch I forgot the canoe, forgot myself. Breathing and paddling and seeing became a single motion, a gliding meditation. Then a rock would loom before us, a gust of wind would jostle us, a hawk would call or a muscle twitch, and suddenly I would be yanked back into myself. There were my hands gripping the paddle, there were the boxy green packs leaning together over the middle thwart, there was Eva with ponytail swaying beneath her plum-colored hat, there was the gulf once more between seer and seen.

What I saw hemming the water on all sides was a low-slung landscape which had been scoured down to bedrock by glaciers, had been thronged with pine and spruce and aspen and birch over the next ten thousand years, had been stripped back again to bedrock by loggers, and was now being slowly reclaimed by forest. Here and there the spiky green humps of islands broke through the gray plane of water. On the portages between lakes, staggering beneath the weight of canoes or rucksacks over trails worn down through mud and roots to stone, we could see how thin the soil was, how precarious the hold of life.

After one of those portages, as we started the long pull down Pipestone Bay, the wind picked up and blew somber clouds from the north. We could see the rain coming, like a translucent scrim wafting toward us over the water. By the time Eva and I put on our slickers, the squall had blown past, and we found ourselves sweating in sunlight. So we peeled off the slickers, only to see another curtain of rain approaching, and behind it another dose of sun. After three or four cloudbursts, wet from without and within, we gave up on rain gear and paddled on through whatever the sky delivered.

"How are you doing?" I asked Eva during a lull between showers.

"So far so good," she answered. "All those years of ballet may have messed up my feet, but at least they've given me stamina."

"You're not chilled, are you?"

"I'm fine, Daddy."

"Don't forget to take your vitamin C."

From the bow came a sigh, and then silence. At twenty, Eva was the youngest in our group, and I was the oldest at forty-seven. She was the only one who had a parent along on the trip, a fact that annoyed her whenever I reminded her of it by some clumsy fatherly gesture. She was also annoyed when any of our companions seemed to coddle her—by urging her to carry a lighter pack on the portages, for example, or by offering her the first food at a meal.

I have called those companions friends, because that is what they became by journey's end; but at the beginning I scarcely knew these four women and four men. Our friendship came about less through the sharing of a landscape than through the sharing of good work. From dawn until dusk, we lifted, carried, paddled, hiked, packed and unpacked, sawed, cooked, and scrubbed. The work was good because every bit of it served an obvious need—to move, to eat, to shelter, to keep warm—and because all of us joined in willingly, taking up whatever job was there to be done, helping one another without being asked. Only when the necessary work was finished did we swim or sing or pick berries or stretch out on sun-warmed stone and talk.

We camped that first night within earshot of Basswood Falls, and as I lay down in the tent on my thin cushion, the steady thrum of water made me feel as though I were still afloat. Waiting for sleep, I heard from a number of muscles and bones I had not thought of for a long time.

I woke in darkness to the wacky, wailing sound of loons, a pair of them calling back and forth like two blues singers demented by love. Listening, I felt the tug of desires I could not name.

Before setting out again, we changed canoeing partners. I knew that Eva would be glad not to have me looking over her shoulder as we paddled. Out from under my gaze, her own gaze grew keener. She was the first to spy a bald eagle perched on a dead tree, as she was the first to spy blueberries and raspberries on our portages, the first to notice the swoop of a peregrine falcon and the pale blue sprays of harebells on shoreline rocks. Since her birth, she had been restoring to me lost pieces of the world or disclosing pieces I had never known.

From its perch, the eagle followed our slow progress, the great white head turning. What did it see? Not food, surely, and not much of a threat, or it would have flown. Did it see us as fellow creatures? Or merely as drifting shapes, no more consequential than clouds? Exchanging stares with this great bird, I dimly recalled a passage from *Walden* that I would look up after my return to the company of books: "Who shall say what prospect life offers to another? Could a greater miracle take place than for us to look through each other's eyes for an instant?" Neuroscience may one day pull off that miracle, giving us access to another set of eyes, another mind. For the present, however, we must rely on our native sight, on patient observation, on hunches and inklings and empathy. By empathy I do not mean the projection of human films onto nature's screen, turning grizzly bears into teddy bears, crickets into choristers, grass into lawns; I mean the shaman's leap, a going out of oneself into the inwardness of other beings.

The longing I heard in the cries of the loons was not just a feathered version of mine, but neither was it wholly alien. It is risky to speak of courting birds as blues singers, or to speak of diving otters as children taking turns on a playground slide. It is even riskier, however, to pretend we have nothing in common with the rest of nature, as though we alone, the chosen species, were centers of feeling and thought. We cannot speak of that common ground without casting threads of metaphor outward from what we know to what we do not know.

An eagle is *other,* but it is also alive, bright with sensation, attuned to the world, and we respond to that vitality wherever we find it, in bird or beetle, in moose or lowly moss. Edward O. Wilson has given this impulse a lovely name, biophilia, which he defines as the urge "to explore and affiliate with life." Of course, like the copulating dragonflies that skimmed past our canoes in iridescent pairs or like ospreys hunting fish, we seek out other creatures for survival. Yet even if biophilia is an exaggeration of an evolutionary trait, like the fiddler crab's claw or the peacock's tail, our fascination with living things carries us far beyond the requirements of eating and mating and sheltering. In that excess energy, that freewheeling curiosity, there may be a healing power. The urge to explore has scattered human beings over the whole Earth, to the peril of many species, including our own; perhaps the other dimension of biophilia, the desire to affiliate with life, could lead us to honor the entire fabric and repair what has been torn.

If you know where to look, you can find ancient tokens of biophilia in the Boundary Waters. Downriver from the eagle's perch we came to a granite cliff that was splotched with iron stains and encrusted with lichens. Grass and ferns sprouted from every fissure. Paddling close and holding our position against the current, we could make out faint red figures on the rock, paintings that had begun to weather long before the first Europeans straggled through here in search of pelts and souls. The pigment of ocher and fish oil had faded to the color of rouge, barely distinguishable from the rusty iron smears.

"There's a moose," Eva called, pointing at a blurry shape on the cliff.

The rest of us agreed that might be a moose, and we also agreed in discerning a bear, a bird, a beaver, a man or woman, a canoe, and, clearest of all, the prints of hands. What those pictures meant to their makers we could only guess. Perhaps—as observers have speculated about the more famous paintings in the caves at Lascaux—they were hunters' icons, images for worship and meditation. Perhaps they were travel signs or territorial markers. Perhaps they were doodles. Without discounting other possible meanings, what I saw in the faint red figures was a group portrait, a way of declaring: Here are the people of this place, those that fly and those that go on four legs and those that go on two. The old artists identified our human tribe by the upright stance, by the canoe, and by the imprint, not of a foot, as for any other beast, but of a hand, that universal tool capable of fashioning canoes and drawings.

If one could paint such an elusive trait, our kind might also be identified by the urge that kept ten members of the human tribe paddling there below the cliff, studying those hazy shapes, trying to read our ancestors' minds, casting threads of meaning from our lives to theirs. Whether our interpretations were right or wrong matters less than the impulse that led us to make them. With over six billion of us now on the planet, and the web of life unraveling under the burden of our appetites, we need to foster in every way we can this countervailing urge to weave, to stitch, to bind.

It may be my craving for a source of hope that persuades me to see in the petroglyphs evidence of biophilia. Certainly I felt a kinship with those vanished artists, even as I sensed in their drawings their own feeling of kinship with bear and beaver and moose. If I were to mix red clay with fish oil and daub pictures on the granite cliff, I would begin with an otter and a loon, and when I came to represent the human tribe I would draw two figures, side by side, a father and a daughter.

Although the petroglyphs are ancient by human measure, they are brand-new by comparison with the rock on which they were painted. As dark as charred bones, as gray as concrete, in places a dull rose, smoky pink, or crystalline white, the bedrock that cradles rivers and lakes in this portion of the Boundary Waters was formed between two and three billion years ago, which makes it half as old as the Earth and a thousand times older than Homo sapiens. How, standing barefooted on such venerable stone, and diving into the river for a swim, can one reach back through the abyss of time without losing hold of the icy, exhilarating present? How can one be fully aware of the moment *and* of the infinite depths on which every moment floats? Fixity of rock, flow of water: we are stretched perennially between the two.

I swam each day of the trip, and each day the first dive was daunting. This was July, I kept reminding myself, and the otters frolicked here in January. Once I made the plunge, I stayed under as long as I could, eyes open to glimpse the otter's realm, mouth closed to protect myself from disease. Until a few years ago, travelers here could safely drink straight from the streams. But now acid rain has fouled even these remote waters, leading to the growth of giardia, an intestinal parasite, and so we filtered every drop we drank and we sealed our lips as we swam. Once the initial shock of cold wore off, it felt good to rinse away the day's sweat. The water scoured me through and through. After the swim, back in camp, where Eva and the other women brushed their long damp hair by the fire, I tingled for hours.

The day we paddled up the meandering Horse River, several of us found ourselves swimming with our clothes on. The water was high from summer-long rains that had swollen the Missouri and Mississippi Rivers with five-hundred-year floods. Throughout much of its length, the channel spread out lazily into marshes of cattails and willows and reeds, but wherever it was pinched in by rock the current was swift. The only way of maneuvering a canoe safely through the fiercest rapids was for one of the paddlers to climb out, grope for footing among the slippery stones, and push or pull the canoe upstream.

As I slogged through the first few riffles, I wore my life vest; but eventually I became so hot from the effort and from the midday sun that I decided to take it off, and I noticed the other waders doing the same. And so it happened that none of us was wearing a vest when we came to the last and worst of the rapids. Eva was in the bow of the lead canoe, and the man in the stern, the strongest paddler in our group, thought they could dig their way up through the central chute without wading. They made one hard run, then another and another, but each time they were stalled in white water and shoved back downstream.

At last Eva decided to climb out and tug from the front while her partner paddled. The canoe inched forward, foam brimming around Eva's knees, then her thighs, her waist, and when she lurched into the narrowest place, where the water pounded between great boulders, suddenly her feet were swept from under her and she fell, barely keeping her chin above water by clutching the gunwale with one hand. The canoe spun crossways to the current and wedged against the boulders, and there Eva dangled, her face jammed against the upstream side of the canoe, her booted feet bobbing up uselessly on the downstream side. Watching her, I had the slow-motion sense from nightmare that something horrible was about to happen, and that I was powerless to intervene. I saw my daughter being sucked under and battered against rocks and tumbled down past me through the bruising rapids.

I *saw* it happen; but it did not happen. While voices all around me shouted advice, Eva clung to the canoe with one hand, worked the other hand free to seize the gunwale, then dragged herself across the roiling water and hauled herself out onto a ledge. Only the top of her head was dry. When I saw her safe, I realized that I had been holding my breath. I opened my throat, letting out stale air and drawing in fresh, but for a long while I could not speak.

Much later, after miles of winding through fragrant water lilies and gliding past the tranquil gaze of basking turtles, their domed shells gleaming in the sun like hubcaps, we arrived at a campsite on Horse Lake. Eva and I were to cook supper that night, and while she was unpacking the food and I was building the fire, she asked me if I had been worried by her dunking.

"I was terrified," I told her. "Weren't you?"

"No," she said. "It was kind of fun."

"What if you had gone under?"

"I didn't go under."

"But what if you had?"

"I would have washed up again sooner or later."

Recalling those fierce waters, those indifferent rocks, again I lost my voice. Eva frowned at her alarmist father, and we both returned to our work.

Near the fire pit, where I knelt to fan the flames, stood a wild cherry tree whose bark had been raked by claws and whose branches, glinting with dark purple fruit, had been twisted and smashed. There were tufts of black hair snagged on twigs, and smudged tracks in the dirt below. We had been instructed to shout or bang on pans and generally raise a ruckus if we spotted a bear. We never spotted one, but if we had, I might not have been able to make a sound, any more than I could cry out when I saw the river snatch my daughter.

There were dangers enough in the Boundary Waters. A few years earlier a father and son were pulling to shore when a black bear came rushing out at them, seized the father and began mauling him; the son beat the bear with a paddle until the father wriggled free, then father and son escaped in their canoe. More recently, two men sleeping in a tent during a thunderstorm were electrocuted when lightning struck nearby and the juice flowed through roots under their sleeping bags; two other men in the same tent were only dazed. The week before our trip, a woman canoeing alone was killed when a tree felled by a beaver crashed down on her as she passed by.

We had not gone seeking danger in the wilderness, as skydivers go to the treacherous air or climbers to steep rock or mercenaries to war, but we had stumbled into danger anyway. We knew the risk from broken bones and drowning, from snakes and leeches and ticks. In the wilds, risk is the underside of beauty. To be a creature is to be vulnerable, to bruise, and sooner or later to break. Unlike most dangers in our cities, where guns or bombs or drunken drivers or heedless sex might kill us, what could harm us in the Boundary Waters had no will behind it, no malign intention.

The Horse River did not mean to hurt my daughter, did not mean to frighten me, did not *mean* anything. Whether the browsing bear meant to harm the wild cherry tree is a harder question, but I suspect the answer is no. Whether the original world itself—the one that precedes and upholds our human world as a billion-year-old stone upholds the petroglyphs—whether the original world means anything, whether it embodies a purpose or direction, is an even harder question, perhaps the most difficult of all. I do not pretend to know the answer, nor even how one might be found, yet I find myself living as if the answer is yes. Arising out of a dead universe, evolving from an original simplicity toward unimaginable complexity, life does seem to be an immense journey—as Loren Eiseley described it—but not one with a human destination. We are not the goal of evolution, nor are we competent guides, despite our tinkering with DNA. If we are voyageurs, then so are the otters and eagles, the dragonflies and spiders, the lichens and pines, along with all the countless species that have gone down into the Earth.

While the Horse River was roaring through its boulder-strewn trough, the Mississippi River was drowning dozens of towns and thousands of farms. Headlines described the Mississippi as rampaging, brutal, cruel, the same words we use for street gangs or packs of feral dogs. After we had spent so many dollars and decades to control it, the television commentators asked, how could the river turn on us this way? How could it defy our levees, our breakwaters, our sandbags and dams? Cancers and hurricanes, earthquakes and the AIDS virus are often described in the same outraged tone as aberrations, as if by shattering the walls of our houses or our cells they were violating some covenant between us and nature.

In defining wilderness as an unruly place where shaggy creatures roam, our language betrays an uneasiness about our own hairy origins and a regret that the original world does not dance to our music. Beyond our campfires, beyond our tents, beyond our makeshift structures, the whole universe is wild, from quarks to quasars, from black bears to black holes, but far from being disorderly, it follows intricate, exquisite rules that we have only begun to decipher. They are not *our* rules, however, no matter how fervently we may desire to legislate, a fact that is dismaying only to those who believe that we should be running the show.

Even such a battered scrap of wilderness as the Boundary Waters reminds us, at every turn, that we are not running the show. On our last evening there, the sky was clear, so Eva and I and several others gathered on a stony point beside the lake to wait for stars. Mosquitoes came droning in as usual at dusk, and the calls of night birds picked up as the calls of day birds dwindled away. Catching the ruddy light of sunset, a V of ripples approached us from the far shore, and this time it was a beaver, carrying in its jaw a stick the size of a baseball bat. The ripples arrowed straight toward us, and the beaver climbed out just below our point, so close that we could see the wet fur slicked back like a greaser's hairdo, and we could hear the scrape of teeth on wood as it gnawed bark from the stick.

I glanced at Eva, to share with her a conspiratorial grin. But she was lost in looking, and soon I was, too. By and by, startled perhaps by our feet stamping the rock and our hands pawing the air to scatter mosquitoes, the beaver nosed away into the lake, gave the water a resounding smack with its tail, and dove. Moments later it emerged again on the opposite side of our point, even closer to us, the wood still clenched in its jaw. One end of the stick was pale and shining, the other end, unchewed, still gray with bark. After a spell of gnawing, the beaver nosed away from shore again, smacked the water, dove, climbed out once more, gnawed, then reversed the procedure several more times, until we lost its movements in the gloom and we lost its sounds in the stir of wind. Only then did we remember the stars, and we looked up to find that the sky had been covered by a quilt of cloud.

The next afternoon we slid our canoes out of Fall Lake onto the same landing from which we had launched them, closing the circle of our journey. Before getting on the bus I picked up a palm-sized chunk of rosy granite, the edges sharp enough for scraping hides, and I stuffed it into my pack as a reminder of this place. I have often reached for the stone while writing these pages, turning and turning it, never quite able to make the hard angles fit my hand.

From inside, the shell of the bus seemed flimsy, the floor unsteady, the windows deceitful. Only my weariness made sense. Eva looked across the aisle at me, shook her head, and said, "More and more like a bum. Now you could beg for change without a greasy blanket."

I stroked my beard, which had begun to feel like fur. "What do you think? Should I let it grow out?"

"Sure," Eva said, "if you want to look like Father Time."

After a week away from clocks, I was beginning to hear time again in the whir of the tires, beginning to see it in the mile markers along the road. To keep time at bay a while longer, I hummed the melody from a song we had sung while paddling, and I shut my eyes. When I opened them again, rain was drumming on the roof and mist from an open window was falling on my face and lightning was cracking the pitch-black sky. This was better than sleep, so I sat up watching the storm.

I was still watching as we cruised through Chicago, the expressways deserted this Sunday morning, the street lamps a bleary yellow. The bus pulled in for a rest stop at a hamburger franchise near the Indiana border, and I made the mistake of going inside. The light and noise were painful, the surfaces too shiny, the smells too coarse. Everywhere I looked, mirrors multiplied the garish colors, the harsh lights, and the feeding faces. Televisions suspended from the ceiling played bouncy cartoons, and at the tables beneath them diners shoveled in fatty food and sucked sweet liquids. Another day, I might have sat down at one of those tables myself, might have shoveled and slurped; but this day, this thundery morning, I backed away feeling sick.

Another day, I might have stayed there to admire the people, in all their shades of skin and shapes of body; I might have listened to their accents and tried to guess where they were from. This was Chicago, after all, my mother's polyglot city, the city where my Assyrian grandfather had practiced medicine among poor immigrants from dozens of lands. But so soon after returning from the original world, I was not ready to see the human world as enough, not even in Chicago. We celebrate our own diversity, as we should. But if we think our rainbow of races, our preferences in making love, our flags, our ways of cooking and speaking and praying, our X or Y chromosomes make us more various, more mysterious, than all the rest of nature, then we flatter ourselves.

Back on the bus, Eva told me she had dreamed of looking out the window to see a great blue bird flying along beside us, a mighty beast with the crooked neck of a heron, the body of an eagle, and the fur of a lion. Mythology teems with such composite beasts. Eva's dream animal, in fact, sounds like a near relative of the griffin. While banishing griffins and centaurs and sphinxes from our textbooks, biologists have revealed that we ourselves are composite creatures, built up over millions of years from ancestral species, part lemur and part lizard, with bacteria in our bellies and mitochondria in our cells. The mountain gorilla and the lowland gorilla differ genetically from one another more than we differ from chimpanzees. Does that make us indistinguishable from apes? No, but our genetic heritage does make us kin, not only with apes and otters, but with frogs and ferns and fritillaries, indeed with every one of Earth's countless organisms.

The fellowship of all creatures is more than a handsome metaphor; it is a fact entwined in our DNA. The appetite for discovering such connections is also entwined in our DNA. Science articulates in formal terms affinities that humans have sensed for ages in direct encounters with wildness. Even while we slight or slaughter members of our own species, and while we push other species toward extinction, we slowly, painstakingly assemble the knowledge that could enable us, indeed require us, to change our ways. If that knowledge begins to exert a steady pressure in us, and we come to feel the fellowship of all creatures as potently as we feel hunger or fear, we may have some prospect of fashioning a truly just and tolerant society, one that cherishes the land and our wild companions along with our brothers and sisters.

In America lately we have been carrying on two parallel conversations, one about respecting human diversity, the other about preserving natural diversity. Unless we merge those two conversations into one, both will be futile. Our effort to honor human differences cannot succeed apart from our effort to honor the buzzing, blooming, bewildering variety of life on Earth. All life rises from the same source, and so does all fellow feeling, whether the fellows move on two legs or four, on scaly bellies or feathered wings. If we care only for human needs, we betray the land; if we care only for Earth and its wild offspring, we betray our own kind. The profusion of creatures and cultures is the most remarkable fact about our planet, and the study and stewardship of that profusion seems to me our fundamental task.

While Eva and I were sorting the week's laundry in the basement at home, the good smell of mud rising from our jeans, she recalled her dream as one of the most powerful events of the week, and so I recall it now. Accounts of wilderness sojourns, like the sojourners themselves, often turn their backs on the human realm. Here is pristine nature, these accounts imply, and over there is corrupt society. In anger or despair, I have written such narratives myself. Likewise, many who write about social problems, about poverty or prejudice or war, turn their backs on nature, as though we were acting out our destiny on a bare stage. But the stage is crowded with life, the stage is teeming, indeed the stage is the main story. The only durable community is the one that embraces the whole planet, wild and tame. We need to find ways of speaking about that great community without drawing lines between nature and society, for such boundaries are just as illusory as the one between Canada and the United States, over which we paddled time and again during our trip without so much as a bump.

At any rate, that is what I am trying to find, a way of speaking and writing and thinking about the whole of life, human as well as nonhuman, in all its dazzling array. Although I am caught much of the time in ego's shiny jar, distracted by my own reflections, there were moments during our wilderness sojourn when I slipped out of that small self and entered, however briefly, into the great community. Those are the moments worth telling.

# Mountain Music

On a June morning high in the Rocky Mountains of Colorado, snowy peaks rose before me like the promise of a world without grief. A creek brimful of meltwater roiled along to my left, and to my right an aspen grove shimmered with freshly minted leaves. Bluebirds kept darting in and out of holes in the aspen trunks. Butterflies flickered beside every puddle, tasting the succulent mud. Sun glazed the new grass and licked a silver sheen along the boughs of pines.

With all of that to look at, I gazed instead at my son's broad back, as he stalked away from me up the trail. Sweat had darkened his gray T-shirt in patches the color of bruises. His shoulders were stiff with anger that would weight his tongue and keep his face turned from me for hours. Anger also made him quicken his stride, gear after gear, until I could no longer keep up. I had forty-nine years on my legs and heart and lungs, while Jesse had only seventeen on his. My left foot ached from old bone breaks and my right knee creaked from recent surgery. Used to breathing among the low muggy hills of Indiana, I was gasping up here in the alpine air, a mile and a half above sea level. Jesse would not stop, would not even slow down unless I asked; and I was in no mood to ask. So I slumped against a boulder beside the trail and let him rush on ahead.

The day, our first full one in Rocky Mountain National Park, had started out well. I woke at first light, soothed by the roar of a river foaming along one edge of the campground, and I looked out from our tent to find half a dozen elk, all cows and calves, grazing so close by that I could see the gleam of their teeth. Just beyond the elk, a pair of ground squirrels loafed at the lip of their burrow, noses twitching. Beyond the squirrels, a ponderosa pine, backlit by sunrise, caught the wind in its ragged limbs. The sky was a blue slate marked only by the curving flight of swallows.

Up to that point, and for several hours more, the day was equally unblemished. Jesse slept on while I sipped coffee and studied maps and soaked in the early light. We made our plans over breakfast without squabbling: walk to Bridal Veil Falls in the morning, raft on the Cache la Poudre River in the afternoon, return to camp in the evening to get ready for backpacking the next day up into Wild Basin. Tomorrow we would be heavy laden, but today we carried only water and snacks, and I felt buoyant as we hiked along Cow Creek toward the waterfall. We talked easily the whole way, joking and teasing, more like good friends than like father and son. Yet even as we sat at the base of the falls, our shoulders touching, the mist of Bridal Veil cooling our skin, we remained father and son, locked in a struggle that I could only partly understand.

For the previous year or so, no matter how long our spells of serenity, Jesse and I had kept falling into quarrels, like victims of malaria breaking out in fever. We might be talking about soccer or supper, about the car keys or the news, and suddenly our voices would begin to clash like swords. I had proposed this trip to the mountains in hopes of discovering the source of that strife. Of course I knew that teenage sons and their fathers always fight, yet I sensed there was a deeper grievance between us, beyond the usual vexations. Jesse was troubled by more than a desire to run his own life, and I was troubled by more than the pain of letting him go. I wished to track our anger to its lair, to find where it hid and fed and grew, and then, if I could not slay the demon, at least I could drag it into the light and call it by name.

The peace between us held until we turned back from the waterfall and began discussing where to camp the following night. Jesse wanted to push on up to Thunder Lake, near eleven thousand feet, and pitch our tent on snow. I wanted to stop a thousand feet lower and sleep on dry dirt.

"We're not equipped for snow," I told him.

"Sure we are. Why do you think I bought a new sleeping bag? Why did I call ahead to reserve snowshoes?"

I suggested that we could hike up from a lower campsite and snowshoe to his heart's content.

He loosed a snort of disgust. "I can't believe you're wimping out on me, Dad."

"I'm just being sensible."

"You're wimping out. I came here to see the backcountry, and all you want to do is poke around the foothills."

"This isn't wild enough for you?" I waved my arms at the view. "What do you need, avalanches and grizzlies?"

Just then, as we rounded a bend, an elderly couple came shuffling toward us, hunched over walking sticks, white hair jutting from beneath their straw hats. They were followed by three toddling children, each one rigged out with tiny backpack and canteen. Jesse and I stood aside to let them pass, returning nods to their cheery hellos.

When they had trooped by, Jesse muttered, "We're in the wilds, huh, Dad? That's why the trail's full of grandparents and kids." Then he quickened his pace until the damp blond curls that dangled below his billed cap were slapping against his neck.

"Is this how it's going to be?" I called after him. "You're going to spoil the trip because I won't agree to camp on snow?"

He glared around at me. "You're the one who's spoiling it, you and your hang-ups. You always ruin everything."

With that, he swung his face away and lengthened his stride and rushed on ahead. I watched his rigid shoulders and the bruise-colored patches on the back of his T-shirt until he disappeared beyond a rise. That was when I gave up on chasing him, slumped against a boulder, and sucked at the thin air. Butterflies dallied around my boots and hawks kited on the breeze, but they might have been blips on a screen, and the whole panorama of snowy peaks and shimmering aspens and shining pines might have been cut from cardboard, for all the feeling they stirred in me.

The rocks that give these mountains their name are ancient, nearly a third as old as the Earth, but the Rockies themselves are new, having been lifted up only six or seven million years ago, and they were utterly new to me, for I had never seen them before except from airplanes. I had been yearning toward them since I was Jesse's age, had been learning about their natural and human history, the surge of stone and gouge of glaciers, the wandering of hunters and wolves. Drawn to these mountains from the rumpled quilt of fields and forests in the hill country of the Ohio Valley, I was primed for splendor. And yet, now that I was here, I felt blinkered and numb.

What we call landscape is a stretch of Earth overlaid with memory, expectation, and thought. Land is everything that is actually *there,* independent of us; landscape is what we allow in through the doors of perception. My own doors had slammed shut. My quarrel with Jesse changed nothing about the Rockies, but changed everything in my experience of the place. What had seemed glorious and vibrant to me when we set out that morning now seemed bleak and bare. It was as though anger had drilled a hole in the world and leached the color away.

I was still simmering when I caught up with Jesse at the trailhead, where he was leaning against our rented car, arms crossed over his chest, head sunk forward in a sullen pose I knew too well, eyes hidden beneath the frayed bill of his cap. Having to wait for me to unlock the car no doubt reminded him of another gripe: I had the only set of keys. Because he was too young to be covered by the rental insurance, I would not let him drive. He had fumed about my decision, interpreting it as proof that I mistrusted him, still thought of him as a child. That earlier scuffle had petered out with him grumbling, "Stupid, stupid. I knew this would happen. Why did I come out here? Why?"

The arguments all ran together, playing over and over in my head as we jounced, too fast, along a rutted gravel road toward the highway. The tires whimped and the small engine whined up hills and down, but the silence inside the car was louder. We had two hours of driving to our rendezvous spot for the rafting trip, and I knew that Jesse could easily clamp his jaw shut for that long, and longer. I glanced over at him from time to time, looking for any sign of détente. His eyes were glass.

We drove. In the depths of Big Thompson Canyon, where the road swerved along a frothy river between sheer rock face and spindly guardrail, I could bear the silence no longer. "So what are my hang-ups?" I demanded. "How do I ruin everything?"

"You don't want to know," he said.

"I want to know. What is it about me that grates on you?"

I do not pretend to recall the exact words we hurled at one another after my challenge, but I remember the tone and thrust of them, and here is how they have stayed with me:

"You wouldn't understand," he said.

"Try me."

He cut a look at me, shrugged, then stared back through the windshield. "You're just so out of touch."

"With what?"

"With my whole world. You hate everything that's fun. You hate television and movies and video games. You hate my music."

"I like some of your music. I just don't like it loud."

"You hate advertising," he said quickly, rolling now. "You hate billboards, lotteries, developers, logging companies, and big corporations. You hate snowmobiles and Jet Skis. You hate malls and fashions and cars."

"You're still on my case because I won't buy a Jeep?" I said, harking back to another old argument.

"Forget Jeeps. You look at any car, and all you think is pollution, traffic, roadside crap. You say fast food's poisoning our bodies and TV's poisoning our minds. You think the internet is just another scam for selling stuff. You think business is a conspiracy to rape the Earth."

"None of that bothers you?"

"Of course it does. But that's the *world*. That's where we've got to live. It's not going to go away just because you don't approve. What's the good of spitting on it?"

"I don't spit on it. I grieve over it."

He was still for a moment, then resumed quietly. "What's the good of grieving if you can't change anything?"

"Who says you can't change anything?"

"*You* do. Maybe not with your mouth, but with your eyes." Jesse rubbed his own eyes, and the words came out muffled through his cupped palms. "Your view of things is totally dark. It bums me out. You make me feel the planet's dying, and people are to blame, and nothing can be done about it. There's no room for hope. Maybe you can get along without hope, but I can't. I've got a lot of living still to do. I have to believe there's a way we can get out of this mess. Otherwise, what's the point? Why study, why work, why do anything if it's all going to hell?"

That sounded unfair to me, a caricature of my views, and I thought of many sharp replies; yet there was too much truth and too much hurt in what he said for me to fire back an answer. Had I really deprived my son of hope? Was this the deeper grievance, the source of our strife—that I had passed on to him, so young, my anguish over the world? Was this what lurked between us, driving us apart, the demon called despair?

"You're right," I finally told him. "Life's meaningless without hope. But I think you're wrong to say I've given up."

"It seems that way to me. As if you think we're doomed."

"No, buddy, I don't think we're doomed. It's just that nearly everything I care about is under assault."

"See, that's what I mean. You're so worried about the fate of the Earth, you can't enjoy anything. We come to these mountains, and you bring the shadows with you. You've got me seeing nothing but darkness."

Stunned by the force of his words, I could not speak. If my gloom cast a shadow over the creation for my son, then I had failed him. What remedy could there be for such a betrayal?

Through all the shouting and then talking and then painful hush, our car hugged the swerving road, yet I cannot remember steering. I cannot remember even seeing the stony canyon, the white mane of the Big Thompson whipping along beside us, the oncoming traffic. Somehow we survived our sashay with the river and cruised into a zone of burger joints and car-care emporiums and trinket shops. I realized how often, how relentlessly, I had groused about just this sort of commercial dreck, and how futile my complaints must have seemed to Jesse.

He was caught between a chorus of voices telling him that the universe was made for us, that the Earth is an inexhaustible warehouse, that consumption is the goal of life, that money is the road to delight—and the stubborn voice of his father saying none of this is so. If his father was right, then most of what humans babble every day—in ads and editorials, in sitcoms and song lyrics, in thrillers and market reports and teenage gab—is a monstrous lie. Far more likely that his father was wrong, deluded, perhaps even mad.

\\\\\\|//

We observed an unofficial truce for the rest of the way to the gas station north of Fort Collins, where we met the rafting crew at noon. There had been record rain and snowfall in the Rockies for the previous three months, so every brook and river tumbling down from the mountains was frenzied and fast. When local people heard that we meant to raft the Cache la Poudre in this rough season, they frowned, advised against it, recounting stories of broken legs, crushed skulls, deaths. Seeing that we were determined to go, they urged us to sign up for the shorter trip that joined the river below the canyon, where the water spread out and calmed down. But Jesse had his heart set on taking the wildest ride available, so we had signed up for the twelve-mile trip through the boulder-strewn canyon.

I was relieved to see a crowd of twenty or so, including scrawny kids and rotund parents, waiting at the rendezvous point. If the outfitters were willing to haul such passengers, how risky could the journey be? The sky-blue rafts, stacked on trailers behind yellow vans, looked indestructible. The guides seemed edgy, however, as they told us what to do if we were flung into the river, how to survive a tumble over rocks, how to get out from under a flipped raft, how to drag a flailing comrade back on board.

Jesse stood off by himself and listened to these dire instructions with a sober face. I could see him preparing, gaze focused inward, lips tight, the way he would concentrate before taking his place in goal at a soccer game.

When the time came for us to board the vans, he and I turned out to be the only customers for the canyon run; all the others, the reedy kids and puffing parents, were going on the tamer trip. Our raft would be filled out by three sinewy young men, students at Colorado State, who were being paid to risk their necks: a guide with a year's experience and two trainees.

The water in Poudre Canyon looked murderous, all spume and standing waves and suckholes and rips. Every cascade, every low bridge, every jumble of boulders reminded the guides of some disaster, which they rehearsed with gusto. It was part of their job to crank up the thrill, I knew that, but I also knew from talking with friends that most of the tales were true.

At the launching spot, Jesse and I wriggled into our black wetsuits, cinched tight the orange flotation-vests, buckled on white helmets. The sight of my son in that armor sent a blade of anxiety through me again. What if he got hurt? Lord God, what if he were killed?

"Hey, Dad," Jesse called, hoisting a paddle in his fist, "you remember how to use one of these?"

"Seems like I remember teaching you," I called back.

He flashed me a grin, the first sign of communion since we had sat with shoulders touching in the mist of Bridal Veil Falls. That one look restored me to my senses, and I felt suddenly the dazzle of sunlight, heard the river's rumble and the fluting of birds, smelled pine sap and wet stone.

One of the trainees, a lithe wisecracker named Harry, would guide our run. "If it gets quiet in back," he announced, "that means I've fallen in and somebody else better take over."

We clambered into the raft—Jesse and I up front, the veteran guide and the other trainee in the middle, Harry in the stern. Each of us hooked one foot under a loop sewn into the rubbery floor, jammed the other foot under a thwart. Before we hit the first rapids, Harry made us practice synchronizing our strokes, as he hollered, "Back paddle! Forward paddle! Stop! Left turn! Right turn!" The only other command, he explained, was "Jump!" Hearing that, the paddlers on the side away from some looming boulder or snag were to heave themselves *toward* the obstruction, in order to keep the raft from flipping.

"I know it sounds crazy," said Harry, "but it works. And remember: from now on, if you hear fear in my voice, it's real."

Fear was all I felt over the next few minutes, a bit for myself and a lot for Jesse, as we struck white water and the raft began to buck. Waves slammed against the bow, spray flew, stone whizzed by. A bridge swelled ahead of us, water boiling under the low arches, and Harry shouted "Duck!" then steered us between the lethal pilings and out the other side into more rapids, where he yelled, "Left turn! Dig hard! Harder!"

He kept barking orders, and soon I was too busy paddling to feel anything except my own muscles pulling against the great writhing muscle of the river. I breathed in as much water as air. The raft spun and dipped and leapt with ungainly grace, sliding through narrow flumes, gliding over rocks, kissing cliffs and bouncing away, yielding to the grip of the current and springing free. Gradually I sank into my body.

The land blurred past. Sandstone bluffs rose steeply along one shore, then the other, then both, hundreds of feet of rock pinching the sky high above into a ribbon of blue. Here and there a terrace opened, revealing a scatter of junipers and scrub cedars, yet before I could spy what else might be growing there it jerked away out of sight. I could tell only that this was dry country, harsh and sparse, with dirt the color of scrap iron gouged by erosion. Every time I tried to fix on a detail, on bird or flower or stone, a shout from Harry yanked me back to the swing of the paddle.

The point of our bucking ride, I realized, was not to see the canyon but to survive it. The river was our bronco, our bull, and the land through which it flowed was no more present to us than the rodeo's dusty arena to a whirling cowboy. Haste hid the country, dissolved the landscape, as surely as anger or despair ever did.

"Forward paddle!" Harry shouted. "Give me all you've got! We're coming to the Widow-maker! Let's hope we come out alive!"

The flooded Poudre, surging through its crooked canyon, was a string of emergencies, each one christened with an ominous name. In a lull between rapids, I glanced over at Jesse, and he was beaming. The helmet seemed to strain from the expansive pressure of his smile. I laughed aloud to see him. When he was little, I could summon that look of unmixed delight into his face merely by coming home, opening my arms, and calling, "Where's my boy?" In his teenage years, the look had become rare, and it hardly ever had anything to do with me.

"Jump!" Harry shouted.

Before I could react, Jesse lunged at me and landed heavily, and the raft bulged over a boulder, nearly tipping, and then righted itself and plunged on downstream.

"Good job!" Harry crowed. "That was a close one."

Jesse scrambled back to his post. "You okay?" he asked.

"Sure," I answered. "How about you?"

"Great," he said. "Fantastic."

For the remaining two hours of our romp down the Poudre, I kept stealing glances at Jesse, who paddled as though his life truly depended on how hard he pulled. His face shone with joy, and my own joy was kindled from seeing it.

This is an old habit of mine, the watching and weighing of my son's experience. Since his birth, I have enveloped him in a cloud of thought. How's he doing? I wonder. Is he hungry? Hurting? Tired? Is he grumpy or glad? Like so many other exchanges between parent and child, this concern flows mainly one way; Jesse does not surround *me* with thought. On the contrary, with each passing year he pays less and less attention to me, except when he needs something, and then he bristles at being reminded of his dependence. That's natural, mostly, although teenage scorn for parents also gets a boost from popular culture. My own father had to die before I thought seriously about what he might have needed or wanted or suffered. If Jesse has children of his own one day, no doubt he will brood on them as I have brooded on him for these seventeen years. Meanwhile, his growing up requires him to break free of my concern; I accept that, yet I cannot turn off my fathering mind.

Before leaving for Colorado, I had imagined that he would be able to meet the Rockies with clear eyes, with the freshness of his green age. So long as he was in my company, however, he would see the land through the weather of my moods. And if despair had so darkened my vision that I was casting a shadow over Jesse's world—even here among these magnificent mountains and tumultuous rivers—then I would have to change. I would have to learn to see differently. Since I could not forget the wounds to people and planet, could not unlearn the dismal numbers—of pollution and population and poverty—that foretold catastrophe, I would have to look harder for antidotes, for medicines, for sources of hope.

Tired and throbbing from the river trip, we scarcely spoke during the long drive back to our campground in the national park. This time the silence felt easy, like a fullness rather than a void.

In that tranquillity I recalled our morning's hike to Bridal Veil Falls, before the first quarrel of the day. No matter how briskly I walked, Jesse kept pulling ahead. He seemed to be in a race, eyes focused far up the trail, as though testing himself against the rugged terrain. I had come to this high country for a holiday from rushing. A refugee from the tyranny of deadlines and destinations, I wished to linger, squatting over the least flower or fern, reading the Braille of bark with my fingers, catching the notes of water and birds and wind. But Jesse was just as intent on covering ground. Although we covered the same ground, most of the time we experienced quite different landscapes, his charged with trials of endurance, mine with trials of perception. Then every once in a while the land brought us together—in the mist of the falls, on the back of the river— and it was as if, for a moment, the same music played in both of us.

Without any quarrel to distract me, I watched the road faithfully as we swerved up through Big Thompson Canyon. We entered the park at dusk and a rosy light glinted on the frozen peaks of the Front Range.

I was driving slowly, on the lookout for wildlife, when a coyote loped onto the road ahead of us, paused halfway across, then stared back in the direction from which it had come. As we rolled to a stop, a female elk came charging after, head lowered and teeth bared. The coyote bounded away, scooted up a bank on the far side of the road, paused, then peered back over its bony shoulder. Again the elk charged; again the coyote pranced away, halted, stared. Jesse and I watched this ballet of taunting and chasing, taunting and chasing, until the pair vanished over a ridge.

"What was that all about?" he asked when we drove on.

"She was protecting a calf, I expect."

"You mean a coyote can eat an elk?"

"The newborns they can."

When I shut off the engine at the campground and we climbed out of the car, it was as though we had stepped back into the raft, for the sound of rushing water swept over us. The sound lured us downhill to the bank of a stream and we sat there soaking in the watery music until our bellies growled. We made supper while the full moon chased Jupiter and Mars up the arc of the sky. The flame on our stove flounced in a northerly breeze, promising cool weather for tomorrow's hike into Wild Basin.

We left the flap of our tent open so we could lie on our backs and watch the stars, which burned fiercely in the mountain air. Our heads were so close together that I could hear Jesse's breath, even above the shoosh of the river, and I could tell he was nowhere near sleep.

"I feel like I'm still on the water," he said after a spell, "and the raft's bobbing under me and the waves are crashing all around."

"I feel it too."

"That's one of the things I wanted to be sure and do before things fall apart."

I rolled onto my side and propped my head on an elbow and looked at his moonlit profile. "Things don't have to fall apart, buddy."

"Maybe not." He blinked, and the spark in his eyes went out and relit. "I just get scared."

"So do I. But the Earth's a tough old bird. And we should be smart enough to figure out how to live here."

"Let's hope." There was the scritch of a zipper and a thrashing of legs and Jesse sprawled on top of his new sleeping bag, which was too warm for this fifty-degree night. "I guess things could be scarier," he said. "Imagine being an elk, never knowing what's sneaking up on you."

"Or a coyote," I said, "never knowing where you'll find your next meal."

A great horned owl called. Another answered, setting up a duet across our valley. We listened until they quit.

"You know," said Jesse, "I've been thinking. Maybe we don't need to sleep on snow. Maybe we can pitch camp in the morning at North St. Vrain, where there ought to be some bare ground, then we can snowshoe on up to Thunder Lake in the afternoon."

"You wouldn't be disappointed if we did that? Wouldn't feel we'd wimped out?"

"Naw," he said. "That's cool."

"Then that's the plan, man."

The stars burned on. The moon climbed. Just when I thought he was asleep, Jesse murmured, "How's that knee?"

"Holding up so far," I told him, surprised by the question, and only then did I notice the ache in my knee and foot.

"Glad to hear it. I don't want to be lugging you out of the mountains."

When he was still young enough to ride in a backpack, I had lugged him to the tops of mountains and through dripping woods and along the slate beds of creeks and past glittering windows on city streets, while he burbled and sang over my shoulder; but I knew better than to remind him of that now in his muscular youth. I lay quietly, following the twin currents of the river and my son's breath. Here were two reasons for rejoicing, two sources of hope. For Jesse's sake, and for mine, I would get up the next morning and hunt for more.

# Wildness

Hope caught me by surprise a couple of weeks ago, when the last snow of winter hit town on the first day of spring. It was a heavy, slashing snow, stinging the skin, driven by a north wind. Because the temperature was near freezing, the flakes clung to everything. A white streak balanced on telephone wires, on clotheslines, on every branch and twig and bud. Many buds had already cracked open after a spell of warm days, so we fretted over the reckless early flowers and eager trees. By noon, snow piled a foot deep, and more kept falling. The few drivers who ventured out usually wound up spinning their wheels in drifts. Soon even the four-wheelers gave up and the city trucks quit plowing and the streets were abandoned to the storm.

I made the first blemish on our street by going out at dusk for a walk. The light was the color of peaches, as if the sky were saturated with juice. The clinging snow draped every bush with a lacy cloak. Even fire hydrants and cars looked rakish in their gleaming mantles. I peeled back my parka hood to uncover my ears, and heard only the muffled crunching of my boots. Now and again a siren wailed, a limb creaked, or wind sizzled through the needles of a pine, but otherwise the city was eerily silent, as though following an evacuation. In an hour I met only three other walkers, each one huddled and aloof. The weight of snow snapped branches and toppled trees onto power lines, leaving our neighborhood without electricity. As I shuffled past the dark houses, beneath unlit street lamps, through blocks where nothing moved except the wind, my mood swung from elation toward dismay. The snow began to seem a frozen burden, like a premonition of glaciers, bearing down from the heedless, peach-colored sky. The world had been radiantly simplified, but at the price of smothering our handiwork and maiming trees and driving warm-blooded creatures into hiding.

Drawn by thoughts of family and candles and woodstove, I hastened back to my street, anxious to retreat indoors. Nearing our porch, however, I heard a low, steady whinnying from the hemlock beside our front door, and I paused. When I had first heard that sound back in January, I took it for a distant machine of some sort, a fan or a pump. But then, listening more closely, I recognized the single-note gargling of a screech owl. My wife, Ruth, and I had been hearing it almost nightly for two months, and one or the other of us would often wake in the small hours to savor this watery song. I never expected to hear it during a blizzard, but there it was, persistent as the purr of a brook. I squinted up through slanting snow into the dark boughs of the hemlock and listened as the screech owl, unruffled by the storm, went about its wooing. My mood swung back from dismay toward joy. At length I went indoors, chilled and reassured.

Bird books describe the screech owl's call as a mournful whistling, quavery and tremulous. To Thoreau it sounded "doleful," like "the dark and tearful side of music." At least since Pliny warned that the "Scritch Owl betokeneth some heavie news," many have taken the sound for an ill omen. A Cajun forklift driver I worked with at a factory in Louisiana once told me that his trailer was haunted by a shivering owl. The blasted thing ruined his sleep with its creepy whispering. Had he ever seen it? I asked him. Yes, indeed, he'd even had it in the sights of his shotgun, but dared not shoot for fear of bad luck. I knew from his description—a ruddy bird as tall as a robin and twice as big around, with ear tufts and piercing yellow eyes—that he was talking about a screech owl. Indeed, "shiver" comes closer than "screech" to describing the soft, murmuring call.

Every night since first hearing it in January, right on through the blizzard in March and up to the last week of April when I write these words, I have been listening to my wild neighbor without ever laying eyes on him. A friend tells me I could spy the owl if I probed the hemlock with a flashlight. But I am content to use my ears. Let it remain hidden, a voice calling out of storm and darkness. I hear no ill omen in that sound. On the contrary, I hear in the screech owl's call an energy and yearning and grit that I find immensely encouraging.

Comets were also once thought to be tokens of ill fortune. Anything unusual in the night sky might prophesy war, invasion, plague, the death of a ruler, or some other calamity. The word *disaster,* after all, means ill-starred. We now understand comets to be frozen chunks of debris from the vast cloud of material left over when the sun and planets coalesced out of dust some four billion years ago. They are very old scrap, recycled from earlier generations of stars. Far from malignant, comets appear to have donated much of our atmosphere and water when they bombarded Earth in its early days, perhaps even delivering the carbon compounds necessary for the emergence of life. Though not so numerous these days, they still pass our way, mementos of our origins, snared by the sun into long, looping orbits.

For a month or so, beginning just before the blizzard and continuing well into April, another celebrated comet blazed through the headlines and through our northern skies, moving from Virgo past the Dippers to Perseus. Named Hyakutake after the Japanese amateur astronomer who discovered it, the comet followed a path that would bring it around once every eighteen thousand years or so, which means that during its previous visit our ancestors were all still hunters and gatherers, not yet having learned how to plant grains or tame sheep and goats. Compared to the length of my life or yours, eighteen thousand years is a long time; compared to the age of the solar system or universe, it's an eye blink. In that eye blink we have learned not only how to sow grains but how to engineer seeds, not only how to tame animals but how to breed new species; we have learned how to transplant trees and hearts, split infinitives and atoms, write sonnets, cure diseases, explore other planets, encode memory on silicon—learned all that and a great deal more, for we are as persistent about inquiring as the screech owl is about wooing.

Much of what we have learned is useful, ingenious, even glorious; but much is dangerous. In exercising our knowledge, we have made over the planet to suit our needs, and in the process we have done grievous damage. Whether our descendants will still flourish here eighteen thousand years from now, and whether millions upon millions of our fellow species will still be around to keep them company, depends on whether our wisdom can overtake our knowledge. Whatever our fate, Hyakutake will sweep by on its appointed rounds, indifferent as a blizzard, and that indifference, like the owl's yearning, is a true face of wildness.

When so many of our actions lead to desolation, we should be glad the comets and stars pay us no mind. Who'd be willing to answer for the twentieth century? To say that the universe takes no heed of our desires is not to say, however, that it is random or crass. The more I learn about the natural world, from science and art and my own senses, the more elegance, order, and splendor I see.

# Wildness

When I ponder the way of wild things I do not think of blind chance; I think of the screech owl calling, resourceful and resolute, and of the hemlock shedding snow. I think of ferns unfurling and comets tracing their clean curves. I think of seeds and spores, eggs and sperm, those time capsules jammed with souvenirs from past lives and brimming with future lives. I think of images beamed down from the Hubble telescope, showing nebulae giving birth to stars.

A couple of days after the snowstorm, Ruth called me from the lab at midmorning, her voice brittle with distress. A colleague who worked in the neighboring lab, she told me, had stopped by earlier to say that he was feeling awful and thought he might go home after finishing a few chores. Usually robust, he looked gray and bent, and everyone urged him to forget the chores and go right home or to a doctor or maybe to the hospital. Somebody would drive him. He shrugged aside the offers and went into his lab, where he collapsed a few minutes later, drowned in his own blood from a split aorta. "He was forty-seven," Ruth told me, "and he left four young kids." Later she would explain that the bursting of his blood vessel was programmed into his cells, a case of genetic fate. His children and widow and friends would scarcely be comforted to know that his death was as natural as his birth, as natural as the owl's calling or the comet's return.

On the eve of our wedding, twenty-nine years ago, Ruth and I were out buying presents for the bridesmaids. As I steered into a parking space at an Indianapolis mall, she reached across the seat, laid her hand on my forearm, and said quietly, "Wait, don't get out. I have to lie down for a minute."

"What's the matter?"

"My heart's racing and I need to be still."

My own heart plunged and bucked. "What should I do?"

"Nothing. It'll pass."

She turned, bent her legs, and lay across the front seat with her head in my lap. I stroked her face. Eyes closed, she told me the name of what was happening to her: tachycardia, pulse madly accelerating, the heart's controls gone haywire. She had suffered rheumatic fever at age four, nearly died from it, and this was her heart's echo of that illness. Usually she carried medicine that would rein it in, but in her excitement over the wedding she had left the pills at home. I smoothed her glistening hair. She was twenty; she was beautiful; she would marry me the next day. How could she ever die?

By and by, Ruth sat up, smoothed her skirt, and looked at me soberly. I felt as though I was meeting her all over again, this time as an adult. Twenty-nine years later, her heart still acts up occasionally, often enough to remind me that she is precious and mortal, and that every cell in our bodies is wild.

Owl, blizzard, comet, heart, all are wild, beyond our will, obedient to their own ways. Clever species that we are, through much of our history we have sought to control wildness, harness it, predict its movements; we have even tried, in our Faustian moments, to abolish it. The same impulse that lifted stones into circles thousands of years ago, to measure the cycles of sun and moon and stars, now lofts telescopes and laboratories into orbit. The same impulse that strung weirs across rapids to snare fish now dams whole rivers. The same impulse that tanned buffalo skins and built fires within the tepee also gives us vinyl siding and gas furnaces. We have labored for millennia to superimpose on original nature a secondary one of our own design. As a result of this prolonged effort, those who are most repulsed by wildness, or most afraid of it, can now move into sealed boxes, eat artificial food, shoot their bodies full of drugs, and plug themselves into virtual worlds where they are boss.

I'm grateful for a furnace and insulated walls in winter, for light to read by at night; I'm grateful for the medicine that keeps Ruth's heart in trim, for the plastic lenses that correct my vision, for the bicycle that wheels me around town, for bread and music, for cameras and shovels and shoes; I'm grateful for many, many fruits of human ingenuity.

But I still hanker for the original world, the one that makes us rather than the one we make. I hunger for contact with the shaping power that curves the comet's path and fills the owl's throat with song and fashions every flake of snow and carpets the hills with green. It is a prodigal, awful, magnificent power, forever casting new forms into existence, then tearing them apart and starting over.

Crews were busy for days after the blizzard, clearing downed trees from the streets, chain saws roaring. When the snow melted, homeowners trudged across their boggy yards, gathering torn branches and piling them by the curb. Before the city trucks got around to collect those heaps, some of the branches turned rusty pink, from redbuds bursting into flower. So for a while the streets seemed to be lined with bonfires, as though for a triumphal procession. But the fires could just as well have been for a funeral procession. Such late snowstorms can wipe out half the population of birds. In our city alone, hundreds of old trees keeled over or split down the middle. The small woods at the end of our block was a havoc of shattered trunks, bark stripped away to reveal the creamy flesh. Along the sidewalks, the severed redbud limbs went on blooming defiantly, yet no seed would come of those blossoms.

Like the tricksters who show up in tales the world over, wildness has many guises, but chief among them are creator and destroyer. Coyote and Spider and Hare bring gifts one day and steal them away the next. Even before we hear their stories, we know the truth of them in our bones. Every form that gathers into existence eventually dissolves, every cell, every star, a diamond as surely as a diatom. Each of us is a wave heaved up, holding shape for a while, maybe widening at the waist and thinning on top as the years go by, then sinking again into the primordial waters. Each heart that beats will one day cease. Knowing that, we have the choice of judging wildness, the very condition of our being, primarily by what it snatches away or by what it gives. We can fix on the brokenness of those redbud limbs, or on their insistent blossoming. We can be most impressed that the owl survives by killing, or that it survives at all, carrying on through sixty million years of storms.

Often in the night, or in grief over a nearby death, I can see nothing of wildness but the destroyer. Most of the time, however, I am struck by the generosity of wild gifts, the fertility of nature, the abundance of creatures and forms constantly rising. Right now I feel the thrum of freshness, for I write these words in spring, while sap rises and green shoots break ground and bright grass licks the air. I keep interrupting work to go outside, stooping over sprouts in the yard, listening to birdsong, moseying through our patch of dirt to see what's new.

One place I check is near the back door, where the hose drips onto a sliced-up block of limestone I rescued from a derelict mill. Last spring I noticed that a little fern had taken root where two saw marks cross in the limestone block, a clutch of feathery green fronds on black stalks as thin as thread. I needed the magnifying glass and the field guide to identify it as an ebony spleenwort. I had brought dozens of other wild plants in from the woods to our lot, but never this one. I had never seen it in our yard before, nor did I know of any in the yards nearby. Yet somehow the spores had found this good spot, on the north side of the house, on damp limestone. It was also a hazardous spot, where feet tromped on their way to the compost bin and the hose dragged. I showed the fern to everyone in the house, so that we could take care not to crush it. From then on, whenever I used the hose I gave the spleenwort a drink. It seemed too flimsy to survive, yet it held on through summer, pushing tiny green tendrils along the saw marks in the stone. In fall I covered it with leaves. Today I peel the leaves aside cautiously, as though unwrapping a fragile present; and sure enough, there's the fern, uncurling its newly minted fronds.

Within days after an explosion blew off the top of Mount St. Helens, spewing ash and flattening trees, the insects reappeared on the slopes, then plants, rodents, and birds. Blackened by fire a few years ago, Yellowstone is once more green. Even volcanic islands, sterile heaps of lava flung up from the ocean floor, soon gather life: birds arrive, carrying seeds in their guts and mites in their feathers, and spiders come drifting on the breeze, and uprooted plants come riding the current, and sometimes even mammals wash up, carried on rafts of weeds. It seems not so much that nature abhors a vacuum as that it adores fullness. There is violence as well as freshness deep down in things, as we are reminded by volcanoes and earthquakes and tornados and fires. But so far, at least, on our green planet, freshness has won out.

When Ruth and I go canoeing on Lake Monroe—a large reservoir near our home in Bloomington, Indiana—we commonly see a great bird wheeling, its white tail and head gleaming against a backdrop of trees or clouds. As recently as ten years ago, there were no bald eagles on the lake, none in Indiana, because they had been wiped out by guns and poisons. DDT had been especially hard on the birds, weakening the shells of their eggs so that chicks died before hatching. After DDT was banned and the shooting of eagles was outlawed by the Endangered Species Act, state wildlife agents and volunteers began reintroducing eagles to the lake, using techniques developed by falconers in the Middle Ages. Eaglets were placed in hacking boxes mounted on towers beside the water, screened from viewing the humans who climbed up daily to feed them. The feeding continued until the young birds could fly well enough to hunt their own food. Soon a few of these hand-reared eagles began rearing their own chicks in the old-fashioned way. This spring, eagles are nesting in more than a dozen sites around the lake.

Right now, in hundreds of places here and abroad, people are at work returning animals and plants to areas from which they had vanished, reflooding wetlands, gathering rare seeds, replanting forests and prairies, cleaning up rivers, helping endangered species and battered lands to recover. In Chicago, for example, every weekend volunteers fan out through parks and forests to plant and weed, restoring patches of the prairie-savanna habitat that once flourished there, on their way toward a goal of reclaiming a hundred thousand acres. Instead of merely grieving over what has been lost, these dedicated people, in Chicago and elsewhere, are working to reverse the devastation. This worldwide movement of ecological restoration shows great promise of mending human as well as wild communities. One of the foremost chroniclers of the movement, Stephanie Mills, describes it as "a science of love and altruism." Informed by ecology, inspired by affection, it couples human intelligence and imagination and sweat with the recuperative powers of nature to begin healing some of the wounds we've made.

Except in harsh terrain, such as desert or tundra, the land responds to care, or even to benign neglect. Large portions of New England and the Appalachian Mountains are now more heavily wooded than at any time since the early days of European settlement. As the trees have returned, so have bear and beaver and coyote and moose, even wolves and mountain lions, along with other less glamorous creatures. On the other hand, arid sections of the American West, where overgrazing or salinization have reduced grasslands to dust, will recover slowly, if ever. Even in moist regions, wherever we have kept up our pressure, through clear cutting or bad farming or paving or pollution, habitats are still being degraded and biodiversity is still declining. A recent tally of threatened species published by the World Conservation Union lists more than a thousand mammals, nearly a quarter of all those we know, and more than a thousand birds. Each year's list is longer. We can reverse those trends, as the movement for ecological restoration shows, by living more lightly and by making way for wildness in our yards and parks and forests and farms. Nothing keeps us from doing so, except habit and haste and lack of faith. Faith in what? In our capacity for decent and loving work, in the healing energy of wildness, in the holiness of creation.

The prime exhibit for the vigor and genius of nature is the creation itself. That the universe exists at all, that it obeys laws, that those laws have brought forth galaxies and stars and planets and—on one planet, at least—life, and out of life, consciousness, and out of consciousness these words, this breath, is a chain of wonders. Wildness is the patterning power in this lavish production; it is orderly, extravagant, inventive. Wildness coils the molecules of DNA; it spirals the chambered nautilus and the nebulae; it shapes the whorls on a fingertip, the grain in wood, the plains of cleavage in stone; it regulates the waves breaking on a beach and the beating of a heart; it designs the amoeba's foot, the zebra's stripes, the dance of the honeybee; it matches the roundness of nipple and lips and fills the baby with a desire to suck. Wildness destroys, to be sure, recycling whole galaxies, but on balance it creates, bringing new and complex forms into existence; and it has brought forth, in us, a creature capable of gazing back at the source.

Although we primates have been gazing at our cosmic home for a few million years, we have only begun to fathom the scope and complexity of the universe. As recently as the 1920s, our best guess was that the whole shebang contained one and only one galaxy, the Milky Way. Since then we have kept enlarging our view, at a speed that dizzies the brain. In the winter of 1996, the Hubble Space Telescope focused for ten days on a point in the sky within the Big Dipper, and the resulting photographs revealed that the universe is far more densely populated with galaxies than we had previously thought. In fact, the Hubble photos increased our estimate of the number of galaxies fivefold, from ten to fifty billion, and thereby also dramatically increased our estimate for the odds of life having evolved elsewhere.

Measured against all those worlds, all that potential life, what do eagles and owls and ferns matter? Why would it matter if they disappeared, not only from my neighborhood but everywhere? The most immediate and personal answer is that, if they were gone, I would grieve. Quite aside from their roles in the web of life, they are companions and teachers; they are unique expressions of the beauty that suffuses the whole creation. Asking what good are eagles and owls, or ebony spleenworts, or black-footed ferrets, or snail darters, or any other of our fellow travelers, is like asking what good are brothers and sisters, or children, or friends. Such questions arise only in the absence of love.

We can study wildness, harness it, worship or waste it, but we cannot create it; nor can we extinguish it, in spite of our worst efforts. Life on Earth will outlast us, as it has survived ice ages, meteor showers, volcanic eruptions, continental drift, parasites and disease. There have been mass extinctions before, and life has always come back. The question is not whether life will go on, with or without us. The question is whether we will continue our reckless use of Earth until we perish, taking innumerable other species down with us, or whether we will work to preserve the intricacy and beauty of our home.

We can make peace with the rest of creation, perhaps more easily than we can make peace with our own kind. Unlike humans, who seethe with resentment over past wrongs, the whales and wolves and rivers and woods hold no grudges. They answer our love with healing. What more joyful and promising work could there be than to help nurture and restore wildness? For that good work we have a powerful ally in wildness itself.

# Beauty

In memory, I wait beside Eva in the vestibule of the church to play my bit part as father of the bride. She is supposed to remain hidden from the congregation until her queenly entrance, but in her eagerness to see what's going on up front she leans forward to peek around the edge of the half-closed door. The satin roses appliquéd to her gown catch the light as she moves, and the toes of her pale silk shoes peep out from beneath the hem. The flower girls watch her every motion. Twins a few days shy of their third birthday, they flounce their unaccustomed frilly skirts, twirl their bouquets, and stare with wide eyes down the great length of carpet leading through the avenue of murmuring people.

Eva hooks a hand on my elbow while the three bridesmaids fuss over her, fixing the gauzy veil, spreading the long ivory train of her gown, tucking into her bun a loose strand of hair, which glows the color of honey filled with sunlight. Clumsy in my rented finery—patent leather shoes that are a size too small and starched shirt and stiff black tuxedo—I stand among these gorgeous women like a crow among doves. I realize they are gorgeous not because they carry bouquets or wear silk dresses, but because the festival of marriage has slowed time down until any fool can see their glory.

Concerned that we might walk too fast, as we did in rehearsal, Eva tries in vain to teach me a gliding ballet step to use as we process down the aisle.

"It's really simple, Daddy," she says, as I botch it over and over.

On an ordinary day, I would have learned the step quickly, but this is no ordinary day, and these few furtive seconds of instruction in the vestibule are not enough for my pinched feet. I fear that I will stagger like a wounded veteran beside my elegant daughter.

Eva, meanwhile, seems blissfully confident, not only of being able to walk gracefully, as she could do in her sleep, but of standing before this congregation and solemnly promising to share her life with the man who waits in thinly disguised turmoil at the far end of the aisle. Poised on the dais, wearing a black ministerial robe and a white stole, is the good friend whom Eva and I know best as our guide on canoe trips through the Boundary Waters. He grins so broadly that his full cheeks push up against the round rims of his spectacles.

"There's one happy preacher," Eva says.

"He believes in marriage," I reply.

"So do I. Remember, Matt and I figured that between you and Mom and his folks, our parents have been married fifty-eight years."

Eva lets go of my arm to lift a hand to her throat, touching the string of pearls she has borrowed from my own bride, Ruth, to whom I've been married thirty years. The necklace was a sixteenth birthday gift to Ruth from her own parents, who have now been married over half a century all by themselves.

Love *can* be durable, I'm thinking, as Eva returns her free hand to my arm and tightens her grip. The arm she holds is my left one, close against my racing heart. On her own left arm she balances a great sheaf of flowers—daisies and lilies, marigolds, snapdragons, bee balm, feverfew—the sumptuous handiwork of a gardening friend, and in her left hand she holds a Belgian lace handkerchief, also borrowed from Ruth, in case she cries. But so far there is no welling of tears in those bold brown eyes.

The organ strikes up Bach's "Jesu, Joy of Man's Desiring" for the bridesmaids' entrance, and down the aisle they skim, those gorgeous women in midnight blue. The organist is another friend, the former choir director of our church, an old pro whose timing and touch are utterly sure, and likewise a generous man, who has postponed open heart surgery until next week in order to play for Eva's wedding. He tilts his head back to read the music through bifocals, then tilts it forward to study the progress of the bridesmaids, then tilts it back again as he raises the volume a notch for the entrance of the flower girls. Overawed by the crowd, the flower girls hang back until their mother nudges them along and they spy their father waving eagerly at them from the third row of seats, and then they dash and skip, carrying their fronds of flowers like spears.

Finally, only the bride and the father of the bride remain in the vestibule. Eva whispers, "Remember, now, don't walk too fast." But how can I walk slowly while my heart races? I have forgotten the ballet step she tried to show me. I want events to pause so that I can practice the step, so that we can go canoeing once more in the wilderness, so that we can sit on a boulder by the sea and talk over life's mysteries, so that I can make up to my darling for anything she may have lacked in her girlhood.

But events do not pause. The organ sounds the first few bars of Purcell's "Trumpet Voluntary," our cue to show ourselves. We move into the open doorway, and two hundred faces turn their lit eyes on us. Eva tilts her face up at me, quirks the corners of her lips into a tight smile, and says, "Here we go, Daddy." And so, lifting our feet in unison, we go.

The wedding took place in Bloomington, Indiana, on a sizzling Saturday in July. Now in early September, I can summon up hundreds of details from that radiant day, but on the day itself I was aware only of a surpassing joy. The glow of happiness had to cool before it would crystallize into memory.

Pardon my cosmic metaphor, but I can't help thinking of the physicists' claim that, if we trace the universe back to its origins in the Big Bang, we find the multiplicity of things fusing into greater and greater simplicity, until at the moment of creation itself there is only pure undifferentiated energy. Without being able to check their equations, I think the physicists are right. I believe the energy they speak of is holy, by which I mean it is the closest we can come with our instruments to measuring the strength of God. I also believe this primal energy continues to feed us, directly through the goods of creation, and indirectly through the experience of beauty. The thrill of beauty is what entranced me as I stood with Eva's hand hooked over my arm while the wedding march played, as it entrances me on these September nights when I walk over dewy grass among the songs of crickets and stare at the Milky Way.

We are seeing the Milky Way, and every other denizen of the sky, far more clearly these days thanks to the sharp eyes of the Hubble Space Telescope, as it orbits out beyond the blur of Earth's atmosphere. From data beamed down by the telescope, for example, I summon onto my computer screen an image of Jupiter wrapped in its bands of cloud like a ball of heathery yarn. Then I call up the Cat's Eye Nebula, with its incandescent swirls of red looped around the gleam of a helium star, for all the world like the burning iris of a tiger. This fierce glare began its journey toward Earth three thousand years ago, about the time my Assyrian ancestors were in their prime. Pushing back deeper in time and farther in space, I summon onto my screen the Eagle Nebula, seven thousand light-years away, a trio of dust clouds upraised like rearing horses, their dark bodies scintillating with the sparks of newborn stars. I study images of quasars giving birth to galaxies, galaxies whirling in the shapes of pinwheels, supernovas ringed by strands of luminous debris, immense tornados of hot gas spiraling into black holes; and all the while I'm delving back and back toward that utter beginning when you and I and my daughter and her new husband and the bright heavenly host were joined in the original burst of light.

On these cool September mornings, I have been poring over two sets of photographs, those from deep space and those from Eva's wedding, trying to figure out why such different images—of supernova and shining daughter, of spinning galaxies and trembling bouquets—set up in me the same hum of delight. The feeling is unusually intense for me just now, so soon after the nuptials, but it has never been rare. As far back as I can remember, things seen or heard or smelled, things tasted or touched, have provoked in me an answering vibration. The stimulus might be the sheen of moonlight on the needles of a white pine, or the iridescent glimmer on a dragonfly's tail, or the lean silhouette of a ladder-back chair, or the glaze on a hand-thrown pot. It might be birdsong or a Bach sonata or the purl of water over stone. It might be a line of poetry, the outline of a cheek, the savor of bread, the sway of a bough or a bow. The provocation might be as grand as a mountain sunrise or as humble as an icicle's jeweled tip, yet in each case a familiar surge of gratitude and wonder wells up in me.

Now and again some voice raised on the stairs leading to my study, some passage of music, some noise from the street, will stir a sympathetic thrum from the strings of the guitar that tilts against the wall behind my door. Just so, over and over again, impulses from the world stir a responsive chord in me—not just any chord, but a particular one, combining notes of elegance, exhilaration, simplicity, and awe. The feeling is as recognizable to me, as unmistakable, as the sound of Ruth's voice or the beating of my own heart. A screech owl calls, a comet streaks the night sky, a story moves unerringly to a close, a child lays an arrowhead in the palm of my hand, my daughter smiles at me through her bridal veil, and I feel for a moment at peace, in place, content. I sense in those momentary encounters a harmony between myself and whatever I behold. The word that seems to fit most exactly this feeling of resonance, this sympathetic vibration between inside and outside, is *beauty*.

What am I to make of this resonant feeling? Do my sensory thrills tell me anything about the world? Does beauty reveal a kinship between my small self and the great cosmos, or does my desire for meaning only fool me into thinking so? Perhaps, as biologists maintain, in my response to patterns I am merely obeying the old habits of evolution. Perhaps, like my guitar, I am only a sounding box played on by random forces.

I must admit that two cautionary sayings keep echoing in my head. "Beauty is only skin deep" I've heard repeatedly, and "Beauty is in the eye of the beholder." Like most proverbs, these two convey partial truths that are commonly mistaken for the whole truth. Appealing surfaces may hide ugliness, true enough, as many a handsome villain or femme fatale should remind us. Some of the prettiest butterflies and mushrooms and frogs are also the most poisonous. It is equally true that our taste may be influenced by our upbringing, by training, by cultural fashion. One of my neighbors plants in his yard a pink flamingo made of translucent plastic and a concrete goose dressed in overalls, while I plant in my yard ox-eye daisies and jack-in-the-pulpits and maidenhair ferns, and both of us, by our own lights, are chasing beauty. The women of one tribe scarify their cheeks, and the women of another tribe paint their cheeks with rouge, while the women of a third tribe hide their cheeks behind veils, each obeying local notions of loveliness.

Mustn't beauty be shallow if it can be painted on? Mustn't beauty be a delusion if it can blink off and on like a flickering bulb? A wedding gown will eventually grow musty in a mothproof box, flowers will fade, and the glow will seep out of the brightest day. I'll grant that we may be fooled by facades, may be led astray by our fickle eyes. But I have been married to Ruth for thirty years, remember. I've watched my daughter grow for twenty-four years, my son for twenty, and these loved ones have taught me a more hopeful possibility. Season after season I have knelt over fiddleheads breaking ground, have studied the wings of swallowtails nectaring on blooms, have spied skeins of geese high in the sky. There are books I have read, pieces of music I have listened to, ideas I have revisited time and again with fresh delight. I have lived among enough people whose beauty runs all the way through, I have been renewed by enough places and creatures, I have fed long enough from certain works of intellect and imagination, to feel absolutely certain that genuine beauty is more than skin deep, that real beauty dwells not in my own eye alone but out in the world.

While I can speak with confidence of what I feel in the presence of beauty, I must go out on a speculative limb if I am to speak about the qualities in the world that call it forth. Far out on that limb, therefore, let me suggest that a creature, an action, a landscape, a line of poetry or music, a scientific formula, or anything else that might seem beautiful, seems so because it gives us a glimpse of the underlying order of things. The swirl of a galaxy and the swirl of a gown resemble one another not merely by accident, but because they follow the grain of the universe. That grain runs through our own depths. What we find beautiful accords with our most profound sense of how things *ought* to be. Ordinarily, we live in a tension between our perceptions and our desires. When we encounter beauty, that tension vanishes, and outward and inward images agree.

Before I climb out any farther onto this limb, let me give biology its due. It may be that in pursuing beauty we are merely obeying our genes. It may be that the features we find beautiful in men or women, in landscape or weather, even in art and music and story, are ones that improved the chances of survival for our ancestors. Put the other way around, it is entirely plausible that the early humans who did *not* tingle at the sight of a deer, the smell of a thunderstorm, the sound of running water, or the stroke of a hand on a shapely haunch, all died out, carrying with them their oblivious genes.

Who can doubt that biology, along with culture, plays a crucial role in tuning our senses? The gravity that draws a man and woman together, leading each to find the other ravishing, carries with it a long history of sexual selection, one informed by a shrewd calculation of fertility and strength. I remember how astonished I was to realize, one rainy spring day in seventh grade, that the girl sitting in the desk beside me was suddenly, enormously *interesting*. My attention was riveted on Mary Kay's long blond hair, which fell in luxuriant waves over the back of her chair, until it brushed against a rump that swelled, in a way I had never noticed before, her green plaid skirt. As a twelve-year-old, I would not have called Mary Kay beautiful, although I realize now that is what she was. And I would have balked at the suggestion that my caveman ancestors had any say in my dawning desire, although now I can hear their voices grunting, Go for the lush hair, the swelling rump.

If we take a ride through the suburbs and study the rolling acres of lawn dotted with clumps of trees and occasional ponds, what do we see but a faithful simulation of the African savanna where humans first lived? Where space and zoning laws permit, the expanse of green will often be decorated by grazing animals, docile and fat, future suppers on the hoof. The same combination of watering holes, sheltering trees, and open grassland shows up in paintings and parks the world over, from New Delhi to New York. It is as though we shape our surroundings to match an image, coiled in our DNA, of the bountiful land.

Perhaps in every case, as in our infatuation with lover or landscape, a sense of biological fitness infuses the resonant, eager, uplifting response to the world that I am calling beauty. Yet I persist in believing there is more to this tingle than an evolutionary reflex. Otherwise, how could a man who is programmed to lust after every nubile female nonetheless be steadily attracted, year after year, to the same woman? Why would I plant my yard with flowers that I cannot eat? Why would I labor to make these sentences fit my thoughts, and why would you labor to read them?

As far back as we can trace our ancestors, we find evidence of a passion for design—decorations on pots, beads on clothes, pigments on the ceilings of caves. Bone flutes have been found at human sites dating back more than thirty thousand years. So we answer the breathing of the land with our own measured breath; we answer the beauty we find with the beauty we make. Our ears may be finely tuned for detecting the movements of predators or prey, but that does not go far toward explaining why we should be so moved by listening to Gregorian chants or Delta blues. Our eyes may be those of a slightly reformed ape, trained for noticing whatever will keep skin and bones intact, but that scarcely explains why we should be so enthralled by the lines of a Shaker chair or a Dürer engraving, or by photographs of meteor impacts on Jupiter.

As it happens, Jupiter is the brightest light in the sky on these September evenings, blazing in the southeast at dusk. Such a light must have dazzled our ancestors long before telescopes began to reveal the planet's husk of clouds or its halo of moons. We know that night-watchers in many cultures kept track of the heavenly dance because the records of their observations have come down to us, etched in stone or inked on papyrus or stitched into stories. Did they watch so faithfully because they believed the stars and planets controlled their fate, or because they were mesmerized by the majesty of the night? I can't speak for them. But when I look at Jupiter, with naked eye or binoculars, or in the magnified images broadcast down from the Hubble telescope, I am not looking for a clue to the morning's weather or to the mood of a deity, any more than I am studying the future of my genes when I gaze at my daughter. I am looking for the sheer bliss of looking.

# Beauty

\\\\//

In a wedding scene that has cooled into memory, I keep glancing at Eva's face as we process down the aisle, trying to match my gawky stride to her graceful one. The light on her skin shimmers through the veil. A ripple of voices follows us toward the altar, like the sound of waves breaking on cobbles. The walk seems to go on forever, but it also seems to be over far too soon. Ready or not, we take our place at center stage, with the bridesmaids to our left, Matthew and his groomsmen to our right. My heart thrashes like a bird in a sack.

The minister gives us both a steadying glance. Then he lifts his voice to inquire of the hushed congregation, "Who blesses this marriage?"

I swallow to make sure my own voice is still there, and say loudly, "The families give their blessing."

I step back, lift Eva's hand from my arm and place it on Matthew's, a gesture that seemed small in rehearsal yesterday but that seems huge today. Now my bit part is over. I leave the stage, carefully stepping around the long train of Eva's dress, and go to my seat beside Ruth, who dabs a handkerchief to her eyes. I grasp her free hand, so deft and familiar. Thirty years after my own wedding, I want to marry her all over again. Despite my heart's mad thrashing, I have not felt like crying until this moment, as I sit here beside my own bride, while Eva recites her vows with a sob in her throat. When I hear that sob, tears rise in me, but joy rises more swiftly.

\\\\//

Judging from the scientists I know, including Eva and Ruth, and those whom I have read about, you cannot pursue the laws of nature very long without bumping into beauty. "I don't know if it's the same beauty you see in the sunset," a friend tells me, "but it *feels* the same." This friend is a physicist, who has spent a long career deciphering what must be happening in the interior of stars. He recalls for me his thrill on grasping for the first time Dirac's equations describing quantum mechanics, or those of Einstein describing relativity. "They're so beautiful," he says, "you can see immediately they have to be true. Or at least on the way toward truth." I ask him what makes a theory beautiful, and he replies, "Simplicity, symmetry, elegance, and power."

When Einstein was asked how he would have felt had the predictions arising from his equations not been confirmed, he answered that he would have pitied the Creator for having failed to make the universe as perfect as mathematics said it could be. Of course, his predictions were confirmed. Experiments revealed that light does indeed bend along the curvature of space, time slows down for objects traveling near the speed of light, and mass transmutes into energy.

Why nature should conform to theories we find beautiful is far from obvious. The most incomprehensible thing about the universe, as Einstein said, is that it is comprehensible. How unlikely, that a short-lived biped on a two-bit planet should be able to gauge the speed of light, lay bare the structure of an atom, or calculate the gravitational tug of a black hole. We are a long way from understanding everything, but we do understand a great deal about how nature behaves. Generation after generation, we puzzle out formulas, test them, and find, to an astonishing degree, that nature agrees. An architect draws designs on flimsy paper, and her buildings stand up through earthquakes. We launch a satellite into orbit and use it to bounce messages from continent to continent. The machine on which I write these words embodies a thousand insights into the workings of the material world, insights that are confirmed by every tap of the keys, every burst of letters on the screen. My vision is fuzzy, but I view the screen clearly through plastic lenses, their curvature obeying the laws of optics first worked out in detail by Isaac Newton.

By discerning patterns in the universe, Newton believed, he was tracing the hand of God. Scientists in our day have largely abandoned the notion of a Creator as an unnecessary hypothesis, or at least an untestable one. While they share Newton's faith that the universe is ruled everywhere by a coherent set of rules, they cannot say, as scientists, how these particular rules came to govern things. You can do science without believing in a divine Legislator, but not without believing in laws.

I spent my teenage years scrambling up the mountain of mathematics, aiming one day to read the classic papers of Einstein and Dirac with comprehension. During my college summers, as I sat on a forklift in a Louisiana factory between trips to the warehouse with loaded crates, I often worked problems in calculus on the backs of shipping pads. Men passing by would sometimes pause to study my scribbles. When they asked what I was doing, I said, Just messing around. I couldn't bring myself to admit that I was after the secrets of the universe. Baffled, my visitors would frown or grin, and then josh me about having my head stuck way up there in the clouds.

I never rose as high as the clouds. Midway up the slope of mathematics, I staggered to a halt, gasping in the rarefied air, well before I reached the heights where the equations of Einstein and Dirac would have made sense. Nowadays I add, subtract, multiply, and do long division when no calculator is handy, and I can do algebra and geometry and even trigonometry in a pinch, but that is about all that I have kept from the language of numbers. Still, I remember glimpsing patterns in mathematics that seemed as bold and beautiful as a sky full of stars on a clear night.

I am never more aware of the limitations of language than when I try to describe beauty. Language can create its own loveliness, of course, but it cannot deliver to us the radiance we apprehend in the world, any more than a photograph can capture the stunning swiftness of a hawk or the withering power of a supernova. Eva's wedding album holds only faint glimmers of the wedding itself. All that pictures or words can do is gesture beyond themselves toward the fleeting glory that stirs our hearts. So I keep gesturing.

Because the creation puts on a nonstop show, beauty is free and inexhaustible, but we need training in order to perceive more than the most obvious kinds. Even fourteen billion years or so after the Big Bang, echoes of that event still linger in the form of background radiation, only a few degrees above absolute zero. Just so, I believe, the experience of beauty is an echo of the order and power that permeate the universe. To measure background radiation, we need subtle instruments; to measure beauty, we need alert intelligence and our five keen senses.

The word *aesthetic* derives from a Greek root meaning sensitive, which derives in turn from a verb meaning to perceive. The more sensitive we are, the more we may be nourished by what Robinson Jeffers called "the astonishing beauty of things." Anyone can take delight in a face or a flower. You need training, however, to perceive the beauty in mathematics or physics or chess, in the architecture of a tree, the design of a bird's wing, or the shiver of breath through a flute. For most of human history, the training has come from elders who taught the young how to pay attention. By paying attention, we learn to savor all sorts of patterns, from quantum mechanics to patchwork quilts.

This predilection brings with it a clear evolutionary advantage, for the ability to recognize patterns helped our ancestors to select mates, find food, and avoid predators. But the same advantage would apply to all species, and yet we alone compose symphonies and crossword puzzles, carve stone into statues, map time and space. Have we merely carried our animal need for shrewd perceptions to an absurd extreme? Or have we stumbled onto a deep congruence between the structure of our minds and the structure of the universe?

I am persuaded the latter is true. I am convinced there is more to beauty than biology, more than cultural convention. It flows around and through us in such abundance, and in such myriad forms, as to exceed by a wide margin any mere evolutionary need. Which is not to say that beauty has nothing to do with survival: I think it has everything to do with survival. Beauty feeds us from the same source that created us. It reminds us of the shaping power that reaches through the flower stem and through our own hands. It restores our faith in the generosity of nature. By giving us a taste of the kinship between our own small minds and the great Mind of the Cosmos, beauty reassures us that we are exactly and wonderfully made for life on this glorious planet, in this magnificent universe. I find in that affinity a profound source of meaning and hope. A universe so prodigal of beauty may actually *need* us to notice and respond, may need our sharp eyes and brimming hearts and teeming minds, in order to close the circuit of creation.

# Silence

finding a traditional Quaker meeting in Indianapolis would not be easy. No steeple would loom above the meetinghouse, no bell tower, no neon cross. No billboard out front would name the preacher or proclaim the sermon topic or tell sinners how to save their souls. No crowd of nattily dressed churchgoers would stream toward the entrance from a vast parking lot filled with late-model cars. No bleat and moan of organ music would roll from the sanctuary doors.

I knew all of that from having worshipped with Quakers off and on for thirty years, beginning when I was a graduate student in England. They are a people who call so little attention to themselves or their gathering places as to be nearly invisible. Yet when I happened to be in Indianapolis one Sunday this past January, I still set out in search of the meetinghouse without street address or map. My search was not made any easier by the snow lilting down on the city that morning. I recalled hearing that the North Meadow Circle of Friends gathers in a house near the intersection of Meridian and Sixteenth Streets, a spot I found easily enough. Although I could not miss the imposing Catholic Center nearby on Meridian nor the Joy of All Who Sorrow Eastern Orthodox Church just a block away on Sixteenth, the only landmark at the intersection itself was the International House of Pancakes. Figuring somebody in there might be able to direct me to the Quakers, I went inside, where I was greeted by the smell of sausage and the frazzled gaze of the hostess. No, she'd never heard of any Quakers.

"But there's the phone book," she told me, gesturing with a sheaf of menus. "You're welcome to look them up."

I thanked her, and started with the yellow pages. No luck under "Churches." Nothing under "Religion." Nothing under "Quakers" or "Friends, Society of." Finally, in the white pages, I found a listing for the North Meadow Circle, with a street address just a couple of blocks away.

As I returned the phone book to its cubbyhole, I glanced across the room, where a throng of diners tucked into heaping platters of food, and I saw through the plate-glass window a man slouching past on the sidewalk. He wore a knit hat encrusted with leaves, a jacket torn at the elbows to reveal several dingy layers of cloth underneath, baggy trousers held up with a belt of rope, and broken leather shoes wrapped with silver duct tape. His face was the color of dust. He carried a bulging gray sack over his shoulder, like a grim Santa Claus. Pausing at a trash can, he bent down to retrieve something, stuffed the prize in his bag, then shuffled north on Meridian into the slant of snow.

I thought how odd it was that none of the diners rushed out to drag him from the street into the House of Pancakes for a hot meal. Then again, I didn't rush out either. I only stood there feeling pangs of guilt, an ache as familiar as heartburn. What held me back? Wouldn't the Jesus whom I try to follow in my own muddled way have chosen to feed that man instead of searching for a prayer meeting? I puzzled over this as I drove the few blocks to Talbott Street, on the lookout for number 1710, the address I had turned up in the phone book. The root of all my reasons for neglecting that homeless man, I decided, was fear. He might be crazy, might be strung out, might be dangerous. He would almost certainly have problems greater than I could solve. And there were so many more like him, huddled out front of missions or curled up in doorways all over Indianapolis this bitterly cold morning. If I fed one person, why not two? Why not twenty? Once I acknowledged the human need rising around me, what would keep me from drowning in all that hurt?

A whirl of guilt and snow blinded me to number 1710, even though I cruised up and down that stretch of Talbott Street three times. I did notice that the neighborhood was in transition, with some houses boarded up and others newly spiffed up. A few of the homes were small enough for single families, but most were big frame duplexes trimmed in fretwork and painted in pastels, or low brick apartment buildings that looked damp and dark and cheap. On my third pass along Talbott I saw a portly man with a bundle of papers clamped under one arm turning in at the gate of a gray clapboard house. I rolled down my window to ask if he knew where the Friends worshipped, and he answered with a smile, "Right here."

I parked nearby in a lot belonging to the Herron School of Art. As I climbed out of the car, a pinwheel of pigeons lifted from the roof of the school and spun across the sky, a swirl of silver against pewter clouds. No artists appeared to be up and about this early on a Sunday, but some of their handiwork was on display in the yard, including a flutter of cloth strips dangling from wire strung between posts, an affair that looked, under the weight of snow, like bedraggled laundry. An inch or two of snow covered the parking lot, and more was falling. Footprints scuffled away from the five or six cars, converged on the sidewalk, then led up to the gate where I had seen the man carrying the bundle of papers. True to form, the Quakers had mounted no sign on the brick gateposts, none on the iron fence, none on the lawn. Twin wreaths tied with red ribbons flanked the porch, and a wind chime swayed over the front steps. Only when I climbed onto the porch did I see beside the door a small painted board announcing that an "Unprogrammed ('Silent') Meeting" is held here every First Day at 10 AM, and that "Each person's presence is reason to celebrate."

There was celebration in the face of the woman who greeted me at the door. "So good to see you," she whispered. "Have you worshipped with Quakers before?" I answered with a nod. "Wonderful," she murmured, pointing the way: "We're right in there."

I walked over creaking floorboards from the narrow entrance hall into a living room cluttered with bookshelves, cozy chairs, and exuberant plants. Stacks of pamphlets filled the mantel above a red brick fireplace. Posters on the walls proclaimed various Quaker testimonies, including opposition to the death penalty and a vow against war. It was altogether a busy, frowzy, good-natured space.

From there I entered the former dining room, which had become the meeting room, and I took my seat on a wooden bench near the bay windows. Five other benches were ranged about, facing one another, to form an open square. Before closing my eyes, I noticed that I was the ninth person to arrive. No one spoke. For a long while the only sounds were the scritch of floorboards announcing latecomers, the sniffles and coughs from winter colds, the rumble and whoosh of the furnace, the calling of doves and finches from the eaves. The silence grew so deep that I could hear the blood beating in my ears. I tensed the muscles in my legs, balled up my fists, then let them relax. I tried stilling my thoughts, tried hushing my own inner monologue, in hopes of hearing the voice of God.

That brazen expectation, which grips me now and again, is a steady article of faith for Quakers. They recite no creed, and they have little use for theology, but they do believe that every person may experience direct contact with God. They also believe we are most likely to achieve that contact in stillness, either alone or in the gathered meeting, which is why they use no ministers or music, no readings or formal prayers, no script at all, but merely wait in silence for inward promptings. Quakers are mystics, in other words, but homely and practical ones, less concerned with escaping to heaven than with living responsibly on Earth.

The pattern was set in the seventeenth century by their founder, George Fox, who journeyed around England amid civil and ecclesiastical wars, searching for true religion. He did not find it in cathedrals or churches, did not hear it from the lips of priests, did not discover it in art or books. Near despair, he finally encountered what he was seeking within his own depths: "When all my hopes in all men were gone, so that I had nothing outwardly to help me, nor could I tell what to do, then, oh then, I heard a voice which said, 'There is one, even Christ Jesus that can speak to thy condition,' and when I heard it my heart did leap for joy."

My heart was too heavy for leaping, weighed down by thoughts of the unmet miseries all around me. The homeless man shuffled past the House of Pancakes with his trash bag, right down the main street of my brain. I leaned forward on the bench, elbows on knees, listening. By and by there came a flurry of sirens from Meridian, and the sudden ruckus made me twitch. I opened my eyes and took in more of the room. There were twelve of us now, eight women and four men, ranging in age from twenty or so to upwards of seventy. No suits or ties, no skirts, no lipstick or mascara. Instead of dress-up clothes, the Friends wore sweaters or wool shirts in earth colors, jeans or corduroys, boots or running shoes or sandals with wool socks. The wooden benches, buffed and scarred from long use, were cushionless except for a few rectangular scraps of carpet, only one of which had been claimed. A pair of toy metal cars lay nose to nose on one bench, a baby's bib and a Bible lay on another, and here and there lay boxes of Kleenex.

Except for those few objects and the benches and people, the room was bare. There was no crucifix hanging on the walls, no saint's portrait, no tapestry, no decoration whatsoever. No candles flickered in shadowy alcoves. The only relief from the white paint were three raised-panel doors that led into closets or other rooms. The only movement, aside from an occasional shifting of hands or legs, was the sashay of lace curtains beside the bay windows when the furnace puffed warm air, and those windows of clear glass provided the only light.

To anyone glancing in from outside, we would have offered a dull spectacle: a dozen grown people sitting on benches, hands clasped in laps or lying open on knees, eyes closed, bodies upright or hunched over, utterly quiet. "And your strength is, to stand still," Fox wrote in one of his epistles, "that ye may receive refreshings; that ye may know, how to wait, and how to walk before God, by the Spirit of God within you." When the refreshing comes, when the Spirit stirs within, one is supposed to rise in the meeting and proclaim what God has whispered or roared. It might be a prayer, a few lines from the Bible or another holy book, a testimony about suffering in the world, a moral concern, or a vision. If the words are truly spoken, they are understood to flow not from the person but from the divine source that upholds and unites all of creation.

In the early days, when hundreds and then thousands of people harkened to the message of George Fox as he traveled through England, there was often so much fervent speaking in the meetings for worship, so much shaking and shouting under the pressure of the Spirit, that hostile observers mocked these trembling Christians by calling them "Quakers." The humble followers of Fox, indifferent to the world's judgment, accepted the name. They also called themselves Seekers, Children of the Light, Friends in the Truth, and, eventually, the Society of Friends.

Most of these names, along with much of their religious philosophy, derived from the Gospel according to John. There in the first chapter of the recently translated King James Version they could read that Jesus "was the true Light, which lighteth every man that cometh into the world." In the fifteenth chapter they could read Christ's assurance to his followers: "Henceforth I call you not servants; for the servant knoweth not what his lord doeth: but I have called you friends; for all things that I have heard of my Father I have made known unto you" (John 1:9 and 15:15).

There was no outward sign of fervor on the morning of my visit to the North Meadow Circle of Friends. I sneezed once, and that was the loudest noise in the room for a long while. In the early years, meetings might go on for half a day, but in our less patient era they usually last about an hour. There is no set ending time. Instead, one of the elders, sensing when the silence has done its work, will signal the conclusion by shaking hands with a neighbor. Without looking at my watch, I guessed that most of an hour had passed, and still no one had spoken.

It would have been rare in Fox's day for an entire meeting to pass without any vocal ministry, as the Quakers call it. But it is not at all rare in our own time, judging from my reading and from my visits to meetings around the country. Indeed, Quaker historians acknowledge that over the past three centuries the Society has experienced a gradual decline in spiritual energy, broken by occasional periods of revival, and graced by many vigorous, God-centered individuals. Quakerism itself arose in reaction to a lackluster Church of England, just as the Protestant Reformation challenged a corrupt and listless Catholic Church, just as Jesus challenged the hidebound Judaism of his day. It seems to be the fate of religious movements to lose energy over time, as direct encounters with the Spirit give way to secondhand rituals and creeds, as prophets give way to priests, as living insight hardens into words and glass and stone.

The Quakers have resisted this fate better than most, but they have not escaped it entirely. Last century, when groups of disgruntled Friends despaired of reviving what they took to be a moribund Society, they split off to form congregations that would eventually hire ministers, sing hymns, read scriptures aloud, and behave for all the world like other low-temperature Protestant churches. In midwestern states such as Indiana, in fact, these so-called "programmed" Quaker churches have come to outnumber the traditional silent meetings.

I could have gone to a Friends' Church in Indianapolis that Sunday morning, but I was in no mood to sit through anybody's program, no matter how artful or uplifting it might be. What I craved was silence—not absolute silence, for I welcomed the ruckus of doves and finches, but rather the absence of human noise. I spend nearly all of my waking hours immersed in language, bound to machines, following streets, obeying schedules, seeing and hearing and touching only what my clever species has made. I often yearn, as I did that morning, to withdraw from all our schemes and formulas, to escape from the obsessive human story, to slip out of my own small self and meet the great Self, the nameless mystery at the core of being. I had a better chance of doing that here among the silent Quakers, I felt, than anywhere else I might have gone.

A chance is not a guarantee, of course. I had spent hundreds of hours in Quaker meetings over the years, and only rarely had I felt myself dissolved away into the Light. More often, I had sat on hard benches rummaging through my past, counting my breaths, worrying about chores, reciting verses in my head, thinking about the pleasures and evils of the day, half hoping and half fearing that some voice not my own would break through to command my attention. It's no wonder that most religions put on a show, anything to fence in the wandering mind and fence out the terror. It's no wonder that only a dozen people would seek out this Quaker meeting on a Sunday morning, while tens of thousands of people were sitting through scripted performances in other churches all across Indianapolis.

Carrying on one's own spiritual search, without maps or guide, can be scary. When I sink into meditation, I often remember the words of Pascal: "The eternal silence of these infinite spaces fills me with dread." What I take him to mean is that the universe is bewilderingly large and enigmatic; it does not speak to us in any clear way; and yet we feel, in our brief spell of life, an urgent desire to learn where we are and why we are and who we are. The silence reminds us that we may well be all on our own in a universe empty of meaning, each of us an accidental bundle of molecules, forever cut off from the truth. If that is roughly what Pascal meant, then I suspect that most people who have thought much about our condition would share his dread. Why else do we surround ourselves with so much noise? We plug in, tune in, cruise around, talk, read, run, as though determined to drown out the terrifying silence of those infinite spaces. The louder this human racket becomes, the more I value those who are willing, like Buddhists and Benedictines and Quakers, to brave the silence.

In the quiet of worship on that snowy First Day, I gradually sank into stillness, down below the babble of thought. Deep in that stillness, time let go its grip, the weight of muscle and bone slid away, the empty husk of self broke open and filled with a pure listening.

A car in need of a muffler roared past the meetinghouse, and the racket hauled me back to the surface of my mind. Only when I surfaced did I realize how far down I had dived. Had I touched bottom? Was there a bottom at all, and if so, was it only the floor of my private psyche, or was it the ground of being?

As I pondered, someone stood up heavily from a bench across the room from me. Although Quakers are not supposed to care who speaks, I opened my eyes, squinting against the somber snowlight. The one standing was the portly man whom I had asked the way to the meetinghouse. A ruff of pearl-gray hair fell to his shoulders, a row of pens weighted the breast pocket of his flannel shirt, and the cuffs of his jeans were neatly rolled. He cleared his throat. In times of prayer, he said, he often feels overwhelmed by a sense of the violence and cruelty and waste in the world. Everywhere he looks, he sees more grief. When he complains to God that he's fed up with problems and would like some solutions for a change, God answers that the solutions are for humans to devise. If we make our best effort, God will help. But God isn't going to shoulder the burden for us. We're called not to save the world but to carry on the work of love.

All of this was said intimately, affectionately, in the tone of a person reporting a conversation with a close friend. Having uttered his few words, the speaker sat down. The silence flowed back over us. A few minutes later, he grasped the hand of the woman sitting next to him, and with a rustle of limbs greetings were exchanged all around the room. We blinked at one another, returned from wherever it was we had gone together, separated once more into our twelve bodies. Refreshed, I took up the sack of my self, which seemed lighter than when I had carried it into this room. I looked about, gazing with tenderness at each face, even though I was a stranger to all of them.

A guest book was passed around for signatures. The only visitor besides myself was a man freshly arrived from Louisiana, who laughed about needing to buy a heavier coat for this Yankee weather. An elder mentioned that donations could be placed in a small box on the mantel, if anyone felt moved to contribute. People rose to announce social concerns and upcoming events. After an hour and a half of nearly unbroken silence, suddenly the air filled with talk. It was as though someone had released into our midst a chattering flock of birds.

Following their custom, the Friends took turns introducing themselves and recounting some noteworthy event from the past week. A woman told about lunching with her daughter-in-law, trying to overcome some hard feelings, and about spilling a milkshake in the midst of the meal. A man told how his son's high school basketball coach took the boy out of a game for being too polite toward the opponents. The father jokingly advised his son to scowl and threaten, like the professional athletes whom the coach evidently wished for him to emulate. This prompted a woman to remark that her colleagues at work sometimes complained that she was too honest: "Lie a little, they tell me. It greases the wheels." The only student in the group, a young woman with a face as clear as springwater, told of an English assignment that required her to write about losing a friend. "And I've spent the whole week in memory," she said. A man reported on his children's troubled move to a new school. A woman told of her conversation with a prisoner on death row. Another told of meeting with a union organizer while visiting Mexico. "They're so poor," she said, "we can't even imagine how poor." A woman explained that she and her husband, who cared nothing for football, would watch the Super Bowl that afternoon, because the husband's estranged son from an earlier marriage was playing for the Green

Bay Packers. When my turn came, I described hiking one afternoon that week with my daughter Eva, how we studied the snow for animal tracks, how her voice lit up the woods. Others spoke about cleaning house, going to a concert, losing a job, caring for grandchildren, suffering pain, hearing a crucial story: small griefs, small celebrations.

After all twelve of us had spoken, we sat for one final moment in silence, to mark the end of our time together. Then we rose from those unforgiving benches, pulled on coats, and said our goodbyes. On my way to the door, I was approached by several Friends who urged me to come again, and I thanked them for their company.

As I walked outside into the sharp wind, I recalled how George Fox had urged his followers to "walk cheerfully over the world, answering that of God in every one." There were still no footprints leading to the doors of the art school, no lights burning in the studios. I brushed snow from the windows of my car with gloved hands. To go home, I should have turned south on Meridian, but instead I turned north. I drove slowly, peering into alleys and doorways, looking for the man in the torn jacket with the bulging gray sack over his shoulder. I never saw him, and I did not know what I would have done if I had seen him. Give him a few dollars? Offer him a meal at the International House of Pancakes? Take him home?

Eventually I turned around and headed south, right through the heart of the city. In spite of the snow, traffic was picking up, for the stores recognized no Sabbath. I thought of the eighteenth-century Quaker John Woolman, who gave up shopkeeping and worked modestly as a tailor, so that he would have time for seeking and serving God. "So great is the hurry in the spirit of this world," he wrote in 1772, "that in aiming to do business quickly and to gain wealth the creation at this day doth loudly groan."

In my Quakerly mood, much of what I saw in the capital was distressing—the trash on curbs, the bars and girlie clubs, the war memorials, the sheer weight of buildings, the smear of pavement, the shop windows filled with trinkets, the homeless men and women plodding along through the snow, the endless ads. I had forgotten that today was Super Bowl Sunday until the woman at meeting spoke of it, and now I could see that half the billboards and marquees and window displays in the city referred to this national festival, a day set aside for devotion by more people, and with more fervor, than any date on the Christian calendar.

"The whole mechanism of modern life is geared for a flight from God," wrote Thomas Merton. I have certainly found it so. The hectic activity imposed on us by jobs and families and avocations and amusements, the accelerating pace of technology, the flood of information, the proliferation of noise, all combine to keep us from that inward stillness where meaning is to be found. How can we grasp the nature of things, how can we lead gathered lives, if we are forever dashing about like water striders on the moving surface of a creek?

By the time I reached the highway outside of Indianapolis, snow was falling steadily and blowing lustily, whiting out the way ahead. Headlights did no good. I should have pulled over until the sky cleared, as the more sensible drivers did. But the snow held me. Rolling on into the whiteness, I lost all sense of motion, lost awareness of road and car. I seemed to be floating in the whirl of flakes, caught up in silence, alone yet not alone, as though I had slipped by accident into the state that a medieval mystic had called the cloud of unknowing. Memory fled, words flew away, and there was only the brightness, here and everywhere.

# The Force of Spirit

y wife's father is dying, and I can think of little else, because I love him and I love my wife. Once or twice a week, Ruth and I drive the forty miles of winding roads to visit him in the nursing home. Along the way we pass fields bursting with new corn, stands of trees heavy with fresh leaves, pastures deep in grass. In that long grass the lambs and calves and colts hunt for tender shoots to nibble and for the wet nipples of their mothers to suck. The meadows are thick with flowers, and butterflies waft over the blossoms like petals torn loose by wind. The spring this year was lavish, free of late frosts, well soaked with rain, and now in early June the Indiana countryside is all juiced up.

On our trip to the nursing home this morning, I drive while Ruth sits beside me knitting. Strand by strand, a sweater grows under her hands. We don't talk much, because she must keep count of her stitches. To shape the silence, we play a tape of Mozart's Requiem from a recent concert in which Ruth sang, and I try to detect her clear soprano in the weave of voices. The car fills with the music of sorrow. The sound rouses aches in me from earlier losses, the way cold rouses pain from old bone breaks.

Yet when I look out through the windows at the blaze of sunlight and the blast of green, I forget for minutes at a time where we're going and what we're likely to see when we get there. Ruth must forget, as well, because every now and again she glances up from her knitting to recall a story or a task or some odd discovery she's read about recently.

As we slow down for a hamlet named Cope—a cluster of frame houses gathered at a bend in the road—she describes a scientific article that she came across at the lab this past week. After puzzling over what distinguishes living organisms from dead matter, the author, a biologist, had concluded that the vital secret is the flow of electrons in association with oxygen.

I tell her that all sounds reasonable enough, but I wonder why oxygen goes hauling electrons around in the first place.

"He hasn't figured that out yet," she replies.

"Wouldn't it be easier," I say, "for oxygen to sit still and leave matter alone? Why stir things up?"

"In other words, why life?"

"Yeah, why life?"

She laughs. "Ask me an easy one."

"All right," I say. "Why corn? Why shagbark hickories? Why moss and wolves? Why not just rock and dust?"

Used to my pestering her with questions, she normally answers with good humor and patience. But now she merely says, "You'll have to read the article."

A fly beats against the inside of the windshield. Suddenly the crazed, buzzing bit of stuff seems bizarre and precious. I lift one hand from the steering wheel, crank down a window, shoo the fly to freedom, and then grip the wheel once more. Now my fingers seem utterly strange. How can they curl so exactly in the shape of my thoughts? The lurching of my heart surprises me, as if a desperate animal has crawled inside my chest. All at once my whole body feels like an implausible contraption, and my skin barely contains the storm of electrons.

What I feel is not exactly panic, because I'm spared for the moment the chill of knowing I will die. What I feel right now is amazement that anything lives, fly or hawk, virus or man. I stare at the radiant fields and woods flowing past our windows, and they seem far-fetched, outrageous. Why all those leaves waving? Why all those juicy stems thrusting at the sky? Why those silky black wings of crows slicing the air? And why am I set moving through this luminous world, only to feel such grief when some patch of woods falls before the saw, when a farm vanishes beneath the pavement of a shopping mall or a valley beneath a reservoir, when a man withers in a nursing home bed?

"What are you thinking?" I ask Ruth, just to make sure my voice works.

"I'm thinking I only need two more inches to finish the front of this sweater."

"About your dad, I mean."

She turns her brown eyes on me, reading my face, which has grown transparent to her gaze over thirty years of marriage. Her own heart-shaped face draws into a frown. "I'm wondering if he'll still know us."

"Surely he's not that far gone," I say.

"Maybe not yet," she agrees.

I turn my attention back to the music, and gradually Mozart restores my composure.

After a while Ruth sets down her knitting and takes up a stack of her father's insurance papers. She's been working on them for months, but the stack keeps growing thicker, each layer of papers recording another bout in the hospital, another round of tests. She circles numbers, places checkmarks beside dates, compares one statement with another, imposing order on this chronicle of illness. Congestive heart failure is the short name for what afflicts him. After coronary seizures, quadruple bypass surgery, the insertion of a pacemaker, and several strokes, and after seventy-eight years of faithfully pumping blood, Earl McClure's heart is simply wearing out.

Every now and again as she works on the insurance forms, Ruth sighs, whether because of the tedious papers, or because of the history they record, I can't tell.

Near a tiny settlement called Bud, we pass a white barn that bears a warning in letters six feet high: AT THE END THERE IS JUDGMENT! One side of the barn is painted with the silhouette of a man hanging on a cross, the figure entirely black except for two white rings marking the eyes, which glare out like searchlights. A caption explains: "He died for you."

Ruth and I have known since childhood who he is, this dangling man, for we both spent nearly all of our childhood Sundays in Methodist churches, singing hymns, memorizing Bible verses, listening to sermons, learning that Jesus saves. Although Ruth still sings regularly in a church choir, and I sit in a pew on the occasional Sunday morning with a Bible in my lap, neither of us any longer feels confident that the man on the cross will preserve us from annihilation, nor that he will reunite us with our loved ones in heaven. The only meetings we count on are those we make in the flesh. The only time we're sure about is right now.

"Whenever we pass by here," Ruth says, "I wonder why anybody would paint such a scary picture on a barn. Who'd want to look every day at those awful eyes?"

"They're meant to keep your mind on ultimate things as you milk the cows."

"They're creepy," she insists.

I agree, but I also understand the attraction of a faith that eases the sting of loss, including the loss of one's own precious life. Until I was twenty or so I embraced that faith, hoping for heaven, then I gradually surrendered it under the assault of science, and in dismay over witnessing so much evil carried out in

Christ's name. I no longer believe that Jesus can do our dying for us; we must do that for ourselves, one by one. Yet I've not given up believing in the power that was supposed to have sent him to redeem us, the Creator who laid the foundations of the world.

For the last few miles of our drive to the nursing home, I study the land. There's a shaping intelligence at work here, I feel sure of it. I sense a magnificent energy in the grasses bowing beneath the wind, in the butterflies flouncing from blossom to blossom, in the trees reaching skyward and the jays haranguing from the topmost branches and the clouds fluffing by. I sense in this rippling countryside a tremendous throb and surge, the same force that squeezes and relaxes my heart. Everything rides on one current. As I listen to the music of grief filling the car, as I go with my wife to visit her dying father, the world, for all its density and weight, seems made of breath.

Legend has it that Mozart died while composing the Requiem, a few measures into the section beginning with the Latin word *lacrimosa*, which means tearful or weeping. "On that day of weeping," the verse proclaims, "again from the ashes will arise / guilty mankind, to be judged." That much he orchestrated, but he never completed the remainder of the verse: "Therefore, spare this one, O God, / Merciful Lord Jesus, / And grant them rest." Officially, the one to be spared from God's wrath was the dearly departed wife of the count who had commissioned this Mass for the Dead, but the ailing Mozart must also have been mourning himself. Another scrap of legend claims that in those final days he said, "It is for myself that I am writing this." I suspect he was grieving as well for his own dearly departed, especially his mother, who had died some years earlier in Paris while he was there looking for work.

Ruth's mother died last October, not long before the chorus began rehearsing the Requiem. By the time of her death, Dessa McClure had been whittled away by Alzheimer's disease for half a dozen years, losing her memory, speech, balance, and strength, becoming again as a little child. This was not the sort of child she had aspired to become, for she meant to find her way to heaven by achieving a clear vision and a simple heart. Toward the end, her vision grew cloudy, and the world became a blur of strange rooms and unknown faces. And at the very end, while she was rising from a bath, her heart quit.

The nurse who'd been helping her at the time told us afterward, "She went limp all of a sudden and dropped right down and was gone."

Ruth's father, still able to get around fairly well back then, had just been to see Dessa in the special care unit, where patients suffering from various forms of dementia drifted about like husks blown by an idle breeze. She had seemed almost happy, he recalled. She even whistled a bit, and showed no signs of pain. And he was sure she'd recognized him by the way she squeezed his finger and smiled. He let that be his last glimpse of her, for he chose not to look at his wife's body after the nurses brought him news of her death.

But Ruth saw her laid out in the nursing home, still crumpled, as if, when breath departed, the body had collapsed like an empty sack. Ruth was so appalled by the image that she insisted on seeing her mother's body one more time before the cremation. And so, after we had finished our business in the funeral home, she and I slipped into a back room to gaze for a moment at the shell of her mother resting on a cart, all but the face hidden by a white sheet, the skin pale except for dark rings under the shut eyes. We knew this face, yet it seemed aloof and slack, for it had been peeled away from the person to whom it once belonged. Beneath the sheet, the body lay as motionless as a piece of furniture covered with drapery in a vacant house. I put my arm around Ruth, not so much to comfort her as to comfort me, to feel the warmth and weight of her. She tilted her head against my shoulder and stood there for a long while without speaking. Then she leaned forward, ran a hand over that forsaken face, and turned to go.

The heart is only a muscle. It's a meaty pump that shoves and sucks the blood that carries the oxygen that carries the electrons that keep us alive. It beats forty or a hundred and forty times a minute, hour after hour, day after day, until, between one contraction and the next, it falters and stops. When surgeons lay the heart open to repair valves and carve out damaged tissue, they find no spirit hiding there, no seat of the soul. Biologists can trace it back down the evolutionary path to the earliest twitching of life in the sea.

Yet who can accept that we're merely meat? Who can shake the suspicion that we're more than two-legged heaps of dust accidentally sprung into motion? Whatever the doctors and biologists claim, we go on using the word *heart* as if it pointed to an emotional center, a core of integrity. We trust those who speak from the heart. We're wary of those who are heartless and hard-hearted. Have a heart, we say, begging for kindness. Home is where the heart is, we say. We're drawn irresistibly to our heartthrob, who knows how to pluck our heartstrings.

We long to feel heart's-ease by fulfilling our heart's desire. In our earnest pronouncements, we appeal to hearts and minds, heart and soul. Swearing most solemnly, we cross our hearts and hope to die, if what we say should be a lie. Heartfelt and heartsick, heartland and heartache, heartwood and heartbreak: the word, like the muscle beating in our chest, is indispensable. The beliefs we truly live by, the ones we'll die for, are those we hold in our heart of hearts.

At the nursing home, we find Ruth's father drowsing on his bed, arms outstretched as if he has fallen there from a great height. He wears a white shirt, brown dress pants, low knit socks that leave his ankles bare, and lace-up leather shoes. His hair, still dark and full, is neatly combed. Except for his gauntness, he might be a man resting after a day at the office. Yet he's too frail even to stand up for more than a few minutes at a time. His wrists are sticks. His cheeks are hollow. Blue veins show through the translucent skin of his jaw.

I can see Ruth hesitate before waking him, because she wonders if he will recognize her. So long as he sleeps, she remains his daughter. At last she lightly touches one of those out-flung arms, and he startles awake. Behind thick spectacles, his eyes are milky and uncertain. He looks bewildered for a moment, and then he beams, reaching out to grasp Ruth's hand.

"Hey, there," he says. "I'd about given up on you."

"Don't you worry," she answers. "If I say I'm coming, I'm coming."

"Well, I was thinking . . ." he begins, then loses his way and falls silent with an embarrassed little shrug.

But he has said enough to assure Ruth that he knows her, that he's still there in his withered body. She asks how he's feeling, how he's eating, whether he's had any visitors, whether the nurses have been treating him well, and he answers each question in two or three words, staring up into her face and squeezing her hand.

To say that he is dying makes it sound as though he's doing something active, like singing or dancing, but really something is being done to him. Life is leaving him. From one visit to the next we can see it withdrawing, inch by inch, the way the tide retreating down a beach leaves behind dry sand. With each passing day he has more and more trouble completing sentences, as if words, too, were abandoning him.

I hang back, awkward before his terrible weakness. Eventually he notices me standing near the foot of his bed.

"Why, here's Scott," he says.

I step closer. "I came to see if you're behaving yourself."

"I am, pretty much," he says. "How was the drive over?"

"It was beautiful," I tell him, lifting my voice because I can see he has left his hearing aids in a dish on the bedside table. "Everything's blooming. The corn's shooting up. Some of the hay is cut and drying."

"Good, good," he murmurs. Then he asks if I've been watching the NBA tournament, which I haven't, and so he tells me, pausing for breath between sentences, how the Indiana Pacers lost to the New York Knicks. The Pacers had a lead going into the fourth quarter, but their legs gave out. "I understand tired legs," he says, and gives a rheumy laugh.

Ruth and I exchange looks, amazed that he's following basketball. He's also following our children, Eva and Jesse, for now he asks what they've been up to since our last visit. After we've told him, he repeats bits of what we've said, as if to pin down memory: "So Jesse's working in the restaurant. Is that right? And Eva's studying birds? She bought a new computer?" His voice is thin and soft, like a trickle of water over smooth stone.

Since we saw him last, Ruth and I have attended a college graduation in Ohio. He remembers this, as well, and asks if we had a good time. We did, I answer. And then I tell him about watching the graduates troop across the stage as each name was called, most of them so young and spry they fairly danced in their black robes, while parents and friends and fellow students cheered. A few waddled heavily or limped stiffly. Two scooted across in electric chairs. Then near the end of the ceremony, one slight woman who'd been waiting in line among those receiving degrees in nursing rose from a wheelchair, labored up the stairs, and slowly crossed the stage while holding on to the arm of a young man. When the president gave her the diploma and shook her hand, the audience broke out in the loudest applause of the afternoon. We clapped because many of us knew she was gravely ill with cancer, she'd not been expected to live until commencement, and yet she'd refused to give up. Now here she was, onstage for a moment, drawing our praise.

When I finish my story, which poured out of me before I thought how it might sound in the ears of a dying man, Ruth's father says, "She's got spunk."

"She does," I answer.

"I like that," he says. "You can never have too much spunk." He rouses a bit to report that he's going once a day to physical therapy. They wheel him down there in his chair, but then they make him stand up and push a walker across the room to build up his legs and make him lift dumbbells to build up his arms.

"Pumping iron, are you?" I say.

"I need to get my strength back." He raises an arm and the sleeve droops down, revealing the tender bruised skin of his wrist.

We learned from a doctor this week that his heart now pumps blood at twenty percent of the normal rate, and it will keep on dwindling. His eyes close, but he doesn't let go of Ruth's hand. She says we'd better let him get some rest. Does he need anything before we go? Yes, he answers, three things: his bathrobe, an extra pair of trousers, and his electric shaver.

I go to fetch them from his apartment on the floor below, a comfortable suite of rooms where he's never likely to stay by himself again. Going there and coming back, I take the stairs two at a time. I rush down the halls past elderly residents who look at me as if I'm a lunatic. There's no reason to race, except that I still can, and so I do, savoring the bounce in my legs and the wild flutter in my chest.

⁘

I want a name for the force that keeps Earl McClure asking questions while the tide of life withdraws from him. I want a name for the force that abandoned the body of Dessa McClure and left it like a piece of shrouded furniture on a cart in the funeral home. I want a name for the force that carried a woman dying of cancer through her studies and across a stage to claim her diploma. I want a name for the force that binds me to Ruth, to her parents, to my parents, to our children, to neighbors and friends, to the land and all its creatures.

This power is larger than life, although it contains life. It is tougher than love, although it contains love. It is akin to the power I sense in lambs nudging the teats of their dams to bring down milk, in the raucous tumult of crows high in trees, in the splendor of leaves gorging on sun. I recognize this force at work in children puzzling over a new fact, in grown-ups welcoming strangers, in our capacity, young and old, for laughter and kindness, for mercy and imagination.

No name is large enough to hold this power, but of all the inadequate names, the one that comes to me now is spirit. I know the risks of using such a churchy word. Believers may find me blasphemous for speaking of the wind that blows through all things without tracing the breath to God. Nonbelievers may find me superstitious for invoking any force beyond gravity, electromagnetism, and the binding energy of atoms. But I must run those risks, for I cannot understand the world, cannot understand my life, without appealing to the force of spirit. If what I feel for my wife or her father and mother is only a by-product of hormones, then what I feel for swift rivers or slow turtles, for the shivering call of a screech owl or the green thrust of bloodroot breaking ground, is equally foolish. If we and the creatures who share the Earth with us are only bundles of quarks in motion, however intricate or clever the shapes, then our affection for one another, our concern for other species, our devotion to wildness, our longing for union with the creation are all mere delusions.

I can't prove it, but I believe we're more than accidental bundles of quarks, more than matter in motion. Our fellowship with other creatures is real, our union with the creation is already achieved, because we all rise and fall on a single breath. You and I and the black-footed ferret, the Earth, the sun, and the far-flung galaxies are dust motes whirling in the same great wind. Whether we call that magnificent energy Spirit or Tao, Creator or God, Allah or Atman or some other holy name, or no name at all, makes little difference, so long as we honor it. Wherever it flows—in person or place, in animal or plant or the whole of nature—we feel the pressure of the sacred, and that alone deserves our devotion.

A gusty breeze is pawing the grass and churning the ponds as Ruth and I drive back from the nursing home over the winding roads. Neither of us can bear to hear the Requiem again right now, so we talk. She remembers stories of her father from when he was strong—how he lifted her in and out of bed when she was down with rheumatic fever, how he laid fires in a charcoal grill when the family went camping, how he dug up the yard to plant roses. She recalls how, in their last house before the nursing home, her father and mother used to stand spellbound at the dining room window and watch birds at the feeders. And she recalls how, even in the final stark days, her mother shuffled to the birdcage in the special care unit and watched the fierce, tiny finches darting about, squabbling and courting. From inside the Alzheimer's daze, her mother would say nothing, but sometimes she whistled at the finches, and sometimes she laughed.

As if summoned by these memories of Dessa and Earl McClure, birds fill this blustery June afternoon here in southern Indiana. We see goldfinches dipping and rising as they graze among the waving seed heads of the tall grasses. We see red-winged blackbirds clinging to the tops of cattails that sway in the breeze. We see a kettle of hawks, a swirl of starlings, a fluster of crows. A great blue heron goes beating by, and six or eight geese plow the ruffled waters of a lake. Near the barn that's painted with the crucified man, more than a dozen turkey vultures spiral over a field, a lazy black funnel pointing down toward carrion.

There's an abundance in this teeming land that promises to make up for anything lost to vultures. The corn seems to have shot up higher since our drive over this morning. In the afternoon heat the woods bristle and the pastures heave and the fields are charged with light.

After a while Ruth takes up her knitting, clacks along for a few stitches, then puts it down again. Gazing out the window, she recalls in a soft voice how she thought of her mother at every rehearsal of the Requiem, and how moved she was at the performance itself when the conductor announced that the concert would be given in memory of Dessa McClure. Ruth had been forewarned of this gesture, but still she had to blink hard to read the opening measures.

We pass a hayfield where a tractor is rolling the cut grass into fat round bales, and I can't help thinking of the verse in Isaiah:

All flesh is grass,
    and all its beauty is like the flower of the field.
The grass withers, the flower fades,
    when the breath of the Lord blows upon it;
surely the people is grass. (40:6–7)

These days, I'm in no danger of forgetting how swiftly every living thing withers. But I also remember that grass, once cut, sprouts up again from the roots. Whatever Lord breathes upon this world of crickets and constellations blows beginnings as well as endings. The Latin word for breath is *spiritus,* which also means courage, air, and life. Our own word *spirit* carries all those overtones for me when I use it to speak of the current that lifts us into this life and bears us along and eventually lets us go.

We pass more fields scattered with round bales of hay like herds of slow, ungainly beasts. When we come up behind a truck on the road sagging under the weight of a single great bale, a stream of chaff comes blowing back at us, and loose bits float in through our open windows.

I reach over to brush some straw from Ruth's lap. She grabs my hand and holds on.

"I hate to think of clearing out Daddy's things," she says. "We'll have to find who wants what, then get rid of the rest."

"Let's hope that won't be for a while yet," I say.

She doesn't answer. We drive on through the lush green countryside. I remember when we cleared out Dessa's things, how we found more than forty Bibles and hundreds upon hundreds of religious books, which she had long since lost the ability to read. In drawers and cupboards and closets we found entry forms for sweepstakes, because she had decided, as her mind began to go, that winning some game of chance might set things right. And we found lists she had made of crucial events in her life—her marriage, her children's births, her surgeries, her husband's heart attack, the death of her parents, the moves from house to house—all the personal history that was slipping away from her. On page after page in a spiral notebook she wrote down in broken phrases what mattered to her, what defined her life, as if words on paper might preserve what the mind no longer could hold.

I make my own lists, in sentences and paragraphs rather than broken phrases, because language has not yet abandoned me. I am making such a list now, here in these pages. You've seen the long version. A short version of the story I've been telling you might say only:

Ruth, Earl, Dessa,
corn, crow, grass,
wind, dirt, sun.

# The Uses of Muscle

When I was a boy growing up on the country roads of Tennessee and Ohio, the men I knew all earned a hardscrabble living with the strength of their hands and arms and backs. They raised corn and cows, felled trees, split wood, butchered hogs, mortared bricks and blocks, built and wired and plumbed houses, dug ditches, hauled gravel, overhauled cars, drove bulldozers and backhoes, welded broken parts. They hunted game for the table in season, and sometimes out of season. Some of them had once mined coal in Appalachia or trawled for fish in the Great Lakes. Many had fought in Europe or Korea. They arm-wrestled at the volunteer fire department, smacked baseballs over fences at the schoolyard, and at the county fair they swung sledgehammers or hefted barrels to see who was the mightiest of the lot.

A brawny, joking, red-haired southern charmer who often won those contests was my father. He had grown up on a farm in Mississippi, had gone to college for a year on a boxing scholarship, had lost the cartilage in his nose during a brief Golden Gloves career. After moving north to Chicago, where he met the woman who would become my mother, he worked by turns as a carpenter, a tire builder, and a foreman in a munitions plant, until he eventually graduated to wearing a white shirt and sitting all day at a desk. He never liked the fit of a desk or a starched shirt, however, so as soon as he came home from the office he would put on overalls and go to work in the shop, garden, or barn. He could fix every machine we owned, from the car to the camera, and he needed to fix them, for we rarely had enough money to buy new ones. Although he grumbled when the tractor threw a belt or the furnace quit, as soon as he grabbed his tools he began to hum. He took pleasure in using his strength and skill, and I took pleasure in watching him. Around our house, whenever anything heavy needed lifting or anything stubborn needed loosening he was the one to do it. He could tame a maverick horse, hoist an oil-slick motor out of a car, balance a sack of oats on his shoulder, plow a straight furrow in stony ground, transplant a tree with its root-ball bundled in burlap, carry my sister and me both at once in his great freckled arms.

My mother had strengths of her own, but they did not depend on muscle. City bred, the daughter of an immigrant physician who had worked his way through night school by helping to dig tunnels for the New York subway, my mother read books to me and gave me drawing lessons and hauled me to and from libraries and science fairs in the fervent hope, later fulfilled, that I would make my way in the world by my wits. She wished the same for my sister, who patterned herself on the women as I patterned myself on the men. Although I have a much greater appreciation now for the bodily strength of women, as a boy I saw only their finesse, their ability to get by on little money, their competence in the face of calamity, their insistence on kindness and fairness, their hunger for beauty. While I valued those traits, and wound up being deeply influenced by them, as a boy I fixed my sights on my burly father and his buddies.

My father, meanwhile, waited for my body to fill out so I could be of some earthly use. As soon as I was big enough, he put me to work raking leaves, weeding the garden, stretching barbed wire, setting fence posts, clearing brush with a hatchet, carrying water to the ponies. At first I staggered between the pump house and the pasture lugging a gallon bucket. After a while I could manage a five-gallon bucket half full of water, then a full bucket, and finally a pair of them, one in each hand, the water lapping at the brim. None of this labor was mere exercise; it all had a purpose as clear as the sound of the ponies lapping at their trough or the taste of sweet corn fresh from the garden.

Before washing off the sweat from chores I studied my scrawny frame in the bathroom mirror, looking for signs of the muscle I saw in my father and the other men. I might think of the welder whose ropy forearms were speckled with scars from drops of molten steel. I might think of the roofer whose shoulders tightened into knots as he carried bundles of shingles up a ladder, or the farrier who stopped by our place twice a year to shoe the ponies. He would gentle the crotchety mare, lift one of her feet, remove the old shoe, clean the hoof, pare the horny surface smooth, then fit a new shoe and tap in the nails, all the while talking mildly to the mare, his own bare arms rippling with a muscularity as impressive as that in the pony's lifted leg. To hurry my body along, I began doing push-ups on the oily floor of the garage, doing chin-ups from a rafter in the barn. Yet no matter how tightly I flexed my arms before the mirror, my biceps hardly bulged, my chest remained a blank slate.

I was impatient to grow strong so that I could work alongside the men. On days off school when my father didn't need me at home I rode my bicycle to nearby farms, offering to do any sort of job for fifty cents an hour. I doubt my labor was worth that much, at least to begin with, but a kindly old Swede paid me anyway to help milk his docile Guernseys, fork silage into their feeding troughs, and shovel their manure. In spring I worked at his sugar camp, hauling buckets of maple sap. In winter I trapped muskrat along the river that ran through his bottomland and sold the skins in the county seat.

The summer I was thirteen, a man who baled hay on contract for other farmers hired me for his crew. I climbed into his pickup at five each morning wearing a long-sleeved shirt to protect my skin from the sharp stubble and to hide my skinny arms. We towed the baling machine to a field where the hay lay combed into windrows and where six or eight older boys and men stood waiting to lift and load and stack the boxy bales onto wagons and then unload the wagons into the barn. We sweltered. Between sunrise and dark we stopped only for a hot lunch served in the farmhouse and a cold drink guzzled between loads in the barn, the men drinking beer and the boys drinking soda. By far the smallest of that sinewy bunch, I struggled to keep up, my back and thighs aflame from heaving bales, my forearms scratched, my hands raw from the twine. But I would have died before quitting. I wasn't just a useless boy any more—I was finally working among the men.

The following summer I got a job setting pins in a bowling alley, the only one in our area that lacked machines to do this hectic job. From a narrow seat between two alleys, I would leap down first to one side and then the other, returning balls along grooved tracks, picking up scattered pins and setting them in overhead racks, all the while dodging the next ball. I went home with shins black-and-blue from flying pins and hands numb from gripping the wooden necks. Those aches and bruises were mild compared to the ones I acquired in later summers as an apprentice carpenter. A local builder, a friend of my father's from the volunteer fire department, hired me to carry lumber, mix mortar, push wheelbarrows, and drive nails. At night I could barely lift my arms to strip the sweat-soaked T-shirt over my head. I would lie in a tub of hot water until the cramps began to ease in my arms and back, my head throbbing with visions of studs and rafters rising against the sky.

After a summer of building houses, I started college with callused hands and a body tuned by hard work. A scholarship carried me to a place filled with young men who had spent their summers clerking or sailing or sightseeing. Overhearing their chatter about ski trips and stock options, about Dad's firm and Mama's trust, I soon realized that muscle did not matter there, except as ornament for attracting mates. Brawn was necessary for laborers, the men who load suitcases onto airplanes or rivet girders on skyscrapers or sweep the streets, but nobody in college aspired to become a laborer. On the contrary, the men I met on campus expected to earn handsome salaries by means of their fingers and tongues, guided by their well-furnished minds. They were training to become surgeons, brokers, attorneys, businessmen, psychiatrists, architects, journalists, salesmen, or teachers.

Even though I worked in a factory during the summers of college, I knew such work was only temporary, a way to pay for books, and that I was destined to earn my living by my wits, as my mother had always hoped. When I returned to school each fall, my calluses soon grew soft and my body grew slack. Following graduate school I became a teacher, rather to the dismay of my father—who held by the view that "Those who can, *do*, and those who can't, *teach*"—but to the satisfaction of my mother. I also became a writer, one who pushes around nothing heavier than words. If all but my neck and jaw were paralyzed, God forbid, and my brain were still nimble, I could carry on my work by holding a pencil in my teeth and pecking at a keyboard.

Since finishing my last shift at the factory, I've had to make an effort to use those muscles I longed for while growing up. Without cows to milk or hay to gather, I dig and weed and rake in our small yard. Without walls to frame or roofs to shingle, I remodel our old house. When time permits, I bicycle to the office, climb stairs, cut and split wood for the stove, fix the washer and change the oil in the car. But when I run short of time, I drive instead of biking, ride upstairs in elevators, hire others to do the heavy work for me, and then I feel as though my body has become a chance appendage, a mere device for transporting my brain.

To fight flab, once again I'm doing push-ups and sit-ups, nowadays on a bedroom carpet rather than on the oily concrete floor of a garage, and I swing dumbbells while watching nature videos, careful not to pinch a nerve. The men I knew while growing up in the country, including my father, would have been amused by this spectacle. Their jobs, their farms, their big families, their ailing machines, gave them more than enough exercise. Why would a grown man need to work out, they might have asked, if he did an honest day's work? Imagine the astonishment that Abraham Lincoln, the gaunt old rail-splitter, might feel at the sight of modern presidents jogging through the streets of Washington with an entourage of panting aides. Like the rest of the nation, our leaders don't run in order to get somewhere, or to toughen their legs for walking or bicycling, but to compensate for a life spent in meetings and banquets, and to redeem their arteries from fat.

In the recreational sports palace at my university, thousands of young men exercise religiously, lifting weights, sculpting their bodies, studying themselves in floor-to-ceiling mirrors. Their goal in cultivating these muscles, so far as I can tell, is to impress their girlfriends and to swell the shoulders of their suits. Except for athletes with dreams—more often delusions—of playing professional sports, these husky young men would shun any career that requires them actually to use their showy strength. Thousands of young women also work out in the gym, but the look they're after is lean instead of bulky, and the muscles they're toning have even less to do with any prospective jobs. The same divorce between work and workout could be witnessed, I'm sure, on campuses from coast to coast. One principal aim of higher education—as evident in the state university where I teach as in the Ivy League college where I studied—is to make irrelevant the kind of strength and skill that I spent my boyhood admiring.

Our machines, likewise, tend to make muscles superfluous. Consider that traditional male chore, the cutting of grass. The scythe gave way to the reel push-mower, which gave way in turn to walk-behind power mowers, then to riding mowers, and more recently, in the fancier suburbs, to hired landscaping crews that roar about on tractors. A job that once required the coordinated power of one's whole body now requires the twitching of a steering wheel or the writing of a check. Who needs strong legs in a world of elevators, escalators, rolling sidewalks, golf carts, and cars? Who needs a strong back or powerful arms when leaves can be gathered with a blower instead of a rake, trees can be felled with a chain saw instead of an ax, and ditches can be dug with a backhoe instead of a shovel?

There is still heavy work to do, of course. As I write these lines early on a December morning, while the temperature hovers around zero, a garbage truck rumbles down our street. Two men balance on platforms near the back of the truck, and at each stop they jump down, jog to the sidewalk, snatch the loaded cans, rush back to the truck and dump the contents, then replace the cans on the sidewalk and climb back on board. They will do this on street after street, for eight hours, lifting tons of trash. Next a tow truck pulls up at a neighbor's house and the driver climbs out and slides on his back underneath a stalled car to hook thick chains to the frame. From a distance I hear the bump and grind of boxcars coupling, the rat-a-tat of a jackhammer, the wail of a fire engine, and all of these sounds remind me how many hard and dangerous jobs remain.

Countless men still labor on farms and roads, in mines and mills and quarries. Yet they form an ever-shrinking portion of the workforce in this cybernetic age, and much of the hardest work, even in these primary trades, has been turned over to machines. Hay is now bundled in fat rolls that are handled entirely by tractors; one man pulling levers can put up more hay in a morning than a crew of six or eight, lifting and stacking the old boxy bales, could put up in a day. Big-time construction crews don't cut rafters for roofs but instead hoist prefabricated trusses into place with cranes and anchor them with nail guns. A single robot on an assembly line supplants a dozen workers who once bolted and welded parts together. An earthmover replaces hundreds of men pushing wheelbarrows. Forklifts do the he-man loading of barrels and crates.

If technology and education alike tend to free us from the need for muscles, what are we to do with our bodies, especially those of us who carry a Y chromosome and a charge of testosterone? I used to wrestle with my two children when they were little. For my daughter it was always a lark, make-believe, hilarious. But for my son, as he got up around twelve or thirteen, it became deadly serious, and he put all his might into throwing me off balance and pinning me to the floor. He would hurl himself at me with a fury and we would thrash around on the living room carpet. These tussles alarmed my wife, who feared that we might smash the furniture or one another. Partly because I was afraid of hurting my son and partly because I could foresee the day when he would get the better of me, eventually I called a halt to the wrestling, much to his regret.

Like sap rising in the trunks of trees in spring, strength still rises in the bodies of boys as they become teenagers, whether or not they grow up among laboring men. Boys today must spend more years in school than their fathers or grandfathers did, and the jobs they eventually find will make more use of their brains than their backs. So what are they to do with all that strength? Some cruise around town in souped-up cars with sound systems blaring. Some tear up phone booths, play violent video games, fight in bars. Some deal drugs, risking a jail sentence or a bullet in the head. Some sit on stoops with their sleeves rolled up, waiting for action. Some beat up their girlfriends or their wives. Some join the armed forces. Some join gangs.

Fortunately for the peace of society, many boys play sports, and thereby gain some of the benefits offered by hard physical work. What sports can't provide, however, is the satisfaction of doing something useful. While they offer entertainment, they don't build anything, raise anything, fix anything, or make anything. At their best, sports teach athletes a respect for discipline, skill, and cooperation. At their worst, they foster a brand of narcissism, most visible in the overpaid and pampered egomaniacs of the professional ranks. Perhaps the ultimate expression of strength without a purpose is weight lifting, where the point is to hoist a mass of iron overhead for a few seconds before letting it drop. Lifting so much weight, hitting so many home runs, throwing so many touchdown passes, making so many dunks, may be impressive, but it is also only a game, a child's pastime even when it is carried on into adulthood.

How might boys and young men—or, for that matter, men of any age—use their muscles for something besides recreation or mischief? Suppose we quit buying the latest "labor-saving" gadgets for our households and do more of the labor with our own hands. There is pleasure in washing dishes, hanging out laundry, shaking rugs, sweeping walks. There is pleasure as well as economy in painting our own walls, fixing a leaky faucet or a stopped-up sink, or changing a part on a car; and if we don't know how to do such things, then let us learn from someone who does. Suppose, instead of playing yet another sport or watching one on television, we dig up a patch of the yard or a plot in the community garden for a crop of vegetables. Suppose we bicycle or walk, whenever possible, instead of driving. Suppose we volunteer to help build or rehabilitate houses for needy people. Suppose we help a land trust maintain its property by clearing trails and picking up trash.

There is no shortage of work to do. We could fix up schools and meeting halls, clean up rivers and streets and parks, restore wetlands, plant trees. We could do small repairs for the elderly, deliver groceries for shut-ins, and shovel snow for folks too weak to do the shoveling themselves. The physical power I saw in my father and in the other men I knew while growing up was not for show, not for playing games, but for carrying on the necessary tasks of life. Since fewer and fewer of our households or jobs demand such power, those of us who still inherit the old hormonal rush, acquired by our male ancestors over thousands of generations, may now use our muscles to serve others. Freed from toil, we may choose to make our strength a blessing for our neighbors and our neighborhoods.

# A Private History of Awe

_W_hen I rise from meditation each morning, I gaze through an uncurtained window at the waking world, and I bow. The gesture is plain enough—hands drawn to my chest, palms pressed together, a slight bend at the waist—but its meaning is elusive. If you asked me to explain my little ritual, to say whom or what I honor with my bow, I would be hard put to answer.

It's a question I ask myself with increasing urgency as the years run by. The urgency is not the same as I felt at the age of ten or fifteen, when I prayed fervently each night, having been persuaded by preachers and Sunday School teachers that there was one and only one combination to the door opening from life into immortality. Nor is it the urgency I felt in my twenties, when the Vietnam War pressed me down to the roots of conscience as I struggled to choose between going into battle, exile, or jail. Nor is it the urgency I felt during my thirties and forties, when my children, still young, looked to me for guidance about ultimate things.

No, the urgency to understand my small bow has nothing to do with dreams of eternal life, with resistance to wars, with setting an example for children. It has to do with feeling called, as if something is required of me. Now and again since early childhood, I have heard such a call in various settings, in company or in solitude, often in darkness or in the midst of wildness, and I have heard it in sundry accents, from the roar of rain or the hoot of an owl to the vibration of a cello string or the whisper of words on a page. Each time the call comes, it stirs me to my depths.

One summer evening in Alaska, I was sitting with friends in a community hall, listening to the performance of a Beethoven string quartet. The four musicians, dressed in black, were framed against a bank of windows that opened onto Sitka Sound, where islands bristled with spruce and fir, and bald eagles soared against a rare blue sky. I must have listened and watched, I must have felt the nearness of my friends, and yet for the length of the concert I lost all sense of my separate self. Only when the instruments fell silent, and the audience recovered from its spell to break into applause, did I realize that for most of an hour I had become the music, the water, the birds, the sky. It was as though the narrow self dammed up within my skin had flowed back to its source, like a brook flowing back to the sea.

As a first inkling of what I'm trying to elucidate in these pages, I would point to such a moment. Thinking back on that concert in Sitka, I find myself wanting not merely to savor the experience but to live in light of the possibility it revealed—this rhyming of human artifice and wildness, this breaching of the wall between inner and outer worlds, this return to the source.

The longing to discern more clearly where I come from is what sits me down on a cushion before daybreak each morning. In meditation, I seek to quiet my inner chatter, still my jittery body, and simply listen. Usually I fail, remaining caught up in the froth of thought, distracted by the twitch of muscle. But every once in a while the fidgety self dissolves, as if it were a wave sliding back into the water, and there is only the swaying, shimmering sea. The moan of a freight train in the switching yard, the wail of an ambulance setting out from the hospital, the dawn chorus of birds, my faint breath, the beating of my heart, all are the pulse of the sea.

Such communion feels like a taste of my true nature. The feeling fades, but the memory of it lingers, beckoning me. So when I rise from meditation and gaze out on the waking world, I bow as if in answer to a summons. Whence does that summons come, and what does it require of me?

Midway through my fifties, having lost friends my own age to heart attacks or cancer, I realize it's high time for me to lay hold of this question and not let go until it blesses me with understanding. I don't expect to understand everything, for life slips through the finest net the mind can make. I don't expect pure enlightenment, for I'm too restless and wayward to court perfection. I merely want to gain every glimmer of insight my mind can hold. And so, on these late winter days, aware of time slipping by, I ponder my bow and its meaning.

\\\|//

Even though it's only the middle of February, three months shy of the custom-
ary date for last frost here in southern Indiana, the winter has been mild, and
the birds and trees and flowers and I carry on as if it were already spring. When
I go outside to fetch the newspaper at dawn, the cardinals, robins, sparrows,
finches, and other tribes are fairly shouting their amorous songs. The maples
break out in flowers the color of cranberries, the pussy willows push out catkins
like furry paws, the pines flaunt their candles, and the black cherries bristle
with spiky buds. The shoots of daffodils burst up through leaf mulch to probe
the air, and crocuses brazenly bloom.

I fully expect that snow will put a damper on all this enthusiasm before long.
Meanwhile, I rush the season by spading up our backyard garden. It's roughly
circular, bordered by flower beds and a limestone terrace, about the size of a
wading pool where fifteen or twenty children could splash. I dig slowly, partly
to save my back, partly to enjoy the digging. As I work across the bed I turn
under the stand of rye grass that we planted last fall to hold the soil. The rye is
a brilliant green, reaching halfway to my knee, and it sways in the wind. Every
time I slice through the turf with my spade, the grass yields a sweet, sharp
smell. I regret having to bury so much vigor, but I know it will rise again in our
spinach and peas.

This afternoon as I dig I sing snatches of a gardening song composed by a
sandy haired friend named Kevin Hanks, a banjo player and bard who rolls
through town once a year or so on a tide of music and stays next door with our
neighbors, Malcolm and Judy. Coming home from an errand, Judy sees me
working in the garden and approaches with a mixture of cheer and distress in
her face. She admires the dirt, saying it looks good enough to eat. Then she tells
me she can't see a garden without thinking of Kevin.

"I was just singing one of his songs," I tell her. The fret in Judy's face keeps
me from laughing at the coincidence.

"Well," she says, her voice going quiet, "they've just found cancer in Kevin's
throat, a kind that's rarely cured. It has already metastasized. By the time he's
finished with chemotherapy and radiation, he'll no longer be able to sing. He
may not be able to speak."

I rest on my shovel and look at Judy, her dark eyes gleaming. My own eyes
smart. Kevin unable to sing? He's a man in the prime of life, a decade younger

255

than I am, with a teenage son, a wife he adores, and enough musical talent for a whole band. It seems an outrage for such a man to be cut down, as if he were no more than the rye grass falling beneath my spade. Neither his family nor his friends will be comforted to think of Kevin's vigor coming back in the voices of other people. It's *his* voice we want, his fingers on the banjo, his particular song.

"That's terrible news," I say.

"I'm sorry to bring it," Judy answers. "But I thought you'd want to know."

I assure her that I'm grateful for knowing, and I promise to write Kevin a letter. She admires the dirt once more before going into her house. I resume digging, watching the spadefuls of soil, black from last year's compost, bury the vibrant grass. Each time I bend to lift the shovel I make another bow.

Kevin's own blood has spread the cancer through his body. In their effort to cure him, doctors will poison many of his good cells along with the cancerous ones. Life and death go everywhere together, hand in hand. As it decays, the rye grass I'm burying will release nutrients for the seeds I sow. The seeds, the soil, my hands, the Earth itself are all made of debris from doomed stars. Virtually all elements heavier than helium—including the oxygen we breathe, the carbon we burn, the calcium that stiffens our bones, the iron in our blood—were forged in the furnaces of supernovas and scattered abroad by explosions. It's as though a cosmic gardener keeps turning under old worlds to fertilize new ones.

This seems extravagant, especially when what's being turned under is your own life or the life of someone you love. At the age of ten, during minor surgery, I nearly died from loss of blood. I remember surfacing from an ether nightmare to realize that one day I would not wake, one day my heart would stop. What then? Would the world go on? Would I? I remember when the first person close to me died, remember seeing his body, slack as an old boot, laid out on a dining room table. He was a crotchety farmer who'd told me once that he was made mostly of ham and beans. Now something else, I realized, would be made out of that farmer. Was it really possible that one day something else would be made out of me?

As a boy, clasping my hands and praying into the darkness, I yearned for some way to dodge this fate. And of course the preachers offered me one. If I believed in Jesus, I would not only escape from death into life everlasting, I would get my old body back, as good as new. In my Bible I still keep a list, written in my schoolboy hand, of passages confirming this promise. I could recite many of them now, for I read the verses over and over, whispering them like charms in the face of midnight panic. Back then, when I bowed my head it was not mainly to give thanks or ask favors, but to beg the mercy of an inscrutable king who could swoop down, according to his fancy, as either the Good Shepherd or the Grim Reaper. I prayed almost entirely out of fear. Lord, let me not vanish. Lord, let me hold on to this sweet life. Lord, let me rise out of this sinful flesh into high heaven, let me join there with everyone I love, and let us all be healthy and joyful forever and ever.

I wanted desperately to believe the promise of eternal life, the way I believed in sunrise, but I never quite could. What I observed in barnyards and grave-yards, in creeks and woods, and what I later learned from science, convinced me that there's no special dispensation for humans, exempting us from death simply because we repeat certain gestures or words. There was no room for heaven in the cosmos described by physics and astronomy. There was no refer-ence to spirit in the equations defining the dance of matter and energy. Even if there were a life after this one—and the chances of that seemed slim—I fig-ured it would take no form I could imagine. Certainly it wouldn't resemble the quirky, precious life I already knew.

Year by year, I let go the dream of immortality. By my twenties, I had quit thinking of Jesus as a shining prince who could plead my case to the king. I had quit imagining God as that fickle king, a dispenser of rewards and punishments who might be persuaded to cut me a better deal. I left the list of comforting verses folded up in my Bible, like child's clothes I had outgrown.

Meanwhile, growing up in the country, I saw in the fields and woods miracles that surpassed anything I had read about in the Bible or heard about in church. Water striders dimpled the surface of the creek with their wiry legs, gliding back and forth across the current. Crows flustered in the treetops, their black feathers polished by sun. Beans in the garden pushed up clods of dirt, unfurled leaves, climbed poles, blossomed, and gave more beans. Snakes slithered from beneath the henhouse and stared with unblinking eyes, their tongues tasting the air. Hens turned grain into eggs. Lilacs cast their syrupy smell upon the air. Thunderstorms swept overhead, lightning spiked the horizon, rain roared down, every pebble and grass blade shone. And on clear nights, the Milky Way stretched across the sky like sugar flung on black velvet, every grain a world.

At the age of fourteen I inherited from my mother's father the brass micro-scope he had purchased while a student in medical school. The plating on the adjustment wheels had been worn off by his blunt fingers over the years, as he looked at blood samples from his patients. On a card table set up in our dining room, I studied a smear of my own blood under the lens, examined a single hair, a dandelion seed, a mite of dust. The detail and finish of the world astounded me. Then I dipped water from the ditch behind our house and placed a drop onto a slide, and for a few seconds, before the moisture evaporated from the heat of the lamp, I saw dozens of minuscule swimmers, each one going its own way, each transparent body as willful and complete as my own. Suddenly, the whirling of those specks, the glow of the lamp, and the intensity of my looking all shimmered with a single energy.

In the presence of such wonders, the boy who cowered in his bed, worrying about eternity, was nowhere to be found. Where my fretful, scheming self had been, there was only amazement. Surely this rapture must be a taste of the kingdom of God, I thought. Surely these marvels must be a glimpse of the glory of God. Yet nobody spoke of them as anything special, nobody honored them in church or school, nobody urged me to shape my life around the power I witnessed in microscope and telescope, in woods and fields. Gradually the miracles became familiar, like the beating of my own heart, and they lost their radiance. But years later, rising in memory, they would prove to be signs pointing me the way toward understanding this life.

Without guidance from religion or encouragement from science, I still felt the impulse to bow, to bend my knee, to pray. What I prayed for during my twenties was direction, because the events of that decade, from 1965 to 1975, bewildered me. I went from being a student to being a teacher, from bachelor to husband, from tenant to homeowner, from son to father. All the while, I was learning about the oppression of native people, black people, poor people, women, and Earth, and I was trying to figure out how to live with my pale skin and male genes and newfound prosperity.

Far and away the most bewildering challenge of that decade for me, however, was the Vietnam War. From the moment in college when I began paying attention to the bloody conflict, it roused in me a deep revulsion. I soon learned to give political and philosophical reasons for my opposition, but feeling came first. The spectacle of my country bombing and strafing one of the world's poorest countries filled me with grief. As we sprayed poison on the jungles, stripping the trees bare to uncover enemies, we seemed to be waging war on the land itself.

After much thought, I declared myself a conscientious objector. I notified my draft board in Louisiana that I would do alternative service, would clean toilets in a hospital or sweep floors in a school, would do any drudge work they chose, but I would not help kill people in Vietnam. The draft board promptly rejected my claim. I appealed their decision, and while I waited for a hearing, I debated what I would do if they ordered me to fight. Go to war as a noncombatant? Flee to Canada, England, or Sweden? Go to jail?

While preparing myself for a grilling before the draft board, I tried to account for my sense of moral revulsion against the war. It was easy to call myself a conscientious objector, but hard to explain the origins of conscience. Was it merely a product of my upbringing? Was it a result of taking seriously the teachings of Jesus and the Hebrew prophets? Was it only cowardice in disguise? Or was conscience a spark of God's own light deep within me?

The need to answer those questions bowed my head and set me praying. No longer hoping to woo favors from the universe, as I had in childhood, now I prayed for clear instruction. I wanted signposts showing me the path I should take. I wanted proof that the Creator loved life more than death. I wanted assurance that my sense of right and wrong was no mere private whim, but was anchored in the ground of being.

God did not oblige. No pillars of cloud arose by day, no pillars of fire by night. No voice proclaimed the unambiguous message I longed to hear. Instead, I heard only the inner tumult of a feverish mind. So I took long, brooding strolls, which were another form of prayer. I walked along a river hemmed in by stone walls, through gardens laid out in geometrical patterns, across pastures grazed by sheep—the wildest places I could find in the tame town of Cambridge, England, where my wife and I were living at the time. In this long-settled place, I was surrounded by human handiwork.

Yet even on the placid River Cam, amid punts jostling upstream and down, swallows cruised for insects. One day I happened to be watching as a swallow glided low over the water, dipped its bill, and took a sip on the fly. Overcome by the splendor of it, I bowed. I had witnessed such aerial drinking before, but until that instant, wrought up as I was about the war, I had never really *seen* it. As in boyhood, I disappeared into the seeing. I felt only the bird's thirst, its hunger, even a hint of its exuberant grace. And I understood absolutely that whatever power brought such creatures into being must indeed love life more than death, and this was the power I wished to serve. Of course I realized that swallows live by devouring mosquitoes and midges, that life feeds on life, but I also realized that such killing is bounded by the limits of hunger and muscle.

Swallows did not invent machines to magnify their killing, did not slaughter insects wholesale to enforce a change of ideology, did not report body counts on the evening news.

This glimpse of careening beauty, there on the River Cam, confirmed me in my fierce opposition to the war. I couldn't have justified by cool reasoning the way my heart moved. Certainly, I couldn't hope to persuade the draft board to see an argument for pacifism in the flight of a swallow. So I armed myself with quotations from Jesus and the Buddha, Meister Eckhart and St. Francis of Assisi, Tolstoy and Thoreau, Gandhi and Martin Luther King, Jr. I prepared answers to every challenge I could imagine coming from a panel of men who believed that the first duty of any red-blooded American male is to go overseas and kill strangers for his country. The question I thought about hardest was the only one they were sure to ask: "Do you solemnly swear, Mr. Sanders, that your objection to this war comes as a direct instruction from God?"

The truthful answer, then and now, would be that I am not a confidant of God. I make no claims to knowing the Creator. My convictions arise from observing and honoring the creation. Why should I marvel at a swallow sipping? Why should one moment shine forth with meaning while the surrounding moments remain dark and dim? I could not give a theological or a scientific argument for loathing war any more than I could explain my love for birds, trees, rivers, or the woman I married. I could only trust and obey the sympathy stirred in me by the creatures I met.

As it turned out, the draft board never asked me to account for my conscience, because on the eve of my hearing they reclassified me, not as a conscientious objector, but as a man unfit for military service. It was their way of dismissing me and my scruples. Instead of feeling relieved, I felt thwarted, like a student who had studied hard, only to be expelled from school right before the final exam. But in struggling over my response to the war, I had learned to heed an authority higher and grander than any government. I had come to understand conscience as a kind of sympathetic vibration, resonant with the force that brings new creatures into being and that lavishes so much beauty on the world.

\\\\|///

Within a few years the voices of my children broke into what up until then had been largely a private search, and those two voices were more compelling than any others I had heard. From the hour of their birth, I trembled at their least murmur or cry. As soon as they learned to talk, they were a clamor of questions, about matters ranging from why we have belly buttons to what happens after we die. Soon they would begin asking me why there is so much pain in the world, how to tell good from evil, where to find heaven, what to think of God. I felt I should have some creed to offer them, some list of tidy answers, as in a catechism, yet no written doctrine seemed to me worthy of the majesty or subtlety of the universe.

Although I had often spoken with my wife about the ancient questions, I felt no need to come up with answers for her, because Ruth had already acquired her own sturdy beliefs through a fusion of Methodist upbringing and scientific training. The children, on the other hand, were brand-new to the universe, surprised and puzzled by everything. They were also readily transfixed by pattern and movement—spinning mobiles over the crib, a face playing peekaboo, the screech of a blue jay, a crescent moon, the kiss of wind. We could have sat them down before a television, which would have offered them moving shapes galore, but instead Ruth and I took them outdoors, because we wanted them to bond, as we had, with the wild world that humans have not made.

We also took them to churches and Quaker meetings, looking for a story that we all could embrace. But the silent Quakers, whom I love, seemed forbidding to the children, and the churches told stories about life and death and a capricious God that Ruth and I could not accept. All the while we kept leading the children outdoors, planting and harvesting vegetables in our yard, stooping over crocuses and woods poppies and fiddlehead ferns, watching monarch butterflies and red-bellied woodpeckers. Further afield, we joined hands with them to measure the girth of great trees, splashed with them along the stony troughs of creeks, spread a blanket in the park and lay down with them to gaze at stars. And in this way, without ever planning to, we taught our children the oldest form of reverence, one that has no creed. Although we could not offer them neat answers to the old questions about paradise and pain, we taught them to honor the impulse in themselves that rises to meet the energy and glory in creation.

I am not saying that nature is God, for at this time in my life, with my children grown and my beard turning white, I have given up all opinions about God. I am saying that what we call nature, this all-embracing power and pattern, fills me with joy and inspires me to act with profound respect for all that lives.

I am saying that mountains and mosquitoes, rivers and rhododendrons, you and I are utterances of this power. I am saying that this pervasive, unnamable, shaping energy, glimpsed in the whorl of skin on a thumb or the spiral of stars in a distant nebula, is what compels me to bow at a brightening window each morning.

In moments now and again, I still sink into the blissful union with things that I knew as a child. The experience may come as I dig in the garden, as I pluck the strings of a guitar, as I watch a red-tailed hawk spiral overhead, as I read a passage in a book. On a recent trip, I was reading in the crowded, noisy lounge of an airport. The words on the page held my attention through the hubbub, until I smelled a piercing fragrance. Looking up, I saw a woman sitting perhaps twenty feet away, slowly peeling an orange. Sunlight pooled in her lap, illuminating the deliberate movement of her hands. When she had stripped away the last curls of rind, the plump orange lay in her palm like an egg. It looked so vibrant, so potent, it might have been the egg from which the whole universe hatched. Then the woman broke it apart, slid one section into her mouth, closed her eyes, and chewed. After a minute or so, she ate another section, then a third, and so on until she had finished. As I watched her eat, I felt as nourished by that orange as by any food I had ever swallowed. The tang and smell and juicy abundance of the fruit filled me to overflowing.

In childhood, I accepted these trances without thinking. Now I realize that the experience of oneness, though fleeting and rare, is life's deepest truth. Like a field of force, this knowledge slowly works in me, realigning each cell, turning me toward the source. I no longer look for salvation, for a highway to heaven, for explicit instructions, for blinding light. I don't look for any reward. While meditating or walking, loafing or working, I simply try to be present, attentive, open. And when I am blessed, my inner ruckus yields to stillness, and I am overcome by awe.

Our neighbors Malcolm and Judy have invited us to go next door on Saturday night for a party. Their plan is to fill a tape with songs and send it to Kevin, to cheer him up as he begins his first round of chemotherapy. When they call Kevin in Massachusetts to tell him of their scheme, he says, "Well, it sounds like I'd better come out to Indiana. How can I miss my own party?" He reports that he has lost his hair, but not yet his voice. And so, when he comes to join in the singing, he'll wear one of the dozen weird hats that friends have given him to cover his sudden baldness.

On the morning of our songfest, I rise from meditation and gaze out on a world glazed with ice. The false February spring has held long enough for our cherry tree to break into bloom and for me to plant lettuce and spinach and peas. Under a sheen of ice, the raised beds of the garden create a rippling landscape of ridges and valleys. Slowed by cold, the seeds wait under the black soil, but soon they will push up toward the sun, bearing in their tendrils all the force of the universe. The prospect draws my hands together at my chest, bends my body at the waist, tilts my head and heart toward the Earth.

Eventually, of course, I will slide back into my skin. My attention will scatter like smoke. Fear and confusion, those grim companions, will crowd me once more. And yet these moments clarify my whole life. They show me where I have come from and they light the way ahead, guiding my speck of being back to the center of Being. I now sense more clearly what I am summoned to do, which is to witness the creation in its detail and grandeur, and to sing praise. That's what I've been trying to do in book after book, I now realize. That's what I'm doing again here in these lines—singing praise with my small voice. Yet nothing I write or say ever quite catches the music I hear. So I go on praising in silence, and my bow becomes like the bending of grass beneath the wind.

# A Road into Chaos and
# Old Night

When I first read a handful of his essays in college, I didn't much care for Ralph Waldo Emerson. He seemed too high-flown, too cocksure, too earnest. I couldn't imagine he had ever sweated or doubted. His sentences rang with a magisterial certainty that I could never muster. In the library, his portrait gazed from the wall with a superior air; his name was carved in stone alongside the names of other literary immortals. More like an angel than a man, he seemed to float above the messy Earth where I labored in confusion. He rarely told stories, rarely framed arguments, rarely focused on any creature or place, but instead he piled one oracular statement atop another like a heap of jewels, each one hard and polished and cold.

While resisting Emerson, I fell under the spell of another citizen of Concord, Henry David Thoreau, who was agreeably cranky and earthy. Here was a man who rode rivers, climbed mountains, ambled through forests, and told of his journeys in wide-awake narratives, as I aspired to do. He built a cabin with his own hands, hoed beans, baked bread, and chopped wood. Thoreau kept his feet on the ground, his eyes and ears alert to the homely world—ants fighting on a stump, mud thawing on a railroad bank, men building a bridge, skunk cabbage perfuming a swamp. He led an outdoor life, keeping his distance from the gossipy town. He stood up against slavery, protested the Mexican war, went to jail for refusing to pay the poll tax, and wrote prose that seemed to me as wild as the loons he chased across Walden Pond.

Inspired by Thoreau, who began keeping a journal at the age of twenty, I began keeping one of my own at the same age. Thoreau's journal opened with an unidentified voice asking, "'What are you doing now?' . . . 'Do you keep a journal?'" Thoreau responded to that challenge by declaring, "So I make my first entry to-day." The questioner, I soon learned, was Emerson, then thirty-four, author of a slender book entitled *Nature,* which Thoreau had read closely during his final year at Harvard. From the opening lines of Thoreau's journal onward, Emerson kept appearing, occasionally by name, often simply as "he," more often as a climate of ideas, a presence so familiar as to need no label. Although rebellious, Thoreau was clearly a disciple of Emerson, returning to his thought as to an ever-flowing spring.

To see what Thoreau found so inspiring, I decided to give Emerson another try. This time I read a selection from his journals, and there I found quite a different man from the ethereal sage of the essays. I found a man acquainted with bewilderment and grief, who could write, after his son died at age five, "He gave up his little innocent breath like a bird. Sorrow makes us all children again,—destroys all differences of intellect. The wisest knows nothing" (January 30, 1842). I found a householder and citizen, immersed in the affairs of his time, who insisted, "A man must have aunts and cousins, must buy carrots and turnips, must have barn and woodshed, must go to market and to the blacksmith's shop, must saunter and sleep and be inferior and silly" (June 8, 1838). I found a judge of character who saw through shams—remarking, soon after a saber-rattling veteran of the Indian wars had presided over the White House, "I do not like to see a sword at a man's side. If it threaten man, it threatens me. A company of soldiers is an offensive spectacle" (November 25, 1838).

In Emerson's journal I found a skeptic who regarded the Bible as a wise but imperfect book, no more worthy of our devotion than the Bhagavad-Gita or the Koran or any of the world's other great scriptures. "This old Bible," he complained, "if you pitch it out of the window with a fork, it comes bounce back again" (November 26, 1842). I found a freethinker who grumbled that "The most tedious of all discourses are on the subject of the Supreme Being" (April 22, 1837). While Emerson often invoked the Supreme Being in his essays—under the name of Over-Soul, Universal Spirit, Original Cause, Unknown Center, Eternal One, or some other alias—in his journals he avoided theology. Instead, he looked for the holy in his own depths and in his everyday surroundings. He was a mystic of the ordinary who could muse, "What is there of the divine in a load of bricks? What is there of the divine in a barber's shop? . . . Much. All"

(August 17, 1834). He was a seeker who did not retreat to monastery or mountaintop, but rather gazed from the windows of his house or walked the streets or rambled through the countryside on the trail of spirit. "To the dull mind all nature is leaden," he concluded. "To the illuminated mind the whole world burns and sparkles with light" (May 20, 1831).

From beginning to end, I found in Emerson's journals a writer struggling to describe what lurked at the edges of perception, what loomed in the depths of consciousness. Instead of the Olympian, cocksure figure who spoke through the essays, here was an explorer who left the well-trodden ways, brushed against mysteries, and tried to describe what he had experienced. "Far the best part . . . of every mind is not that which he knows, but that which hovers in gleams, suggestions, tantalizing, unpossessed, before him" (November 1846; day not specified). Over the course of more than fifty years and some two hundred and fifty notebooks, Emerson pursued those tantalizing suggestions. In these unrehearsed pages, you can see him searching for language to evoke "the upheaving principle of life" (July 13, 1833) that he sensed in the *Jardin des Plantes* of Paris, in the dazzle of light on a man's hat or a child's spoon, in the gleam of pine needles or the scintillation of dust motes.

Emerson followed the nib of his pen across the blank pages of his journal as across uncharted space, never knowing where the trail might lead. In his own way, he was as bold as Lewis and Clark, even when he did not stir from his study. Whatever else he sought, he was always tracking that most elusive of quarries—the shaping, luminous power that burns in mind and nature and in human works, a power he called by many names, including Beauty, Divinity, and Unity. In his most daring pages, he pushed language to the frontiers of what words can convey, and then he pushed a bit beyond. His own description of how such writing feels is the best I've ever read: "The maker of a sentence . . . launches out into the infinite and builds a road into Chaos and old Night, and is followed by those who hear him with something of wild, creative delight" (December 19, 1834).

It's true, we do feel a thrill of recognition when we hear Thoreau say, "In Wildness is the preservation of the World"; or when we hear Pascal say, "Man is only a reed, the weakest in nature, but he is a thinking reed"; or when we hear Whitman say, "I think I could turn and live with animals, they are so placid and self-contain'd"; or when we hear Emerson say, "Tell me where is the manufactory of this air, so thin, so blue, so restless, which eddies around you, in which your life floats, of which your lungs are but an organ, and which you coin into musical words" (November 6, 1837). An original writer is one who ventures into the darkness of the unsaid and draws into the light something vital that has been hidden from us.

A young writer commonly begins by imitating the writers he or she admires, as Emerson began by imitating Goethe, or Thoreau by imitating Emerson, and as I began by aping Thoreau and Faulkner and Frost. If the young writer hopes to keep learning, however, and to have any prospect of doing original work, eventually he or she must let go of the models and launch out, solo, into unknown terrain. It's a scary moment for any artist, leaving behind the familiar patterns and opinions, trying to discern a new truth, however small. Many pull back out of laziness or fear; many try and fail; a few succeed. And so we have Walt Whitman, giving up strict rhyme and meter, reaching out in his sinewy lines to embrace the whole of America. So we have Emily Dickinson, stretching the prim quatrains of hymns to contain insights never sung in church. So we have Samuel Clemens, smuggling the speech of riverfront and backwoods into high literature. So we have Toni Morrison, drawing African American memory and lore out of the shadows to reveal the immense agony of slavery.

Those who embark on a spiritual quest often follow a path similar to that of the young writer. We begin by echoing our ancestors, reading their scriptures, learning their stories about encounters with the divine, repeating their rituals and creeds. Many people stop there, fully satisfied by hand-me-down religion. For other people, the meaning leaks away, but they keep going through the motions anyway, reciting verses and repeating gestures, not knowing what they would put in place of this comforting habit. Still others, no longer nourished by the tradition they've been taught, abandon religion altogether as an empty shell.

In any generation, a relative few let go of secondhand accounts and seek their own direct experience of the power that flows through all things. Instead of groping "among the dry bones of the past," they demand "an original relation to the universe," as Emerson urged us all to do in his first book, *Nature*. These are the radical seekers, the ones who dig down to the roots of life, and they are the figures who appealed to Emerson, either among the famous dead—the Buddha, Plato, Jesus, Martin Luther, George Fox, Emanuel Swedenborg—or among his contemporaries—Thomas Carlyle, Bronson Alcott, Margaret Fuller, Walt Whitman, Henry Thoreau. Like the adventurous writer, these determined seekers turn away from the well-lit clearings where others have already camped, and they launch out into Chaos and old Night.

From reading Emerson's journals, therefore, I realized that the seeming confidence of the essays had been hard won. The magisterial pronouncements in his public writings had been culled from thousands of sentences tried out in private, many of them false starts and failures, much as the tidy equations of science derive from years of experiments. By the time his journal entries had been filtered for delivery as lectures, and then filtered again for publication in books, Emerson had removed nearly all of the struggles, puzzles, and doubts. After all, people did not pay to read an author or hear a lecturer confess his confusion, any more than they welcomed a minister questioning his faith.

And yet if we read carefully, we can see that the greatest of his essays were those he wrote not to proclaim certainties but to overcome uncertainties. Few passages could appear more confident than this often-quoted one from *Nature:* "Standing on the bare ground,—my head bathed by the blithe air, and uplifted into infinite space,—all mean egotism vanishes. I become a transparent eye-ball; I am nothing; I see all; the currents of the Universal Being circulate through me; I am part or particle of God." A few lines earlier in the same essay, however, we hear quite a different note: "Crossing a bare common, in snow puddles, at twilight, under a clouded sky, without having in my thoughts any occurrence of special good fortune, I have enjoyed a perfect exhilaration. I am glad to the brink of fear."

Why should fear cling to good fortune like a shadow? At least part of the answer in Emerson's case, I suspect, is that he had fallen deliriously in love with his first wife, Ellen, only to lose her to tuberculosis within a year and a half of their wedding; and he had made heroes and confidants of his two younger brothers, Edward and Charles, only to lose them soon after to the same disease. The wounds from these losses were still raw at the time Emerson was writing *Nature*. Whatever public business he may have been conducting in that book, his private business included asking why a universe that could inspire such exhilaration could also inflict such pain. Cast in religious terms, the question was the same as Job's: How could a just God make the innocent suffer? As in God's answer to Job, Emerson consoled himself by appealing to the grandeur and glory of creation: "The misery of man appears like childish petulance, when we explore the steady and prodigal provision that has been made for his support and delight on this green ball which floats him through the heavens." However petulant, the misery was real. Time and again it stung him into taking up his pen.

We miss something crucial in Emerson's achievement if we hear only the assurance he was offering his readers, and not the reassurance he was offering himself. Let me mention just one more example, an essay which on first reading appears to be the very epitome of confidence. "Trust thyself," Emerson admonishes us in "Self-Reliance." He goes on to say, "Nothing is at last sacred but the integrity of your own mind. . . . What I must do is all that concerns me, not what the people think. . . . Let us stun and astonish the intruding rabble of men and books and institutions, by a simple declaration of the divine fact." What could be more confident, indeed arrogant, than such announcements?

But an undercurrent of doubt runs through "Self-Reliance." "We but half express ourselves, and are ashamed of that divine idea which each of us represents," Emerson admits. Or again: "I am ashamed to think how easily we capitulate to badges and names, to large societies and dead institutions. Every decent and well-spoken individual affects and sways me more than is right. I ought to go upright and vital, and speak the rude truth in all ways." That word *ought* discloses the gap between Emerson's values and his life. Listen closely, and you hear him lamenting his lapses, as when he says, "At times the whole world seems to be in conspiracy to importune you with emphatic trifles. Friend, client, child, sickness, fear, want, charity, all knock at once at thy closet door, and say,—'Come out unto us.' But keep thy state; come not into their confusion. The power men possess to annoy me, I give them by a weak curiosity." As soon as you notice the murmur of questioning and recrimination, you realize that Emerson was not merely delivering advice to his readers, he was exhorting himself to live up to his own ideals.

Read in this light, every grand claim in "Self-Reliance" becomes a challenge, which the essayist may fail to meet. Every instruction is a reminder addressed as much to himself as to the reader. Let us not worship the Old World, Emerson insisted, while he eagerly read the books and magazines of Europe. Let us not gad about restlessly, he urged, after making the first of several European tours, and after beginning the lecture career that would carry him the length and breadth of the United States. He urged us to protect our genius by shunning family obligations, yet he supported his brothers and his mother, funded the endeavors of friends, edited and promoted the books of acquaintances. He urged us to avoid social obligations, yet he served on the school committee, donated money and words and his weighty name to many good causes. He urged us to beware the burdens of property, as he bought land for woodlot and orchard, as he enlarged and renovated his old house. He urged us to scorn convention, while pursuing a largely conventional life.

Emerson wrote "Self-Reliance" at a time when he was trying to throw off the authority of the Bible and the church, the weight of European culture, and the manacles of polite opinion. This was an era, mind you, when the editor of a newspaper or the president of a college or a prominent minister could denounce a lecturer for impiety, as Emerson was denounced after delivering his scandalous address to the graduating class at the Harvard Divinity School in 1838. That episode had taught Emerson how "for nonconformity the world whips you with its displeasure." Sometimes the whipping could be not merely verbal but literal, as in the case of certain outspoken abolitionists and women's rights advocates, who were heckled and beaten even in the relatively civilized precincts of Boston, leading Emerson to fear what he called the "the unintelligent brute force that lies at the bottom of society," or simply the "mob."

In "Self-Reliance," you can see him facing down that fear. He marshaled all his arguments for trusting one's inner light not because such trust came easily to him, but because it came so hard. He called for simplicity in one's affairs because his own had become so complicated. He called for concentrating one's efforts on the essential questions because his energy had been scattered by the demands of family and village and friends. He called on us to wake up because he knew from his own experience how much easier it is for us to sleepwalk through our days.

I am not saying that Emerson was a hypocrite, but rather that he wrote essays in an effort to lay out a path for himself, to set himself standards. Because those standards were so exacting, neither he nor any of us could live up to them consistently. In a characteristically generous entry from his journal, he observed that Thoreau came closer than anyone else to achieving his ideals: "Thoreau gives me, in flesh and blood and pertinacious Saxon belief, my own ethics. He is far more real, and daily practically obeying them, than I" (July 1852; day not specified). Thus, returning to Thoreau by way of Emerson, I came to see that the very qualities I admired in the young rebel were those championed by his stately and courageous mentor.

Two centuries after his birth, if we are going to feel the liberating impact of Emerson's work, as it was felt by Thoreau or Whitman or by countless of his contemporaries, we need to strip him of his halo, remove the muffling cloak of fame from his shoulders, and see him once again as a man caught in the midst of an often frantic life, assailed by duties and doubts, struggling to find his way forward through confusion.

You can trace the pattern of profound questioning and provisional answering through all of his finest essays. This is the quality that makes them *essays,* in the sense imagined by the inventor of the term, one of Emerson's heroes, Michel de Montaigne, who adapted a French word meaning to weigh out, to conduct a trial. Emerson's essays are experiments in making sense of things.

He wrestled with the most consequential puzzles that each of us has to face, the very puzzles that intrigued me as a young man and that intrigue me still: Is our brief time in the world an accident or a gift? Is the universe merely matter in motion, within which life and consciousness are chance side effects? Or is there a greater Being in whom each individual being participates, like a wave rising from the sea? Is mind an essential feature of reality, or is it a marginal quirk? If mind is essential, does it give us access to the source of things? And if mind gives us access to the source, what does it discover about how we should live?

In *Nature* Emerson wrote, with a brashness that had once fooled me, "Let us interrogate the great apparition, that shines so peacefully around us. Let us inquire, to what end is nature?" We may inquire until the cows come home, but nature is not going to oblige us with an answer. However peaceful the apparition may seem on a sunny day or a starry night, it will eventually tear down whatever we build and reclaim whatever we love, including our own precious life. Yet we cannot help inquiring.

We betray Emerson's memory if we merely echo his answers to the perennial questions. What he would have us emulate, I believe, is his patient, passionate search. We must find our own answers. We must dive into our own depths. While learning all we can from books and teachers and the witness of other seekers, we must treasure our own spark of the one great fire, striving to see, and to say, what it reveals to us.

# Words Addressed to
# Our Condition Exactly

In the fall of 1971, seeing that I was floundering, a veteran teacher who had floundered himself when he was twenty-five gave me a book by a writer he knew down in Kentucky. "You might find some guidance here," he said, handing me *The Long-Legged House*.

It was a paperback edition, small enough to fit in a coat pocket, printed on cheap paper, unassuming, not the sort of book one would expect to confirm or change the course of a life. The cover illustration showed a cabin perched on a steep riverbank, with a view across the stream toward green ridges fading away into the distance; a curving flight of stone steps led to the uphill side of the cabin, which rested on the ground, while the downhill side rested on poles, evoking the long legs of the title.

The author's name, Wendell Berry, was unknown to me, but his photograph on the back recalled men I'd known while growing up in rural Tennessee and Ohio. He wore a work shirt unbuttoned at the throat, with a T-shirt underneath and striped coveralls on top; beneath a billed cap, his face lay in shadow, the mouth slightly open and jaw set as if he were catching his breath in the midst of sawing or plowing. In the faint background of the photograph, instead of the usual desk littered with papers or shelves of books, there were blossoms, as of hollyhocks or fruit trees in flower. The biographical note identified him as a teacher and farmer, as well as the author of three collections of poetry, two novels, and the slender book of essays I held in my hand.

I was floundering that fall of 1971 because I had just returned to the United States after four years in England, where I had earned my doctorate at Cambridge, where I had helped organize protests against the war in Vietnam, and where I had begun to write stories. I knew my writing was clumsy and shallow, but that knowledge only made me determined to go deeper and write better. When my wife and I chose to decline the offer of a teaching position in England and sail home to America, our friends told us we were fools. Why give up a career in the motherland of English and return to a land bitterly divided over a war, smoldering with race riots, rife with political corruption and corporate greed? I was all the more a fool, our friends assured me, for choosing to settle in the godforsaken Midwest and for imagining I could find anything worth writing about in the hills of southern Indiana, where I had accepted a job.

Didn't I know that for generations the most talented writers born and reared in the Midwest had moved away as soon as they found their traveling legs? Mark Twain, Theodore Dreiser, Sinclair Lewis, T. S. Eliot, F. Scott Fitzgerald, Willa Cather, Hart Crane, Sherwood Anderson, Ernest Hemingway, Langston Hughes, Kenneth Rexroth, Wright Morris, Theodore Roethke, Wallace Stegner, Kurt Vonnegut, Jr., and sundry others had left. What writers of note had stayed? Saul Bellow, I suggested. Sure, my friends conceded, but he lived in Chicago, a cosmopolitan city immune to the deadening effects of the provinces. Whereas I would be lost in the boondocks, my friends warned me, and if I did manage to write books, nobody would care to read them.

My wife and I shared our friends' dire view of what America had become during the Vietnam War, but that seemed all the more reason to return from exile and lend our hands to mending what was so grievously broken. I felt my own misgivings about settling in the Midwest. I had been reared on the back roads of Ohio, where I'd met little encouragement for the life of the mind. A scholarship carried me to an Ivy League college, where the Midwest, if mentioned at all, was spoken of as a vast expanse of corn and beans and hogs, a region topographically and intellectually flat. Another scholarship carried me from New England to graduate school in old England, where the Midwest hardly figured in anyone's imagination, except as another one of those forbidding hinterlands, like the frozen wastes of Siberia, the Australian outback, or the South African veldt.

For my wife, a biochemist, the move was less troubling. Given adequate laboratories, one could do good science anywhere. She had been reared in Indiana; her parents, grandparents, and most of her aunts, uncles, and cousins lived there still. As teenagers, she and I had met at a science camp in the very town where I was going to teach. We both felt at home among the forested hills and limestone creeks; we knew the birdsongs, the burly clouds, the teeth-rattling thunderstorms and sudden snows, the flash of fireflies and rasp of cicadas; we knew the habits of speech, the shapes of churches and barns; we knew the smells of thawing soil in the spring and hard frost in the fall; and those were all good reasons for moving there.

But moving to Indiana was a far milder step than deciding to settle there, to rear a family and make a life and ground my writing in this unfashionable place. I gained the courage to put down roots largely from reading books by writers who had chosen to settle in other seemingly out-of-the-way places. And for me, the most encouraging of these writers turned out to be the man whose publicity photo showed him wearing coveralls and a feed store cap. Unlike Thoreau, Faulkner, Eudora Welty, Flannery O'Connor, William Carlos Williams, Gary Snyder, and other deeply rooted souls, Wendell Berry lived in my home region; the water that rolled off his hillside farm in northern Kentucky, like the rain that drummed on my roof in southern Indiana, flowed into the Ohio River. His home state came in for as much scorn from literary potentates as did Indiana, yet he had defied those opinions to gaze at the world from the banks of the Kentucky River and to publish, so far, six books about what he had seen. His example inspired me to imagine that I might become a writer and a useful citizen in the hills of southern Indiana as well as anywhere else. And that imagining began with my reading of *The Long-Legged House*.

I don't need to recollect the look and feel of *The Long-Legged House* in its cheap paperback edition, for I am leafing through the book now, thirty-four years after it was given to me. From my several readings, passage after passage has been underlined, and the margins have been riddled with comments, all in ink, for the paper is too soft to record the marks of pencils. Tape holds together the cracked spine. The pages have turned yellow and stiff. I can't help sensing an affinity between this battered book and my own body, now on the verge of sixty. I can't help reading *The Long-Legged House* with a dual perspective—part of me my present age, author of some twenty books, firmly committed to my midwestern home ground; part of me still the young man wondering how and where and if to become a writer.

What struck me most vividly when I first read *The Long-Legged House* in 1971 were the confidence, clarity, high aspirations, and moral passion of the voice on the page. The aspirations had to do not with making a name or a fortune but with leading a meaningful life: "My aim is to imagine and live out a decent and preserving relationship to the earth." The moral passion showed in the narrator's willingness to condemn behavior he saw as destructive—strip mining, aimless mobility, war—but even more so in his efforts to clarify and act on his own values: "If one disagrees with the nomadism and violence of our society, then one is under an obligation to take up some permanent dwelling place and cultivate the possibility of peace and harmlessness in it." While admitting that a perfectly harmless and peaceful relation to place might be impossible, the narrator stood by his ideal: "It is a spiritual ambition, like goodness. The wild creatures belong to the place by nature, but as a man I can belong to it only by understanding and by virtue. It is an ambition I cannot hope to succeed in wholly, but I have come to believe that it is the most worthy of all." I could have imagined such words coming out of Emerson, Thoreau, Whitman, or some other nineteenth-century American sage, but I was surprised and thrilled to hear them coming from one of my contemporaries.

Berry had written most of these essays when he was in his early thirties, only about half a dozen years older than I was on first reading them, and yet he spoke with the authority of an elder. Thus he could say about a strip mine in eastern Kentucky: "Standing and looking down on that mangled land, one feels aching in one's bones the sense that it will be in a place such as this—a place of titanic disorder and violence, which the rhetoric of political fantasy has obstructed from official eyesight—that the balance will finally be overcast and the world tilted irrevocably toward its death." He could respond to the roar of motor boats on the Kentucky River by pronouncing judgment on our industrial way of life: "Man cannot be independent of nature. In one way or another he must live in relation to it, and there are only two alternatives: the way of the frontiersman, whose response to nature was to dominate it, to assert his presence in it by destroying it; or the way of Thoreau, who went to the natural places to become quiet in them, to learn from them, to be restored by them."

Even back in my twenties, eager for a clear diagnosis of the world's ailments, I realized there were more than two ways of relating to nature; yet I relished such decisive proclamations. I welcomed a narrator who could bluntly denounce the Vietnam War: "We say that America is a Christian and a democratic country.

But I find nothing in the Gospels or in the Declaration of Independence or in the Constitution to justify our support of puppet tyrants, or our slaughter of women and children, or our destruction of crops and villages and forests, or our herding of civilians into concentration camps in Vietnam. We do these things because we have forsaken our principles and abandoned ourselves to the inertia of power." In an age of cynicism, here was an Ohio Valley neighbor who spoke with utmost seriousness about principles, virtues, and spiritual ambition. In an age of irony, here was a man who spoke with the solemn indignation of the Hebrew prophets.

Indeed, biblical cadences and allusions ran through the book: "The most exemplary nature is that of the topsoil. It is very Christ-like in its passivity and beneficence, and in the penetrating energy that issues out of its peaceableness." Such prose rhythms and sentiments were utterly out of keeping with the most celebrated nonfiction of the day, which I read carefully in my search for literary models. Norman Mailer's *The Armies of the Night* (1968), Tom Wolfe's *The Electric Kool-Aid Acid Test* (1968), and Hunter S. Thompson's *Fear and Loathing in Las Vegas* (1971)—to choose three distinctive examples—featured brash, hip, slangy, irreverent narrators preoccupied with drugs and deals and politics. One could not imagine them brooding on the fate of the biosphere, let alone the fate of hillside farms, nor could one imagine them citing the Bible to illustrate their points or speaking forthrightly, as Wendell Berry did, of our need for reverence: "We must abandon arrogance and stand in awe. We must recover the sense of the majesty of creation, and the ability to be worshipful in its presence." The narrators created by Mailer, Wolfe, and Thompson were urban and secular, not so much hostile to rural communities and religion as oblivious to them. Speaking in a swaggering first-person singular, each of these narrators seemed to strive for an idiosyncrasy of voice that would make him stand out in the crowded literary marketplace.

By contrast, the narrator of *The Long-Legged House* was formal, dignified, and reserved. He showed no inclination to display his personality, or to reveal more about his private life than was necessary to explain his principles. What little he had to say about cities was mostly a lament over the estrangement of urban people from nature. Instead, his points of reference and his sympathies lay in the countryside, among people who worked with their hands, among plants and animals both wild and domestic. His framing vision was ecological and moral, rather than political or technological: "I must attempt to care as much for the world as for my household. Those are the poles between which a competent morality would balance and mediate: the doorstep and the planet.

The most meaningful dependence of my house is not on the U.S. government, but on the world, the earth." He showed no interest in the culture broadcast on television, on radio, or in cinemas, but he cared deeply about the culture embodied in the skills and lore of farming communities.

When this narrator employed the first-person singular, he did so in a spare, measured, almost impersonal way: "I had been a native; now I was beginning to belong. There is no word—certainly not *native* or *citizen*—to suggest the state I mean, that of belonging willingly and gladly and with some fullness of knowledge to a place." He also deflected attention from himself by using the indefinite pronoun: "Knowing this valley, once one has started to know it, is clearly no casual matter. . . . Its wonders are commonplace and shy. Knowing them is an endless labor and, if one can willingly expend the labor, an endless pleasure." And often he used the first-person plural, as a way of speaking not just about himself but about all of us:

> We have lived by the assumption that what was good for us would be good for the world. And this has been based on the even flimsier assumption that we could know with any certainty what was good even for us. We have fulfilled the danger of this by making our personal pride and greed the standard of our behavior toward the world—to the incalculable disadvantage of the world and every living thing in it. And now, perhaps very close to too late, our great error has become clear. It is not only our own creativity—our own capacity for life—that is stifled by our arrogant assumption; the creation itself is stifled.

On first reading such passages back in 1971, I admired the boldness and reach of this narrator, who was always gesturing beyond himself, toward our collective fate and our shared planet. I was smitten by his voice. The elegant balance of his periodic sentences, the gravity of his diction, the reticence about private matters, and the prophetic tone set him apart from his flashy contemporaries, and linked him to such predecessors as Jefferson, Lincoln, and Thoreau. Amidst so much writing that seemed petulant and perishable, Wendell Berry sounded like a grown-up, like someone whose words would last.

Although I still value the clarity, confidence, and fervor of this voice, what I perceive more clearly now, as I look back on *The Long-Legged House* from the neighborhood of sixty, is the narrator's uncertainty, his emotional and intellectual struggle, and his search for literary ancestors. I notice the young man's effort to persuade himself, along with the reader, that what he has chosen to do with his life is honorable and sensible. I hear him acknowledging his doubts, as when he confesses "the suspicion that pursued me for most of my life, no matter where I was, that there was perhaps another place I *should* be, or would be happier or better in." I see how wary he is of appearing to be "something of an anachronism," as when he concedes that the ideas he is advocating have been "allowed to grow old-fashioned, so that in talking about them now one is always on the verge of sounding merely wishful or nostalgic or absurd." I sense the grief that weighs on him constantly: "The pristine America that the first white man saw is a lost continent, sunk like Atlantis in the sea. The thought of what was here once and is gone forever will not leave me as long as I live. It is as though I walk knee-deep in its absence."

Having become a father—and recently a grandfather—I read the few references to Berry's own children with a piquancy I could not have felt in my childless twenties: "I am the father of two young children whose lives are hostages given to the future. Because of them and because of events in the world, life seems more fearful and difficult to me now than ever before. But it is also more inviting, and I am constantly aware of its nearness to joy." And I see more clearly now the scars left by passages in Berry's own childhood, such as his having been sent away from home at the age of fourteen to attend a military boarding school: "The highest aim of the school was to produce a perfectly obedient, militarist, puritanical moron who could play football. That aim, of course, inspired a regime that was wonderfully vindictive against anything that threatened to be exceptional. And having a lively and independent mind, I became a natural enemy of the regime."

Having made my break with the metaphysical claims, as opposed to the ethical instructions, of Christianity, I now see Berry himself wrestling with the shadow side of the religious tradition he invokes. While he acknowledges that his thinking and rhetoric have been shaped by the Bible, he also challenges much of what passes for "religion": "I am uneasy with the term, for such religion as has been openly practiced in this part of the world has promoted and fed upon a destructive schism between body and soul, heaven and earth. It has encouraged people to believe that the world is of no importance, and that their only obligation in it is to submit to certain churchly formulas in order to get to heaven."

And having sought for more than three decades to make sense of things from a home base in southern Indiana, a place that many people consider a backwater, I now see the narrator of *The Long-Legged House* striving to justify his decision not merely to live and farm beside the Kentucky River, but to reflect on America, indeed on the Earth and the universe, from that vantage point: "Against a long-standing fashion of antipathy, I will venture to suggest that the best model we have of a community is still the small country town of our agricultural past." Here and elsewhere, in words such as *venture* and *suggest,* behind the voice of authority I now hear a defensive note.

In one of the book's most eloquent passages, Berry describes the impact of watching, on a slew near his cabin, a pair of blue geese stopping over on their way south from Hudson's Bay:

> They made me realize that the geography of this patch of riverbank takes in much of the geography of the world. It is under the influence of the Arctic, where the winter birds go in summer, and of the tropics, where the summer birds go in winter. It is under the influence of forests and of crop-lands and of strip mines in the Appalachians and it feels the pull of the Gulf of Mexico. How many nights have the migrants loosened from their guide stars and descended here to rest or to stay for a season or to die and enter this earth? The geography of this place is airy and starry as well as earthy and watery. It has been arrived at from a thousand other places, some as far away as the poles. I have come here from great distances my-self, and am resigned to the knowledge that I cannot go without leaving it better or worse. Here as well as any place I can look out my window and see the world. There are lights that arrive here from deep in the universe. A man can be provincial only by being blind and deaf to his province.

That is beautifully said; but no young writer who lived in New York, say, or Chicago, San Francisco, London, or Rome would have felt the need to say it.

Before settling on his hillside farm, Berry had tried out some of the certified literary places. He had spent two years as a Stegner Fellow at Stanford, lived for a year in Italy, and taught for two years at New York University. When he decided to give up his job at NYU and return to Kentucky, his friends and academic mentors greeted the decision with incredulity, reflecting "the belief, long honored among American intellectuals and artists and writers, that a place such as I came from could be returned to only at the price of intellectual death; cut off from the cultural springs of the metropolis, the American countryside is Circe and Mammon." During his time away from Kentucky, he admitted, "I had been enough influenced by the cultural fashion to have become compulsively suspicious both of my origins and of myself for being unwilling to divide

myself from them." Only a writer who has made a home in the provinces—
which means anywhere outside the great cities and beyond the ken of travel
brochures—needs to defend himself against the charge of being provincial.
Only such a writer would assert the relevance of his home place by appealing to
the migratory patterns of birds and the wheeling of stars.

The narrator of *The Long-Legged House* knows that if he is to avoid "intellectual death" in the provinces he must face what is most shameful and para-
lyzing in the history of his province: "I am forever being crept up on and newly
startled by the realization that my people established themselves here by killing
or driving out the original possessors, by the awareness that people were once
bought and sold here by my people, by the sense of the violence they have done
to their own kind and to each other and to the earth, by the evidence of their
persistent failure to serve either the place or their own community in it." Indeed, this brutal history goes a long way toward explaining the "long-standing
fashion of antipathy" that questions whether "the small country town of our
agricultural past" can be a worthy model for community.

To make matters worse, the few predecessors who had written about any portion of Kentucky had either ignored or sentimentalized this legacy of slaughter,
slavery, selfishness, and waste: "My problem as a writer, though I didn't clearly
know it yet, was that I had inherited a region that had as a literary tradition only
the corrupt and crippling local colorism of the 'Kentucky' writers. This was
both a mythologizing chauvinism and a sort of literary imperialism, tirelessly
exploiting the clichés of rural landscape, picking and singing and drinking and
fighting lazy hillbillies, and Bluegrass Colonels. That is a blinding and tongue-
tying inheritance for a young writer."

About his own portion of Kentucky, no one had written at all, a blankness
that posed challenges of its own:

> And this place I am related to not only shared the state's noxious literary
> inheritance, but had, itself, never had a writer of any kind. It was, from
> a writer's point of view, undiscovered country. I have found this to be
> both an opportunity and a disadvantage. The opportunity is obvious. The
> disadvantage is that of solitude. Everything is to be done. No beginnings
> are ready-made. One has no proof that the place can be written about,
> no confidence that it can produce such a poet as one suspects one might
> be, and there is a hesitance about local names and places and histories
> because they are so naked of associations and assigned values—none of
> which difficulties would bother a poet beginning in Concord, say, or the
> Lake District.

Bereft of local models, he drew encouragement from American writers who proved that an unheralded place could be written about, as William Carlos Williams did in Paterson: "I saw how his poems had grown out of his life in his native city in New Jersey, and his books set me free in my own life and my own place as no other books could have. . . . Reading them, I felt I had a predecessor, if not in Kentucky then in New Jersey, who confirmed and contemporized for me the experience of Thoreau in Concord."

More clearly now than on my first reading of *The Long-Legged House*, I see that Thoreau is the pervasive influence behind the book, not merely as someone who chose to make his native place the lens through which he viewed the world, but as a prose stylist and contrarian thinker. Many of the sentences might have been written by Thoreau: "It was fishing that paid well, though not always in fish." "Does the hope of peace lie in waiting for peace, or in being peaceable? If I see what is right, should I wait for the world to see it, or should I make myself right immediately, and thus be an example to the world?" "It is certain, I think, that the best government is the one that governs least. But there is a much-neglected corollary: the best citizen is the one who least needs governing. The answer to big government is not private freedom, but private responsibility." As Thoreau apologizes on the opening page of *Walden* for speaking in the first person, so Berry defends his own right to offer a personal vision: "I am writing with the assumption that this is only one of several possibilities, and that I am obligated to elaborate this particular one because it is the one that I know about and the one that is attractive to me."

In tracing these resemblances, I don't mean to suggest that the writer from Kentucky merely imitated the writer from Massachusetts, but that Berry found in him an essential predecessor. Thoreau was the prime example for Berry, as Emerson was for Thoreau, of someone thinking and writing about fundamental questions in a place with no literary history. In subsequent books, Berry would have his quarrels with the philosopher of Walden Pond, and would go beyond him in significant ways, but in *The Long-Legged House* Thoreau is still his tutelary spirit, one who blesses a chancy endeavor.

Any writer could be proud of having written *The Long-Legged House* as a culminating book, let alone as a first collection. Knowing what Wendell Berry has accomplished in the four decades since writing those earliest essays, one might be tempted to imagine, as I did when I first read them, that his triumph was inevitable. But of course it was not; he might have failed, might have sunk into silence, as many aspiring artists have done, defeated by geography or lack of talent or loss of hope. Instead, he has gone on to write many more essays, poems, novels, and stories, gradually building up a comprehensive vision of what is wrong with our present way of life and what a finer, fairer, more reverent, and more enduring way of life might be. By way of some forty books, his hill farm, the nearby town of Port Royal, and the lower Kentucky River now find their place on the American literary map, along with Concord, Paterson, Mark Twain's Mississippi River and William Faulkner's Mississippi, Flannery O'Connor's Georgia, Willa Cather's Nebraska, and John Steinbeck's California.

Even as Berry's thought has grown more complex over the years and his style more assured, his work has shown remarkable consistency. Open any of his fifteen or so books of essays, and you will recognize a distinctive voice pondering a distinctive set of concerns, and you might conclude that neither voice nor vision has changed much between the earliest published essays from the 1960s and those appearing in the twenty-first century. And yet, a close reading of *The Long-Legged House* reveals that there is more searching, more testing, more trying-out of ideas—in short, more *essay*ing—in the early essays than in the later ones. There is a freshness here, a sense of discovery, as he glimpses possibilities that would later harden into certainties; and there is a disarming candor, as he questions the adequacy of his cultural inheritance and of his own powers for the great task he has set himself, that of challenging the industrial worldview and rethinking our whole way of life.

I still read everything Berry publishes, because I never tire of watching this fine mind grapple with the central questions of our time—as in the magisterial *Citizenship Papers* (2003), where he confronts terrorism, biotechnology, the latest American wars, and the decay of democracy. But I'm stirred more deeply by the early essays, where the young man was still trying to find his way. His marriage was new; his two children were young; he had only recently convinced himself to settle down for good in his native place, and the possibility of making significant art there was still unproved, as was the relevance of his agrarian worldview. His ideal of achieving "a more indigenous life" was still an aspiration and not yet an accomplishment. This first gathering of essays tells more poignantly than any of the later ones the story of his wandering and his settling down—what he calls "the myth of my search and my return"—and this overarching myth is as crucial to Berry's self-understanding as the tale of escape from Egypt and wandering in the desert and return to the Promised Land was for the Israelites.

Wendell Berry's story, in turn, helped me begin to understand my own. *The Long-Legged House,* this gift from a wise older teacher, came into my hands precisely when I needed it. Distraught over what had become of my country during the Vietnam War, wary of settling in the Midwest, uneasy about my rural and religious upbringing, uncertain how to lead my life, I found in this book a clarifying intelligence. It confirmed my anguish and my hope, calling to mind the promise Thoreau offered in *Walden:* "There are probably words addressed to our condition exactly, which, if we could really hear and understand, would be more salutary than the morning or the spring to our lives, and possibly put a new aspect on the face of things for us. How many a man has dated a new era in his life from the reading of a book." *Walden* has been such a book for many readers, as I suspect Thoreau devoutly hoped it would be. *The Long-Legged House* has been such a book for me.

# Honoring the Ordinary

or years, I could ignore the charges raised against the memoir, just as I could ignore the charges raised against burglary, because I had no intention of committing either offense. But then the circumstances of my life and the sad state of my country prompted me to write a book called *A Private History of Awe,* which I thought of as an extended essay about my life-long spiritual search, but which my editor informed me was, indeed, a memoir. When the book was published in 2006, it bore that label on the jacket for all to see. And so, having joined the suspect company of memoirists, I began to take a personal interest in the accusations leveled against this literary form.

The most common accusations often appear in the guise of two blunt questions: How could you write a whole book about yourself? And how much of it did you make up? The questioners assume that a memoir must be an exercise in narcissism, and that it is likely to be dishonest to boot. One can easily find published examples that would justify either suspicion. There has never been a shortage of egotists or frauds, so it's no wonder that some of them compose and peddle books. Although these two human failings often go together, for the sake of clarity I'm going to separate them, speaking first about the dangers of deceit and then about the dangers of narcissism.

Making up a fabulous story and calling it true is a practice as old, I suspect, as human speech. In literature, the deceit is customarily disclosed by a wink of irony, as in the work of such fabulists as Cervantes, Defoe, Mark Twain, and Borges. Outright fraud, such as writing a crassly commercial novel and calling it a memoir, may be considered tacky or even despicable, but it should not be surprising. In any case, such dishonesty tells us nothing distinctive about the memoir, only about the influence of merchandizing and greed.

We have a name for writing that begins from the impulse to make things up, to spin a colorful yarn, to invent a situation and see how it unfolds, to create characters and see what they do. Since around 1600, such writing has been called fiction, from a Latin root meaning to feign or counterfeit. In making fiction, the writer freely goes wherever imagination leads. The only requirement is that the counterfeit be sufficiently compelling to engage the reader's attention from the first line to the last.

Writing may also begin from a contrary impulse, not to make things up but to record and examine something the writer has witnessed, lived through, learned about, or pondered. Such writing can range from memoirs to manifestos, from the formality of footnoted tomes to the pizzazz of slangy blogs. What all such writing has in common is an allegiance to some reality that the writer did not invent—to a shared history, to real people, to actual events, to places one can visit, to facts one can check. For better or worse, this wildly diverse range of writing has come to be called, by contrast with the freely invented kind, *non*fiction.

Dividing the realm of prose literature into fiction and nonfiction is clumsy at best, rather like dividing the realm of animals into birds and non-birds. It might be technically correct to describe giraffes and June bugs as non-birds, but it would not be very instructive. Nor is it useful to lump together a four-volume saga of the Crusades and a four-paragraph reminiscence of a car wreck under the single label of nonfiction. Judging from the earliest citations of the word in the *Oxford English Dictionary,* the label was imposed by nineteenth-century librarians, who began dividing their books into the twin categories of fiction and non-fiction (originally with a hyphen). I suspect they did so, at least in America, to emphasize the portion of a library's holdings that were solid, sober, practical, uplifting, and, above all, *true,* such as encyclopedias and repair manuals and religious tracts, as opposed to the romances, mysteries, fantasies, westerns, pirate adventures, thrillers, dime novels, and other frivolous books that wasted readers' time and corrupted youth and made no millwheels turn.

Whatever the origins of the nonfiction label, the publishers soon picked it up, and then so did bookstores, critics, and teachers, and now, clumsy though it may be, we are stuck with it. One virtue of the term is that the crafty little prefix *non-* implies a promise—that such literature is neither feigned nor counterfeit; it is answerable not merely to the writer's imagination but to a world beyond the page, a world that precedes and surrounds and outlasts the act of writing.

Of course these two contrary impulses—to freely invent a world or to report on the actual world—rarely exist in pure form. The literature we call fiction emphasizes the first impulse, and the literature we call nonfiction emphasizes the second, but neither impulse appears in isolation. Fiction must draw on the familiar world if it is to be comprehensible, and nonfiction must draw on the writer's imagination if it is to come alive. Ask a roomful of memoirists how far a work may be shaped by imagination before it no longer deserves to be called nonfiction, and you'll receive a roomful of answers. Most likely all will agree on the necessity of choosing, from the myriad of possible details, those that are essential to the story and leaving out the rest; many writers will accept the filling-in of memory's blank spaces with vivid details; some will permit the merging of incidents or characters to streamline the account; and a few will claim the right to add, drop, change, or invent anything that enlivens the work.

While we may debate where the line should be drawn, at some point along that spectrum, nonfiction gives way to fiction. When a writer crosses over the line and still claims to be offering nonfiction, it is usually for the sake of selling more books. Why does it sell more books? Because, in a culture awash with phoniness, we hunger for authenticity. We're so weary of hucksters, talk-show ranters, ideological hacks, inane celebrities, sleazy moralists, and posturing politicians that we long to hear voices speaking from the heart rather than from a script. Amid so much fakery, hypocrisy, and sham, we long for the genuine. Knowing this, television producers manufacture "reality" shows, filmmakers promote movies as "based on a true story," and some authors, with the connivance of their publishers, fabricate a sensational tale and call it a memoir. In a culture besotted by marketing, such deception is routine.

Within American letters, the most famous advocate of fibbing, fabricating, and outright lying for the sake of a good yarn was Mark Twain. In his *Notebook* he quipped: "I have not professionally dealt in truth. Many when they come to die have spent all the truth that was in them, and enter the next world as paupers. I have saved up enough to make an astonishment there." About the fallibility of memory, that chief resource of memoirists, he had this to say: "When I was younger I could remember anything, whether it had happened or not; but my faculties are decaying now and soon I shall be so I cannot remember any but the things that never happened. It is sad to go to pieces like this but we all have to do it."

When Mark Twain delivered his tongue-in-cheek talk "On the Decay of the Art of Lying" to the Historical and Antiquarian Club of Hartford, Connecticut, in 1882, he assured his audience that the art of lying—"this finest of the fine arts"—would be in no danger of decline if it "had everywhere received the attention, encouragement, and conscientious practice and development which this Club has devoted to it." Having praised his audience as inveterate liars, he went on to warn more soberly about the dangers of "the *silent* lie,—the deception which one conveys by simply keeping still and concealing the truth."

We know from Mark Twain's other writings that among the "silent lies" he had in mind were those that accommodated slavery, Jim Crow laws, and war. In the late and never-finished manuscript called *The Mysterious Stranger*, composed in phases during the Spanish-American War and the lead-up to the First World War, he remarked that whenever one nation invades another, "statesmen will invent cheap lies, putting the blame upon the nation that is attacked, and every man will be glad of those conscience-soothing falsities and will diligently study them, and refuse to examine any refutations of them, and thus he will by and by convince himself that the war is just and will thank God for the better sleep he enjoys after this process of grotesque self-deception."

He might have been speaking here of the American invasions of Iraq and Vietnam. He might also have been speaking of the way Americans have repeatedly justified the persecution of minorities within our country by blaming those who were persecuted, beginning with native tribes and African slaves, and extending through the Japanese-Americans interned during the Second World War and right up to the latest vilified immigrants. The master of playful lies solemnly cautioned us that murderous lies, whether issued by politicians or preachers or pundits, wreak havoc when citizens embrace the deception or quietly allow it to spread.

\|//

When measured against such monstrous deceptions, what's the harm in peddling fiction under the guise of nonfiction? The harm is that it violates the reader's trust. It devalues a literary currency. It corrupts the arena of public speech by pretending to bear witness to a shared world while treating that world as raw material for the writer's trifling and profit. Dressing up a fabrication as a true report is not essentially different from costuming an actor in a white coat to peddle a drug or wrapping a military invasion in the flag to make it appear a blow for freedom. Lying to sell a book is not as grave an offense as lying to sell a drug or a war, but it's a lie nonetheless.

There are no literary police, thank goodness, so the only two parties capable of holding the memoir to a high standard of integrity are the readers and writers of memoirs. Vigilant readers can—and frequently do—check the veracity of a memoir against knowledge available from other sources. They can also judge the plausibility of literary devices, such as the rendering of lengthy dialogue supposedly recollected verbatim from years before. Writers, for their part, can abide by the promise implied in the nonfiction label. They can limit themselves to recording the truth as they honestly remember it or carefully construe it, while acknowledging the imperfections of memory and the inevitability of bias. They can keep faith not merely with their own imagination but with a reality inhabited and shaped by other lives.

We may approach the second danger besetting the memoir, that of narcissism, by way of a remark in a letter of Wallace Stevens. In answer to a correspondent who evidently had asked about the role of egotism in the writing of poetry, Stevens replied: "The truth is that egotism is at the bottom of everything everybody does, and that, if some really acute observer made as much of egotism as Freud has made of sex, people would forget a good deal about sex and find the explanation for everything in egotism" (January 10, 1936).

Whether or not "egotism is at the bottom of everything," surely it is among the motives that prompt any writer to set down words in a carefully chosen order and send them out into the world for others to read. But it need not be the only motive, or even the primary one. While the yearning for praise, fortune, or fame might have driven Dante, Shakespeare, Milton, Whitman, Faulkner, or Stevens himself, none of those writers took *himself* as the subject of art. In literature that endures, the ego of the artist is never the main subject, however much it may have inspired the effort of writing.

But what about the patron saints of the memoir, such as Augustine, Rousseau, and Thoreau? They all might have proclaimed, as Thoreau did on the opening page of *Walden:* "In most books, the *I,* or first person, is omitted; in this it will be retained; that, in respect to egotism, is the main difference. We commonly do not remember that it is, after all, always the first person that is speaking. I should not talk so much about myself if there were any body else whom I knew as well. Unfortunately, I am confined to this theme by the narrowness of my experience." If Thoreau's experience were truly narrow, and if his reflections on that experience were shallow, we would not still be reading his work, any more than we would still be reading Augustine or Rousseau if the same were true of their work.

What keeps us reading these and other durable first-person narratives, beyond the writer's literary skill and the appeal of his or her character, is what the writer says about the universe *beyond* the ego—about nature or God, about the wheeling cosmos, about race or gender or poverty or crime, about love or loss, about the baffling and enthralling struggle to be human. The most compelling first-person accounts, whether we call them memoirs, autobiographies, or essays, are those in which the small self of the author is the lens through which a greater reality is revealed.

Of course, an author whose life is sufficiently famous, colorful, or bizarre may dwell complacently on his or her ego, and may sell truckloads of books. But then, a season after their publication, the life stories of movie stars, rock idols, sports heroes, retired presidents, and other celebrities show up in the remainder bins, along with the breathless accounts of mountain climbers who sawed off an arm to free themselves from fallen rocks or the confessions of reformed drug dealers who conversed with aliens or the testimonies of would-be suicides who've been plucked from the jaws of death. In America, the marketplace for books, like the marketplace for cars, clothes, movies, TV shows, and virtually everything else, is infatuated with celebrity and novelty. And so, again, it's no wonder that some writers of memoir will supply just what the market is looking for.

Thanks to electronic technology, each of us may live, and increasing numbers of us do live, inside a custom-selected media bubble that shuts out the past, the future, other people, and the planet. Unlike the actual world, which pays no regard to us, the virtual world is designed to amuse, flatter, or otherwise gratify the ego. A self sequestered within a media bubble makes an ideal target for advertising, which proclaims that nothing matters except the viewer's or the listener's pleasure, power, status, and comfort. A self thus isolated fulfills the capitalist ideal of the atomized individual, in competition with everyone else, striving for personal advantage, devoted to piling up money and stuff.

Since love of the self, above and beyond the love of anything else, saturates our culture, it's not surprising that essayists and memoirists—like pro athletes or talk-show hosts or blowhards at the local bar—may be narcissists. The remarkable fact is not that some writers of personal narrative indulge in narcissism but that many do not. To document this minor miracle, I go through my shelves pulling out books that speak in distinctive voices from personal experience without dwelling on the author's ego. I quickly gather an armful, by authors ranging from the worthies already mentioned, such as Thoreau, to John Muir, Virginia Woolf, Aldo Leopold, George Orwell, Rachel Carson, James Baldwin, Thomas Merton, Primo Levi, Annie Dillard, Peter Matthiessen, Gary Snyder, N. Scott Momaday, Terry Tempest Williams, J. M. Coetzee, Joan Didion, Barry Lopez, and Wendell Berry.

There are more examples on my shelves, but I content myself with stacking up these books beside the keyboard and studying their spines, as I might study the faces of old friends. What do they have in common? Not geography, not subject matter, not form or style, not political or ethical views. What they share, aside from a high degree of literary skill, is a passionate engagement with a reality so large as to render the perceiving self insignificant. For Lopez, Williams, or Leopold, as for Muir and Thoreau, this greater reality might be nature; for Woolf or Dillard or Didion, it might be the vagaries of perception or the rude fact of death; it might be colonialism, totalitarianism, racism, or genocide, as for Orwell, Baldwin, or Levi; it might be the way of things, the mystery and grain of existence itself, as in Merton, Momaday, Snyder, or Berry.

Off the page, any of these writers might be as prone to egotism as anyone else, but on the page, at their best, their egos melt away. Each of them becomes, in Emerson's famous phrase, a "transparent eye-ball." The grandiose passage from the opening chapter of *Nature* in which this phrase appears is easily and frequently mocked, but the context makes clear that Emerson is speaking of the way an element of nature—a landscape, a sunset, a breeze—can draw us momentarily from our self-preoccupation. Surely we have all felt such transport, if not from nature then from music or meditation or literature or sex or some other captivating force.

When we return from such a momentary trance and sink again into the small self, how do we speak of what we tasted? Having encountered too much sleazy religious language, we might be skeptical of anyone today who, like Emerson, claimed to be "part or particle of God," let alone a conduit for "the currents of the Universal Being." But whether we know how to speak of it or not, the fact remains that in such moments—which may be our truest moments—the *I* disappears. We might describe this egoless insight as *clairvoyance*, but that term has been compromised by association with Ouija boards and palm readers. We might apply the term *epiphany*, popularized by Joyce, but that metaphor has grown stale from overuse in literary circles, and it carries a lot of theological baggage. From Buddhism we might borrow the terms *kensho* and *satori*, which refer to the realization of the true nature of things, *kensho* signifying an initial or tentative awareness and *satori* signifying a profound and lasting enlightenment. But these Buddhist terms, despite their long history of use in Asia, still seem alien to most American readers.

So let me introduce here a modest but fruitful metaphor borrowed from the Quakers. Beginning with George Fox in the seventeenth century, Quakers have described their moments of egoless vision as *openings*. The truths revealed in such openings might be small and private, having to do with the right conduct of one's own life; they might be large and social, having to do, say, with the iniquity of slavery or poverty or war; or they might be the grandest of all truths, having to do with the source of creation and the meaning of life.

If our moments of egoless insight are openings, then, by implication, our routine state of mind, bound up inside the ego, is a kind of enclosure or imprisonment. In his parable of the cave, Plato gave us the most familiar image of mind cut off from ultimate reality; only by leaving the cave and entering the sunlight can the prisoner see things as they truly are. Blake gave us a similar image in "The Marriage of Heaven and Hell," when he proclaimed: "If the doors of perception were cleansed every thing would appear to man as it is, infinite. For man has closed himself up, till he sees all things thro' narrow chinks of his cavern." And Whitman may have been recalling Plato's parable when he wrote in "Song of Myself":

> Long enough have you dream'd contemptible dreams,
> Now I wash the gum from your eyes,
> You must habit yourself to the dazzle of the light and of every
>     moment of your life.

The cavern that encloses the mind might be a creed, a haze of habit, or a cramped imagination; or it might be the mirrored walls of the ego that give back, wherever one looks, reflections of one's own small self. The narcissist preens inside that tiny chamber, wondering constantly how he looks, how he ranks, how he feels, mistaking his ego for the universe. The surest antidote to narcissism is to do as the authors whose works I've stacked beside my keyboard have done, which is to engage with some great and abiding reality. So engaged, we are more likely to experience openings, to cleanse the doors of perception, rub the gum from our eyes, and glimpse the true nature of things.

In Buddhism, as in Taoism, the true nature of things is often spoken of as the Way. Unlike the disembodied, transcendent Ideas of Plato, the Way is earthy and immanent; it is a patterning and flow manifest in mountains and rivers, in creatures and artifacts, in our unadorned flesh and everyday mind. A favorite Zen story tells of a disciple who asks his master, "What is the Way?" and the master answers, "Ordinary mind is the Way." That is to say, we do not need to go anywhere special, do not need to dress up in fancy robes or recite creeds or do spiritual gymnastics, in order to attain a true understanding of existence. That understanding is available right here, right now, by seeing clearly into nature and our own depths. Nothing is more important than such lucid seeing, yet it is nothing special.

The relation of Zen to the rest of Buddhism is roughly the same as the relation of Quakerism to the rest of Christianity. Both Zen and Quakerism emphasize the simple and plain, the nearby rather than the distant, the commonplace rather than the exotic, the homely rather than the showy or sophisticated, the peaceful rather than the violent; both endorse equality rather than hierarchy; both aim at direct rather than hand-me-down knowledge; both insist that ordinary people can see into the heart of things without mediation from gurus or priests. Writing inspired by either tradition, needless to say, would be about as ill-suited to a marketplace fixated on celebrity, sensationalism, and posturing as it could possibly be.

It would certainly be unfashionable, and it might seem paradoxical, to write a memoir in the spirit of Quakerism or Zen. After all, a conventional memoir sets out to dramatize what is idiosyncratic, what is extraordinary, what is captivating about a "self" defined by a skein of deeds, words, thoughts, and qualities. A conventional memoir celebrates those features and circumstances that distinguish the author from everyone else; the more colorful the details, and the more tantalizingly they can be summed up on a dust jacket, the better. What if a memoir set out to dramatize instead the great and abiding Way that is glimpsed *through* the small self? What if a memoir set out to record those moments in a life when the *I* disappears and the undivided, eternal source of things shines forth?

Many in our culture would call the source God, but this word carries a vexed history, and an otherworldly air, that I wish to avoid. I prefer the Buddhist term *emptiness,* which does not mean nothingness, but rather undifferentiated wholeness, fecundity, the brimming, inexhaustible, undifferentiated fullness of being that perpetually casts up new shapes and dissolves them again. Our most direct inward experience of this creative emptiness is the spontaneous arising of thoughts, memories, speculations, and emotions in the mind; our most direct outward experience of the ceaseless upwelling is nature, what the ancient Chinese poets called "mountains-and-rivers," or what we might call wildness. Even hard-headed physicists tell us that the universe itself springs from a fertile void they call the quantum vacuum, in which virtual particles constantly arise and disappear.

Borrowing another metaphor from physics, we might think of emptiness as a pervasive energy field that generates and sustains and eventually reclaims everything—quarks, galaxies, mountains, mice, thimbles, and thoughts. Within this all-encompassing energy field, there are no separate "things"; our labels and categories evaporate; there is only undivided being. Glimpsing this emptiness, we realize that the seeming solidity of the world is an illusion. Not only are all things constantly in flux, but all apparently separate things are aspects of a single reality, like waves on the sea. Nothing is separate, nothing is permanent, least of all that flattering illusion we call the self.

If anything is holy—that is, of ultimate importance—then surely the source of being is holy. And of all our experiences, the rare intuitions of this holy source are surely among the ones most worth recording. That is what I set out to do in *A Private History of Awe,* to record the small openings in an ordinary life. To what extent I succeeded, others will have to decide. Or, rather, others will have to judge the degree of my failure, since in striving to convey the ineffable, one is bound to fail. The best one can do is to point, to say, *Look, see where we are, see what we are?*

The likelihood of failure should not keep one from trying; after all, that is the essence of the essay, to make a trial, to lay out a trail of words in search of greater understanding. E. F. Schumacher, a subversive British economist, observed in *Good Work:* "I think you are put into this life with the task of learning to distinguish between that which is really real and really important and permanent and of true value on the one hand, and things trivial, amusing, ephemeral, and of no real value on the other hand. Your intellect has to make that distinction. The world has to attach itself to the things that really matter and not to those ephemeral trivialities which make the most noise." Whether we are "put into this life" I cannot say; but certainly our culture bombards us with trivialities and noise. A good many books of all sorts, including memoirs, simply add to the gossip and ruckus. I see no point in reading such books, let alone in writing them.

Flannery O'Connor once remarked in a letter, "I don't think you should write something as long as a novel around anything that is not of the gravest concern to you and everybody else and for me this is always the conflict between an attraction for the Holy and the disbelief in it that we breathe in with the air of the times" (September 13, 1959). Allowing for differences between what O'Connor meant by the holy and what I mean by it, I would echo her words in saying that I was moved to write a memoir by my own gravest concern, which is to discover, amidst life's trivialities and noise, what really matters, what endures, what shapes and sustains the ten thousand things of this world. Such discernment requires no special equipment, no exotic location, no learned degrees. It requires only openness to what *is*, always and everywhere.

In *A Private History of Awe*, I wished to honor ordinary experience, not by making it seem exotic, but by peeling away the rind of familiarity that keeps us from seeing the true power and beauty and wonder and terror of it. Honoring the ordinary is akin to the Buddhist and Quaker teaching that we should dwell with full mindfulness in the present moment. Instead of lingering over the past or yearning toward the future, we should fully attend to what is happening right here, right now, whether we are washing dishes or eating an apple or talking with a friend. Wind and rain, sunshine refracted through a blue glass on the windowsill, the voice of a child waking from a nap, the smell of bread, the feel of a loved one's heartbeat against your chest—these may be commonplace, but they are splendid. Whatever the story of the birth of Jesus might mean religiously, with its manger and shepherds, what it means *mythically* is the inbreaking of ultimate value and significance into the humblest of circumstances. The words *humble, homely,* and *humility* all derive from an Indo-European root meaning dirt, earth, soil. The same root gave us *human.* A reasonable translation of *Homo sapiens* would be "dirt able to know" or "wise earth."

What higher aspiration could there be for creatures made of dust than to gaze back with some degree of understanding at the universe that made us? No one lives continuously as a transparent eyeball. Ego keeps reclaiming the spotlight. Appetite and ambition rouse up to cloud one's vision, and no doubt they have done so in *A Private History of Awe*. Whatever the outcome of my own experiment in recounting openings, the experiment itself seems to me worthwhile, if only because it serves as a powerful antidote to dishonesty and narcissism. There is no practice more clarifying or humbling than to ignore the outward trappings of one's life, the facts that might appear on a curriculum vitae, and to consider what one has actually learned about this mysterious world and our brief sojourn here.

In trying to name the complex feeling evoked in me by glimpsing the Way of things, I settled on *awe*, a word that combines wonder and fear. The power one senses outwardly in nature and inwardly in the depths of mind is infinitely creative and implacably destructive. The mind capable of perceiving this truth is itself wondrously inventive and yet fleeting. The self built up from memories and from the testimony of other selves is a convenient illusion that enables one to ride the current for a spell before dissolving. The words one sets down so painstakingly in a certain order to make a paragraph or a book are also temporary stays against dissolution, bound sooner or later to disappear in fire, flood, or forgetfulness. If one nonetheless continues to write, it is with an awareness that our handiwork is no more significant, in the grand scheme of things, than a grain of sand or a blade of grass. And yet writing just may be, along with music, painting, science, dance, and other modes of expression, our modest way of mimicking and honoring the great and deathless Way.

# Speaking for the Land

*G*t the dedication ceremony for the University of Wisconsin Arboretum in June 1934, the pioneering ecologist Aldo Leopold began his
remarks by declaring: "For twenty centuries and longer, all civilized
thought has rested upon one basic premise: that it is the destiny of man to
exploit and enslave the earth. The biblical injunction to 'go forth and multiply' is merely one of many dogmas which imply this attitude of philosophical
imperialism."

Leopold was not shy about making such grand claims, especially when, as
in this brief talk, he wished to distill a complex argument into a few words.
One could cite many examples of "civilized thought," including the teachings
of Hinduism, Buddhism, Taoism, and Native American cultures, that do not
advocate enslavement of the Earth. And one could cite biblical injunctions that
urge us to be caretakers rather than exploiters of the creation. Still, there was
ample evidence in Leopold's time that the majority of his fellow citizens regarded the Earth as purely a source of raw materials, to be mined, dammed, defor-
ested, plowed, paved, and otherwise manipulated to suit human needs, without
regard for the needs of other species and with scant regard for the needs of future generations. This attitude of "philosophical imperialism," which wrought
so much damage in the Dust Bowl years, remains powerful in our day, and is
now wreaking havoc on a global scale.

In his remarks at the dedication ceremony, Leopold went on to say that the
drive for human dominion over the Earth had produced "ecological destruction on a scale almost geological in magnitude." For illustration, he pointed to

the wildfires and dust storms that were afflicting Wisconsin and other prairie states, a disaster brought on by the clearing of forests, draining of wetlands, overgrazing of rangelands, careless plowing, and drought. One of the most severe storms had swept the Great Plains the previous month, in May 1934, blackening the sky and blowing soil all the way to the Atlantic Ocean. Crops were buried. Some roads had to be cleared with snowplows. In Chicago, motorists used headlights at midday. Before the drought broke, later in the decade, half a million people had been rendered homeless, several million had been forced to migrate in search of jobs, and a legacy of fertility built up on the prairie over thousands of years had been squandered.

It would be easy to compile a list of ecological disasters from our own day that are comparable in magnitude to the Dust Bowl. One recalls, for example, the devastation of New Orleans and other cities along the Gulf coast by Hurricane Katrina, a hurricane likely rendered more violent by ocean warming, and floodwaters rendered more lethal by the dredging of coastal wetlands for oil production and by the channeling of the Mississippi River for shipping. One thinks of Prince William Sound in Alaska smeared with oil from the Exxon Valdez, and of the Great Lakes despoiled by sewage, industrial pollution, and invasive species. One thinks of the oxygen-starved region in the Gulf of Mexico where no fish can survive, a dead zone the size of New Jersey caused by the runoff of agricultural fertilizer from the Mississippi basin. One thinks of mountains in Appalachia blasted open in the search for cheap coal, and the resulting debris sliding downhill to clog rivers and bury homes. One thinks of forests killed by acid rain, the fat of polar bears and the milk of nursing mothers laced with toxins, a thinning ozone layer allowing passage of more ultraviolet rays, the leaching and death of coral reefs from offshore pollution and rising water temperatures, the exhaustion of ocean fisheries, and the accelerating pace of species extinction. One thinks of global climate disruption, which threatens to cause an order of suffering that will make the Dust Bowl seem mild by comparison. One thinks, alas, of all too many examples of what happens when a domineering attitude toward the Earth, unconstrained by prudence or reverence, employs ever more powerful technology to serve the appetites of ever more people.

Aldo Leopold remains a vital figure for us today because he analyzed the sources of ecological damage with unprecedented clarity, and he wrote about possible remedies as compellingly as any American ever has. Although he was among the earliest champions of wilderness protection, he thought and wrote mainly about land that has been turned to human use. Given that we must eat, how should we manage our farms? Given that we must build houses, how should we manage our forests? Given that we enjoy outdoor activities, how should we manage our parks? How can we gauge the health of land, and how can we restore land that is ailing?

The argument that Leopold sought to distill into his remarks at the dedication ceremony was one he had begun articulating two decades earlier, as a young forester puzzling over the erosion of public lands in the Southwest, and one he would continue refining right up to his last hours, as he revised the book that would become *A Sand County Almanac* (1949). At the risk of oversimplifying the long and subtle development of Leopold's thought, I would summarize his main argument as follows:

· The soils, waters, and air, with all of the plants and animals that draw their life from them, form one integrated whole, which might be called, collectively, the land.
· We abuse the land because we see it as a commodity belonging to us rather than as a community to which we belong, and on which we depend entirely for our well-being.
· We do not understand the consequences of our actions because we are ignorant of the land's evolutionary history and its ecological functioning.
· Our ignorance of the land is compounded by our increasing alienation from nature, abetted by technology that allows us to dwell almost entirely within human artifacts.
· Government agencies and regulations can be helpful in protecting the land, but the only sure antidote to the exploitative view is the widespread cultivation among the citizenry of a land ethic, grounded in an ecological conscience.
· Such an ethic arises from intimate experience of nature, from an enlarged perception of land's non-economic values, and from a deep awareness of our membership in the land community.

Leopold was convinced that no combination of enlightened laws, clever technology, economic incentives, or patchwork fixes would rescue us from ecological ruin. What was required, he declared in his speech at the Arboretum, was "the reorganization of society," a fundamental shift in values and conduct at all levels, from individuals and households to communities, nations, and ultimately the entire human species. That is a tall order. More than once he confessed his doubt that such a radical shift in worldview could come about any time soon, especially in a society, such as the United States, which is so thoroughly dominated by an industrial and materialistic mindset. But such doubts did not keep him from devoting his life to the effort.

In striving to bring about the "reorganization of society" along ecological lines, Leopold relied as much on the art of writing as on the discipline of science. Writing was not an occasional sideline for him, but a sustained practice throughout his career. The list of his publications runs to over five hundred items, ranging from technical reports to newspaper columns, from speeches for business groups to articles for farmers and essays for the general reader. In addition he wrote thousands of letters, and he left behind at his death numerous unpublished drafts, proposals, lectures, and notes. Anyone who has sampled this large body of work would be hard put to find a single dull page.

Rather than reporting findings in a neutral voice, as scientists are trained to do, Leopold wrote in a personal, often witty, always passionately engaged voice about the implications of ecological research, about his own outdoor experiences, about the faults he saw in American culture, and about the actions he deemed necessary for nurturing the health of the land. Despite his strong feelings, he was never dogmatic; he wrote in a spirit of inquiry rather than certainty. In this regard he was a true essayist, one who tries out ideas, who asks questions.

During his speech at the Arboretum, he raised a series of questions about the history of the land on which he and his audience were standing. How had the tamarack bog, which had occupied this spot from the melting of the most recent glacier until the days of the fur trade, given way in a few years to grass and brush? What role had humans played in the transition? What state of the land here would be "of greatest use to the animal community"? Such questions about the history and condition of land, he asserted, "are of national importance. They determine the future habitability of the earth, materially and spiritually."

The "habitability of the earth, materially and spiritually," was Leopold's overriding concern, already evident in the letters he sent home from boarding school as a teenager, and still evident in the book he was revising at the time of his death in 1948. How the prospects for human flourishing, or even survival, might be compromised by human actions would have been evident to his listeners on that June day in 1934. One quarter of the population was out of work, mainly because of reckless land use and financial speculation. With Social Security not yet enacted, half of all elderly persons were living in poverty. Hundreds of banks were failing. Breadlines spread through cities from coast to coast. News of the Dust Bowl arrived by way of headlines and radio broadcasts and grit on the dining room table. As a result of this calamity and a century of land abuse, Leopold told his audience, "It can be stated as a sober fact that the iron-heel attitude has already reduced by half the ability of Wisconsin to support a cooperative community of men, animals, and plants during the next century. Moreover, it has saddled us with a repair bill, the magnitude of which we are just beginning to appreciate."

Gloomy as that assessment may seem, the notion of a repair bill coming due implies that the healing of damaged land is possible, a possibility that Leopold and his colleagues at the University of Wisconsin hoped to demonstrate in the new Arboretum, where they would pioneer the discipline that has come to be known as restoration ecology. In his speech, Leopold outlined the rationale for such a project:

> If civilization consists of cooperation with plants, animals, soil, and men, then a university which attempts to define that cooperation must have, for the use of its faculty and students, places which show what the land was, what it is, and what it ought to be. This Arboretum may be regarded as a place where, in the course of time, we will build up an exhibit of what was, as well as an exhibit of what ought to be. It is with this dim vision of its future destiny that we have dedicated the greater part of the Arboretum to a reconstruction of original Wisconsin, rather than to a "collection" of imported trees.

He knew well that "original Wisconsin" could not be wholly reconstructed here. Wolves and bears, for example, could not be relocated to a few hundred acres on the shores of Lake Wingra, even if the citizens of Madison could have been persuaded to put up with such wily neighbors. The restoration plan faced other challenges, such as how to establish in southern Wisconsin a sample of the boreal forest native to the far northern reaches of the state. And what habitat types and what stage in their history should be identified as representative of "original Wisconsin"? Once those exemplary habitats were identified, should they be artificially maintained in a more or less static condition, even though wild landscapes change over time? How should invasive species be dealt with? Since the use of fire would be risky in an area surrounded by city, how could fire-dependent biomes be managed? How could fragile plant communities be protected from admirers as well as vandals? No doubt members of the Arboretum staff are still wrestling with these problems today.

*　　　　＊*

The greatest challenge to the restoration scheme was one that Leopold confronted over and over in his career—namely, how to move from *is* to *ought*, from ecological knowledge to ethical imperative. The Arboretum might provide samples of the way Wisconsin's prairies, savannas, forests, and marshes used to be in the past; but how, from such glimpses, could one decide on the proper treatment of any piece of land in the present, or the ideal condition to aim for in the future? Philosophers from David Hume onward have demonstrated that there is no logical way of arguing from descriptive statements about the way things *are* to prescriptive statements about the way things *ought to be*.

Let me illustrate the point by recounting an analogous dilemma from the debate over health-care reform. During a public meeting in my hometown, our congressman explained to an overflow crowd that some fifty million Americans lack health insurance, and another fifty million or so are hesitant to use the insurance they do have for fear of losing coverage. At this point a woman in the audience stood up and shouted, "I work hard for my money and I've got good insurance through my job. Why should I pay to help other people?" Her words won loud applause. Setting aside the question of whether she is already unwittingly paying to help other people through inflated insurance premiums, and setting aside the question of what she would do if she lost her job, the challenge she poses is not a factual one. She is not disputing the data about how many Americans are uninsured or precariously insured. She is demanding to know why she should make any concessions, suffer any inconvenience, pay any taxes, to aid those who lack access to health care. That is not an empirical question, which could be answered by diligent study, scientific or otherwise. It is an ethical question, which could be answered only by conscience or compassion.

Again and again, Leopold encountered similar challenges. How could he persuade ranchers to stop shooting wolves or poisoning hawks; how could he persuade farmers to quit draining wetlands and pasturing cows in their wood-lots; how could he persuade road crews not to mow the last remnants of wild-flowers along the highways; how could he persuade motorists to climb out of their cars and experience the land at a walking pace rather than glimpsing it through a windshield at sixty miles per hour; how could he convince state game boards to value wildlife that hunters wouldn't pay to shoot; how could he move public land managers to see forests as more than timber, grasslands as more than pasture, rivers as more than sources of irrigation and electricity?

In these and numerous other instances, Leopold's view of how the land should be treated came up against the deep-seated desire for money, conve-nience, and comfort. In every case he was in effect being asked: Why shouldn't I exploit and enslave the Earth, if doing so benefits me? Why should I make any concessions from what I regard as my self-interest in order to care for dirt, trees, swamps, flowers, or animals?

He knew a range of answers to that question, most of them variations on the argument that if you despoil the land, if you drive other species to extinc-tion, you and your descendants will suffer dire consequences. That answer hap-pens to be true. But it appeals primarily to fear, and fear is an exhausting emo-tion. We can bear it for only so long before we grow numb. Besides, we tend to discount the future, so that a catastrophe predicted for a decade or a century hence, such as the likely disruption of living systems due to continued heating of the atmosphere, matters less to us than the amount of this month's electricity bill. Likewise, Leopold knew from observing the effects of New Deal conserva-tion programs that changes in behavior prompted solely by government rules and subsidies ended abruptly when the law looked the other way or the pay-ments ceased.

The only durable way of moving people to treat the land responsibly, Leop-old came to realize, was by appealing not to fear, greed, or duty, but to intellect, imagination, and love. His most concise statement of this view appears in the final essay of *A Sand County Almanac:* "We can be ethical only in relation to something we can see, feel, understand, love, or otherwise have faith in." Here he is cataloguing the ways in which something becomes *present* to us—through our senses, through our emotions, through reason, affection, and trust. By *faith,* here, I suspect he does not mean the sort of belief we commonly associate with religion, one based on scriptures, revelation, creeds, or the pronounce-ments of gurus and priests. I suspect he is thinking rather of *keeping faith*—as in the trust that arises between lovers or friends, or the loyalty of a person to a place or a craft or a cause—the enduring commitment we call fidelity.

Leopold's lifework, as conservationist and scientist and writer, was devoted to making the soils, waters, atmosphere, plants, and animals vividly *present* to us, and thereby a focus of our care. So he championed the protection of land which had not been wholly subdued to human purposes, whether remote wilderness or a patch of prairie in a cemetery. In the name of democracy, he defended parks, state and national forests, wildlife refuges, and other public lands against those who sought to privatize every acre. He called for the provision of wild margins in cultivated regions, such as hedgerows between plowed fields and ponds fenced off from livestock and riparian borders along streams. He helped organize cooperative endeavors among farmers who wished to increase the abundance of wildlife on their property. He advocated the preservation or reconstruction of natural biomes within reach of city dwellers, as in the Arboretum. He promoted the restoration of degraded habitats, such as the eroded farm along the Wisconsin River where he and his family planted thousands of trees, shrubs, and wildflowers. His goal in all of these efforts was to provide places where people of every age and condition could experience the land directly, as a living presence.

Through his writing, Leopold sought to make the land a living presence by appealing to imagination as well as to reason, offering a host of metaphors to communicate ecological ideas. And so you will find him describing the land as a round river, a biotic pyramid, a machine made up of cogs and wheels, a food chain, a fountain of energy, an electrical circuit, a hydraulic system, a symphony, a play, a web, an organism, a community, and a variety of other things. Likewise you will find anecdotes from history and mythology, literary allusions, stories of his nature excursions, and lyrical portraits of mountains, rivers, animals, and plants. In *A Sand County Almanac*, for example, you will read of bur oaks withstanding fire and tamaracks turning smoky gold in the fall, a chickadee enduring six Wisconsin winters, a wolf dying from gunshot, a rare compass plant blooming in the corner of a graveyard, the last grizzly bear on an Arizona mountain being killed in the name of progress, and woodcocks performing their sky dance, along with many other memorable stories.

By dealing in stories and metaphors, Leopold ventured beyond the realm of science into art. Using every device that a poet, novelist, or essayist might use, he sought to convey a sense of the land as an unfolding drama, radiant with beauty, and endlessly fascinating. Here, for example, is a passage from *A Sand County Almanac* describing the return of sandhill cranes to a Wisconsin marsh in spring:

A dawn wind stirs on the great marsh. With almost imperceptible slowness it rolls a bank of fog across the wide morass. Like the white ghost of a glacier the mists advance, riding over phalanxes of tamarack, sliding across bog-meadows heavy with dew. A single silence hangs from horizon to horizon.

Out of some far recess of the sky a tinkling of little bells falls soft upon the listening land. Then again silence. Now comes a baying of some sweet-throated hound, soon the clamor of a responding pack. Then a far clear blast of hunting horns, out of the sky into the fog.

High horns, low horns, silence, and finally a pandemonium of trumpets, rattles, croaks, and cries that almost shakes the bog with its nearness, but without yet disclosing whence it comes. At last a glint of sun reveals the approach of a great echelon of birds. On motionless wing they emerge from the lifting mists, sweep a final arc of sky, and settle in clangorous descending spirals to their feeding grounds. A new day has begun on the crane marsh.

These birds have flown thousands of miles to reach this place, and they have been doing so, generation after generation, since the retreat of the glaciers. But the day may come, and soon, Leopold warns us, when the last marshes and bogs will be drained for the growing of crops, and the cranes will return no more. By making us feel the allure of their ancient lineage, their graceful movements, their clamorous voices, he clearly hoped we might be moved to treasure cranes and therefore to defend the wetlands they need for survival. Elsewhere in *A Sand County Almanac,* lamenting the loss of a rare prairie plant, he remarked, "We grieve only for what we know." And so he wrote of many species and habitats, some of them rare, others commonplace, all of them, in his eyes, worthy of our attention and concern.

In spite of his considerable powers as a writer, Leopold despaired of ever fully conveying what captivated him about the greater-than-human world. After describing the sandhill cranes so eloquently, he observed: "Our ability to perceive quality in nature begins, as in art, with the pretty. It expands through successive stages of the beautiful to values as yet uncaptured by language. The quality of cranes lies, I think, in this higher gamut, as yet beyond the reach of words."

The limitations of language did not keep Leopold from trying to evoke these elusive qualities. In another essay from *A Sand County Almanac,* for instance, he recounted a journey on the Rio Gavilan, in Mexico's Sierra Madre, a river so unsullied, so brimming with life, that it made the rivers on the American side of the border appear sick by comparison. Here is how he described the aura of the Gavilan:

> This song of the waters is audible to every ear, but there is other music in these hills, by no means audible to all. To hear even a few notes of it you must first live here for a long time, and you must know the speech of hills and rivers. Then on a still night, when the campfire is low and the Pleiades have climbed over rimrocks, sit quietly and listen for a wolf to howl, and think hard of everything you have seen and tried to understand. Then you may hear it—a vast pulsing harmony—its score inscribed on a thousand hills, its notes the lives and deaths of plants and animals, its rhythms spanning the seconds and the centuries.

At times, in seeking to communicate a sense of the land's wholeness, he could sound like Thoreau or Emerson in their most transcendental moments, as in a 1923 essay entitled "Some Fundamentals of Conservation in the Southwest," where he envisioned the Earth "as a living being, vastly less alive than ourselves in degree, but vastly greater than ourselves in time and space—a being that was old when the morning stars sang together, and, when the last of us has been gathered unto his fathers, will still be young." More often, and especially in the later essays, Leopold avoided transcendental language and pointed toward the "higher gamut" of values in nature by speaking of health, integrity, resilience, and beauty, all shorthand terms for qualities that could never be adequately named.

Leopold was not a religious man in any church-going, creed-embracing sense. Nor did he treat nature as divine. But he was imbued with a mystic's feeling for the unity of all things, human and nonhuman. In speaking of this unity as an "organism," a "living being," or "a vast pulsing harmony," he could only gesture with a metaphor toward a mystery, yet such writing might awaken readers to the possibility of experiencing this unity for themselves.

Of course I cannot pretend to say clearly what Leopold declared to be unsayable, nor can I presume to know exactly what he felt on the crane marsh or the Rio Gavilan. But I have a hunch. I suspect that anyone who has spent much time in wild country has experienced such moments of communion, when the ordinary sense of self dissolves. One might be watching a bird, or listening to a creek, or feeling the brush of wind, or smelling the approach of rain, and for a spell there is only pure awareness. Such moments strip away the illusion that we are separate from and superior to the rest of nature. They humble us. They place our lives in perspective. They reveal what Buddhists call interdependence, an insight which is also key to the science of ecology.

Thus we can see why, for Leopold, healthy land is vital for our spiritual as well as our material well-being. When forests are leveled, when farmland is paved, when the waters and soils and atmosphere are poisoned, when other species are driven to extinction by our actions, we lose not only the emotional richness of all that vanished beauty; we lose our bearings. We stop hearing voices other than our own. Swaddled in the artificial world that humans have made, we forget that we depend entirely on the original world, the one that made us. We succumb to the illusion that we are masters rather than members of Earth.

The greatest theme in American literature is the search for right relations between humankind and nature, between civilization and wildness. Leopold's writing belongs squarely in this tradition, which runs from Audubon, Emerson, and Thoreau, up through Melville, Muir, Faulkner, Carson, and such contemporaries as Wendell Berry and Gary Snyder. This lineage continues to inspire those of us who seek to articulate a conservation ethic for our own time.

The challenges to the health of the land in our day are even more severe than those that troubled Leopold. Since his death in 1948, the human population has more than doubled; the power of technology has dramatically increased, and so has the rate of habitat disturbance and resource exhaustion. We know in greater detail than Leopold could have known that human activities are polluting the waters and atmosphere, depleting the life of the oceans, accelerating the extinction of species, and upsetting the climate. Deserts are spreading, forests are dwindling, aquifers are drying up. The amount of human suffering—from poverty, epidemics, and wars, as well as from environmental degradation—has increased decade by decade, along with population. The attitude of "philosophical imperialism" that Leopold spoke of during the Dust Bowl era has become even more firmly entrenched in our current economic system, which pursues consumption rather than stewardship, profit rather than health. The largest corporations now surpass all but a few nations in the amount of wealth they control, and they wield ever greater power over governments and the mass media. Citizens of industrialized countries have less and less direct contact with nature, and young people in particular spend more and more of their waking hours inside an electronic cocoon.

In hopeful counterpoint to these disturbing trends, the fields of conservation biology and ecology, which Leopold pioneered, have become steadily more sophisticated, and our capacity for gauging the condition of the Earth has become more robust. Just at the moment in our evolutionary history when humans have begun to degrade living systems on a planetary scale, we have developed the capacity to monitor and model the biosphere, and to communicate our findings everywhere on Earth at the speed of light. We are an exceedingly clever species; it remains to be seen whether we are also wise. We understand in some detail how we ought to conduct our lives, generate energy, produce food, manufacture commodities, and care for the land. And we possess much of the technology we need to move toward a sustainable way of life. What we lack is a culture of conservation, which would guide individuals, households, communities, nations, and our entire species to live in a durable fashion.

Recalling his impressions of the Sierra Madre in "Conservationist in Mexico," Leopold speculated that these mountains could still offer "so lovely a picture of ecological health" because the Apache had kept settlers from moving there in large numbers. Once the Apache were subdued, however, and settlers moved in, what could keep this pristine land from suffering the fate of mountains just across the border in Arizona and New Mexico, mountains which had lost much of their vegetation, topsoil, wildlife, and beauty to the onslaught of axes, plows, and livestock? His answer was "that we seem ultimately always thrown back on individual ethics as the basis of conservation policy. It is hard to make a man, by pressure of law or money, do a thing which does not spring naturally from his own personal sense of right and wrong."

He elaborated on this insight in his justly famous essay "The Land Ethic," the final piece in *A Sand County Almanac*. There he argued that over the centuries we have gradually enlarged our sense of the human community, and therefore our sphere of moral concern, to encompass not only the members of our tribe, our sex, our race, class, nation, or religion, but all people. Dismayed by two world wars, with their concentration camps and wholesale slaughter, he knew that humans still fell far short of treating all members of our species with respect and care. Nonetheless, he foresaw the possibility, and indeed the necessity, of extending our sphere of moral concern beyond our species to embrace fields and forests, rivers and mountains, animals and plants. "Obligations have no meaning without conscience," he wrote, "and the problem we face is the extension of the social conscience from people to land."

Some argue that we should endeavor to take good care of our fellow humans before we fret about how we treat the land. But that is a false dichotomy. The well-being of people is inseparable from the well-being of Earth. Moreover, if we treat with indifference or contempt one portion of the living world, such as trees or topsoil, we are likely to treat other portions in the same way, including humans. The willingness to exterminate another species by destroying its habitat may translate into the willingness to exterminate another people. Conversely, if we embrace the land ethic, an attitude of generosity, fellow feeling, and stewardship may come to permeate all our actions.

But how do we develop a sense of right and wrong in our treatment of the land? Although philosophers may reason their way to an ethic, most of us must feel our way there. Evolutionary psychologists suggest that some of what we label as conscience may be inborn, an evolutionary inheritance—our tendency to cooperate, for example, to value fairness, to empathize with the pain of others. But surely the greater part of conscience is learned; it is a product of culture.

So how do we cultivate an ecological conscience in ourselves and how do we nurture it in society? As individuals, we spend more time outdoors, free from electronic devices. If we are parents we take our children outside with us. We learn the names and habits of local animals and plants, and we support organizations that are devoted to their protection. We patronize farmers' markets and agricultural co-ops. We grow vegetables and native plants in our yards. We learn where our water comes from, where our trash goes. We support politicians who understand ecology and who care about the health of the land. We inquire about the true cost, to Earth and its creatures, of our purchases, our travels, our pastimes, and our jobs.

As a society, we provide natural areas within reach of everyone, the poor as well as the rich, through gardens in schoolyards, parks in neighborhoods, green belts along rivers, through land trusts and community forests. We embody ecological principles in legislation and in the curriculum of our schools. We hold corporations responsible for their impact on the land. We ask of our religious traditions what they can teach us about taking care of Earth and not merely of individual souls. We protect wilderness and the roadless areas of our national forests, so as to place a limit on human dominion, to preserve habitat for other species, and to provide a standard for healthy land.

Leopold saw the University of Wisconsin Arboretum as a means of providing within a populated area, and in miniature, what wilderness provides on a grand scale. Visitors could glimpse in these tended acres the possibility of a more benign relationship between humans and the rest of nature. In his speech at the dedication ceremony, the only time he used the first-person singular was when he declared "I am here to say that the invention of a harmonious relationship between men and land is a more exacting task than the invention of machines, and that its accomplishment is impossible without a visual knowledge of the land's history."

Since those words were spoken in June of 1934, we have invented countless new machines, but we have made only halting progress toward achieving a harmonious relationship between ourselves and the land. This remains our great task. The need to envision a way of life that harmonizes with the way of nature, and to set about creating such a life, has never been more urgent. If we do create a culture of conservation, it will be in no small measure thanks to Aldo Leopold, for helping us to imagine and to relish our proper place on Earth.

# The Mystique of Money

nyone who pays attention to the state of the planet realizes that all natural systems on which human life depends are deteriorating, and they are doing so largely because of human actions. By natural systems I mean the topsoil, forests, grasslands, wetlands, rivers, lakes, oceans, atmosphere, the host of other species, and the cycles that bind them together into a living whole. By human life I mean not merely the survival of our species, although in the long run that will surely be in question; rather I mean the *quality* of our existence, the prospects for adequate food, shelter, work, education, health care, conviviality, intellectual endeavor, and spiritual growth for our kind far into the future.

So the crucial question is, Why? Why are those of us in the richest countries acting in such a way, individually and collectively, as to undermine the conditions on which our own lives, the lives of other species, and the lives of future generations depend? And why are we so intent on coaxing or coercing the poorer countries to follow our example? There are many possible answers, of course. It may be that on average we humans are too short-sighted and dim-witted to take stock of our situation and change our behavior. It may be that evolution has ill-fitted us to restrain our appetites. It may be that selfish genes and tribal instincts prompt us to define our interests too narrowly, excluding regard for people whom we perceive as different from ourselves, not to mention other species and unborn generations. It may be that the otherworldly religion preached so fervently across our land has convinced many believers that Earth, indeed the whole universe, is merely a backdrop for the drama of human salvation, destined to evaporate once the rapture comes. It may be that we have been so stupefied by consumerism and around-the-clock entertainment that we have lost the ability to think clearly and take sensible actions. It may be that global corporations have achieved such a stranglehold over the mass media and the political system as to thwart all efforts at reforming our way of life. It may be that the logic of capitalism, based on perpetual growth, is incompatible with a finite planet. It may be that preachers, pundits, pitchmen, and politicians have deluded us into thinking that financial wealth represents real wealth.

The list of factors that help to explain why we are degrading the Earth could easily be extended, but let me focus on the last one—our confusion of financial wealth with real wealth. To grasp the impact of that confusion, think of someone you love. Then recall that if you were to reduce a human body to its elements—oxygen, carbon, phosphorous, copper, sulfur, potassium, magnesium, iodine, and so on—you would end up with a few dollars' worth of raw materials. The estimates vary, some lower, some higher. But even with inflation, and allowing for the obesity epidemic, this person you cherish still would not fetch as much as ten dollars on the commodities market. A child would fetch less, roughly in proportion to body weight.

Such calculations seem absurd, of course, because none of us would consider dismantling a human being for any amount of money, least of all someone we love. Nor would we entertain the milder suggestion of lopping off someone's arm or leg and putting it up for sale, even if the limb belonged to our worst enemy. Our objection would not be overcome by the assurance that the person still has another arm, another leg, and seems to be getting along just fine. We'd be likely to say that it's not acceptable under any circumstances to treat a person as a commodity, worth so much per pound.

And yet this is how our economy treats every portion of the natural world—as a commodity for sale, subject to damage or destruction if enough money can be made from the transaction. Nothing in nature has been spared—not forests, grasslands, wetlands, mountains, rivers, oceans, atmosphere, nor any of the creatures that dwell therein. Nor have human beings been spared. Through its routine practices, this economy subjects people to shoddy products, unsafe working conditions, medical scams, poisoned air and water, propaganda dressed up as journalism, and countless other assaults, all in pursuit of profits.

When tobacco or pharmaceutical companies suppress research that shows their products are killing people, they may not single out particular human beings for execution, yet they deliberately sentence a large number of strangers to premature death. Likewise, when banks launder drug money, when the insurance industry opposes public health care, when the auto industry lobbies against higher fuel efficiency standards, when arms manufacturers fight any restraint on the trade in guns, when agribusiness opposes limits on the spraying of poisons, when electric utilities evade regulations that would clean up smoke from power plants, when chambers of commerce lobby against efforts to reduce greenhouse gas emissions, they are just as surely condemning vast numbers of people to illness, injury, and death.

We all participate in this economy, to one degree or another, if only by shopping at chain stores or driving cars. I will consider our own complicity later. Right now I want to focus on those people who actually decide to blow the tops off mountains and bury streams in search of coal, or to level forests and ravage millions of acres of wilderness in pursuit of oil sands, or to drill for oil a mile below sea level, or to pump a toxic brew underground and foul aquifers in order to release natural gas from shale, or to sell weapons to dictators and thugs. I want to think about those people who give the orders to suppress damning research reports or ignore safety requirements or thwart environmental legislation or dump toxic waste or broadcast lies.

What drives them to make such harmful decisions? And how might they be stopped? Would they be chastened by having to choose from a lineup of children, for example, which ones should die of asthma attacks caused by smog, or from a group of pregnant women which ones should pass on lethal doses of carcinogens to their babies? Would they ponder their decisions more carefully if they had to pick out which workers should be crushed or drowned because of shortcuts on safety, or which poor people should die for lack of health insurance, or which policemen should be shot by drug dealers wielding assault rifles? It might be comforting to think so, but it's unlikely the autocrats would change their priorities, even if they had to look their victims in the eyes. For what ethical difference is there between knowingly causing harm to particular individuals and knowingly causing harm to strangers? Either way, you are trading the health, and often the lives, of human beings for money, as surely as if you were selling people for so much per pound.

We should be clear that it is money, and money's offspring, power, that the owners and managers of such businesses are seeking. Mining companies, for instance, have no interest in coal or oil, in uranium or gold, except as a material they can sell, and the same is true of corn and hogs for industrial farms, of trees for timber companies, of bundled mortgage securities for financial traders. Such enterprises are not devoted to heating our homes or filling our pantries, any more than the purveyors of trash on television are devoted to enlightening us. Their only goal is private profit. On a small scale, there is nothing wrong with that. But on a large scale, especially among global corporations, the relentless pursuit of profit can become pathological, overriding all regard for the well-being of people, places, or nature, eluding the control of governments, operating as if nothing matters except piling up more money. This is as it should be, according to free-market economists, because the only legal requirement of corporations is that they maximize the return to their shareholders. The best-known and most influential of such economists, Milton Friedman, stated flatly in a 1970 *New York Times* op-ed piece: "There is one and only one social responsibility of business—to use its resources and engage in activities designed to increase its profits so long as it stays within the rules of the game, which is to say, engages in open and free competition without deception or fraud."

The second half of Friedman's sentence would place a curb on the first half only in a universe where enterprises motivated entirely by greed never engaged in deception or fraud. This may have seemed like a possibility in the rarefied atmosphere of the Chicago School of Economics, where Friedman held sway and helped to shape the free-market ideology that has dominated American society in recent decades. But in the world where the rest of us live, deception and fraud have been commonplace among corporate giants, from Enron to Exxon, from United Fruit to Union Carbide. Consider a short list of recent malefactors: Halliburton, Philip Morris, WorldCom, Wachovia, Arthur Andersen, Adelphia, Blackwater, Monsanto, Massey Energy, Tyco, HealthSouth, Wal-Mart, Global Crossing, Citigroup, Goldman Sachs, Countrywide Financial, AIG, and BP. These companies, and legions of others, have cooked the account books, misrepresented their financial condition with end-of-quarter window dressing, abused their employees, cheated their investors, sold lethal products, violated safety regulations, lied, bribed, swindled, or otherwise refused to stay within "the rules of the game."

In our country, when the rules become a nuisance or do not sufficiently favor their interests, big companies purchase enough support in the White House or Congress or regulatory agencies to have the rules revised or abolished. Examples of this abuse could be cited from all industries, but none are more egregious than those in finance. Until the mid-1980s, the U.S. financial sector never accounted for more than 16 percent of all corporate profits, but over the past decade it has averaged more than 41 percent, and it has done so while contributing only modestly to social needs, chiefly through local banks and credit unions, and while doing a great deal of harm, chiefly through the creation and trade of financial paper. Most of the economic advisers for President Obama as for President Bush have come straight from Wall Street, and, not surprisingly, they have shaped government policy to benefit the biggest Wall Street firms and the richest investors. The global economic meltdown was largely a result of such rigging of the system, which freed commercial and investment banks, trading companies, and rating agencies to gamble recklessly with other people's money.

In spite of the worldwide suffering caused by this casino capitalism, the financial reform bill passed by Congress in the summer of 2010 does little to rein it in. The managers of hedge funds, for example, have kept their operations essentially free of oversight, while preserving the loophole that treats their earnings as capital gains, taxed at 15 percent, rather than as regular income, which would be taxed in the top bracket at 35 percent. In 2009, when the CEOs of the twenty-five largest American hedge funds split over $26 billion, this cozy arrangement cost the Treasury, and therefore the rest of us, several billion dollars in lost tax revenue. When President Obama urged Congress to close this tax loophole, the billionaire chairman of one hedge fund responded by comparing such a move with the Nazi invasion of Poland.

Now, why would a billionaire want more money, and why have some billionaires sought to increase their fortunes by purchasing television networks and newspapers, funding think tanks, hiring armies of lobbyists and propagandists, and setting up phony front groups, all to spread the gospel of no-holds-barred capitalism? You might say that such behavior is natural, because everybody wants more money. But consider: Suppose you keep a billion dollars under your mattress, where it will earn no income, and you set out to spend it; in order to burn through it all within an adult lifetime of, say, fifty years, you would have to spend $1.7 million per month, or $55,000 per day. If you took your billion dollars out from under the mattress and invested it in long-term U.S. Treasury bonds at current rates, you could spend $40 million per year, or $110,000 per day, forever, without touching your capital. It so happens that $110,000 is a bit more than twice the median household income in the United States. If you do the math, you will find that the twenty-five hedge fund managers who pulled in $26 billion last year claimed an income equivalent to roughly 500,000 households, or some two million people.

What are Rupert Murdoch, David and Charles Koch, Adolph Coors, Richard Mellon Scaife, and other billionaire advocates of unbridled capitalism after? They certainly are not worrying about sending their kids to college or paying their medical bills. Then what are they seeking? A psychiatrist might be better qualified to answer the question, but let me offer an amateur's hunch, which arises from six decades of watching our legislatures, regulatory agencies, judiciary, public lands, mass media, and schools come under the influence, and often under the total control, of the richest Americans. What the free-enterprise billionaires are greedy for is not money but power, and not merely the power to take care of themselves and their families, which would be reasonable, but the power to have anything they want and do anything they want without limit, which is decidedly unreasonable. Anyone who has shared a house with a two-year-old or a fifteen-year-old has witnessed such a craving to fulfill every desire and throw off every constraint. Most children grow beyond this hankering for omnipotence. Those who carry the craving into adulthood may become sociopaths—incapable of sensing or caring for the needs of other people, indifferent to the harm they cause, reacting aggressively toward anyone or anything that blocks their will.

I'm not saying that all billionaires, or mega-millionaires, are sociopaths. Bill Gates and Warren Buffett clearly aren't, for example, for they are using their fortunes to serve the public good, including funding programs for those who dwell at the other end of the money spectrum. In June of 2010, Gates and Buffett invited the richest individuals and families in America to sign a pledge to donate the majority of their wealth to philanthropic causes. As of this writing, fifty-seven have accepted the invitation, including Michael Bloomberg, mayor of New York; Martin Zuckerberg, co-founder of Facebook; Paul Allen, co-founder of Microsoft; and Ted Turner, founder of CNN. Perhaps they have signed the pledge out of pure altruism. But I would like to believe they also understand that they themselves did not *create* their financial wealth, however skillful and hardworking they may be; they amassed their money by drawing on the efforts of countless people, living and dead; by drawing on public resources, such as schools and courts; by reaping the benefits of madcap bidding on the stock market; and by drawing on the natural resources of the planet. I would like to believe that, having derived their riches from the commons, they feel obliged to return a substantial portion of those riches for the benefit of the commons.

Whatever their motives, the signers of the Giving Pledge are following the example of Andrew Carnegie. Although he acquired his fortune by methods as ruthless as any employed by buccaneer capitalists today, having made his money, Carnegie gave it all away, except for a modest amount left to his family. We associate his name especially with the more than 2,500 libraries he endowed, but he also funded many other public goods, including a university, a museum, and a foundation for promoting, not free enterprise, but education and world peace. In an essay published in 1889 called "The Gospel of Wealth," he argued that the concentration of great fortunes in the hands of a few was an inevitable result of capitalism, but also a dangerous one, because the resulting disparity between the haves and have-nots would cause social unrest. And so, he insisted, these great fortunes should be restored to society, either through philanthropy or through taxation.

In view of the current efforts, backed by many of the richest Americans, to abolish the estate tax, it is striking to read Carnegie's view of the matter:

> The growing disposition to tax more and more heavily large estates left at death is a cheering indication of the growth of a salutary change in public opinion. . . . Of all forms of taxation, this seems the wisest. Men who continue hoarding great sums all their lives, the proper use of which for public ends would work good to the community, should be made to feel that the community, in the form of the state, cannot thus be deprived of its proper share. By taxing estates heavily at death, the state marks its condemnation of the selfish millionaire's unworthy life.

That is not a passage you are likely to find cited by the Cato Institute, Free Enterprise Fund, Heritage Foundation, Club for Growth, or any of the other strident opponents of the federal estate tax, a tax that under current regulations affects only the richest 1 percent of Americans—the very citizens, by coincidence, who fund the Cato Institute, etc., etc.

Now let us return to pondering the richest of our fellow citizens who show no inclination to share their wealth, but rather seem intent on growing richer by hook or crook, regardless of the consequences for our democracy, the environment, or future generations. Unlike Andrew Carnegie, unlike Bill Gates or Warren Buffett, these individuals use their wealth only to increase their power, and use their power only to guard and increase their wealth, and so on in an upward spiral toward infinity. Their success in this endeavor can be measured by the fact that by 2010 the top 1 percent of earners were receiving 24 percent of all income in the United States, the highest proportion since the eve of the Great Depression in 1929.

Giant corporations operate in a similar way, using their wealth to increase their power over markets and governments, and using their power to increase their wealth. When I say *giant*, I am not referring to retailers, banks, factories, or other firms that operate on a modest scale and in one or a few locations. I am referring to the behemoths of business. Of the one hundred largest economies in the world, more than half are multinational corporations. Exxon alone surpasses in revenues the economies of 180 nations. These gigantic empires, spanning the globe, answer to no electorate, move jobs and money about at will, keep much of their operations secret, and oppose any regulation that might cut into their profits. Thus over the past several decades, Exxon has used its enormous might to oppose higher fuel efficiency standards, to resist safety regulations that might have prevented the catastrophic oil spill in Prince William Sound, to push for drilling in the Arctic National Wildlife Refuge, and to thwart legislation aimed at controlling carbon emissions. In doing so, the managers of Exxon have simply obeyed the logic of capitalism, which is to maximize profits regardless of social and environmental costs. Through trade organizations such as the American Petroleum Institute and numerous front groups, Exxon, Shell, BP, and other energy titans have spent millions of dollars trying to persuade the public that the climate isn't shifting dangerously, or if it is shifting then humans play no part in the change, or if humans do play a part then nothing can be done about it without stifling the economy.

Saving the economy is the slogan used to defend every sort of injustice and negligence, from defeating health-care legislation to ignoring the Clean Water Act to shunning the Kyoto Protocol on Climate Change. But should we save an economy in which the finance industry claims over 40 percent of all corporate profits and a single hedge fund manager claims an income equivalent to that of 20,000 households? Should we save an economy in which the top 1 percent of earners rake in a quarter of all income? Should we embrace an economy in which one in ten households faces foreclosure, 44 million people live in poverty, and 51 million lack health insurance; an economy in which the unemployment rate for African Americans is above 17 percent and for all workers is nearly 10 percent? Should we defend an economy that even in a recession generates a gross domestic product (GDP) over $14 trillion, a quarter of the world's total, and yet is supposedly unable to afford to reduce its carbon emissions? Should we serve an economy that represents less than 5 percent of Earth's population and yet accounts for nearly half of world military spending? A reasonable person might conclude that such an economy is fatally flawed, and that the flaws will not be repaired by those who profit from them the most.

The accumulation of money gives the richest individuals and corporations godlike power over the rest of us. Yet money itself has no intrinsic value; it is a medium of exchange, a token that we have tacitly agreed to recognize and swap for things that do possess intrinsic value, such as potatoes or poetry, salmon or surgery. Money is a symbolic tool, wholly dependent for its usefulness on an underlying social compact. It is paradoxical, therefore, that those who have benefitted the most financially from the existence of this compact have been most aggressive in seeking to undermine it, by attacking unions, cooperatives, public education, independent media, social welfare programs, nonprofits that serve the poor, land-use planning, and every aspect of government that doesn't directly serve the rich. For the social compact to hold, ordinary people must feel that they are participating in a common enterprise that benefits everyone fairly, and not a pyramid scheme designed to benefit a few at the very top. While the superrich often pretend to oppose government as an imposition on their freedom, they are usually great fans of government contracts, crop subsidies, oil depletion allowances, and other forms of corporate welfare, and even greater fans of military spending.

War is calamitous for people and Earth, but it is highly profitable for many businesses, as we know from the $1 trillion spent so far on the tragic invasions of Afghanistan and Iraq, a figure that is predicted to triple by the time all the costs have been reckoned. War is also a potent instrument for protecting and advancing corporate interests, which is why those who clamor for smaller government never clamor for a smaller military. While they invoke the principle of fiscal conservatism to oppose federal spending on public television, national endowments for the arts and humanities, childhood inoculation, endangered species, and other social and environmental programs, they are great boosters of spending for America's worldwide military empire, with its 2.5 million soldiers and hundreds of thousands of private contractors on some seven thousand bases in more than sixty nations.

Among those who have grasped this link between U.S. militarism and the cult of money was Martin Luther King, Jr. In a speech entitled "A Time to Break Silence," delivered a year to the day before he was assassinated, Dr. King went against the counsel of his friends and advisers by denouncing the Vietnam War. Like the wars in Iraq and Afghanistan, indeed like every U.S. military operation from the 1950s onward, the war in Vietnam was justified as an effort to promote freedom and democracy and to protect American security. What our military was actually protecting, Dr. King argued, were "the privileges and the pleasures that come from the immense profits of overseas investments." For saying so, he was denounced as a communist or socialist by newspapers and self-proclaimed patriots nationwide, just as President Obama has been denounced as a socialist for proposing national health care.

The slur is an old one, going back to the late nineteenth century, when movements to organize unions or end child labor in factories or secure votes for women were decried as socialist by the robber barons and their henchmen in politics and journalism. Since the Bolshevik Revolution of 1917, the labels *communist* and *socialist* have been used interchangeably by the superrich to condemn any cooperative efforts by citizens to secure basic rights or to serve common needs. These twin labels have been used to vilify the income tax, the estate tax, unemployment insurance, Social Security, Medicare, Medicaid, the Civil Rights Act, every major piece of environmental legislation, American participation in the U.N., disarmament treaties, aid to the poor, humanitarian aid to other nations—any endeavor by government, in short, that might reduce the coffers or curb the power of those who sit stop the greatest heaps of capital.

That power is steadily increasing, as witness the Supreme Court's decision in early 2010, by a 5–4 vote, in the *Citizens United vs. Federal Election Commission* case, which holds that corporate funding of political broadcasts during elections cannot be limited. The majority based their argument on the twin claims, never mentioned in the U.S. Constitution, that corporations are entitled to be treated as persons under the law and that money is a form of speech, and therefore any constraint on spending by corporations to influence elections would be a denial of their right to free speech guaranteed by the First Amendment. The decision means that our electoral process, already corrupted by big money, will fall even more under the sway of corporations and their innocuous-sounding front groups, such as "Citizens United." The nearly unanimous view among the nation's leading First Amendment scholars, voiced at a meeting in March of 2010, was that the case was wrongly decided. But the only five opinions that count are those of the judges in the majority, who were appointed to the Supreme Court by administrations that have benefited most handsomely from corporate financing.

So how do we break the spell of money? First, we need to recognize that it *is* a spell; if we kowtow to money, we are worshipping a phantom. For example, Rupert Murdoch's billions, with which he peddles anti-government ideology to a large fraction of the Earth's newspaper readers and television viewers, are only numbers stored in databases, numbers that stand for various currencies, every one of which derives its value from national and international laws, courts, regulatory agencies, police forces, armies, and other elements of government. Without those supports, he might be able to heat a penthouse for a while by burning stacks of $100 bills in the fireplace, but otherwise his money would be worthless. You might object that he also owns real wealth, such as buildings and boats, broadcast studios and newsrooms; but his claim to ownership of things tangible as well as intangible also depends wholly on social institutions and social consent. If those institutions were destroyed, as they have been in places lacking government, such as Somalia, or if the consent were withdrawn, as it has been in periods of revolution, then Murdoch and his fellow moguls would be left with a trove of meaningless papers and numbers.

Money derives its meaning from society, not from those who own the largest piles of it. Recognizing this fact is the first move toward liberating ourselves from the thrall of concentrated capital. We need to desanctify money, reminding ourselves that it is not a god ordained to rule over us, nor is it a natural force like gravity, which operates beyond our control. It is a human invention, like baseball or Monopoly, governed by rules that are subject to change, and viable only so long as we agree to play the game. We need to see and to declare that the money game as it is currently played in America produces a few big winners, who thereby acquire tyrannical power over the rest of us as great as that of any dictator or monarch; that they are using this power to skew the game more and more in their favor; and that the net result of this money game is to degrade the real sources of our well-being.

It is just as important that we shake off the spell of consumerism. In a 1955 essay for *The Journal of Retailing,* an industry analyst named Victor Lebow bluntly described what an ever-expanding capitalism would require of us: "Our enormously productive economy demands that we make consumption our way of life, that we convert the buying and use of goods into rituals, that we seek our spiritual satisfaction, our ego satisfaction, in consumption. The economy needs things consumed, burned, worn out, replaced, and discarded at an ever-increasing rate." And so it has come to pass. Americans, by and large, *have* made consumption a way of life, and a prime source, if not of spiritual satisfaction, then of compensation for whatever else might be missing from our lives, such as meaningful work, intact families, high-quality schools, honest government, safe streets, a healthy environment, a nation at peace, leisure time, neighborliness, community engagement, and other fast-disappearing or entirely vanished boons.

Advertisers maintain the consumerist illusion by appealing to our every impulse, from lust and envy to love of family and nature. The estimates for annual spending on advertising in the U.S. hover around $500 billion. This is roughly the amount we spend annually on public education. While taxpayers complain about the cost of schools, they do not protest the cost of advertising, which inflates the price of everything we purchase, and which aims at persuading us to view the buying of stuff as the pathway to happiness. A current ad for Coke, showing a frosty bottle, actually uses the slogan "Open Happiness." The promise is false, and all of us know it, yet we keep falling for the illusion. We can begin to free ourselves from that illusion by reducing our exposure to those media, such as commercial television and radio, that are primarily devoted to merchandizing. We can laugh at advertising. We can distinguish between our needs, which are finite, and our wants, which are limitless. Beyond meeting our basic needs, money cannot give us any of the things that actually bring happiness—family, community, good health, good work, experience of art and nature, service to others, a sense of purpose, spiritual insight.

When we do spend money, so far as possible we should put it in the hands of our neighbors—local merchants, professionals, growers, craft workers, artists, chefs, and makers of useful things—and we should put as little as possible in the coffers of distant corporations and plutocrats, who know and care nothing about our communities. We should encourage efforts to restore local economies, through small-scale manufacturing, sustainable agriculture and forestry, distributed energy generation, credit unions, public access television and radio, nonprofits, and cooperatives. We should experiment with local currencies, as a number of cities across the U.S. have done. When possible, we should barter goods and services, avoiding the use of money altogether.

As a nation, we need to quit using the flow of money as the chief measure of our well-being. The U.S. gross domestic product is the dollar value of our nation's economic output in a given period, without regard to the purpose of that output. So the cost of cleaning up an oil spill in the Gulf of Mexico adds to the GDP, as does an epidemic of cancer, a recall of salmonella-laced eggs, a bombing campaign in Afghanistan, lawsuits against Ponzi schemers, prison construction, and every other sort of ill. The GDP does not reflect work done at home without pay, volunteer work in the community, or mutual aid exchanged between neighbors. It counts junk food you buy on the highway but not food you grow in your backyard. It counts the child care you purchase but not the care you provide. If you lead a healthy life, you contribute little to GDP through medical expenditures, but if you smoke, become addicted to drugs or alcohol, become dangerously obese, neglect your health in any way at all, you're sure to boost the GDP. War also swells the GDP, but peacemaking does not. We need to devise measures of well-being that take into account the actual quality of life in our society, from the rate of incarceration (currently the highest in the world) to the rate of infant mortality (currently 33rd in the world), from the condition of our soils and rivers and air to the safety of our streets.

One need not be an economist—as I am not—to see that our economic system is profoundly unjust in its distribution of benefits and damage, that it relies on violence toward people and planet, and that it is eroding the foundations of democracy. What should we do? Not as any sort of expert, but as a citizen, I say we need to get big money out of politics by publicly financing elections and strictly regulating lobbyists. We need to preserve the estate tax, for its abolition would lead to rule by an aristocracy of inherited wealth, just the sort of tyranny we threw off in our revolt against Britain. We need to defend the natural and cultural goods we share, such as the oceans and the internet, from those who seek to exploit the common wealth for their sole profit. We need to stop private-sector companies from dictating research agendas in our public universities. We need legislation that strips corporations of the legal status of persons. We need to restore the original definition of a corporation as an association granted temporary privileges for the purpose of carrying out some socially useful task, with charters that must be reviewed and renewed periodically by state legislatures. We need to enforce the anti-trust laws, breaking up giant corporations into units small enough to be answerable to democratic control. We need to require that the public airwaves, now used mainly to sell the products of global corporations, serve public interests.

To recover our democracy, relieve human suffering, and protect our planet, we need to do a great many things that may seem unlikely or impossible. But they seem so only if we define ourselves as isolated consumers rather than citizens, if we surrender our will and imagination to the masters of money. Over the next few generations, we will either create a civilization that treats all of its members compassionately and treats the Earth respectfully, or we will sink into barbarism. Whatever the odds, I say we should work toward that just and ecologically wise civilization, with all our powers.

# Buffalo Eddy

rom pristine headwaters in Yellowstone National Park, the Snake River flows through western Wyoming, across Idaho, and into Washington before joining the Columbia River near the Hanford Nuclear Site, a destination as toxic as any on Earth. Hanford, repository for two-thirds of our nation's high-level radioactive waste, has leaked its lethal brew into air and water and soil since reactors there began making fuel for bombs during World War II. Despite its pure beginnings, by the time it reaches the Columbia, the Snake bears its own load of pollution, mainly runoff from irrigated croplands, feedlots, and fish farms. Such a fall from innocence to corruption is a common fate for American rivers, but few have fallen as dramatically as the Snake.

Over its thousand-mile course, the Snake cuts through mountain ranges, surges across sagebrush plains, and roars through canyons—or at least it did cut and surge and roar, until a series of fifteen dams built during the past century reduced the river to a string of lakes. The dams have been profitable for ranchers, farmers, barge companies, and electric utilities, but they have proven disastrous for salmon. Huge numbers of returning coho, chinook, and sockeye perish at each dam, chiefly from the strain of climbing fish ladders. Of those that survive the climb, many die from the higher temperatures and increased predation in the reservoirs, and others lose their way in the slack water, where the current is too weak to offer direction, and where silt blocks the light and pollution muffles the smells they need to guide them to their spawning grounds.

Before the dams, before the bomb factories, before the spraying of poisons on farms, the Snake was a muscular river and a bountiful one, hosting runs of salmon that numbered in the hundreds of thousands. And fish were not the only bounty. In those free-flowing days, at a sharp bend in the river south of Lewiston, Idaho, the current curled back on itself, forming an eddy that gathered whatever had fallen or leapt or been hurled into the water. According to oral tradition, native hunters used to drive herds of buffalo over a cliff upstream from here, and the dead or dying animals were ensnared by this whirlpool long enough for the bodies to be hauled out. Whether the stories are based on fact or legend, the river bend has come to be called Buffalo Eddy. The name summons up the spectacle of bulls, cows, and calves, some of them still thrashing, with broken legs, crushed skulls, and shattered ribs, the whole mass whirling slowly, like a spiral galaxy made of fur.

Buffalo drives occurred at favorable sites throughout the intermountain West and Great Plains, usually in autumn, when the oncoming cold would preserve meat through the hungry moons of winter. In May of 1805, while traveling up the Missouri near present-day Great Falls, Montana, the Lewis and Clark Expedition came upon what they took to be the remains of a recent kill. Meriwether Lewis described the scene in his journal (and in his wayward spelling) for May 29:

> today we passed on the Stard. side the remains of a vast many mangled carcases of Buffalow which had been driven over a precipice of 120 feet by the Indians and perished; the water appeared to have washed away a part of this immence pile of slaughter and still their remained the fragments of at least a hundred carcases they created a most horrid stench. in this manner the Indians of the Missouri destroy vast herds of buffaloe at a stroke. . . .

Four other members of the expedition remarked on the scene in their journals, including Joseph Whitehouse, who noted:

> about one oC. P. M. we passed high Steep clifts of rocks on the N.S. where the natives had lately drove a gang of buffaloe off from the plains they fell So far on the uneven Stone below that it killed them dead. they took what meat they wanted, & now the wolves & bears are feasting on the remains, which causes a horrid Smell.

In his entry, Lewis went on to give a detailed account of how the drives were carried out, including the role of a daredevil young man in a buffalo disguise who served as a decoy to lure the bulls toward a cliff.

## Buffalo Eddy

The reigning hunters along that stretch of the Missouri when the Corps of Discovery passed through were the Blackfeet, whose name for a buffalo jump is *pishkun,* which has been translated as "deep blood kettle." Among their jump sites is one in Alberta, Canada, known as Head-Smashed-In, where bones piled up, layer after layer, hunt after hunt, over more than five thousand years. The practice was abandoned only when the Blackfeet and other tribes of this region acquired horses and could hunt buffalo year-round.

No bones are visible when I visit Buffalo Eddy on a drizzly October morning. The rain is unusual in this country, which receives only about twelve inches of precipitation a year, most of it snow. To eyes like mine, imprinted on the dense broadleaf forests of the Ohio Valley, the hills along the Snake appear stark. Scrubby trees fringe the riverbanks, thickets bristle in the draws, sagebrush and grasses dot the slopes, but otherwise the land is bare. So exposed, the dun hillsides appear to be sculpted into giant stair steps or terraces, a pattern resulting from the erosion of successive volcanic flows that spread across the Columbia River Plateau, layer upon layer, like the bones of buffalo at Head-Smashed-In, only here the deposition occurred over a period of some ten or fifteen million years, ending about six million years ago.

As the basalt from these lava flows cooled, it fractured along cleavage planes, forming great faceted chunks like massive gemstones. There are outcroppings of such basalt monoliths on both sides of the river at Buffalo Eddy, and many of the stones present surfaces nearly as flat and large as schoolroom chalkboards. Humans began leaving their marks on these inviting surfaces as early as forty-five hundred years ago, carving figures and abstract designs by chipping through the dark patina of desert varnish to reveal the lighter stone beneath. Hands continued this work for millennia, until the flanks of the basalt were tattooed with imagery. Whether or not whole tribes once drew their meat from this spot, the host of images would mark Buffalo Eddy as a sacred place.

The guide who has brought me to see the petroglyphs is a poet, naturalist, and teacher named Bill Johnson, native to this dry terrain in the intermountain West. Tall and lean, moving easily in conversation from the virtues of hackberry trees to Romantic theories of imagination, Bill is rangy in mind as well as body. He and I are roughly of an age, mid-sixties, both craggy of face and long of limb, although his limbs are noticeably longer than mine. Both of us are grandfathers who fret about the world the young ones will inherit, and we both would rather look at rocks and rivers and hills, and at whatever may live there, than stay indoors out of the rain.

We approach Buffalo Eddy along the western shore by way of a sinuous trail that leads down from the river road. Against the gray of earth and sky, the only bright colors are the scarlet of sumac leaves turning with the season, purple disks of asters nodding in the rain, rusty patches of lichens on rocks, and green tufts of moss. Unfazed by the drizzle, chickadees pluck seeds from thistles beside the path, their black caps bobbing. Except for the chickadees and us, the only animate presence is the river, which glints as it swirls, like molten pewter.

I peer at every large stone we pass, on the lookout for designs other than those made by lichen and moss, but I see nothing that seems to be a human mark. Then Bill pauses beside an inky slab of basalt. "There," he says, pointing at a pale shape on the rock face. "See the bighorn?"

With a thrill I recognize the silhouette of a bounding sheep, its forelegs and hindlegs stretched out in a gallop, mouth open wide as if panting, horns curled back over the head. The figure is a light aquamarine, contrasting with the dusky brown of the desert varnish. I reach up, longing to lay my fingers in the shallow carving, but then I draw back, afraid the oil from my skin might sully the stone.

Trained by that first pale silhouette, my eyes discern glyphs everywhere on the rocks we pass as we make our way to the trail's end, where angular chunks of basalt form a spit reaching out into the stream at Buffalo Eddy. For the next hour, Bill and I clamber among the stones, careful where we set our boots to avoid slipping and also to avoid stepping on any of the figures. Among the ghostly images we discover a few burly four-legged animals that might represent buffalo, and a scattering of slender, hornless ones that might represent elk or deer. We find a zigzag design that could be a bolt of lightning, a snake, or the meandering river itself, but we find no fish, despite the former abundance of salmon here. We come across an etching of concentric circles, like ripples spreading out from a pebble dropped into still water. Other circles appear in isolation, suggesting sun or moon. And there are spirals that inevitably make us think of the eddy's whirl, but we also wonder if they might speak of something grander, such as the circling movement of seasons or stars.

By far the most common figures, repeated on one rock face after another, are bighorn sheep, identified by their backswept horns, and whole tribes of humans. The typical human figure has stubby, splayed legs, a broad-shouldered torso, and arms outstretched in the pose of a weightlifter displaying his biceps. The brawny comparison comes to mind because many of the human figures hold objects that look for all the world like barbells. Others hold long shafts that might be spears. Still others brandish hoops that could be lassos or snares. The heads of some human figures are topped by stalks, like giant antennae, and others are wreathed in spikes that suggest horns or shaggy manes. They might be men wearing masks, Bill and I conjecture, or shamans taking on the guise of other animals, or hybrid creatures from the time before humans and the other living tribes drifted apart.

We struggle to reach across the gulf of cultures and years to read this lost language, but we can only speculate about its meaning. The images themselves are fading, for the older the carvings, the darker they are, and the harder to see, as desert varnish reclaims them. Long thought to be the result of chemical weathering, this brown-to-black stain is now thought to be the work of bacteria, which metabolize manganese and iron leached from the rock and lay on a thin coating of oxides at a measurable rate, thus providing a way of gauging how long a rock face—or a rock carving—has been exposed to the air. The images are also being erased by lichens, which draw minerals from the basalt and break it down, grain by grain, to form soil, thus making way for moss, sumac, hackberry, willow, and other plants.

It does not trouble me that tough desert organisms are gradually effacing these human marks. But a much more sudden, and disturbing, erasure is evident at Buffalo Eddy, in patches of newly bared stone where thieves have pried away sections of petroglyphs. Although Bill forewarned me about the vandalism, I am stunned by these naked gaps, as if pages have been ripped from a holy scripture. Whoever stole the carvings could not have seen them as holy, could only have seen them as objects readily turned into money or private trophies. Applied on an industrial scale, reverence for money justifies damming salmon rivers for cheap electricity, drilling for oil in wildlife refuges, blasting mountaintops for coal. All such vandalism would be as perplexing to the ancient carvers, I suspect, as their carvings are to us.

Bill and I puzzle longest over designs that show a series of dots trailing across the stone, like tracks in sand or snow. In one place, the dots trace out shapes like upside-down Vs, which remind us of volcanic peaks in the Cascade Mountains to the west. In another place, the dots lead from a hoop held by one human figure to a hoop held by another, as if marking the trajectory of something thrown. Elsewhere, human figures hovering near a string of dots might be following a trail, but they might equally well be counting kills, reckoning distances, telling stories, or mapping the night sky. We can only guess. Even the archaeologists must guess, when they propose that the images tell about hunting practices, religious rituals, battles, or beliefs. All we can say for certain is that the people who garnered their livelihood from this river felt a compelling need, sustained over several thousand years, to leave a record of their actions, observations, and thoughts precisely here, not upstream or down, but here where the current curls back on itself and gathers whatever drifts by.

Responding to the world in symbols is a hallmark of human presence everywhere, from the caves at Altamira to the petroglyphs at Buffalo Eddy to the internet. All of our symbolic languages—words, music, dance, painting, earthworks, mathematics, sculpture, architecture, photography, formulas, graphs, on and on—are ways of ensnaring what would otherwise drift by—an event or idea, a melody or feeling, a person, perception, or place. In our age of round-the-clock, round-the-globe communications, with its flood of images and words, it is hard for us to recover a sense of the power that symbols carried when they were still made, patiently and singly, by hand. Paintings on shields and robes, animal shapes worked into pipes and pots, beadwork designs on dresses and moccasins, images inscribed onto skin or rock, all expressed the makers' feelings for the beautiful and mysterious way of things, the patterns in nature, the movements of mind. By taking in these expressions of what our ancestors saw and thought and felt, our own minds are enlarged, our sympathies expanded.

The two roots of the word *hieroglyphics* are the Greek *hieros,* meaning sacred, and *glyphein,* meaning to carve or hollow out. Although we associate this term with the picture writing of ancient Egypt, the word applies just as well to the figures at Buffalo Eddy. In their presence, one senses these are sacred carvings. Like the Psalms, they bear witness to what is holy, not in the humans who made them, but in the creation.

We cannot know what moved those vanished artists to carve their language into stone, but I imagine it is akin to the impulse that will move Bill to write a poem about our visit to Buffalo Eddy and will prompt me to write this essay. Such writing is like breathing, an exhaling that follows inhaling, as natural as that. We wish to express what we perceived there, what we felt, what thoughts the place inspired. Although far less physical effort is required to lay down a line of words than to chisel a bighorn sheep or a pattern of dots into basalt, the mental effort may be just as great. Seeking the right shape for a sentence or a paragraph, one may labor for an hour, a day, or off and on for a year. And still the result may not satisfy one's ear or one's desire for congruence between language and experience. No matter how painstaking the writing, the reality one seeks to convey is always larger, subtler, and more highly charged than what one has managed to set down.

As it flows, an essay creates its own current, which bears the mind along, through twists and turns, past unforeseen tributaries, into country unknown to the writer. While working on this essay, I chance upon a *New York Times* article headlined "Colombian Woman Salvages Corpses at River Bend." Immediately I recall the story about buffalo salvaged from the Snake, but I learn that the bodies hauled from an eddy in Colombia's Cauca River are human, the victims of drug lords, death squads, guerrillas, and gangs. They are often dismembered, a farrago of heads, arms, legs, and torsos. For more than a decade, a woman named Maria Ines Mejia, who lives near the eddy, took it as her mission to retrieve corpses from the river, ninety-five bodies in all, and to see that they received a proper burial. Hardest of all, she told a reporter, was to haul out the body of a child. She kept careful descriptions of the victims' clothing, hair, tattoos, anything that might help next of kin identify their missing loved ones. Thugs who did not want their handiwork documented burned down Maria Mejia's cottage and threatened to kill her, and only then did she abandon her service to the dead.

Soon after learning about the grisly eddy in the Cauca River, I come across references to a much larger and in some respects more appalling whirlpool, this one in the ocean. Covering an area the size of the continental United States, by one estimate, the North Pacific Gyre   or, as it is unofficially known, the Great Pacific Trash Vortex—gathers litter carried by wind-driven currents from the surrounding sea. The debris, weighing millions of tons, has been dumped from ships or washed from river mouths and beaches. It's mainly plastic, which has been abraded into small particles known fancifully as mermaid tears and more prosaically as nurdles. Although the name sounds benign, nurdles are proving to be malignant. The particles do not biodegrade, but they do break down from exposure to sunlight, releasing their constituent compounds, many of which are toxic. They also absorb organic pollutants, such as DDT and PCBS, from seawater. When nurdles are ingested by seabirds and turtles and other marine organisms, they can cause blockages, disrupt hormones, or poison the creatures outright. Each year untold millions of animals are killed by this trash, including thousands of albatross chicks, whose parents feed them flecks of plastic.

Of the three whirlpools I have noted here, this noxious ocean gyre may be the most disturbing. The Indians who drove buffalo over cliffs ate the animals they killed, used the hides and horns and bones for shelter and clothing, and left no poisons behind. True, the lumbering beasts must have suffered as they died, but the buffalo herds were soon replenished, and their kind flourished alongside humans for thousands of years. Thugs who dump human bodies into the Cauca River do their killing not for sustenance but for money or vengeance or spite. While their consciences may not be troubled, at least they know that murder is against the law, which is why they threaten Señora Mejia. But those of us who through our daily living add to the world's garbage—and who, reading these lines, does not?—most likely never imagine that our leavings cause so much havoc. Even if we faithfully recycle whatever comes into our hands, by purchasing anything at all from the industrial system we empower networks of mines, factories, railroads, ships, trucks, and stores that generate debris on our behalf. Sooner or later much of that debris will end up in the sea, and not only in the Great Pacific Trash Vortex, but in gyres scattered across the world's oceans.

Sooner or later, everything we do will have an effect, and the more of us there are, the greater the effect. All too often, the summing together of billions of seemingly innocent actions causes damage we never intended. None of us set out to fill the oceans with trash. None of us set out to heat the atmosphere, melt glaciers, drown coastlines, or expand deserts. None of us set out to extinguish the thousands of species that vanish every year. None of us, in lighting our houses and running our appliances, meant to kill salmon or level mountains or add to the toll of radioactive waste. But that is what we are doing. Such knowledge might be cause for despair, if it were not equally true that the summing together of countless acts of healing could restore the health of individuals, communities, and planet.

Bill's poem arrives the week following our visit to Buffalo Eddy. In it, after evoking the day and the place, he asks, "Lord, what doesn't come to mind?" The making of this essay takes months rather than weeks, for so much comes to mind. The writing feels at times as I imagine the hammering of shapes into stone must have felt to those ancient artisans—achingly slow, the medium recalcitrant, the eventual shape only gradually revealing itself. And when the hammering is finished, one's meaning may still be lost.

Any language may be misinterpreted, words as well as glyphs, especially when reading requires translation from one age or culture to another. The people whom Lewis and Clark encountered along the Snake River were given the name Nez Perce by a white translator. But they called themselves—and still call themselves—Nimi'ipuu, which the tribal website translates as "the real people" or "we the people." Likewise the river itself was misnamed by outsiders. On first encountering white explorers in this region, the Northern Shoshone identified themselves by making swimming motions with their hands. The explorers read the sign as meaning snake, and gave this name to the Shoshone and to the river; but the sign actually meant fish. So the Shoshone were likely saying: We are people of the river filled with fish. After learning this, I reconsider photographs of the carvings at Buffalo Eddy. Some of the figures I took to be human have legs so abbreviated and splayed that they might not be legs at all but tail fins, and the figures might be salmon people.

So I read the hieroglyphs at Buffalo Eddy cautiously, aware how likely I am to be misreading. Inevitably, I see everything through the lens of my time, and this is a time of human-caused extinctions and disruptions. Humans have been killing other animals and slaughtering our own kind for as long as we have stood upright. But only in the last half century or so have we developed the capacity to extinguish, not merely a species or a tribe, but whole floras and faunas. With the burning of fossil fuels, the splitting of atoms, the synthesizing of chemicals unknown in nature, the genetic engineering of organisms, and the headlong growth of our own population, we are disrupting all the life-sustaining processes on Earth.

As our actions throw into disarray the conditions that have nurtured humankind for hundreds of thousands of years, what conditions will replace them? "Whirl is king, having driven out Zeus," a character in Aristophanes' *Clouds* declares. The line implies that once the familiar order breaks down, it will be succeeded by chaos. And whirl may indeed bring about devastation, as a tornado does in tearing up houses and trees, as a hurricane does in pummeling a city, as a black hole does in swallowing matter and light. Yet for all the disorder it may cause, a vortex itself is orderly. In fact, it is one of the fundamental organizing patterns in nature. On this blue planet, there are gyres in the air, in the sea, in rivers, and in the finest grain of matter, where clouds of electrons spin about the nuclei of atoms. Our solar system whirls about the sun, our sun rides a spiraling arm of the Milky Way, and our galaxy spins through space that is curved by the gravity of everything in the universe, visible and invisible.

The artisans who recorded their visions in the rocks at Buffalo Eddy must have returned to that spot again and again as they pursued buffalo and salmon and sheep. And when the orbit of their lives carried them away from the river, they could have summoned up those carved figures in memory, as talismans, as companions on their journeys. Just so, a man living long after the artisans left their marks may return to those figures, to that place, leaping thousands of miles, leaping centuries, as his mind, seeking to gather meaning, creates an eddy of words.

# Mind in the Forest

I touch trees, as others might stroke the fenders of automobiles or finger silk fabrics or fondle cats. Trees do not purr, do not flatter, do not inspire a craving for ownership or power. They stand their ground, immune to merely human urges. Saplings yield under the weight of a hand and then spring back when the hand lifts away, but mature trees accept one's touch without so much as a shiver. While I am drawn to all ages and kinds, from maple sprouts barely tall enough to hold their leaves off the ground to towering sequoias with their crowns wreathed in fog, I am especially drawn to the ancient, battered ones, the survivors.

Recently I spent a week in the company of ancient trees. The season was October and the site was the H. J. Andrews Experimental Forest, a 15,800-acre research area defined by the drainage basin of Lookout Creek, within Willamette National Forest, on the western slope of the Cascade Mountains in Oregon. It's a wet place. At higher elevations, annual precipitation averages 140 inches, and even the lower elevations receive 90 inches, twice the amount that falls on my well-watered home region of southern Indiana. Back in Indiana the trees are hardwoods—maples and beeches and oaks, hickories and sycamores—and few are allowed to grow for as long as a century without being felled by ax or saw. Here in Andrews Forest, the ruling trees are Douglas firs, western hemlocks, western red cedars, and Pacific yews, the oldest of them ranging in age from five hundred to eight hundred years, veterans of countless fires, windstorms, landslides, insect infestations, and floods.

333

On the first morning of my stay, I follow a trail through moist bottomland toward Lookout Creek, where I plan to spend half an hour or so in meditation. The morning fog is thick, so the treetops merge with gray sky. Condensation drips from every needle and leaf. My breath steams. Lime-green lichens, some as long as a horse's tail, dangle from branches. Set off against the somber greens and browns of the conifers, the yellow and red leaves of vine maples, bigleaf maples, and dogwoods appear luminous in spite of the damp. Shelf fungi jut from the sides of old stumps like tiny balconies, and hemlock sprigs glisten atop nurse logs. The undergrowth is as dense as a winter pelt.

Along the way, I reach out to brush my fingers over dozens of big trees, but I keep moving, intent on my destination. Then I come upon a Douglas fir whose massive trunk, perhaps four feet in diameter at chest height, is surrounded by scaffolding, which provides a stage for rope-climbing by scientists and visiting schoolchildren. Something about this tree—its patience, its generosity, its dignity—stops me. I place my palms and forehead against the furrowed, moss-covered bark, and rest there for a spell. Gradually the agitation of travel seeps out of me and calm seeps in. Only after I stand back and open my eyes, and notice how the fog has begun to burn off, do I realize that my contact with this great tree must have lasted fifteen or twenty minutes.

I continue on to a gravel bar on Lookout Creek, a jumble of boulders, cobbles, pebbles, and grit scoured loose from the volcanic plateau that forms the base of the Cascade Mountains. Because these mountains are young, the slopes are steep and the water moves fast. Even the largest boulders have been tumbled and rounded. Choosing one next to a riffle, I sit cross-legged and half close my eyes, and I am enveloped in water sounds, a ruckus from upstream and a burbling from downstream. Now and again I hear the thump of a rock shifting in the flow, a reminder that the whole mountain range is sliding downhill, chunk by chunk, grain by grain.

Although I have tried meditating for shorter or longer stretches since my college days, forty years ago, I have never been systematic about the practice, nor have I ever been good at quieting what Buddhists call the "monkey mind." Here beside Lookout Creek, however, far from my desk and duties, with no task ahead of me but that of opening myself to this place, I settle quickly. I begin by following my breath, the oldest rhythm of flesh, but soon I am following the murmur of the creek, and I am gazing at the bright leaves of maples and dogwoods that glow along the thread of the stream like jewels on a necklace, and I am watching light gleam on water shapes formed by current slithering over rocks, and for a spell I disappear, there is only this rapt awareness.

☀

When the H. J. Andrews Experimental Forest was established in 1948, what we now call "old-growth" was labeled on maps as "large saw-timber." The original purpose of the forest was to determine the best methods of harvesting big trees. The assumption was that they should be cut down—the only question was how. Fortunately, since 1948, many people, both inside and outside the U.S. Forest Service, have come to see that venerable trees possess values other than supplying lumber.

Research conducted at the Andrews has taught us much of what we know about old-growth in the Pacific Northwest. In addition to stands of ancient trees, the watershed contains naturally burned areas, open glades, recovering clear-cuts, and managed research plots. Some of these plots are devoted to studying the effects of various harvesting practices. But of the more than one hundred experiments currently under way, many focus on the role of forests in protecting water quality, controlling stream flow and sedimentation, cycling and storing carbon, and providing habitat for wildlife, including endangered species such as the northern spotted owl.

Aside from these ecological gifts, what does an old-growth forest offer to the human heart and mind? Science is not set up to answer that question—but art may be. In 2004, the Spring Creek Project at Oregon State University, in collaboration with the Andrews Forest Long-Term Ecological Research Group, began inviting a series of writers to spend weeklong residencies here, in order to provide ways of observing the land that might complement the ways of science. Writers' responses—poems, stories, essays, field notes, journals—will be added to the stream of instrument data, technical reports, scientific papers, aerial photographs, statistics, and maps, to give a more comprehensive vision of this place. And a vision not only of the present, but of the forest evolving through time, for the sponsors have designed the series of residencies to extend over two centuries.

Designing any human enterprise to last two hundred years may seem brash in an era of headlong haste. Yet precisely because we live in a culture addicted to instant results, such a long-term plan strikes me as visionary and generous, for it seeks to free our thoughts from present needs and to accumulate knowledge that will benefit our descendants. Colleges, museums, and libraries have been founded in the same spirit, to serve the needs not only of the living but of those not yet born.

Without benefit of planning, the oldest trees in the Andrews have survived since the time of the Crusades, and those along the trail to Lookout Creek have endured since Spaniards first set foot in the New World. These veterans haven't had to contend with wars, religious schisms, economic depressions, regime changes, corrupt government, or the other ills that humans fall prey to, but they have withstood countless natural hazards. And now they must contend with a destabilized climate, a tattered ozone layer, invasive species, and other hazards imposed by humans. At this perilous moment, I have traveled here from Indiana to add my observations to a record that is designed to be kept for generations. I suspect I will come away with far more questions than answers, but that proportion seems in keeping with the spirit of science as well as art.

Each morning at first light I repeat the journey to Lookout Creek, and each time I stop along the way to embrace the same giant Douglas fir, which smells faintly of moist earth. I wear no watch. I do not hurry. I stay with the tree until it lets me go.

When at length I lean away, I touch my forehead and feel the rough imprint of the bark. I stare up the trunk and spy dawn sky fretted by branches. Perspective makes the tops of the surrounding, smaller trees appear to lean toward this giant one, as if conferring. The cinnamon-colored bark is like a rugged landscape in miniature, with flat ridges separated by deep fissures. Here and there among the fissures, spiderwebs span the gaps. The plates are furred with moss. A skirt of sloughed bark and fallen needles encircles the base of the trunk. Even in the absence of wind, dry needles the color of old pennies rain steadily down, ticking against my jacket.

I don't imagine that my visits mean anything to the Douglas fir. I realize it's nonsensical to speak of a tree as patient or generous or dignified merely because it stands there while researchers and children clamber up ropes into its highest limbs. But how can I know a tree's inwardness? Certainly there is intelligence here, and in the forest as a whole, if by that word we mean the capacity for exchanging information and responding appropriately to circumstances. How does a tree's intelligence compare with ours? What can we learn from it? And why, out of the many giants thriving here, does this one repeatedly draw me to an embrace?

The only intelligence I can examine directly is my own and, indirectly, that of my species. We are a contradictory lot. Our indifference to other species, and even to our own long-term well-being, is demonstrated everywhere one looks, from the depleted oceans to the heating atmosphere, from poisoned wetlands to eroding farmlands and forests killed by acid rain. Who can bear in mind this worldwide devastation and the swelling catalogue of extinctions without grieving? And yet it's equally clear that we are capable of feeling sympathy, curiosity, and even love toward other species and toward the Earth. Where does this impulse come from, this sense of affiliation with rivers and ravens, mountains and mosses? How might it be nurtured? What role might it play in moving us to behave more caringly on this beleaguered planet?

These are the questions I find myself brooding about as I sit in meditation beside Lookout Creek. One is not supposed to brood while meditating, of course, so again and again I let go of thoughts and return my awareness to the water sounds, the radiant autumn leaves, the wind on my cheek, the stony cold chilling my sitting bones. And each morning, for shorter or longer spells, the fretful *I* quiets down, turns transparent, and vanishes.

Eventually I stir, roused by the haggle of ravens or the chatter of squirrels or the scurry of deer—other minds in the forest—and I make my way back along the trail to the zone of electricity and words. As I walk, it occurs to me that meditation is an effort to become for a spell more like a tree, open to whatever arises, without judging, without remembering the past or anticipating the future, fully present in the moment. The taste of that stillness refreshes me. And yet I do not aspire to dwell in such a condition always. For all its grandeur and beauty, for all its half-millennium longevity, the Douglas fir cannot ponder me, cannot reflect or remember or imagine—can only *be*. Insofar as meditation returns us to that state of pure, unreflective being, it is a respite from the burden of ceaseless thought. When we surface from meditation, however, we are not turning from reality to illusion, as some spiritual traditions would have us believe; we are reclaiming the full powers of mind, renewed by our immersion in the realm of mountains and rivers, wind and breath.

\\|//

At midday, sunlight floods the gravel bar on Lookout Creek, illuminating strands of spider filament that curve from one boulder to another over an expanse of rushing water. At first I can't fathom how spiders managed this engineering feat. The wind might have blown them one direction but not back again, and yet at least a dozen gossamer threads zigzag between the massive stones. Then

I guess that the spiders, after attaching the initial strand, must climb back and forth along the filaments they have already spun, adding to the skein. The stones they stitch together are as knobby and creased as the haunches of elephants. Even in still air, butter-yellow maple leaves come sashaying down. A pewter sheen glints from the bark of young Douglas firs tilting out over the stream.

Unconsciously, I resort to human terms for describing what I see, thus betraying another quirk of our species. We envision bears and hunters and wandering sisters in the stars. We spy dragons in the shapes of clouds, hear mournfulness in the calls of owls. Reason tells us that such analogies are false. For all its delicious sounds, the creek does not speak, but merely slides downhill, taking the path of least resistance, rubbing against whatever it meets along the way. Boulders have nothing to do with elephants, lichens are not horsetails, moss is not fur, spiders are not engineers, ravens do not haggle, and trees do not confer. Scientists are schooled to avoid such anthropomorphism. Writers are warned against committing the "pathetic fallacy," which is the error of projecting human emotions or meanings onto nature. The caution is worth heeding. Yet if we entirely forgo such analogies, if we withhold our metaphors and stories, we estrange ourselves from the universe. We become mere onlookers, the sole meaning-bearing witnesses of a meaningless show.

But who could sit here, on this gravel bar beside Lookout Creek, and imagine that we are the sole source of meaning? Against a halcyon blue sky, the spires of trees stand out with startling clarity, their fringe of lichens appearing incandescent. Moths and gnats flutter above the stream, chased by dragonflies. The creek is lined by drift logs in various states of decay, from bone-gray hulks to rotting red lumps. Wet boulders gleam as if lit from within. Cobbles jammed against one another look like the heads of a crowd easing downstream. The muscular current, twisting over rocks, catches and tosses the light. The banks on either side blaze with the salmon-pink leaves of dogwoods, those western relatives of the beloved understory tree of my Indiana forests. Everything in sight is exquisite—the stones of all sizes laid against one another just so, the perforated leaves of red alders, the fallen needles gathered in pockets along the shore, the bending grasses, the soaring trees.

Only cosmic arrogance tempts us to claim that all this reaching for sunlight, nutrients, and water means nothing except what we say it means. But if it bears a grander significance, what might that be, and what gives rise to such meaning? What power draws the elements together and binds them into a spider or a person, a fern or a forest? If we answer "Life," we give only a name, not an explanation.

# Mind in the Forest

Those who fancy that humans are superior to the rest of nature often use "tree-hugger" as a term of ridicule, as if to feel the allure of trees were a perverted form of sensuality or a throwback to our simian ancestry. Of course, many who decry tree-hugging don't believe we *have* a simian ancestry, and so perhaps what they fear is a reversion to paganism. And they may have a point. The religions that started in the Middle East—Judaism, Christianity, Islam—are all desert faiths, created by people who lived in the open. Theirs is a sky god, who would be eclipsed by a forest canopy. In every civilization influenced by these faiths, trees have been cut down not merely to secure wood for cooking and building or to clear ground for agriculture or to open vistas around settlements where predators might lurk, but to reveal the heavens.

Worship of a sky god has been costly to our planet. Religions that oppose the heavenly to the earthly, elevating the former and scorning the latter, are in effect denying that we emerge from and wholly depend on nature. If you think of the touchable, eatable, climbable, sexy, singing, material world as fallen, corrupt, and sinful, then you are likely to abuse it. You are likely to say that we might as well cut down the last old-growth forests, drain the last swamps, catch the last tuna and cod, burn the last drops of oil, since the end-time is coming, when the elect few will be raptured away to the immortal realm, and everything earthly will be erased.

But our language preserves a countervailing wisdom. In Latin, *materia* means stuff, anything substantial, and in particular it means wood. *Materia* in turn derives from *mater,* which means mother. In the collective imagination that gave rise to these meanings, trees were understood to epitomize matter, and matter was understood to be life-giving. Perhaps we could tap into this wisdom by recovering another word that derives from *mater: matrix,* which means womb. Instead of speaking about "nature" or "the environment," terms which imply some realm apart from us, perhaps we should speak of Earth as our matrix, our mother, the source and sustainer of life.

It is easy to feel nurtured among these ancient trees. I breathe the forest. I drink its waters. I take in the forest through all my senses. In order to survive here for any length of time, I would need to wear the forest, its fur and skin and fiber; I would need to draw my food from what lives here alongside me; I would need to burn its fallen branches for cooking and for keeping warm; I would need to frame my shelter with its wood and clay and stone. Above all, I would need to learn to *think* like the forest, learn its patterns, obey its requirements, align myself with its flow.

There are no boundaries between the forest and the cosmos, or between myself and the forest, and so the intelligence on display here is continuous with the intelligence manifest throughout the universe and with the mind I use to apprehend and speak of it.

One morning beside Lookout Creek, enveloped as usual in watery music, I sit leaning against a young red alder that has sprouted in the gravel bar, its leaves nibbled into lace by insects. Everything here either starts as food or winds up as food. None of the alders growing on this ever-shifting bank is thicker than a baseball bat. The next big flood will scour them away. Beside me, the sinewy roots of an upturned stump seem to mimic the muscular current in the stream. The bar is littered with gray and ruddy stones pockmarked by holes that betray the volcanic origins of this rubble.

Where better than such a place to recognize that the essence of nature is *flow*—of lava, electrons, water, wind, breath. *Materia,* matter, the seemingly solid stuff we encounter—trees, stones, bears, bones—is actually fluid, constantly changing, like water shapes in the current. The Psalmist tells us, "The mountains skipped like rams, and the little hills like lambs," and Dōgen, a thirteenth-century Zen teacher, proclaims that mountains are always walking. Both speak truly. Mountains do move, arising and eroding away over geological time, just as organisms grow and decay, species evolve, tectonic plates shift, stars congeal and burn and expire, entire galaxies shine for a spell and then vanish. Nothing in nature is fixed.

Conservationists have often been accused of wishing to freeze the land in some favored condition—for example, the American continent as it was before European colonization. Back when maps described old-growth as large saw-timber, scientists spoke of forests reaching climax, as if at some point the flow would cease. But we now realize that no such stasis is possible, even if it were desirable. If flux is the nature of nature, however, we still must make distinctions among the *kinds* of change. We cannot speak against the damage caused by human behavior unless we distinguish between *natural* change— for example, the long history of extinctions—and *anthropogenic* change—for example, the acceleration in extinctions due to pollution, habitat destruction, climate disruption, and other disturbances caused by humans. The capacity to make such a distinction, and to act on it, may be as unique to our species as the capacity to use symbolic language.

Thoughts flow, along with everything else, even in the depths of meditation. And yet the human mind seems compelled to imagine fixity—heaven, nirvana, Plato's ideal realm, eternal God—and the human heart yearns for permanence. Why else do we treasure diamonds and gold? Why else do creationists cling to the notion that all species were made in exactly their present form? Why else do we search for scientific "laws" underlying the constant flux of the universe?

Our yearning for the fixed, like our craving for dominion over nature, may be another expression of our fear of aging and death. This occurs to me as I sit, entranced, beside the rowdy riffles on Lookout Creek. A dozen dead snags tilt above my head, their bare limbs like the sparse whiskers on an old man's chin. Upstream, a gigantic Douglas fir has fallen across the creek, its trunk still as straight as when it was alive. Downstream, another giant has fallen, this one snapped in the middle. I can't help imagining one of the looming snags suddenly toppling onto me and snapping my thread of thought, scattering this congregation of elements and notions bearing my name.

Higher up the valley of Lookout Creek, in a grove of five-hundred-year-old Douglas firs and western hemlocks, dozens of logs have been placed side by side on the ground, labeled with aluminum tags, and fitted with instruments to measure their rate and manner of decay. Designed to continue for two centuries, this research aims to document, among other things, the role of dead wood in forest ecology and in the sequestering of carbon.

On a visit to the site, I stroke the moss-covered logs, touch the rubbery fungi that sprout from every surface, peer into the boxy traps that catch flying insects and fallen debris, and lean close to the tubes that capture the logs' exhalations. The only breathing I detect is my own. I'm intrigued that scientists are studying decomposition, for as an artist I usually think about *composition*—the making of something shapely and whole out of elements. A musician composes with notes, a painter with colors, a writer with letters and words, much as life orchestrates carbon, oxygen, nitrogen, and other ingredients into organisms. These organisms—trees, fungi, ravens, humans—persist for a while, change over time, and eventually dissolve into their constituents, which will be gathered up again into living things.

Art and life both draw energy from sunlight, directly or indirectly, to counter entropy by increasing order. Right now, for example, I'm running on the sunshine bound up in pancakes and maple syrup. Organisms interact biophysically with everything in their ecosystem, and ultimately with the whole universe. By contrast, the symbolic structures that humans create—songs, stories, poems, paintings, photographs, films, diagrams, mathematical formulas, computer codes—convey influence only insofar as they are read, heard, or otherwise perceived by humans. What happens when we turn our interpretive powers on living organisms? Does raven, Douglas fir, spider, or lichen mean anything different, or anything more, when it is taken up into human consciousness?

What we think or imagine about other species clearly influences our behavior toward them—as notions about the wickedness of wolves led to their extermination throughout much of their historic range, and as new understanding about the role of predators has led to the reintroduction of wolves in Yellowstone and elsewhere. But aside from this practical impact, does our peculiar sort of mind bear any greater significance in the scheme of things? Is it merely an accidental result of mechanical processes, an adaptive feature that has powered our—perhaps fleeting—evolutionary success? Would the universe lose anything vital if our species suddenly vanished?

We can't know the answer to those questions, despite the arguments of prophets and philosophers. We can only form hunches, and, right or wrong, these will influence the spirit of our work and the tenor of our lives. For what it's worth, my hunch is that what we call mind is not a mere side effect of material evolution, but is fundamental to reality. It is not separate from what we call matter, but is a revelation of the inwardness of things. I suspect that our symbol-wielding intelligence is a manifestation of the creative, shaping energy that drives the cosmos, from the dance of electrons to the growth of trees. If this is so, then our highest calling may be to composition—paying attention to some portion of the world, reflecting on what we have perceived, and fashioning a response in words or numbers or paint or song or some other expressive medium. Our paintings on cave walls, our photos of quasars, our graphs and sonnets and stories may be the gifts we return for the privilege of sojourning here on this marvelous globe.

If intelligence means the ability to take in and respond to information, then all organisms possess it, whether animal or plant, for they exchange signals and materials with their surroundings constantly. If intelligence means the capacity for solving puzzles or using language, then surely the ravens that clamor above me or the wolves that roam the far side of the mountains possess it. But if we are concerned with the power not merely to reason or use language, but to discern and define meanings, to evaluate actions in light of ethical principles, to pass on knowledge across generations through symbolic forms—then we are speaking about a kind of intelligence that appears to be the exclusive power of humans, at least on this planet.

Some contemplative traditions maintain that this meaning-making capacity is a curse, that it divorces us from reality, enclosing us in a bubble of abstractions. It's easy to sympathize with this view, when one considers our history of feuds and frauds. Cleverness alone does not make us wise. Yet here among these great trees and boisterous mountain streams, I sense that our peculiar sort of mind might also be a blessing, not only to us but to the forest, to other creatures, to life on Earth, and even to the universe.

I recognize the danger of hubris. It is flattering to suppose, as many religions do, that humans occupy a unique place in the order of things. The appeal of an idea is not evidence for its falsity, however, but merely a reason for caution. Cautiously, therefore: Suppose that the universe is not a machine, as nineteenth-century science claimed, but rather a field of energy, as twentieth-century science imagined. Suppose that mind is not some private power that each of us contains, but rather a field of awareness that contains us—and likewise encompasses birds, bees, ferns, trees, salamanders, spiders, dragonflies, and all living things, permeates mountains and rivers and galaxies, each kind offering its own degree and variety of awareness, even stars, even stones.

What if our role in this all-embracing mind is to gaze back at the grand matrix that birthed us, and translate our responses into symbols? What if art, science, literature, and our many other modes of expression feed back into the encompassing mind, adding richness and subtlety? If that is our distinctive role, no wonder we feel this urge to write, to paint, to measure and count, to set strings vibrating, to tell stories, to dance and sing.

# NOTES AND ACKNOWLEDGMENTS

These notes record, for each essay, when it was composed, where it was first published, and a few of the intellectual and practical circumstances that influenced the writing. I also list the sources of selected quotations, and the names of magazine editors who have been especially supportive of my work. When identifying previous books of mine in which some of these essays were collected, I use the following abbreviations:

FOS  *The Force of Spirit*
(Boston: Beacon Press, 2000)

HFH  *Hunting for Hope: A Father's Journeys*
(Boston: Beacon Press, 1998)

POB  *The Paradise of Bombs*
(Boston: Beacon Press, 1993)

SOU  *Secrets of the Universe: Scenes from the Journey Home*
(Boston: Beacon Press, 1991)

SP  *Staying Put: Making a Home in a Restless World*
(Boston: Beacon Press, 1993)

WFTC  *Writing from the Center*
(Bloomington: Indiana University Press, 1995)

"The Singular First Person" was composed in June 1987 for delivery at a conference on the art of the essay. Although I had been publishing essays for nine years, this was my first attempt to describe my practice or the tradition in which I saw myself working. I note with dismay that the U.S. population, cited here from 1987 as roughly 250 million, has grown by February of 2011, when I write this note, to

312 million, an increase of 62 million or 25 percent. My gloomy comments on the state of American fiction were made during the heyday of minimalism, an impoverished mode that has been succeeded by several richer ones. I now see much to admire in contemporary fiction from the United States and the Anglophone world. Montaigne's practice of inserting layered revisions into his essays is clearly delineated in Donald M. Frame's translation of *The Complete Essays of Montaigne* (Stanford, Calif.: Stanford University Press, 1958). Lewis Thomas's essay on Montaigne appears in his *The Medusa and the Snail: More Notes of a Biology Watcher* (New York: Viking, 1979). The essay was first published in *The Sewanee Review* 96, no. 4 (Fall 1988) and was collected in *sou*.

"At Play in the Paradise of Bombs," written in July 1983, was one in a series of essays I contributed to *North American Review* between 1981 and 1992, at the invitation of the editor, Robley Wilson, Jr. I owe a great deal to his encouragement of my work and to the hospitality of this venerable magazine (Thomas Jefferson was an early subscriber). Of all my essays, this one comes closest to expressing a primal myth—the struggle, within myself and within the world, between the wild energies of nature and the ingenious, often murderous, works of humankind. The Ravenna Arsenal, now used by the Ohio National Guard for training, is a real place, but it is viewed in these pages through the wide eyes of a child, with corresponding exaggeration of incident and metaphor. First published in *North American Review* 268, no. 3 (September 1983), pp. 53–58, this became the title essay in *POB*.

One of the shortest of my essays, "The Men We Carry in Our Minds" is also one of the most frequently reprinted—in part because of that brevity, handy for classrooms, but also, I suspect, because it enlarges the typical discussion of gender roles to include the issue of class. It was composed in May 1984; first published in *Milkweed Chronicle* 5, no. 2 (Spring/Summer 1984), pp. 34–35; and collected in *POB*.

During the trial recounted in "Doing Time in the Thirteenth Chair," I took detailed notes on the proceedings, using legal pads provided by the bailiff, and each night I elaborated the day's notes into a narrative. The resulting essay, composed in the last week of 1982 and the first week of 1983, has been used in seminars for federal judges. Against my usual practice, I told the story in present tense, in order to reproduce for the reader the juror's experience of watching the parade of witnesses, hearing testimony, and struggling to decide whether the defendant is guilty or innocent. The weighing of evidence and searching for patterns in a trial is akin to the inquiring method of the essay. Under the title of "The Thirteenth Chair," it was first published in *North American Review* 268, no. 1 (March 1983), pp. 47–53, and it was collected in *POB*.

My father died in February 1981; "The Inheritance of Tools" was composed in December 1985. During the nearly five intervening years, I kept looking for a way of writing about his death as the loss of a *particular* human being, but not only as a loss, for I also wanted to honor the gifts he had passed along to me. While making notes about tools, for what I had imagined would be a quite different essay, I finally discovered a key to the man and his legacy—the hand-me-down tools themselves, the instructions in how to use them, and the standards of craft. Only in writing the essay did I realize how my father's teachings about the proper use of tools and the respectful use of wood had shaped my own standards for the craft of writing. Published in *North American Review* 271, no. 1 (March 1986), pp. 55–58, and collected in POB, "The Inheritance of Tools" was the first essay of mine to be reprinted in the annual *Best American Essays* volume.

"Under the Influence" was composed in January–February 1989, three years after "The Inheritance of Tools." I am often asked whether I deliberately omitted from the earlier essay my father's shadow side. The answer is no; I simply needed those three additional years to develop the literary skill and emotional distance required to offer a more complete picture of the man and of my relationship to him. In writing the later essay, I wanted to record what it felt like to be the child of an alcoholic while placing that experience within larger cultural and social contexts. As with any personal story, this one is significant only insofar as it offers insight into experiences that others have shared. I hope it is clear that I do not regard myself as a victim of my father's illness. His illness affected me, along with my entire family, but the healthy rest of him shaped me more profoundly. "My Papa's Waltz" can be found in *The Collected Poems of Theodore Roethke* (New York: Doubleday, 1966). Variations on the story of Jesus, the lunatic, and the swine appear in Matthew 8, Mark 5, and Luke 8. "Under the Influence" was first published in *Harper's Magazine* 279, no. 1674 (November 1989), pp. 68–75, and was collected in SOU. It was a finalist for the National Magazine Award.

"Looking at Women" was written in May–June 1988, the year my son turned eleven, on the verge of adolescence, and perhaps that is why I began remembering my own experiences from that age. I didn't choose to find girls—and later, women—attractive; the desire came to me unbidden. Because I was brought up in a flesh-fearing version of Christianity (see St. Paul), and because my mother regarded sex as shameful, the desire carried with it a great deal of confusion and guilt. I wrote this essay as an effort to reduce both the guilt and the confusion, by trying to understand, from the perspective of a securely married, heterosexual male, how to behave as a sexual as well as a responsible creature. I am fully aware that there are other perspectives, all offering their own truths. An essay that pursues a theme or an idea is riskier, and harder to write, than one that pursues a narrative. Fortunately, *The Georgia Review*—under the editorship of Stanley W. Lindberg and Stephen Corey—has been especially open to my attempts at combining storytelling with reflection, including "Looking at Women," which appeared in vol. 43, no. 1 (Spring 1989), pp. 80–91. It was collected in sou.

I began "Reasons of the Body" in July 1990, while teaching a workshop in Vermont, and I finished it the following month. The essay arose from a concern about the amount of time and attention my son was devoting to sports—to the neglect of music, science, art, and other pursuits—and, more generally, from my dismay over the obsession with sports in American society. While the writing did not banish those concerns, it did help me see more clearly how I had been nurtured, in relationships with my father and son, by playing games such as baseball and basketball—playing not for victory, and certainly not for money, but for the pleasure of skillfully using eye, muscle, and bone. The essay was first published in *The Georgia Review* 44, no. 4 (Winter 1990), pp. 603–615, and it was collected in sou.

"After the Flood" was composed in January 1991. In the previous November, during a residency at Hiram College, I returned for the first time in almost thirty years to see what had become of my childhood landscape since the building of a dam on the West Branch of the Mahoning River. Like many another willing or unwilling migrant, I learned the importance of place from having been uprooted. My first uprooting, from a farm in Tennessee, occurred before I was old enough to realize what I had lost, but my exile from the land I came to know while growing up in Ohio left a deep and lasting ache, moving me to write not only this essay but also "Wayland" and "Buckeye," which appear later in this volume. "After the Flood" was first published in Michael Martone, ed., *Townships* (Iowa City: University of Iowa Press, 1992), pp. 157–164, and it became the opening chapter in sp.

"House and Home" was composed in December 1991, while my wife and I waited for our daughter to return from her first semester in college. Her absence set me thinking about the difference between the physical structure we call a house and the emotional reality we call a home. In the writing, I discovered how thoroughly my own sense of being at home was bound up with the work we had done on our old house, not to make it look better but to make it a more wholesome haven for rearing children. For "The Death of the Hired Man," see *Complete Poems of Robert Frost* (New York: Holt, Rinehart and Winston, 1962) and for "The Design of a House," see Wendell Berry, *Collected Poems: 1957–1982* (San Francisco: North Point, 1985). A condensed version of "House and Home" appeared under the title of "A Perfect Place" in *Notre Dame Magazine* 21, no. 1 (Spring 1992), pp. 35–38; it became the second chapter in sp.

"Staying Put," written in June–July 1991, gave rise to the book of the same title. I had been brooding for years on the American penchant for pulling up stakes instead of putting down roots. Working as I often do against the grain of our dominant culture, I set out to describe the erosive effects of mobility, and to propose an alternative vision, one that emphasizes stability and community over novelty and drift. Because this essay includes quotations from a wide range of authors—more than in any other essay in this volume—I list here the principal sources: Wendell Berry, *Standing by Words* (San Francisco: North Point, 1980); John Berryman, *Henry's Fate & Other Poems* (New York: Farrar, Straus and Giroux, 1977); Bruce Chatwin, *The Songlines* (New York: Viking, 1987) and *What Am I Doing Here* (New York: Viking, 1989); Aldo Leopold, *A Sand County Almanac* (New York: Oxford University Press, 1949); Salman Rushdie, *Imaginary Homelands* (New York: Viking, 1991); Gary Snyder, *The Old Ways: Six Essays* (San Francisco: City Lights, 1977), *The Practice of the Wild* (San Francisco: North Point, 1990), and *The Real Work: Interviews and Talks, 1964–1979* (New York: New Directions, 1980). "Staying Put" was first published in *Orion* 11, no. 1 (Winter 1992), pp. 40–48; under the title "Settling Down" it became chapter 5 of *SP*. *Orion* will show up as the place of first publication for many of the remaining essays in this volume, because from 1990 until the time of this writing—spring 2011—it has been the single most inspiring and welcoming home for my work. I am grateful to several editors at *Orion*, especially Aina Niemela, H. Emerson Blake, and Jennifer Sahn.

"Wayland" was composed in December 1990, following a return visit to my childhood landscape in northeastern Ohio, the same visit recorded in "After the Flood." While tramping around Wayland—the true name of this crossroads hamlet, no matter how symbolic it sounds—I had no plans to write an essay, so I didn't make notes. After leaving, however, I kept retracing my steps in memory, and by the time I reached home in Indiana, six hours later, the haphazard tour had come to feel like a pilgrimage, and the various stops along the way—parsonage, cider mill, horse farm, and so on—had become charged with meaning. To discover what those meanings might be, I wrote the essay. Where the closing paragraphs came from is still a mystery to me. "Wayland" appeared first in *Gettysburg Review* 5, no. 4 (Autumn 1992), pp. 670–681. It became the final chapter in *SP*, and it was reprinted in *Best American Essays 1993*.

"Letter to a Reader" was written in April–May 1991, in response to an invitation for an essay about my development as a writer. Without such an invitation, I would not have considered rehearsing my history, for while I had been writing steadily for twenty years at that point, I had been publishing regularly for only ten, and that seemed to me too modest a record to justify such an accounting. I overcame my misgivings by imagining I was responding not to a generous editor but to a curious reader. While addressing that imaginary reader, I discovered patterns in my life and work that I would not otherwise have seen. The essay was first published in Eve Shelnutt, ed., *My Poor Elephant: 27 Male Writers at Work* (Atlanta: Longstreet Press, 1992), pp. 237–254. With some later additions, it was collected in *WFTC*.

"Buckeye," written in January 1994, really did spring from that walnut box, which still rests on my writing desk, holding my father's last handful of buckeyes. Most of my essays are preceded by extensive note-making and reflection, but this one was unpremeditated. I was sitting at my keyboard one morning, stalled on a piece of fiction, when I took down the box to run my fingers over the wood. Opening the box, I also opened memory, and piece by piece the essay unfolded. The incident with the red-tailed hawk had occurred over two years earlier, in the fall of 1991, and it had baffled me ever since. When that scene came back to me in the composing process, at first I resisted, but finally the memory won its place on the page. This essay, perhaps my clearest expression of grief for the despoiling of Earth, appeared first in *Orion* 14, no. 2 (Spring 1995), pp. 10–13, and became the opening essay in *WFTC*.

"The Common Life" was composed in March–April 1993. Like a number of my essays, it was written in response to an invitation for a keynote address, in this case for a symposium entitled "Community Reconsidered." I only accept such an invitation when the announced theme speaks to one of my concerns, as this one did. I wanted to examine a larger vision of community as embracing not merely humans but all of life, and also to consider how our culture's obsession with private wealth and privilege threatens to squeeze out a concern for the common good. Tocqueville's *Democracy in America* is now available in a new translation by Arthur Goldhammer (New York: Library of America, 2004). This essay appeared first in *The Georgia Review* 48, no. 1 (Spring 1994), pp. 7–22; it was collected in *WFTC*.

Beginning as notebook entries jotted down during a canoe trip in July 1993, "Voyageurs" was transmuted into an essay in September of that year. One way to think of an essay is as a journey, for the writer as well as the reader. It need not recount a physical journey, as this one does, in order to provide a psychological one—the mind's movement outward from the familiar into strange, even mysterious territory, and then back again, slightly or profoundly changed, to the beginning place. The word Edward O. Wilson coined to name our affiliation with life provided the title for his book, *Biophilia* (Cambridge: Harvard University Press, 1984). "Voyageurs" was my contribution to a volume aimed at raising money for relief of hunger: William H. Shore, ed., *The Nature of Nature: New Essays from*

*America's Finest Writers on Nature* (New York: Harcourt Brace, 1994), pp. 257–272; it was collected in wftc.

"Mountain Music" is another essay that began with notes taken during a journey, in this case a June 1995 backpacking trip in Rocky Mountains National Park. It was completed over the following two months. Jesse's challenge—to give him reasons for resisting despair—moved me to write *Hunting for Hope*. This is the sort of essay that prompts readers to ask how my family, especially my son and daughter, feel about showing up in my writing. My answer is that any person I write about is the first one to read what I've written, and to comment on or correct the portrait. I wish to avoid hurting anyone through my writing. When I showed Jesse the draft of "Mountain Music," he told me he was surprised and gratified that I had taken him so seriously. He admitted that he came across as somewhat immature, but he was okay with that, because, after all, he had been only seventeen at the time, while his father, pushing fifty, also appeared immature, and had far less excuse. The essay first appeared in Jodi Daynard, ed., *The Place Within: Portraits of the American Landscape by Twenty Contemporary Writers* (New York: Norton, 1996), pp. 117–130. It later became the second chapter of hfh.

After Jesse challenged me in the manner described in "Mountain Music," I began listing in my notebook sources of healing and renewal. The first item on that list was "Wildness." The essay bearing that title was composed between April and October 1996. Its structure is typical of those in which a central theme or concern establishes an imaginative force field, drawing images, ideas, memories, and metaphors from all directions—here, the notion of wildness gathers blizzards, owls, comets, ferns, the birth of stars, haywire hearts, volcanic eruptions, ecological restoration, and much else. Instead of tracing a clean arc, of the sort that fiction writers aspire to and writing teachers endorse, the essay dramatizes a series of mental excursions, all radiating from the central concern, like petals looping out from the yellow heart of a daisy. "Wildness" first appeared in *Orion* 16, no. 3 (Summer 1997), pp. 9–13, and became the fourth chapter of hfh.

The word *beauty* was high on my list of sources of hope. The essay of that title was written in September 1997. I began with my daughter's wedding not only for the obvious doting father's reasons, but because the occasion was filled with elements we readily think of as beautiful—bride and bridesmaids, gowns, music, flowers, vows of love. From there, I pursued beauty into less and less familiar domains, trying to discover its essence. In doing so, I wound up thinking about ancient questions: Why is there a universe, what drives its evolution, why do its patterns move us so deeply, and what role, if any, do we symbol-using beings play in this great drama? The same questions had led me in my early years to study mathematics and physics, noble disciplines that proved to be, for me, the wrong arenas in which to ask them. "Beauty" appeared first in *Orion* 17, no. 2 (Spring 1998), pp. 16–23, and it became the twelfth chapter of HFH. It was reprinted in *Best American Essays 1999*.

"Silence" was written in February–March 1997. I became acquainted with the Society of Friends as a graduate student in England during the late 1960s, when I sought counseling about my conscientious objection to the Vietnam War. Although I have never formally joined the Society, I have often worshipped with Quakers, and I have long admired them for their peace witness, their work on behalf of social justice, and their practice of collective meditation. I give a fuller account of my indebtedness to the Quaker tradition in my memoir, *A Private History of Awe*. My quotations from George Fox are drawn from the following books: Rufus M. Jones, *The Faith and Practice of the Quakers* (Richmond, Ind.: Friends United Press, n.d.); and two by Howard H. Brinton, *Friends for 300 Years* (Wallingford, Pa.: Pendle Hill, 1964) and *The Religious Philosophy of Quakerism* (Wallingford, Pa.: Pendle Hill, 1973). "Silence" was first published in *Witness* 11, no. 2 (1997), pp. 82–90, and it became the closing essay in FOS.

"The Force of Spirit" was written in June 1999. I had promised to deliver a speech at the Orion Society's Millennium Conference, Fire & Grit, in Shepherdstown, West Virginia, on the 23rd of that month, and I had imagined writing a more discursive essay for the occasion, about our obligation to care for the Earth on behalf of future generations. But in the weeks preceding the event, my father-in-law's failing health had so preoccupied my wife and me that I could think of little else, as the essay declares. So I wrote what I was moved to write, an account of a visit to my father-in-law in the nursing home, an essay that became both requiem and celebration. "The Force of Spirit" first appeared in *Orion* 18, no. 4 (Autumn 1999), pp. 26–35, and it became the title essay in FOS. It was reprinted in *Best American Essays 2000*.

"The Uses of Muscle," composed in December 2000, is the sole example in this book of a type of essay I have written occasionally over the years—one commissioned for a specific publication, with a length requirement (usually short), to fit a column or to illustrate a theme. In this instance, the commission was for the "A Man's Life" column in *Wabash Magazine,* where the essay appeared in the Winter/Spring 2001 issue, pp. 36–39. Like the essays that follow in this volume, this one has not previously been collected in any of my books.

"A Private History of Awe" was composed in February–March 2002. Like "Staying Put," "Mountain Music," and "Writing from the Center," this essay opened questions that spurred me to write a book, in this case my memoir, *A Private History of Awe* (New York: Farrar, Straus and Giroux, 2006). The book, like the essay, reflects on those moments in life that evoke both wonder and terror, moments that reveal an essential truth about our existence: we are fragile, fleeting creatures, vanishingly small in proportion to the universe, and yet we have been blessed with minds capable of responding to this vast cosmos in a host of languages, from poetry and painting to music and mathematics. The essay first appeared in *Orion* 22, no. 1 (January/February 2003), pp. 52–58.

"A Road into Chaos and Old Night" was composed in May 2003, for delivery at the bicentennial celebration of Emerson's birth. Literary critics have made much of the "anxiety of influence," arguing that writers seek to deny or defy their predecessors. My experience has been quite otherwise. I am grateful for my teachers, for those writers who have challenged, instructed, and inspired me. Emerson is one of them—not for his prose, nor for the method of his essays, but for the courageous, probing quality of his thought. *Nature,* "Self-Reliance," and his other major writings can be found in Joel Porte, ed., *Ralph Waldo Emerson: Essays and Lectures* (New York: Library of America, 1983). A convenient selection from the journals is Bliss Perry, ed., *The Heart of Emerson's Journals* (Boston: Houghton Mifflin, 1926). For an intelligent sampling of Thoreau's voluminous journal, see Jeffrey S. Cramer, ed., *I to Myself: An Annotated Selection from the Journal of Henry D. Thoreau* (New Haven, Conn.: Yale University Press, 2007). "A Road into Chaos and Old Night" was first published in *The Journal of Unitarian Universalist History* 29 (2003), pp. 19–28.

"Words Addressed to Our Condition Exactly" was composed in September 2005. I had quoted Wendell Berry in previous essays, and had dedicated *Writing from the Center* to him, but this was my first sustained effort to identify the qualities in his work that spoke most deeply to me. As Berry's readers know, his work includes poetry, short stories, and novels, as well as essays and book-length works of nonfiction. Although the tone and approach vary from one genre to another, and from one piece to another within a genre, Berry's distinctive vision and voice are present throughout. I quote from the original paperback edition of *The Long-Legged House* (New York: Ballantine, 1971). Long unavailable, the book was reprinted in 2003 by Counterpoint. This essay was first published in Jason Peters, ed., *Wendell Berry: Life and Work* (Lexington: University Press of Kentucky, 2007), pp. 34–44.

"Honoring the Ordinary" was composed in February 2007, as the keynote address for a conference on the art of the memoir. I had never thought of myself as a memoirist—and still do not—but rather as an essayist who sometimes tells autobiographical stories; so I set out to distinguish the two modes, and then to discover what they have in common. Along the way, I found myself driven to think about the meaning of "truth" in literature, about the contested boundary between fiction and nonfiction, and about the deepest concerns that have impelled my own writing. "Honoring the Ordinary" may be read as a reconsideration, from late in my work as an essayist, of the matters explored early on in "The Singular First Person." "On the Decay of the Art of Lying" and two thousand additional pages of inimitable prose can be found in the two-volume edition, Louis J. Budd, ed., *Mark Twain: Collected Tales, Sketches, Speeches, & Essays 1852–1890* and *1891–1910* (New York: Library of America, 1992). The letters I quote from Stevens and O'Connor can be found, respectively, in Holly Stevens, ed., *Letters of Wallace Stevens* (Berkeley: University of California Press, 1996) and Sally Fitzgerald, ed., *Letters of Flannery O'Connor: The Habit of Being* (New York: Farrar, Straus and Giroux, 1979). "Honoring the Ordinary" appeared first in *Arts & Letters*, no. 18 (Fall 2007), pp. 160–174.

"Speaking for the Land" was composed in August–September 2009, for delivery at a ceremony marking the seventy-fifth anniversary of the founding of the University of Wisconsin Arboretum. I took the occasion to acknowledge my debt to one of my heroes, Aldo Leopold, who had spoken at the original dedication. He was a rare combination of skillful scientist, accomplished writer, and tireless organizer of efforts to protect and restore the land. "The Arboretum and the University," "Some Fundamentals of Conservation in the Southwest," and "Conservationist in Mexico" can all be found in Susan L. Flader and J. Baird Callicott, eds., *The River of the Mother of God and Other Essays by Aldo Leopold* (Madison: University of Wisconsin Press, 1991). In its original edition, Leopold's most famous book was published as *A Sand County Almanac and Sketches Here and There* (New York: Oxford University Press, 1949). "Speaking for the Land" first appeared in *The Leopold Outlook* 10, no. 1 (Spring 2010), pp. 2–10.

"The Mystique of Money" was composed in September 2010, for delivery at the annual Prairie Festival, held at the Land Institute in Salina, Kansas. I include it here as an example of a less personal, more overtly topical and political sort of essay that I have occasionally written over the years. Although I do not participate in the essay in the guise of narrator, my values and concerns shape every line. The statistics cited here, all current as of February 2011, as well as the names of corporations and individuals, belong to a particular historical moment; yet the underlying issues are perennial ones—unjust disparities in the distribution of wealth, the worship of money, the spell of consumerism, the illusion of perpetual growth, and the social and environmental damage caused by unbridled capitalism. I'm grateful to Wes Jackson and Ken Warren for inviting me to speak at the Prairie Festival. Milton Friedman's "The Social Responsibility of Business Is to Increase Its Profits" appeared in *The New York Times Magazine*, September 13, 1970. Andrew Carnegie's "The Gospel of Wealth" was published in *North American Review*, no. 391 (June 1889). Martin Luther King, Jr.'s "A Time to Break Silence" is collected in *I Have a Dream: Writings and Speeches That Changed the World* (San Francisco: Harper, 1992). Under the title "Breaking the Spell of Money," this essay was first published in *Orion* 30, no. 4 (July/August 2011), pp. 58–63.

"Buffalo Eddy" was composed in January–February 2010. Like a number of my essays, it was inspired by an encounter with a powerful place, the sort of place that a culture more reverent than ours, more respectful of Earth, would regard as holy. This charismatic spot on the Snake River set me thinking about other sorts of eddies—vortices, whirlpools, circles—and about the human impulse to respond to the universe in symbols. I am grateful to Bill Johnson for taking me there. *The Journals of the Lewis and Clark Expedition*, edited by Gary E. Moulton and published in thirteen volumes by the University of Nebraska Press, 1983–2004, can be accessed online: http://lewisandclarkjournals.unl.edu/index.html. The *New York Times* article cited here, "Colombian Woman Salvages Corpses at River Bend," appeared on January 9, 2010. "Buffalo Eddy" is forthcoming in *Orion* in 2012.

"Mind in the Forest" began as field notes in October 2008 and was transformed into an essay in January–February 2009. On the surface, it follows a traditional pattern: a solitary man goes to a wild place, describes what he sees, and reflects on the nature of nature. But of course I was not alone; I bore in mind loved ones and friends; I carried in my head and backpack the findings of countless scientists, historians, poets, novelists, and prior visitors; every line I wrote was an effort to translate what I had seen and thought into words that would be meaningful to others. I never felt isolated, immersed as I was in a living web that stretched from the soil to the sky, and in a human lineage that stretches back to the beginnings of human language. I am grateful to Kathleen Dean Moore, Charles Goodrich, and Fred Swanson for arranging my sojourn among the ancient trees. For information: http://andrewsforest.oregonstate.edu/. Reflections by other writers on their time in the Andrews can be found here: http://andrewsforest.oregonstate.edu/research/related/writers/template.cfm?next=wir&topnav=169. "Mind in the Forest" was first published in *Orion* 28, no. 6 (November/December 2009), pp. 48–53. It won the 2009 John Burroughs Nature Essay Award.

Born in Tennessee and reared in Ohio, **Scott Russell Sanders** studied at Brown University, where he was valedictorian, and earned his Ph.D. as a Marshall Scholar at Cambridge University. He is a Distinguished Professor Emeritus of English at Indiana University, where he taught from 1971 to 2009, and where he earned the university's highest teaching award. Among his twenty books are novels, collections of stories, and works of personal nonfiction, including *Staying Put* (1993), *Writing from the Center* (1995), and *Hunting for Hope* (1998). His most recent books are *A Private History of Awe* (2006) and *A Conservationist Manifesto* (2009). For his writing, Sanders has won the Associated Writing Programs Creative Nonfiction Award, the John Burroughs Essay Award, the Lannan Literary Award, the Mark Twain Award, and the Indiana Authors Award, as well as fellowships from the Guggenheim Foundation and the National Endowment for the Arts. His work has appeared in such magazines as *Orion, Audubon,* and *The Georgia Review,* and it has been reprinted in *The Art of the Essay, The Norton Reader,* and more than a hundred other anthologies, including the annual *Best American Essays.* His writing examines the human place in nature, the character of community, the relation between culture and geography, and the search for a spiritual path. He and his wife, Ruth, a biochemist, have reared two children in their hometown of Bloomington in the hardwood hill country of Indiana's White River Valley.